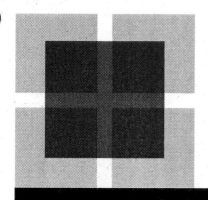

Table of Contents

Your Complete Learning Package

■ The Complete Package

Your *Foundations of Macroeconomics* package consists of:

- Textbook
- Study Guide
- MyEconLab Access Kit

MyEconLab is a powerful and tightly integrated homework and tutorial system that puts you in control of your own learning. MyEconLab includes

- Practice Tests that let you test your understanding and identify where you need to concentrate your studying
- A personalized Study Plan that evaluates your test results and provides further practice
- Tutorial instruction that will guide you through the areas you have difficulty with
- eText—the entire textbook online with animated figures accompanied by audio explanations prepared by us and with hyperlinks to all the other components of the Web site.
- Economics in the News updated daily during the school year
- Online "Office Hours"—ask a question via e-mail, and one of us will respond within 24 hours!
- Economic links—links to sites that keep you up to date with what's going on in the economy and that enable you to work end-of-chapter Web Exercises

Each new textbook arrives with a MyEconLab Student Access Card that unlocks protected areas of the Web site.

■ Checklist and Checkpoints: The Glue That Holds Your Tools Together

Each chapter of your textbook opens with a Chapter Checklist that tells you what you'll be able to do when you've completed the chapter. The number of tasks varies from two to five and most often is three or four. Begin by reviewing this list thoughtfully and get a good sense of what you are about to learn.

Each part of a chapter in the textbook, Study Guide, and MyEconLab Web site is linked directly to a Checklist item to enable you to know exactly what you're studying and how it will enable you to accomplish your learning objective.

Each part of a chapter in the textbook ends with a Checkpoint—a page that offers you Practice Problems to test your understanding of the key ideas of the part. For each Practice Problem there is a worked and illustrated solution. The Checkpoints enable you to review material when it's fresh in your mind—the most effective and productive time to do so. The Checkpoints guide you through the material in a step-by-step approach that takes the guesswork out of learning. The Study Guide reinforces each Checkpoint by providing Additional Practice Problems. Use these if you're still not sure you understand the material or if you want to review before an exam.

The self-test questions in the Study Guide, the Study Plan Exercises on the MyEconLab Web site, and the chapter resources on the MyEconLab Web site are organized by Checkpoint so that you can maintain your focus as you work through the material.

■ Practice Makes Perfect

As you study, distinguish between *practice* and *self-test*. Practice is part of the learning process, learning by doing. Self-test is a check. It shows you where you need to go back and reinforce your understanding, and it helps you build confidence in your knowledge of the material.

The Checkpoint Practice Problems and Exercises, the end-of-chapter Exercises, and the Checkpoint Exercises in MyEconLab are designed for practice. The self-test questions in the Study Guide, the pre- and post-tests, and Study Plan Exercises in MyEconLab are designed to reveal your gaps in understanding and to target your final examination of the material.

■ Learn Your Learning Style

It is unlikely that you'll need to use all the tools that we've created all of the time. Try to discover how you learn best. Then exploit what you discover.

If you learn best by reading with a marker or pencil in your hand, you'll use the textbook and Study Guide more often than the other items. If you learn best by seeing the action, you'll often use the eText and MyEconLab tutorials. If you learn best by hearing, you'll use the eText audio explanations of the action in key figures. If you learn best by participating and acting, you'll often use the Study Plan Exercises.

■ Tell Us What Works for *You*

Please tell us the tools that you find most helpful. And tell us what you think we can improve. You can email us at robin@econ100.com or michael.parkin@uwo.ca, or use the Office Hours in your MyEconLab Web site.

Robin Bade
Michael Parkin
Ontario, Canada
January, 2012

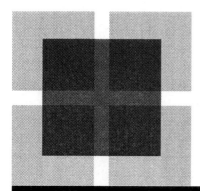

Your Course and Your Study Guide

◼ Introduction

My experience has taught me that what students want most from a study guide is help in mastering course material in order to do well on examinations. This Study Guide has been created to respond specifically to that demand. Using this Study Guide alone, however, is not enough to guarantee that you will earn an A or do well in your course. In order to help you overcome the problems and difficulties that most students encounter, I have some general advice on how to study, as well as some specific advice on how best to use this Study Guide.

Economics requires a different style of thinking than what you may encounter in other courses. Economists make extensive use of assumptions to break down complex problems into simple, analytically manageable parts. This analytical style, while ultimately not more demanding than the styles of thinking in other disciplines, feels unfamiliar to most students and requires practice. As a result, it is not as easy to do well in economics on the basis of your raw intelligence and high school knowledge as it is in many other courses. Many students who come to my office are frustrated and puzzled by the fact that they are getting A's and B's in their other courses but only a C or worse in economics. They have not recognized that economics is different and requires practice. In order to avoid a frustrating visit to your instructor after your first test, I suggest you do the following.

◼ Don't rely solely on your high school economics.

If you took high school economics, you have seen the material on supply and demand which your instructor will lecture on in the first few weeks. Don't be lulled into feeling that the course will be easy. Your high school knowledge of economic concepts will be very useful, but it will not be enough to guarantee high scores on exams. Your college or university instructors will demand much more detailed knowledge of concepts and ask you to apply them in new circumstances.

◼ Keep up with the course material on a weekly basis.

Skim or read the appropriate chapter in the textbook before your instructor lectures on it. In this initial reading, don't worry about details or arguments you can't quite follow — try to get a general understanding of the basic concepts and issues. You may be amazed at how your instructor's ability to teach improves when you come to class prepared. After the lecture, return to the book and read the material more thoroughly and completely. As soon as your instructor has finished covering a chapter, complete the corresponding Study Guide chapter. Avoid cramming the day before or even just the week before an exam. Because economics requires practice, cramming is an almost certain recipe for failure.

■ Keep a good set of lecture notes.

Good lecture notes are vital for focusing your studying. Your instructor will only lecture on a subset of topics from the textbook. The topics your instructor covers in a lecture should usually be given priority when studying. Also give priority to studying the figures and graphs covered in the lecture.

Instructors differ in their emphasis on lecture notes and the textbook, so ask early on in the course which is more important in reviewing for exams — lecture notes or the textbook. If your instructor answers that both are important, then ask the following, typical economic question: which will be more beneficial — spending an extra hour re-reading your lecture notes or an extra hour re-reading the textbook? This question assumes that you have read each textbook chapter twice (once before lecture for a general understanding, and then later for a thorough understanding); that you have prepared a good set of lecture notes; and that you have worked through all of the problems in the appropriate Study Guide chapters. By applying this style of analysis to the problem of efficiently allocating your study time, you are already beginning to think like an economist!

■ Use your instructor and/or teaching assistants for help.

When you have questions or problems with course material, come to the office to ask questions. Remember, you are paying for your education and instructors are there to help you learn. Don't be shy. The personal contact that comes from one-on-one tutoring is professionally gratifying for instructors as well as (hopefully) beneficial for you.

■ Form a study group.

A very useful way to motivate your studying and to learn economics is to discuss the course material and problems with other students. Explaining the answer to a question out loud is a very effective way of discovering how well you understand the question. When you answer a question only in your head, you often skip steps in the chain of reasoning without realizing it. When you are forced to explain your reasoning aloud, gaps and mistakes quickly appear, and you (with your fellow group members) can quickly correct your reasoning. The Exercises at the end of each textbook chapter are extremely good study group material. You might also get together after having worked the Study Guide problems, but before looking at the answers, and help each other solve unsolved problems.

■ Work old exams.

One of the most effective ways of studying is to work through exams your instructor has given in previous years. Old exams give you a feel for the style of question your instructor might ask, and give you the opportunity to get used to time pressure if you force yourself to do the exam in the allotted time. Studying from old exams is not cheating, as long as you have obtained a copy of the exam legally. Some institutions keep old exams in the library, others in the department. If there is a class web page, check there—many instructors now post old exams on their class web pages. Students who have previously taken the course are usually a good source as well. Remember, though, that old exams are a useful study aid only if you use them to understand the reasoning behind each question. If you simply memorize answers in the hopes that your instructor will repeat the identical question, you are likely to fail. From year to year, instructors routinely change the questions or change the numerical values for similar questions.

■ Use All Your Tools

The authors of your book, Robin Bade and Michael Parkin, have created a rich array of learning tools that they describe in the preceding section, "Your Complete Learning Package." Make sure that you read this section because it makes sense to use *all* your tools!

USING THE STUDY GUIDE

You should only attempt to complete a chapter in the Study Guide after you have read the corresponding textbook chapter and listened to your instructor lecture on the material. Each Study Guide chapter contains the following sections.

Chapter Checklist

This first section is a short summary of the key material. It is designed to focus you quickly and precisely on the core material that you must master. It is an excellent study aid for the night before an exam. Think of it as crib notes that will serve as a final check of the key concepts you have studied.

Additional Practice Problems

In each checkpoint in the textbook there are practice problems. These problems are extremely valuable because they help you grasp what you have just studied. In the Study Guide are additional Practice Problems. These Practice Problems are either similar to the one in your textbook, extend the Practice Problem in your textbook, or cover another important topic from the Checkpoint. Although the answer is given to the additional Practice Problem, try to solve it on your own before reading the answer.

Following the additional Practice Problem is the Self Test section of the Study Guide. This section has fill in the blank, true or false, multiple choice, complete the graph, short answer and numeric questions, and additional exercises. The questions are designed to give you practice and to test skills and techniques you must master to do well on exams. Before I describe the parts of the Self Test section, here are some general tips that apply to all parts.

First, use a pencil to write your answers in the Study Guide so you have neat, complete pages from which to study and recall how you answered a question when the test approaches. Draw graphs wherever they are applicable. Some questions will ask explicitly for graphs; many others will not but will require a chain of reasoning that involves shifts of curves on a graph. Always draw the graph. Don't try to work through the reasoning in your head — you are much more likely to make mistakes that way. Whenever you draw a graph, even in the margins of the Study Guide, label the axes. You might think that you can keep the labels in your head, but you will be confronting many different graphs with many different variables on the axes. Also, be sure to understand what the axes are measuring. After finishing Chapter 4, some students think that the vertical axis always shows the price. That belief is simply not so. Hence you must be careful with the axes. In other words, avoid confusion and label. As an added incentive, remember that on exams where graphs are required, instructors often will deduct points for unlabelled axes.

Do the Self Test questions as if they were real exam questions, which means do them without looking at the answers. This is the single most important tip I can give you about effectively using the Study Guide to improve your exam performance. Struggling for the answers to questions that you find difficult is one of the most effective ways to learn. The adage — no pain, no gain — applies well to studying. You will learn the most from right answers you had to struggle for and from your wrong answers and mistakes. Only after you have attempted all the questions should you look at the answers. When you finally do check the answers, be sure to understand where you went wrong and why the right answer is correct.

Fill in the Blanks

This section covers the material in the checkpoint and has blanks for you to complete. Often suggested phrases are given but sometimes there are no hints—in that case you are on your own! Well, not really, because the answers are given at the end of each Study Guide chapter. This section also can help you review for a test because, once completed, they serve as a *very* brief statement of the important points within the important points within the checkpoint.

True or False

Next are true or false questions. Some instructors use true or false questions on exams or quizzes, so these questions might prove very valuable. The answers to the questions are given at the end of the chapter. The answer also has a page reference to the textbook. If you missed the question or did not completely understand the answer, definitely turn to the textbook and study the topic so that you will not miss similar questions on your exams.

Multiple Choice

Many instructors use multiple choice questions on exams, so pay particular attention to these questions. Similar to the true or false questions, the answers are given at the end of the Study Guide chapter and each answer references the relevant page in the text. If you had any difficulty with a question, use this page reference to look up the topic and then study it to remove this potential weakness.

Complete the Graph

The complete the graph questions allow you to practice using one of economists' major tools, graphs. If you will have essay questions on your exams, it is an extremely safe bet that you will be expected to use graphs on at least some of the questions. This section is designed to ensure that you are well prepared to handle these questions. Use the graph in the Study Guide to answer the questions. Although the answer is given at the end of the Study Guide chapter, do *not* look at the answer before you attempt to solve the problem. It is much too easy to deceive yourself into thinking you understand the answer when you simply look at the question and then read the answer. Involve yourself in the material by answering the question and then looking at the answer. If you cannot answer the question or if you got the answer wrong, the Study Guide again has a reference to the relevant page number in the text. Use the text and study the material!

Short Answer and Numeric Questions

The next set of questions are short answer and numeric questions. Short answer and numeric questions are classic exam questions, so pay attention to these questions. Approach them similarly to how you approach all the other questions: Answer them before you look at the answers in the back of the Study Guide. These questions are also excellent for use in a study group. If you and several friends are studying for an exam, you can use these questions to quiz your understanding. If you have disagreements about the correct answers, once again there are page references to the text so that you can settle these disagreements and be sure that everyone has a solid grasp of the point!

Additional Exercises

The final set of questions are exercises that link very closely to the Checkpoint material. These questions (and answers) are also available in your MyEconLab Test A, so you can practice with these questions using either your Study Guide or your computer! Regardless of how you tackle them, as always answer them before you look at the answers. These questions are similar to the short answer and numeric questions because they work very well in a study group.

FINAL COMMENTS

This Study Guide combines the efforts of many talented individuals. For Chapters 1 through 4 and Chapter 18, the author of the Chapter Checklists and many of the additional Practice Problems and answers is Tom Meyer, from Rochester Community and Technical College. It was a pleasure to work with Tom; I always looked forward to his emails and the resulting conversations. For the remaining chapters, the authors of the Chapter Checklists and many of the additional Practice Problems and answers are Neil Garston, from California State University, at Los Angeles, and Tom Larson, also from California State University, at Los Angeles. It was a pleasure to work with these fine scholars.

For the multiple choice questions, we assembled a team of truly outstanding teachers:

- Ali Ataiifar, Delaware County Community College
- Diego Mendez-Carbajo, Illinois Wesleyan University
- William Mosher, Assumption College
- Cynthia Tori, Valdosta State University
- Nora Underwood, University of California, Davis

- Seemi Ahmad, Dutchess Community College
- Susan Bartlett, University of South Florida
- Jack Chambless, Valencia Community College
- Paul Harris, Camden County Community College
- William Mosher, Assumption College
- Terry Sutton, Southeast Missouri State University

I added a few multiple choice questions and wrote the fill in the blank, true or false, complete the graph, and short answer and numeric questions. I also served as an editor to assemble the material into the book before you.

The Study Guide and other supplements were checked for accuracy by a team of instructors. For previous editions, the team included:

- David Bivin, Indiana University-Purdue University
- Geoffrey Black, Boise State University
- Jeffrey Davis, ITT Technical Institute
- Ken Long, New River Community College
- Barbara Wiens-Tuers, Penn State University, Altoona
- Joachim Zietz, Middle Tennessee State University
- Armand Zottola, Central CT State University
- Carol Conrad, Cerro Coso Community College
- Marie Duggan, Keene State University

- Steven Hickerson, Mankato State University
- Douglas Kinnear, Colorado State University
- Tony Lima, California State University, at Eastbay (Tony, I believe you were one of my instructors when I was an undergraduate—thanks for helping excite me about economics!)
- Michael Milligan, Front Range Community College
- Barbara Ross-Pfeiffer, Kapiolani Community College
- John Daly and his class at St. Andrews

Jeannie Shearer-Gillmore, University of Western Ontario, checked every word, every sentence, every paragraph, and every page of the first edition of this book and many of the words, sentences, paragraphs, and pages of the third edition. She made a huge number of corrections and comments. The easiest way to distinguish her work and mine is to determine if there is an error in a passage. If there is, it's my work; if there is not, it's her work.

Looking over this edition of the book have been Alison Eusden and Sarah Dumouchelle, both with Pearson Publishers. Both played a key role in finding blunders, errors, and typos and for that I am eternally grateful. However, beyond that, both also were remarkable in how they remained so chipper and cheerful even in face of what I had presumed were insurmountable obstacles.

Students and professors who have used this book in earlier editions also have found errors that I did not catch. I think we owe them a special thanks for their conscientious work and generous initiative to report the errors:

- Lisa Salazar-Rich, at Cal Poly Pomona
- Professor Tom McCaleb's class at Florida State University and Professor McCaleb himself.
- Professor Lisa Gladstone, at St. Louis University

Robin Bade and Michael Parkin, the authors of your book, also need thanks. Not only have they written such a superior book that it was easy to be enthusiastic about writing the Study Guide to accompany it, both Robin and Michael played a very hands-on role in creating this Study Guide. They corrected errors and made suggestions that vastly improved the Study Guide.

I want to thank my family: Susan, Tommy, Bobby, and Katie, who, respectively: allowed me to work all hours on this book; helped me master the intricacies of FTPing computer files; let me postpone working on our trains with him until after the book was concluded; and would run into my typing room to share her new discoveries. Thanks a lot!

Finally, I want to thank Pearl, Lucky Tu, and Sphynx (and the late, beloved Butterscotch, Snowball, Mik, and Lucky Bunny) who, while I typed, sometimes sat on my lap and sometimes sat next to the computer in a box peering out the window (and occasionally meowed).

We (well, all of us except the cats) have tried to make the Study Guide as helpful and useful as possible. Undoubtedly I have made some mistakes; mistakes that you may see. If you find any, I, and following generations of students, would be grateful if you could point them out to me. At the end of my class at the University of Florida, when I ask my students for their advice, I point out to them that this advice won't help them at all because they have just completed the class. But comments they make will influence how future students are taught. Thus just as they owe a debt of gratitude for the comments and suggestions that I received from students before them, so too will students after them owe them an (unpaid and unpayable) debt. You are in the same situation. If you have questions, suggestions, or simply comments, let me know. My address follows, or you can reach me via e-mail at MARK.RUSH@CBA.UFL.EDU. Your input probably won't benefit you directly, but it will benefit following generations. And if you give me permission, I will note your name and school in following editions so that any younger siblings (or, years down the road, maybe even your children!) will see your name and offer up thanks.

Mark Rush
Economics Department
University of Florida
Gainesville, Florida 32611
January, 2012.

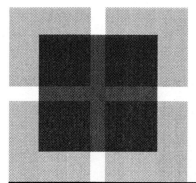

CHAPTER CHECKLIST

Chapter 1 defines economics, microeconomics and macroeconomics; discusses the three major questions of *what, how,* and *for whom;* covers the six core economic ideas that shape how economists think about issues; and, examines methods used by economists.

1 **Define economics and explain the kinds of questions that economists try to answer.**

Economic questions exist because of scarcity, the point that wants exceed the ability of resources to satisfy them. Economics is the social science that studies the choices that individuals, businesses, government, and entire societies make as they cope with scarcity, the incentives that influence those choices, and the arrangements that coordinate them. The field of economics is divided into microeconomics, the study of the choices that individuals and businesses make and the way these choices interact and are influenced by governments, and macroeconomics, the study of the aggregate effects on the national economy and the global economy of the choices that individuals, businesses, and governments make. Economics studies how choices wind up determining: *what* goods and services get produced?; *how* goods and services are produced?; and *for whom* goods and services are produced? Economics also studies when choices made in a person's self-interest also serve the social interest. For instance, do the self-interested choices made about globalization, the information age, climate change and social security also promote the social interest?

2 **Explain the ideas that define the economic way of thinking.**

The six ideas that are the core of the economic approach: a choice is a tradeoff; people make rational choices by comparing benefits and costs; benefit is what you gain from something; cost is what you must give up to get something; most choices are "how much" choices made at the margin; and choices respond to incentives. Choices are tradeoffs—giving up one thing to get another. A rational choice uses the available resources to most effectively meet the objective of the person making the choice. The benefit from something is the gain or pleasure it brings. Benefit is measured by what someone is willing to give up to get something. The opportunity cost of something is the best thing that must be given up. Making choices on the margin means comparing all the relevant alternatives systematically and incrementally to determine the best choice. The marginal cost is the opportunity cost of a one-unit increase in an activity; the marginal benefit is the gain from a one-unit increase in an activity. Rational choices compare the marginal benefit of an activity to its marginal cost and undertake it if the marginal benefit exceeds or equals the marginal cost. Statements about "what is" are positive statements; statements about "what ought to be" are normative statements. Economists are interested in positive statements about cause and effect so they develop economic models. Economists use natural experiments, statistical investigations, and economic experiments to test if their models are making correct predictions.

CHECKPOINT 1.1

■ **Define economics and explain the kinds of questions that economist try to answer.**

Quick Review

- *Self-interest* The choices that people make that they think are the best for them.
- *Social interest* The choices that are best for society as a whole.

Additional Practice Problems 1.1

1. Which of the following headlines deals with *what, how,* and *for whom* questions?:
   a. A new government program is designed to provide high-quality school lunches for children from poorer families.
   b. Intel researchers discover a new chip-making technology.
   c. Regis Hairstyling sets a record for hairstylings in month of July

2. Which of the following headlines concern social interest and self interest?
   a. A new government program is designed to provide high-quality school lunches for children from poorer families.
   b. Intel researchers discover a new chip-making technology.
   c. Regis Hairstyling sets a record for hairstylings in month of July.

Solutions to Additional Practice Problems 1.1

1a. "More lunches" is a *what* question and "for children from poorer families" is a *for whom* question.
1b. "New chip-making technology" is a *how* question because it deals with how computer chips will be manufactured.
1c. "Record for hairstylings" is a *what* question because it notes that a record number of hairstylings have taken place in July.

2a. The decision to implement a new government program is a decision that is most likely made in the social interest. The self-interest of the government bureaucrat who made the decision might also be involved, particularly if the bureaucrat also will help manage the program.
2b. Intel's decision to research new chip-making technology is made in Intel's self-interest.
2c. Regis's decision to offer hairstylings is made in its self-interest as are the decisions of the people who had their hair styled by Regis.

■ **Self Test 1.1**

Fill in the blanks

Economic questions arise because ____ (human wants; resources) exceed the ____ (human wants; resources) available to satisfy them. Faced with ____, people must make choices. (Macroeconomics; Microeconomics) ____ is the study of the choices the individuals and businesses make and the way these choices interact and are influenced by governments. Choices that are the best for the person who makes them are made in ____ (self-interest; social interest).

True or false

1. Faced with scarcity, we must make choices.
2. The question of *what* refers to what production method should a firm use?
3. The answers to the *what, how* and *for whom* questions depend on the interactions of the choices people, businesses, and governments make.
4. If Sam buys a pizza because she is hungry, her choice is made in the social interest.
5. Because everyone is a member of society, all choices made in self-interest are also in the social interest.

Multiple choice

1. The characteristic from which all economic problems arise is
   a. political decisions.
   b. providing a minimal standard of living for every person.
   c. how to make a profit.
   d. hunger.
   e. scarcity.

2. Scarcity results from the fact that
   a. people's wants exceed the resources available to satisfy them.
   b. not all goals are desirable.
   c. we cannot answer the major economic questions.
   d. choices made in self-interest are not always in the social interest.
   e. the population keeps growing.

3. To economists, scarcity means that
   a. limited wants cannot be satisfied by the unlimited resources.
   b. a person looking for work is not able to find work.
   c. the number of people without jobs rises when economic times are bad.
   d. there can never be answers to the *what, how* or *for whom* questions.
   e. unlimited wants cannot be satisfied by the limited resources.

4. Which of the following is a microeconomic issue?
   a. Why has unemployment risen nationwide?
   b. Why has economic growth been rapid in China?
   c. What is the impact on the quantity of Pepsi purchased if consumers' tastes change in favor of non-carbonated drinks?
   d. Why is the average income lower in Africa than in Latin America?
   e. Why did overall production increase within the United States last year?

5. The question "Should we produce LCD televisions or computer monitors?" is an example of a _____ question.
   a. what
   b. how
   c. for whom
   d. where
   e. why

6. The question "Should we produce houses using bricks or wood?" is an example of a _____ question.
   a. what
   b. how
   c. for whom
   d. where
   e. why

7. The question "Should economics majors or sociology majors earn more after they graduate?" is an example of a _____ question.
   a. what
   b. how
   c. for whom
   d. where
   e. why

8. If a decision is made and it is the best choice for society, the decision is said to be
   a. a valid economic choice.
   b. made in self-interest.
   c. made in social interest.
   d. consistent with scarcity.
   e. a want-maximizing choice.

Short answer and numeric questions

1. Will there ever come a time without scarcity?

2. If there was no scarcity, would there be a need for economics?

3. Explain the difference between microeconomics and macroeconomics.

4. What are the three major questions answered by people's economic choices?

5. Why is the distinction between choices made in self-interest and choices made in social interest important?

Additional Exercises (also in MyEconLab Test A)

1. Every day, we make many choices. Why can't we avoid having to make choices?

2. Which of the following headlines deals with *what, how*, and *for whom* questions?
   a. "Major league baseball's turf keepers earn about $85,000, umpires earn about $350,000, and players make millions a year"

b. "Many full-service gas stations are switching to self-serve"

c. "Retail trends analysts make as much as $300,000 a year, while retail salespeople make less than $10 an hour"

3. Explain how the following headlines concern self-interest and social interest:

a. "Former-president George W. Bush powers his Texas ranch with solar electricity"

b. "Today's upper-class traveler goes on safari in southern Africa or stays at eco-resorts that cost $1,000 a night but do not have electricity"

CHECKPOINT 1.2

■ **Explain the ideas that define the economic way of thinking.**

Quick Review

- *Opportunity cost* The opportunity cost of something is the best thing you must give up to get it.
- *Marginal cost* The opportunity cost from a one-unit increase in an activity.
- *Marginal benefit* The benefit that arises from a one-unit increase in an activity.
- *Rational choice* A choice that compares the marginal benefit and marginal cost of the activity and takes the action if the marginal benefit exceeds or equals the marginal cost.
- *Positive statement* A statement that tells what is currently believed about the way the world operates. Positive statements can be tested.
- *Normative statement* A statement that tells what ought to be. It depends on values and cannot be tested.

Additional Practice Problems 1.2

1. What are the opportunity costs of *using* this *Study Guide*?

2. Kate usually plays tennis for two hours a week and her grade on each math test is usually 70 percent. Last week, after playing two hours of tennis, Kate thought long and hard about playing for another hour. She decided to play another hour of tennis and cut her study time by one additional hour. But the grade on last week's math test was 60 percent.

a. What was Kate's opportunity cost of the third hour of tennis?

b. Given that Kate made the decision to play the third hour of tennis, what can you conclude about the comparison of her marginal benefit and marginal cost of the second hour of tennis?

c. Was Kate's decision to play the third hour of tennis rational?

3. Classify each of the following statements as positive or normative:

a. There is too much poverty in the United States.

b. An increase in the gas tax will cut pollution.

c. Cuts to social security in the United States have been too deep.

Solutions to Additional Practice Problems 1.2

1. The opportunity cost is mainly the time spent using the *Study Guide* because that time could be devoted to other activities. The best activity given up, be it studying for another class, or sleeping, or some other activity, which is lost because of the time spent using the *Study Guide* is the opportunity cost. Once you have purchased this *Study Guide*, its price is not an opportunity cost of *using* the *Study Guide* because you have already paid the price.

2a. The opportunity cost of the third hour of tennis was the 10 percentage point drop on her math test grade because she cut her studying time by one hour to play an additional hour of tennis. If Kate had not played tennis for the third hour, she would have studied and her grade would not have dropped.

2b. Kate chose to play the third hour of tennis, so the marginal benefit of the third hour of tennis was greater than the marginal cost of the third hour. If the marginal benefit of the third hour of tennis was less than the marginal cost of the third hour, Kate would have chosen to study rather than play tennis.

2c. Even though her grade fell, Kate's choice used the available time to most effectively satisfy her wants because the marginal benefit of the third hour of playing tennis exceeded the marginal cost of the third hour. This was a choice made in her self-interest.

3a. A normative statement because it depends on the speaker's values and cannot be tested.

3b. A positive statement because it can be tested by increasing the gas tax and then measuring the change in pollution.

3c. A normative statement because it depends on the speaker's values (someone else might propose still deeper cuts) and cannot be tested.

■ Self Test 1.2

Fill in the blanks

A _____ choice uses the available resources to most effectively satisfy the wants of the person making the choice. The opportunity cost of an activity is _____ (all of the activities given up; the best alternative given up). The benefit of an activity is measured by what you _____ (are willing to; must) give up. We make a rational choice to do an activity if the marginal benefit of the activity _____ the marginal cost. A statement that tells "what is" is a _____ (positive; normative) statement. A statement that tells "what ought to be" is a _____ (positive; normative) statement.

True or false

1. Instead of attending his microeconomics class for two hours, Jim can play a game of tennis or watch a movie. For Jim the opportunity cost of attending class is forgoing the game of tennis *and* watching the movie.

2. Marginal cost is what you gain when you get one more unit of something.

3. A rational choice involves comparing the marginal benefit of an action to its marginal cost.

4. A change in marginal benefit or a change in marginal cost brings a change in the incentives that we face and leads us to change our actions.

5. The statement, "When more people volunteer in their communities, crime rates decrease" is a positive statement.

Multiple choice

1. Jamie has enough money to buy either a Mountain Dew, or a Pepsi, or a bag of chips. He chooses to buy the Mountain Dew. The opportunity cost of the Mountain Dew is
   a. the Pepsi and the bag of chips.
   b. the Pepsi or the bag of chips, whichever the best alternative given up.
   c. the Mountain Dew.
   d. the Pepsi because it is a drink, as is the Mountain Dew.
   e. zero because he enjoys the Mountain Dew.

2. The benefit of an activity is
   a. purely objective and measured in dollars.
   b. the gain or pleasure that it brings.
   c. the value of its opportunity cost.
   d. measured by what must be given up to get one more unit of the activity.
   e. not measurable on the margin.

3. The marginal benefit of an activity is
   i. the benefit from a one-unit increase in the activity.
   ii. the benefit of a small, unimportant activity.
   iii. measured by what the person is willing to give up to get one additional unit of the activity.
   a. i only.
   b. ii only.
   c. iii only.
   d. i and iii.
   e. ii and iii.

4. The cost of a one-unit increase in an activity
   a. is called the total one-unit cost.
   b. is called the marginal cost.
   c. decreases as more of the activity is done.
   d. is called the marginal benefit/cost.
   e. is called the unit cost.

5. If the marginal benefit of the next slice of pizza exceeds the marginal cost, you will
   a. eat the slice of pizza.
   b. not eat the slice of pizza.
   c. be unable to choose between eating or not eating.
   d. eat half the slice.
   e. More information is needed about how much the marginal benefit exceeds the marginal cost to determine if you will or will not eat the slice.

6. When people make rational choices, they
   a. behave selfishly.
   b. do not consider their emotions.
   c. weigh the costs and benefits of their options and act to satisfy their wants.
   d. necessarily make a decision in the social interest.
   e. are necessarily making the best decision.

7. A positive statement
   a. must always be right.
   b. cannot be tested.
   c. can be tested against the facts.
   d. depends on someone's value judgment.
   e. cannot be negative.

Short answer and numeric questions

1. What is an opportunity cost?

2. You have $12 and can buy a pizza, a movie on a DVD, or a sketch pad for drawing. You decide to buy the pizza and think that if you hadn't been so hungry, you would have purchased the DVD. What is the opportunity cost of your pizza?

3. What is benefit and how is it measured?

4. What is a marginal cost? A marginal benefit? How do they relate to rational choice?

5. Becky is writing an essay about the law that requires all passengers in a car to use a seat belt and its effectiveness. What might be a positive statement and a normative statement that she will include in her essay?

Additional Exercises (also in MyEconLab Test A)

1. Bill Gates has donated billions of dollars through the Bill and Melinda Gates Foundation to support universities, cancer research, a children's hospital, the Seattle Symphony, etc. Are his donations rational? In making these donations, might Bill Gates have responded to any incentive? Does he make his decision about his donations on the margin?

2. Tony is an engineering student, who is considering taking an extra course in history. What things might be part of his costs and benefits of the history course? Think of an incentive that might encourage him to take the course.

SELF TEST ANSWERS

■ CHECKPOINT 1.1

Fill in the blanks

Economic questions arise because <u>human wants</u> exceed the <u>resources</u> available to satisfy them. Faced with <u>scarcity</u>, people must make choices. <u>Microeconomics</u> is the study of the choices the individuals and businesses make and the way these choices interact and are influenced by governments. Choices that are the best for the person who makes them are made in <u>self-interest</u>.

True or false

1. True; page 2
2. False; page 3
3. True; page 4
4. False; page 4
5. False; page 5

Multiple choice

1. e; page 2
2. a; page 2
3. e; page 2
4. c; page 2
5. a; page 3
6. b; page 3
7. c; page 4
8. c; page 4

Short answer and numeric questions

1. There will never be a time without scarcity because human wants are unlimited; page 2.

2. If there was no scarcity, then there likely would be no need for economics. Economics studies the choices that people make to cope with scarcity, so if there was no scarcity, then people's choices would not be limited by scarcity; page 2.

3. Microeconomics studies individual units within the economy, such as a consumer, a firm, a market, and so forth. Macroeconomics studies the overall, or aggregate, economy, such as the overall unemployment rate, or overall economic growth rate; pages 2-3.

4. The questions are "*What* goods and services get produced and in what quantities?", "*How* are goods and services produced?", and "*For whom* are the goods and services produced?" pages 3-4.

5. In general economists believe that people make choices according to their self-interest. These choices might or might not be in the social interest. Part of what economists study is when choices made in people's self-interest also further the social interest; page 5.

Additional Exercises (also in MyEconLab Test A)

1. The only way to avoid making choices is to either limit our wants or conjure up unlimited resources. Because neither is possible, we will always face choices; page 2.

2. a. The differences in incomes between turf keepers, umpires, and players is directly a *for whom* question. In addition, because it's likely that the consumption choices of the turf keepers, umpires, and players are different, there is also a *what* question involved; pages 3-4.

   b. The switch to self serve directly reflects a *how* question, that is, how will gasoline be delivered. In addition, because the switch means people previously employed at gas stations will be fired, there is a *for whom* question also involved; pages 3-4.

   c. The differences in incomes between retail trend analysts and retail salespeople is directly a *for whom* question. Because it's likely that the consumption choices of the analysts and salespeople are different, there is also a *what* question involved; pages 3-4.

3. a. Former-president Bush's decision to power his ranch with solar power is in his self interest because it affects what he pays for power; pages 4-5.

   b. The travelers' decisions are in their self interest. And, if they are also best for society, then they are in the social interest; pages 4-5.

■ CHECKPOINT 1.2

Fill in the blanks

A <u>rational</u> choice uses the available resources to most effectively satisfy the wants of the person making the choice. The opportunity cost of an activity is <u>the best alternative given up</u>. The benefit of an activity is measured by what you <u>are willing to</u> give up. We make a rational choice to do an activity if the marginal benefit of the activity <u>exceeds</u> the marginal cost. A statement that tells "what is" is a <u>positive</u> statement. A statement that tells "what ought to be" is a <u>normative</u> statement.

True or false

1. False; page 9
2. False; page 10
3. True; page 11
4. True; page 11
5. True; page 13

Multiple choice

1. b; page 9
2. b; page 9
3. d; page 10
4. b; page 10
5. a; page 11
6. c; page 11
7. c; page 13

Short answer and numeric questions

1. The opportunity cost of something is the best thing that must be given up. The opportunity cost is only the *single* best thing, not *all* the other things given up; page 9.
2. The opportunity cost of the pizza is the best thing given, which in this case is the DVD. The opportunity cost is *not* the DVD and the sketch pad because you would not have been able to purchase both of them with your $12; page 9.

3. The benefit of something is the gain or pleasure that it brings. Economists measure the benefit of something by what a person is willing to give up to get it; pages 9-10.
4. Marginal cost is the cost of a one-unit increase in an activity. Marginal benefit is the benefit of a one-unit increase in an activity. A rational choice is made by comparing the marginal cost and marginal benefit, so that if the marginal benefit of an activity exceeds or equals the marginal cost, the activity is undertaken; pages 10-11.
5. A positive statement is "People who wear seat belts are involved in fewer road deaths." This statement can be tested. A normative statement is "People should be free to choose whether to wear a seat belt or not." This statement cannot be tested; page 13.

Additional Exercises (also in MyEconLab Test A)

1. As long as Mr. Gates compares the marginal benefits and marginal costs of his donations and made the best decision he could, his donations are the result of rational decisions. Mr. Gates perhaps responded to incentives when making these donations. For example, by making these donations, he reduced his taxable income. Mr. Gates made his decisions on the marginal as long as he compared all the alternatives available to him. For instance, he could consider giving more or less money to AIDs initiatives or more or less money to cancer research.
2. The costs of any extra course include the extra tuition as well as less time available for studying for other courses, for work, or for leisure. The benefits include increased knowledge of history. An incentive to taking the course might be the promise of a better job or perhaps the fact that he is required to take a history class as a general education requirement in order to graduate.

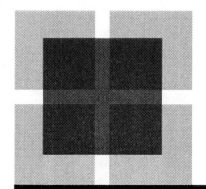

Appendix: Making and Using Graphs

Chapter 1

After you have completed the appendix, you will have thoroughly reviewed the graphs used in your economics course.

▮ Making and using graphs.

Graphs represent quantities as distances. The vertical axis is the *y*-axis and the horizontal axis is the *x*-axis. A scatter diagram plots a graph of one variable against the value of another variable. A time-series graph measures time along the *x*-axis and the variable (or variables) of interest along the *y*-axis. A cross-section graph shows the values of an economic variable for different groups in the population at a point in time. Graphs can show the relationship between two variables in an economic model. Variables that move in the same direction have a positive, or direct, relationship. Variables that move in the opposite direction have a negative, or inverse, relationship. Some relationships have minimum or maximum points. The slope of a relationship is the change in the value of the variable measured on the *y*-axis divided by the change in the value of the variable measured on the *x*-axis. Using the symbol "Δ" to mean "change in", the slope of a relationship equals $\Delta y \div \Delta x$. To graph a relationship among more than two variables, we use the *ceteris paribus* assumption and graph the relationship between two of the variables, holding the other variables constant.

CHECKPOINT 1

■ Making and using graphs.

Additional Practice Problems

1. You have data on the average monthly rainfall and the monthly expenditure on umbrellas in Seattle, Washington. What sort of graph would be the best to reveal if any relationship exists between these variables?

2. In Figure A1.1, draw a straight line showing a positive relationship and another straight line showing a negative relationship.

■ FIGURE A1.1

Year	Price (dollars per gallon)
1998	1.12
1999	1.22
2000	1.56
2001	1.53
2002	1.44
2003	1.64
2004	1.92
2005	2.34
2006	2.64
2007	2.85
2008	3.32

3. The table has the average price of a gallon of gasoline, including taxes, for eleven years. In Figure A1.2, measuring years along the horizontal axis, label the axes and then plot these data. What type of graph are you creating? What is the general trend of gas prices during this decade?

■ **FIGURE A1.2**

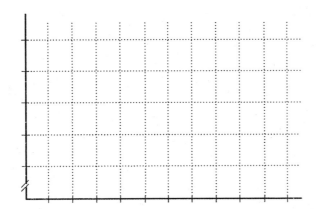

4. Figure A1.3 shows the relationship between the price of a paperback book and the quantity of paperback books a publisher is willing to sell. What is the slope of the line in Figure A1.3?

■ **FIGURE A1.3**

Price (dollars per paperback book)

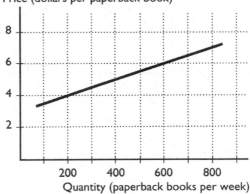

Quantity (paperback books per week)

Solutions to Additional Practice Problems 1

1. A scatter diagram would be the best graph to use. A scatter diagram would plot the monthly value of, say, rainfall along the vertical axis (the y-axis) and the monthly value of umbrella expenditure along the horizontal axis (the x-axis).

■ **FIGURE A1.4**

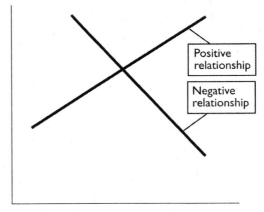

Positive relationship

Negative relationship

2. Figure A1.4 has two lines, one showing a positive relationship and the other showing a negative relationship. Your figure does not need to have identical lines. The key point your figure needs is that the line for the positive relationship slopes up as you move rightward along it and the line for the negative relationship slopes down as you move rightward along it.

■ FIGURE A1.5
Price (dollars per gallon)

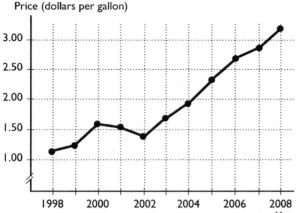

3. Figure A1.5 labels the axes and plots the data in the table. The graph is a time-series graph. The trend is positive because gas prices generally increased during these years.

■ FIGURE A1.6

Price (dollars per paperback book)

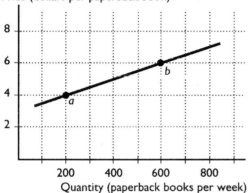

Quantity (paperback books per week)

4. The slope of a line is the change the variable measured on the y-axis divided by the change in the variable measured on the x-axis. To calculate the slope of the line in the figure, use points a and b in Figure A1.6. Between a and b, y rises by 2, from 4 to 6. And x increases by 400, from 200 to 600. The slope equals $2/400 = 0.005$.

■ Self Test 1

Fill in the blanks

In a graph, the vertical line is called the ____ (x-axis; y-axis) and the horizontal line is called the ____ (x-axis; y-axis). A ____ (scatter diagram; time-series graph; cross-section graph) is a graph of the value of one variable against the value of another variable. A ____ (scatter diagram; time-series graph; cross-section graph) measures time along the x-axis and the variable along the y-axis. A ____ (scatter diagram; time-series graph; cross-section graph) shows the values of an economic variable for different groups in the population at a point in time. If the graph of a relationship between two variables slopes up to the right, the two variables have a ____ (positive; negative) relationship. If the graph between two variables is a vertical line, the two variables ____ (are; are not) related. The slope of a relationship is the change in the value of the variable measured along the ____ (x-axis; y-axis) divided by the change in the value of the variable measured along the ____ (x-axis; y-axis). By using the *ceteris paribus* assumption, it ____ (is; is not) possible to graph a relationship that involves more than two variables.

True or false

1. A point that is above and to the right of another point will have a larger value of the x-axis variable and a larger value of the y-axis variable.

2. A scatter diagram shows the values of an economic variable for different groups in a population at a point in time.

3. A time-series graph compares values of a variable for different groups at a single point in time.

4. A trend is a measure of the closeness of the points on a graph.

5. A positive relationship is always a linear relationship.

6. A relationship that starts out sloping upward and then slopes downward has a maximum.

7. A graph that shows a horizontal line indicates variables that are unrelated.

8. The slope at a point on a curve can be found by calculating the slope of the line that touches the point and no other point on the curve.

Multiple choice

1. Demonstrating how an economic variable changes from one year to the next is best illustrated by a
   a. scatter diagram.
   b. time-series graph.
   c. linear graph.
   d. cross-section graph.
   e. trend-line.

2. To show the values of an economic variable for different groups in a population at a point in time, it is best to use a
   a. scatter diagram.
   b. time-series graph.
   c. linear graph.
   d. cross-section graph.
   e. trend diagram.

3. If whenever one variable increases, another variable also increases, then these two variables are _____ related.
   a. positively
   b. negatively
   c. inversely
   d. cross-sectionally
   e. not

4. A graph of the relationship between two variables is a line that slopes down to the right. These two variables are _____ related.
   a. positively
   b. directly
   c. negatively
   d. not
   e. trend-line

5. Two variables are unrelated if their graph is
   i. a vertical line.
   ii. a 45 degree line.
   iii. a horizontal line.
   a. i only.
   b. ii only
   c. iii only
   d. i and iii.
   e. i, ii, and iii.

■ **FIGURE A1.7**

Price (dollars per pound of rutabagas)

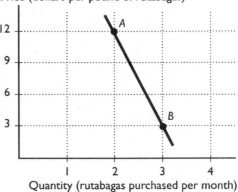

Quantity (rutabagas purchased per month)

6. In figure A1.7, between points A and B, what is the slope of the line?
   a. 12
   b. 3
   c. 9
   d. –9
   e. 0

■ **FIGURE A1.8**

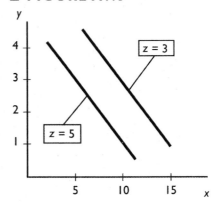

7. In Figure A1.8, an increase in z leads to a
   a. movement up along one of the lines showing the relationship between x and y.
   b. movement down along one of the lines showing the relationship between x and y.
   c. rightward shift of the line showing the relationship between x and y.
   d. leftward shift of the line showing the relationship between x and y.
   e. trend change in both x and y.

8. In Figure A1.8, *ceteris paribus*, an increase in x is associated with
   a. an increase in y.
   b. a decrease in y.
   c. an increase in z.
   d. a random change in z.
   e. no change in either y or z.

Complete the graph

Year	Workers (millions)
1999	7.9
2000	8.1
2001	8.3
2002	8.4
2003	8.5
2004	8.7
2005	9.0
2006	9.2
2007	9.5
2008	9.7

1. The table above gives the number of people working in restaurants and bars in the United States during 10 previous years.

■ **FIGURE A1.9**

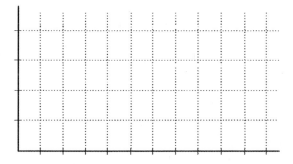

In Figure A1.9, measure time on the horizontal axis and the number of workers on the vertical axis, and then plot these data.
a. What type of graph are you creating?

b. Using your figure, what was the trend in the number of people working in restaurants and bars during these years?

Year	Revenue (billions of dollars)	Workers (millions)
1999	285	7.9
2000	306	8.1
2001	318	8.3
2002	332	8.4
2003	350	8.5
2004	372	8.7
2005	393	9.0
2006	418	9.2
2007	438	9.5
2008	453	9.7

2. The table above gives the annual revenue for restaurants and bars and the number of people employed in restaurants and bars in the United States during 10 previous years. In Figure A1.10, measure the revenue along the horizontal axis and the number of workers along the vertical axis and plot the data.

a. What type of graph are you creating?
b. What relationship do you see in your figure between the revenue and the number of workers?

■ **FIGURE A1.10**

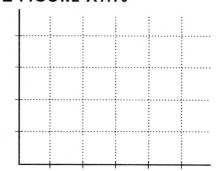

Price (dollars per sack of cat food)	Quantity (sacks of cat food per month)
1	10,000
2	8,000
3	7,000
4	4,000

3. The number of sacks of premium cat food that cat lovers will buy depends on the price of a sack of cat food. The relationship is given in the table above. In Figure A1.11, plot this relationship, putting the price on the vertical axis and the quantity on the horizontal axis.

■ **FIGURE A1.11**

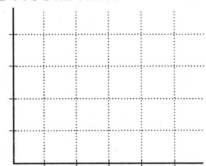

a. If the price of a sack of cat food is $2, how many sacks will be purchased?
b. If the price of a sack of cat food is $3, how many sacks will be purchased?
c. Is the relationship between the price and the quantity positive or negative?

4. In Figure A1.12, label the maximum and minimum points.

■ **FIGURE A1.12**

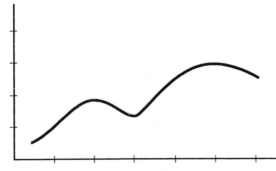

5. In Figure A1.13, draw a line through point *A* with a slope of 2. Label the line "1." Draw another line through point *A* with a slope of –2. Label this line "2."

■ **FIGURE A1.13**

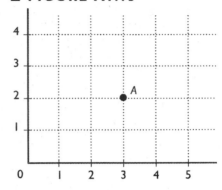

x	y	z
1	4	0
2	3	2
3	1	6
4	0	8

■ **FIGURE A1.14**

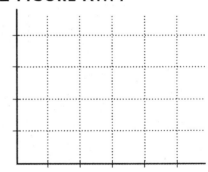

6. The table above contains data for three variables.
   a. In Figure A1.14, put *y* on the vertical axis and *x* on the horizontal axis. Show the relationship between *x* and *y*. Is this relationship positive or negative?
   b. What is the slope between $x = 2$ and $x = 3$?
   c. In Figure A1.15 (on the next page), put *z* on the vertical axis and *x* on the horizontal axis. Show the relationship between *x* and *z*. Is this relationship positive or negative?

■ **FIGURE A1.15**

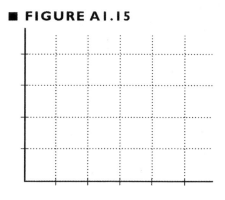

Price (dollars per DVD)	Quantity of DVDs purchased, low income	Quantity of DVDs purchased, high income
11	4	5
12	3	4
13	1	3
14	0	2

7. Bobby says that he buys fewer DVDs when the price of a DVD is higher. Bobby also says that he will buy more DVDs after he graduates and his income is higher. The table above shows the number of DVDs Bobby buys in a month at different prices when his income is low and when his income is high.

■ **FIGURE A1.16**

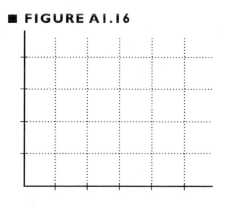

a. In Figure A1.16, put the price on the vertical axis and the quantity purchased on the horizontal axis. Show the relationship be-

tween the number of DVDs purchased and the price when Bobby's income is low.

b. On the same figure, draw the relationship between the number of DVDs purchased and the price when his income is high.

c. Does an increase in Bobby's income shift the relationship between the price of a DVD and the number of DVDs purchased rightward or leftward?

Short answer and numeric questions

1. What are the three types of graphs?

2. If two variables are positively related, will the slope of a graph of the two variables be positive or negative? If two variables are negatively related, will the slope of a graph of the two variables be positive or negative?

3. If a line slopes upward to the right, is its slope positive or negative? If a line slopes downward to the right, is its slope positive or negative?

4. In Figure A1.17, what is the slope of the curved line at point A? At point B?

■ **FIGURE A1.17**

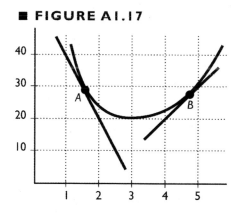

SELF TEST ANSWERS

■ CHECKPOINT I

Fill in the blanks

In a graph, the vertical line is called the <u>y-axis</u> and the horizontal line is called the <u>x-axis</u>. A <u>scatter diagram</u> is a graph of the value of one variable against the value of another variable. A <u>time-series graph</u> measures time along the x-axis and the variable along the y-axis. <u>A cross-section graph</u> shows the values of an economic variable for different groups in the population at a point in time. If the graph of a relationship between two variables slopes up to the right, the two variables have a <u>positive</u> relationship. If the graph between two variables is a vertical line, the two variables <u>are not</u> related. The slope of a relationship is the change in the value of the variable measured along the <u>y-axis</u> divided by the change in the value of the variable measured along the <u>x-axis</u>. By using the *ceteris paribus* assumption, it <u>is</u> possible to graph a relationship that involves more than two variables.

True or false

1. True; page 21
2. False; page 22
3. False; page 22
4. False; page 22
5. False; page 24
6. True; page 26
7. True; page 26
8. True; page 27

Multiple choice

1. b; page 22
2. d; page 22
3. a; page 24
4. c; page 25
5. d; page 26
6. d; page 27
7. d; page 28
8. b; page 28

Complete the graph

■ FIGURE A1.18

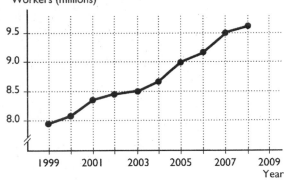

Workers (millions)

1. Figure A1.18 plots the data.
   a. This is a time-series graph; page 22.
   b. The trend is positive. During these 10 years there is an increase in the number of people working in restaurants and bars; page 22.

■ FIGURE A1.19

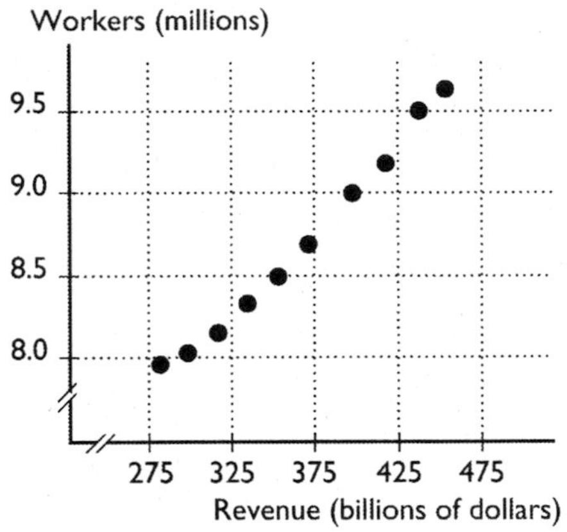

Workers (millions)

2. Figure A1.19 plots the data.
   a. The figure is a scatter diagram; page 22.
   b. The relationship between the revenue and the number of workers is positive; page 24.

■ **FIGURE A1.20**
Price (dollars per sack)

Sacks of cat food (per month)

3. Figure A1.20 plots the relationship.
   a. If the price is $2 per sack, 8,000 sacks are purchased; page 21.
   b. If the price is $3 per sack, 7,000 sacks are purchased; page 21.
   c. The relationship between the price and quantity of sacks is negative; page 25.

■ **FIGURE A1.21**

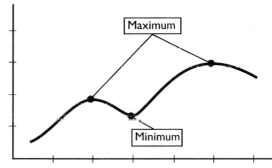

4. Figure A1.21 labels the two maximum points and one minimum point; page 26.

■ **FIGURE A1.22**

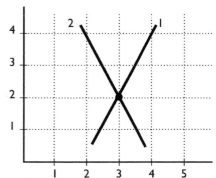

5. Figure A1.22 shows the two lines; page 27.

■ **FIGURE A1.23**

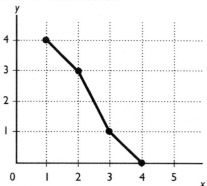

6. a. Figure A1.23 plots the relationship. The relationship is negative; page 25.
   b. The slope equals $(3 - 1) \div (2 - 3)$, which is -2; page 27.

■ **FIGURE A1.24**

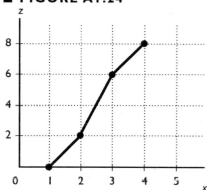

   c. Figure A1.24 plots the relationship. The relationship is positive; page 24.

■ **FIGURE A1.25**
Price (dollars per DVD)

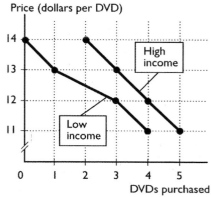

DVDs purchased

7. a. Figure A1.25 plots the relationship; page 28.

b. Figure A1.25 plots the relationship; page 28.

c. An increase in Bobby's income shifts the relationship rightward; page 28.

Short answer and numeric questions

1. The three types of graphs are scatter diagram, time-series graph, and cross-section graph; page 22.

2. If two variables are positively related, a graph of the relationship will have a positive slope. If two variables are negatively related, a graph of the relationship will have a negative slope; pages 24, 25, 27.

3. If a line slopes upward to the right, its slope is positive. If a line slopes downward to the right, its slope is negative; page 27.

4. The slope of a curved line at a point equals the slope of a straight line that touches that point and no other point on the curve. The slope of the curved line at point A is -20 and the slope of the curved line at point B is 10; page 27.

Chapter

2

The U.S. and Global Economies

Chapter 2 introduces the circular flow model which shows how goods and services and expenditures flow from and to households, firms, the government, and the rest of the world.

1   Describe what, how, and for whom goods and services are produced in the United States.

The production of goods and services, the "what" question, is divided into four broad categories defined in terms of the ultimate buyer: individuals (consumption goods and services), businesses (capital goods), governments (government goods and services), and other countries (export goods and services). The "how" of production involves the factors of production: land, labor, capital, and entrepreneurship. Goods and services are sold to those who have income, so the personal distribution of income is one way of showing who ends up with our national output. The functional distribution of income shows how much is paid to the owners of each type of productive resource. The largest share of national income is wages, so workers get the largest share of our nation's goods and services.

2   Describe what, how, and for whom goods and services are produced in the global economy.

Countries are divided into advanced economies, the richest 29 countries, and emerging market and developing economies. The advanced economies produce 53 percent of the world's total output, with 20 percent produced in the United States. The advanced economies have more human capital and physical capital than the developing countries. In the world, the lowest-paid 20 percent of the population receives 2 percent of world income and the highest-paid 20 percent receives 70 percent of world income. Inequality of incomes across the entire world has decreased during the past twenty years, primarily because incomes in China have grown rapidly

3   Use the circular flow model to provide a picture of how households, firms, and governments interact in the U.S. economy and how the U.S. and other economies interact in the global economy.

The circular flow model shows that households provide the services from the factors of production, and firms hire these services in factor markets. The circular flow also shows that households purchase goods and services and firms sell goods and services in goods markets. In the circular flow, the government purchases goods and services in goods markets. It makes transfers to firms and households and also taxes them. The decisions made by households and firms in these markets determine the answers to the "what," "how," and "for whom" questions. Households and firms in the United States buy goods and services from firms in other countries (U.S. imports) and U.S. firms sell goods and services to households and firms in other countries (U.S. exports). Using financial inflows, we borrow from other countries (when the value of imports exceeds that of exports) and using financial outflows, we lend to other countries (when the value of exports exceeds that of imports).

CHECKPOINT 2.1

■ **Describe what, how, and for whom goods and services are produced in the United States.**

Quick Review

- *Consumption goods and services* Goods and services that are bought by individuals and used to provide personal enjoyment and contribute to a person's standard of living.
- *Capital goods* Goods that are bought by businesses to increase their productive resources.
- *Government goods and services* Goods and services that are bought by governments.
- *Exports* Goods and services produced in the United States and sold in other countries.

Additional Practice Problems 2.1

1. Tell whether the following goods and services are consumption goods and services, capital goods, government goods and services, or exports.
   a. A taco at Taco Bell purchased for lunch by Shaniq.
   b. An HP printer manufactured in Idaho purchased by Maria in Peru.
   c. A new grill purchased by Taco Bell.
   d. A tour down the Colorado river from Rimrock Adventures purchased by the Miller family.
   e. CamelBak drinking packs purchased by the U.S. Marine Corp.
   f. CamelBak drinking packs purchased by Rimrock Adventures for use by their customers during tours.
   g. A CamelBak drinking pack purchased by Anne for use while mountain biking.
   h. A CamelBak drinking pack purchased by Sebastian, a German racing in the Tour de France.

2. How much labor is there in the United States? What determines the quantity of labor?

Solutions to Additional Practice Problems 2.1

1a. Shaniq's taco is a consumption good.
1b. Maria's printer is an export good.
1c. The new grill is a capital good.
1d. The tour is a consumption service.
1e. The drinking pack purchased by the Marines is a government good because it is purchased by the government.
1f. The drinking pack purchased by Rimrock Adventures is a capital good because it is purchased by a business.
1g. The drinking pack purchased by Anne is a consumption good.
1h. The drinking pack purchased by Sebastian is an export good.

2. In the United States, in 2011 about 153 million people had jobs or were available for work and they provided about 250 billion hours of labor a year. The quantity of labor depends on the size of the population, the percentage of the population that takes jobs, and on social relationships that influence things such as how many women take paid work. An increase in the proportion of women who have taken paid work has increased the quantity of labor in the United States over the past 50 years.

■ **Self Test 2.1**

Fill in the blanks

Goods and services that are bought by individuals and used to provide personal enjoyment and to contribute to a person's standard of living are ____ (consumption; capital; export) goods. Goods that are bought by businesses to increase their productive resources are ____ (consumption; capital; export) goods. Goods that are produced in the United States and sold in other countries are ____ (consumption; capital; export) goods. Of the four large groups of goods and services in the United States, ____ (consumption goods and services; capital goods; government goods and services; export goods and services) have the largest share of total production. Productive resources are called ____ and are grouped into four categories: ____,

____, ____, and ____. In 2010, ____ (labor; capital) received 69 percent of total income. The distribution of income among households is called the ____ (functional; personal) distribution of income.

True or false

1. Consumption goods and services include a slice of pizza purchased to eat at home.

2. A gold mine is included in the "land" category of productive resources.

3. Michael Dell, the person who founded and manages Dell computers, is an example of an entrepreneur.

4. In the United States, the factor of production that earns the most income is labor.

5. In the United States, the richest 20 percent of individuals earn approximately 30 percent of total income.

Multiple choice

1. When the total U.S. production of goods and services is divided into consumption goods and services, capital goods, government goods and services, and export goods and services, the largest component is
   a. consumption goods and services.
   b. capital goods.
   c. government goods and services.
   d. export goods and services.
   e. capital goods and government goods and services tie for the largest component.

2. An example of a capital good is
   a. a fiber optic cable TV system.
   b. an insurance policy.
   c. a hair cut.
   d. an iPod.
   e. a slice of pizza.

3. Goods and services produced in the United States and sold in other countries are called
   a. consumption goods and services.
   b. capital goods.
   c. government goods and services.
   d. export goods and services.
   e. import goods and services.

4. Which of the following correctly lists the factors of production?
   a. machines, buildings, land, and money
   b. hardware, software, land, and money
   c. capital, money, and labor
   d. owners, workers, and consumers.
   e. land, labor, capital, and entrepreneurship

5. Human capital is
   a. solely the innate ability we are born with.
   b. the money humans have saved.
   c. the knowledge humans accumulate through education and experience.
   d. machinery that needs human supervision.
   e. any type of machinery.

6. Wages are paid to ____ and interest is paid to ____.
   a. entrepreneurs; capital
   b. labor; capital
   c. labor; land
   d. entrepreneurs; land
   e. labor; entrepreneurs

7. Dividing the nation's income among the factors of production, the largest percentage is paid to
   a. labor.
   b. land.
   c. capital.
   d. entrepreneurship.
   e. labor and capital, with each receiving about 41 percent of the total income.

8. The personal distribution of income shows
   a. that labor earn the largest percentage of total income.
   b. how profit accounts for the largest fraction of total income.
   c. that the richest 20 percent of households earn 23 percent of total income.
   d. that interest accounts for most of the income of the richest 20 percent of households.
   e. that the poorest 20 percent of households earn 3 percent of total income.

Short answer and numeric questions

1. Is an automobile a consumption good or a capital good?

2. Compare the incomes received by the poorest and richest 20 percent of individuals.

Additional Exercises (also in MyEconLab Test A)

1. What is the distinction between consumption goods and services and capital goods? Which one of them brings an increase in productive resources?

2. If everyone in the United States were to consume an equal quantity of goods and services, what percentage of total income would the poorest 20 percent of households have to receive from higher-income groups?

3. Compare the percentage of total U.S. income that labor earns with the percentage earned by all the other factors of production combined.

CHECKPOINT 2.2

■ **Describe what, how, and for whom goods and services are produced in the global economy.**

Quick Review

- *Advanced economies* The 29 countries (or areas) that have the highest living standards.

- *Emerging markets and Developing economies* Emerging markets are the 28 countries in Europe and Asia that were until the early 1990s part of the Soviet Union or its satellites and are changing the way they organize their economies. Developing economies are the 119 countries in Africa, the Middle East, Europe, and Central and South America that have not yet achieved a high standard of living for their people.

Additional Practice Problems 2.2

1. What percentage of the world's population live in developing economies? In places such as China, India, and Africa, what was the average income per day?

2. What percentage of the world's population live in advanced economies? In countries such as the United States, Canada, and Japan, what was the average income per day?

3. How does the total production within the advanced economies, the emerging market economies, and the developing economies compare?

4. How is it possible that income inequality within most countries has increased in recent years yet income inequality across the whole world has decreased in recent years?

Solutions to Additional Practice Problems 2.2

1. The world's population is about 7 billion. More than 5 billion of the people live in developing economies. So, approximately 80 percent of the world's population lives in developing economies. Average daily income in China is $16, in India is $8, and in Africa is $7. Because these are the average, many people live on less than these amounts.

2. About 1 billion people, or 15 percent of the world's population live in the 28 advanced economies. The average income per day in the United States was $129, in Canada was $126, and in Japan was $116.

3. Of the world's total production, the advanced economies produce 53 percent (20 percent is produced in the United States). The emerging market economies produce 8 percent of the world's production and the developing economies produce the remainder, 39 percent.

4. While income inequality within nations has been increasing, the difference in incomes among different nations has been decreasing. In particular, China has seen extremely rapid growth in income. The growth in income for this poor but populous nation has decreased income inequality in the world as a whole.

■ **Self Test 2.2**

Fill in the blanks

Most of the world's population lives in the ____ (advanced economies; emerging market economies; developing economies). The lowest average income is in the ____ (advanced economies; emerging market economies; developing economies). Advanced economies produce about ____ (24; 53; 72) percent of the world's total production and the United States, alone, produces about ____ (6; 20; 33) percent of the world's total production. As a fraction of total output, agricultural is a ____ (larger; smaller) part of the economy in developing economies than in advanced economies. Factories in advanced economies generally are much ____ (less; more) capital intensive than in developing economies. During the past 20 years, the distribution of income in the world economy has become ____ (more; less) equal.

True or false

1. About 50 percent of the world's population lives in the advanced economies.

2. Mexico is classified as an emerging market economy.

3. Taken as a group, the 119 developing economy nations produce a larger percentage of total world production than do the 29 advanced economy nations.

4. Most of the world's electricity is generated by coal.

5. Workers in the advanced economies have much more human capital than workers in the developing economies.

6. Income inequality within most nations has increased over the past years.

Multiple choice

1. The world population is approximately ____ people.
   a. 7 million
   b. 2 trillion
   c. 7 billion
   d. 1.4 trillion
   e. 70 million

2. The percentage of the world's population that lives in the advanced economies is
   a. more than 71 percent.
   b. between 51 percent and 70 percent.
   c. between 31 percent and 50 percent.
   d. between 20 percent and 30 percent.
   e. less than 20 percent.

3. Which of following groups of countries are *all* advanced economies?
   a. Australia, Brazil, and the United States
   b. Hong Kong, Japan, France, and the United Kingdom
   c. Italy, the United States, China, and Russia
   d. Singapore, Russia, France, and Chad
   e. Mexico, Canada, Germany, and Egypt

4. The emerging market economies are
   a. the largest grouping including the nations of China and India.
   b. in transition from state-owned production to free markets.
   c. most of the nations of Western Europe.
   d. the nations that are currently agricultural in nature.
   e. the nations with the highest standards of living.

5. As a percentage of total world production, production in the 29 advanced economies is about ____ percent of total world production and in the 119 developing economies is about ____ percent of total world production.
   a. 53; 39
   b. 23; 62
   c. 53; 12
   d. 30; 46
   e. 19; 73

6. Compared to the developing economies, the advanced economies have ____ human capital and ____ physical capital.
   a. more; more
   b. more; less
   c. the same; the same
   d. less; more
   e. less; less

7. In the advanced economies, ____ of the factories use advanced capital equipment and in the developing economies ____ of the factories use advanced capital equipment.
   a. virtually all; virtually all
   b. some; some
   c. virtually all; none
   d. some; none of
   e. virtually all; some

8. Among the United States, Canada, Russia, India, and the United Kingdom, the country with the highest average income per person is
   a. the United States.
   b. Russia.
   c. India.
   d. Canada.
   e. the United Kingdom.

Short answer and numeric questions

1. What are the groups the International Monetary Fund uses to classify countries? Describe each group. Which group has the largest number of countries? The largest number of people?

2. As a fraction of total world production, how does production within the advanced economies compare to production within the developing economies? As a fraction of total population, how does the population within the advanced economies compare to the population within the developing economies?

3. How does the amount of human capital in the advanced economies compare to that in the developing economies?

4. How does the distribution of income within the United States compare to the distribution of income in the world economy?

Additional Exercises (also in MyEconLab Test A)

1. Describe how inequality around the world has changed over the past few decades.

CHECKPOINT 2.3

■ **Use the circular flow model to provide a picture of how households, firms, and governments interact in the U.S. economy and how the U.S. and other economies interact in the global economy.**

Quick Review

• *Circular flow model* A model of the econ-

omy, illustrated in Figure 2.1, that shows the circular flow of expenditures and incomes that result from firms', households', and governments' choices.

■ **FIGURE 2.1**

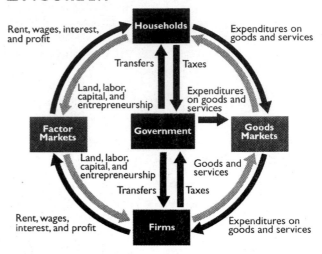

Additional Practice Problems 2.3

1. Describe where the following money flows fit in the circular flow.
   a. Shaniq pays for a taco at Taco Bell.
   b. Sam receives his monthly Social Security payment.
   c. Jennifer gets a $10,000 end of the year bonus from Bank of America, where she works.
   d. Exxon pays landowners in Texas $20,000 for the oil under their land.
   e. Bill pays property tax of $6,000.

2. In the circular flow, what is the relationship between the flow of expenditures into the goods markets (from households and the government) and the flow of revenues out of the goods markets to firms?

Solutions to Additional Practice Problems 2.3

1a. Shaniq's payment is an expenditure on a good that flows from households through the goods market to Taco Bell, a firm.

1b. Sam's check is a transfer payment from the government to households.

1c. Jennifer's payment is wages flowing from a firm, Bank of America, through the factor market to households.

1d. Exxon's payment is rent flowing from a firm, Exxon, through the factor market to households.

1e. Bill's payment is a tax flowing from households to government.

2. The flow of expenditures into the goods markets–the funds that households and the government spend on the goods and services they purchase–equals the flow of revenue out of the goods markets.

■ Self Test 2.3

Fill in the blanks

The ____ model shows the flows of expenditure and incomes. An arrangement that brings buyers and sellers together is a ____ (firm; household; market). A market in which goods and services are bought and sold is a ____ (goods; factor) market and a market in which the services of the factors of production are bought and sold is a ____ (goods; factor) market. In 2010, the federal government spent about ____ (24; 13) percent of the total value of the goods and services produced in the United States. A large part of what the federal government spends is ____ (social security benefits; personal income taxes). The two components that account for most of the federal government's tax revenue are ____. The largest part of the expenditures of state and local governments is spending on ____ (education; highways). When the value of U.S. imports exceeds the value of U.S. exports, U.S. residents ____ (borrow from; lend to) the rest of the world.

True or false

1. Firms own the factors of production.

2. A market is any arrangement where buyers and sellers meet face-to-face.

3. Factors of production flow from households to firms through goods markets.

4. Rent, wages, interest, and profit are the payments made by firms to households through factor markets.

5. Social security payments are made by state and local governments.

6. The largest part of the expenditures of state and local government is on education.

Multiple choice

1. Within the circular flow model, economists define households as
   a. families with at least 2 children.
   b. families living in their own houses.
   c. individuals or groups living together.
   d. married or engaged couples.
   e. individuals or groups within the same legally defined family.

2. A market is defined as
   a. the physical place where goods (but not services) are sold.
   b. the physical place where goods *and* services are sold.
   c. any arrangement that brings buyers and sellers together.
   d. a place where money is exchanged for goods.
   e. another name for a store.

3. In the circular flow model,
   a. only firms sell in markets.
   b. only households buy from markets.
   c. some firms only sell and some firms only buy.
   d. the money used to buy goods and the goods themselves travel in the same direction.
   e. both firms and households buy or sell in different markets.

4. ____ choose the quantities of goods and services to produce, while ____ choose the quantities of goods and services to buy.
   a. Households; firms
   b. Firms; households and the government
   c. The government; firms
   d. Firms; only households
   e. Households; the government

5. A circular flow model shows the interrelationship between the ____ market and the ____ markets.
   a. household; goods
   b. household; factor
   c. business; household
   d. expenditure; income
   e. goods; factor

6. In the circular flow model, the expenditures on goods and services flow in the
   a. same direction as goods and services in all cases.
   b. same direction as goods and services *only if* they both flow through the goods market.
   c. same direction as goods and services *only if* they both flow through the factor market.
   d. opposite direction as goods and services.
   e. same direction as factor markets.

7. Of the following, the largest source of revenue for the federal government is
   a. personal income taxes.
   b. sales taxes.
   c. corporate income taxes.
   d. property taxes.
   e. lottery revenue.

8. U.S. exports of goods and services flow to households and firms in ____ and U.S. financial inflows of capital flow to households and firms in ____.
   a. the United States; the United States
   b. the United States; the rest of the world
   c. the rest of the world; the United States
   d. the rest of the world; the rest of the world
   e. the United States; the rest of the world and the United States

Complete the graph

■ **FIGURE 2.2**

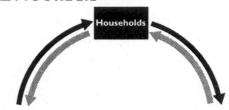

1. Figure 2.2 ignores the government and shows the flows into and out of households. Label the flows and identify who they come from and who they go to.

■ **FIGURE 2.3**

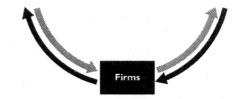

2. Figure 2.3 ignores the government and shows the flows into and out of firms. Label the flows and identify who they come from and who they go to.

■ **FIGURE 2.4**

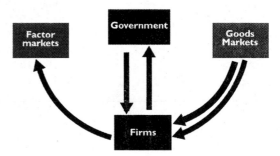

3. Figure 2.4 now includes the government and shows the money flows into and out of firms. Label the money flows.

Short answer and numeric questions

1. Ignoring taxes and transfer payments, what funds flow into firms and what funds flow out of them?

2. Is it possible for something to affect households and not firms? To affect firms and not households? Explain your answers.

3. The circular flow reveals that which two groups interact to determine what will be the payments to the factors of production?

4. In the circular flow model, what are the sources of expenditures on goods and services?

5. In recent years, which spent more, the federal government or state and local governments?

Additional Exercises (also in MyEconLab Test A)

1. What are the choices made by households and firms that determine what, how, and for whom goods and services are produced? Where, in the circular flow model, do those choices appear?

2. How do the actions of governments modify what, how, and for whom goods and services are produced? Where, in the circular flow model, do those choices appear?

SELF TEST ANSWERS

■ CHECKPOINT 2.1

Fill in the blanks

Goods and services that are bought by individuals and used to provide personal enjoyment and to contribute to a person's standard of living are <u>consumption</u> goods. Goods that are bought by businesses to increase their productive resources are <u>capital</u> goods. Goods that are produced in the United States and sold in other countries are <u>export</u> goods. Of the four large groups of goods and services in the United States, <u>consumption goods and services</u> have the largest share of total production. Productive resources are called <u>factors of production</u> and are grouped into four categories: <u>labor</u>, <u>land</u>, <u>capital</u>, and <u>entrepreneurship</u>. In 2010, <u>labor</u> received 69 percent of total income. The distribution of income among households is called the <u>personal</u> distribution of income.

True or false

    1. True; page 32
    2. True; page 34
    3. True; page 36
    4. True; page 37
    5. False; page 37

Multiple choice

    1. a; page 32
    2. a; page 32
    3. d; page 32
    4. e; page 34
    5. c; page 35
    6. b; page 37
    7. a; page 37
    8. e; page 37

Short answer and numeric questions

    1. An automobile might be either a consumption or a capital good. It is a consumption good if it is purchased by a household. It is a capital good if it is purchased by a business for use within the business; page 32.
    2. The richest 20 percent of households receive 51 percent of the total U.S. income. The poorest 20 percent of households receive 3 percent of the total U.S. income; page 37.

Additional Exercises (also in MyEconLab Test A)

    1. Consumption goods and services are items that are bought by individuals and used to provide personal enjoyment. They contribute to a person's standard of living. Capital goods are goods that are bought by businesses to increase their productive resources and thereby help produce additional goods and services. Capital goods increase the nation's capital, which is a productive resource; page 32.
    2. If everyone were to consume an equal quantity of goods and services, the poorest 20 percent of individuals would need to receive about 17 percent of total income from the higher-income groups; page 37.
    3. Labor earns by far the largest share of the nation's total income, about 69 percent. The other factors of production earn only 31 percent of the nation's total income; page 37.

■ CHECKPOINT 2.2

Fill in the blanks

Most of the world's population lives in the <u>developing economies</u>. The lowest average income is in the <u>developing economies</u>. Advanced economies produce about <u>53</u> percent of the world's total production and the United States, alone, produces about <u>20</u> percent of the world's total production. As a fraction of total output, agricultural is a <u>larger</u> part of the economy in developing economies than in advanced economies. Factories in advanced economies generally are much <u>more</u> capital intensive than in developing economies. During the past 20 years, the distribution of income in the world economy has become <u>more</u> equal.

True or false

    1. False; page 39
    2. False; page 39

3. False; page 40
4. True; page 42
5. True; page 42
6. True; page 44

Multiple choice
1. c; page 39
2. e; page 39
3. b; page 39
4. b; page 39
5. a; page 40
6. a; pages 42-43
7. e; page 43
8. a; pages 43-44

Short answer and numeric questions
1. The groups are the advanced economies and the emerging market and developing economies. Advanced economies have the highest standard of living. Emerging market and developing economies have yet to achieve a high standard of living. The emerging market economies are changing their economies from government management and state-ownership of capital to market-based economies similar to that in the United States. There are more nations, 119, and more people, almost 5 billion, in developing economies; page 39.

2. Production in the advanced and emerging economies accounts for 61 percent of world production and production in the developing economies accounts for 39 percent. The population within the advanced and emerging economies accounts for 22 percent of the world's population and the developing economies account for 78 percent of the world's population; page 40.

3. The human capital possessed by workers in the advanced economies is *much* larger than that in the developing economies. People in the advanced economies have vastly more education, more on-the-job training and, in general, better health than in the developing economies; page 42.

4. The distribution of income within the United States is more equal than the distribution of income in the world economy. In the United States, the poorest 20 percent of households receive about 3 percent of the total income and the richest 20 percent of households receive about 50 percent of total income. In the world economy, the poorest 20 percent of households receive about 2 percent of total income and the richest 20 percent receive about 70 percent of total income; page 43.

Additional Exercises (also in MyEconLab Test A)
1. Inequality around the world has decreased over the past few decades. Extreme poverty has fallen, largely because of income growth in China, the largest nation in the world and a nation that was the source of much of the extreme poverty of a few decades ago; page 44.

■ CHECKPOINT 2.3

Fill in the blanks
The circular flow model shows the flows of expenditures and incomes. An arrangement that brings buyers and sellers together is a market. A market in which goods and services are bought and sold is a goods market and a market in which the services of the factors of production are bought and sold is a factor market. In 2010, the federal government spent about 24 percent of the total value of the goods and services produced in the United States. A large part of what the federal government spends is social security benefits. The two components that account for most of the federal government's tax revenue are personal income tax and social security tax. The largest part of the expenditures of state and local governments is spending on education. When the value of U.S. imports exceeds the value of U.S. exports, U.S. residents borrow from the rest of the world.

True or false
1. False; page 46
2. False; page 46
3. False; pages 46-47

4. True; pages 46-47
5. False; page 48
6. True; page 51

Multiple choice
1. c; page 46
2. c; page 46
3. e; pages 46-47
4. b; pages 47, 49
5. e; pages 46-47
6. d; page 47
7. a; page 50
8. c; page 53

Complete the graph
■ FIGURE 2.5

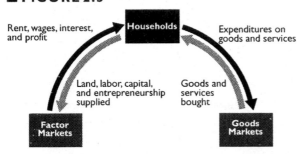

1. Figure 2.5 labels the flows. Rent, wages, interest, and profits (or losses) flow from the factor markets while the services from land, labor, capital, and entrepreneurship flow to the factor markets. In addition, expenditures on goods and services flow to the goods market, and goods and services flow from the goods market; page 47.

■ FIGURE 2.6

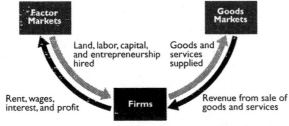

2. Figure 2.6 labels the flows. Revenue from the sale of goods and services, which are the expenditures on goods and services, flow to firms from the goods market and payments of rent, wages, interest, and profit (or loss) flow from firms into the factor market. The services from land, labor, capital, and entrepreneurship flow to firms from the factor markets, and goods and services flow from firms into the goods markets; page 47.

■ FIGURE 2.7

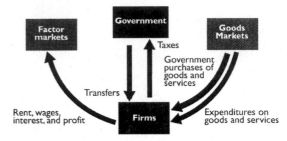

3. Figure 2.7 labels the money flows into and out of firms. The difference between this figure and Figure 2.6 is the addition of transfers and taxes; page 49.

Short answer and numeric questions
1. Funds that flow into firms are households' expenditures and government purchases of goods and services. Funds that flow out of firms are payments for rent, wages, interest, and profit (or loss) to households in exchange for the factors of production; pages 47, 49.

2. The circular flow shows that at the macroeconomic level it is impossible for something to influence only firms or only households. An influence that changes households' buying behavior in goods markets affects firms because they sell to households in goods markets; page 47.

3. Payments to the factors of production are determined by the interaction of households, who own and provide the services from the factors of production, and firms, who employ the services from these factors; page 47.

4. The circular flow identifies two sources of expenditures on goods and services, expenditures by households and expenditures by the government; page 49.

5. In 2010, the federal government spent $3.5 trillion and in 2008 state and local governments spent $2.1 trillion. The federal government spends significantly more than state and local governments; page 48.

Additional Exercises (also in MyEconLab Test A)

1. Households choose the quantities of land, labor, capital, and entrepreneurship services to provide to firms. Households decide what goods and services they will buy. Firms choose the quantities of services of the factors of production to hire and the quantities of goods and services to produce. Households decide what to buy in goods markets and what quantities of the services of factors of production to provide in factor markets. Firms decide the quantities of services of factors of production to hire in factor markets and the quantity of goods and services to produce in goods markets; pages 46-47.

2. Governments modify the answers to the "what," "how," and "for whom" questions by their interactions with firms and households. In the goods market, governments decide what goods to buy, thereby affecting the "what" question. Governments also tax firms and households and give firms and households transfer payments. These directly effect the "for whom" question because taxes decrease the payer's ability to buy goods and services while transfers enhance the recipient's buying power. The taxes and transfer payments also affect households' and firms' decisions about what services of the factors of production to provide and what services to buy, so these taxes and transfer payments also affect the "how" question; page 49.

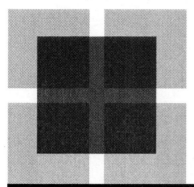

The Economic Problem

Chapter 3

Chapter 3 develops an economic model, the production possibilities frontier, or *PPF*, model. The *PPF* shows how the opportunity cost of a good or service increases as more of the good or service is produced. It can be used to illustrate economic growth and to demonstrate societies and individuals gain by specializing according to comparative advantage.

1 Explain and illustrate the concepts of scarcity, production efficiency, and tradeoff using the production possibilities frontier.

The production possibilities frontier, *PPF*, is the boundary between the combinations of goods and services that can be produced and those that cannot be produced, given the available factors of production and technology. Production points outside the *PPF* are unattainable. Points on and inside the *PPF* are attainable. Production points on the *PPF* are production efficient while production points within the *PPF* are inefficient. Moving along the *PPF* producing more of one good, less of another good is produced—a tradeoff. Moving from inside the *PPF* to a point on the *PPF*, more of some goods and services can be produced without producing less of others—a free lunch.

2 Calculate opportunity cost.

Along the *PPF* all choices involve a tradeoff. Along the *PPF*, the opportunity cost of the good on the *x*-axis is the loss of the good measured along the *y*-axis and is equal to the decrease in the good on the *y*-axis divided by the increase in the good on the *x*-axis. As more of a good is produced, its opportunity cost increases, so the *PPF* is bowed outward. The opportunity cost increases because resources are not equally productive in all activities. In the real world, most activities have increasing opportunity cost.

3 Explain what makes production possibilities expand.

Economic growth is the sustained expansion of production possibilities. If more capital is accumulated production possibilities increase and the *PPF* shifts outward. The (opportunity) cost of economic growth is that resources used to increase capital cannot be used to produce current consumption goods and services.

4 Explain how people gain from specialization and trade.

A person (or nation) has an absolute advantage when the person (or nation) is more productive than another—needs fewer inputs or less time to produce the good. A person (or nation) has a comparative advantage in an activity or producing a good if the person (or nation) can perform the activity or produce the good at lower opportunity cost than another. A person (or nation) can have an absolute advantage in all activities but cannot have a comparative advantage in all activities. People can gain from specializing in production according to comparative advantage and then trading with others. In this situation people (and nations) can consume combinations of goods and services that lie beyond their production possibilities frontiers.

■ **Explain and illustrate the concepts of scarcity, production efficiency, and tradeoff using the production possibilities frontier.**

Quick Review

- *Production possibilities frontier* The boundary between combinations of goods and services that can be produced and combinations that cannot be produced, given the available factors of production and the state of technology.
- *Unattainable points* Production points outside the *PPF* are unattainable.
- *Tradeoff* A constraint or limit to what is possible that forces an exchange or a substitution of one thing for something else.

Additional Practice Problem 3.1

Possibility	Fish (pounds)		Fruit (pounds)
A	0.0	and	36.0
B	4.0	and	35.0
C	7.5	and	33.0
D	10.5	and	30.0
E	13.0	and	26.0
F	15.0	and	21.0
G	16.5	and	15.0
H	17.5	and	8.0
I	18.0	and	0.0

1. The table above shows Crusoe's *PPF*. Can Crusoe gather 21 pounds of fruit and catch 30 pounds of fish? Explain your answer. Suppose that Crusoe discovers another fishing pond with more fish, so that he can catch twice as many fish as before. Now can Crusoe gather 21 pounds of fruit and catch 30 pounds of fish? Explain your answer.

Solution to Additional Practice Problem 3.1

1. Initially, Crusoe cannot gather 21 pounds of fruit and catch 30 pounds of fish. This production point lies outside his *PPF* and so is unattainable. Once Crusoe discovers the new pond, however, he can gather 21 pounds of fruit and catch 30 pounds of fish. (In Row *F*, double the

amount of Crusoe's fish.) The *PPF* depends on the available factors of production and when the factors of production increase, Crusoe's production possibilities change.

■ **Self Test 3.1**

Fill in the blanks

The ____ is the boundary between the combinations of goods and services that can and that cannot be produced given the available ____ (goods; factors of production) and ____ (number of services; state of technology). Production points outside the *PPF* ____ (are unattainable; are attainable; represent a free lunch). Production points ____ (on; beyond; within) the *PPF* are production efficient. Society has the possibility of a free lunch if production occurs ____ (inside; on; outside) the *PPF*. When resources are fully employed we face a ____ (free lunch; tradeoff).

True or false

1. A point outside the production possibilities frontier is unattainable.
2. If all the factors of production are fully employed, the economy will produce at a point on the production possibilities frontier.
3. Moving from one point on the *PPF* to another point on the *PPF* illustrates a free lunch.
4. All production points on the *PPF* are production efficient.

Multiple choice

1. The production possibilities frontier is a graph showing the
   a. exact point of greatest efficiency for producing goods and services.
   b. tradeoff between free lunches.
   c. maximum combinations of goods and services that can be produced.
   d. minimum combinations of goods and services that can be produced.
   e. resources available for the economy's production uses.

2. The production possibilities frontier is a boundary that separates
   a. the combinations of goods that can be produced from the combinations of services.
   b. attainable combinations of goods and services that can be produced from unattainable combinations.
   c. equitable combinations of goods and services that can be produced from inequitable combinations.
   d. fair combinations of goods and services that can be consumed from unfair combinations.
   e. affordable production points from unaffordable points.

3. Points inside the *PPF* are all
   a. unattainable and have fully employed resources.
   b. attainable and have fully employed resources.
   c. unattainable and have some unemployed resources.
   d. attainable and have some unemployed resources.
   e. unaffordable.

4. Points on the *PPF* are all
   a. unattainable and have fully employed resources.
   b. free lunches.
   c. inefficient.
   d. attainable and have some unemployed resources.
   e. production efficient.

5. During a time with high unemployment, a country can increase the production of one good or service
   a. without decreasing the production of something else.
   b. but must decrease the production of something else.
   c. and must increase the production of something else.
   d. by using resources in the production process twice.
   e. but the opportunity cost is infinite.

6. Moving along the production possibilities frontier itself illustrates
   a. the existence of tradeoffs.
   b. the existence of unemployment of some factors of production.
   c. the benefits of free lunches.
   d. how free lunches can be exploited through trade.
   e. how tradeoffs need not occur if the economy is efficient.

Complete the graph

■ **FIGURE 3.1**

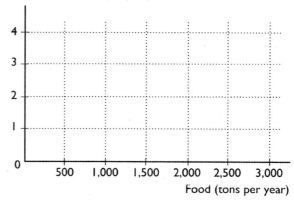

Computers (millions per year)

1. In Figure 3.1, draw a production possibilities frontier showing combinations of computers and food. Label the points that are attainable and unattainable. Label the points that have full employment and the points that have unemployment.

Short answer and numeric questions

1. What factors limit the amount of production in the United States?
2. What points are production efficient? Moving between these points, is there a tradeoff or a free lunch?
3. What is the relationship between unemployment of a resource and a free lunch? Between full employment of all factors of production and a tradeoff?

Additional Exercises (also in MyEconLab Test A)

The table shows the production possibilities frontier of a small Pacific island economy.

Possibility	Fish (pounds)		Berries (pounds)
A	0	and	20
B	1	and	18
C	2	and	15
D	3	and	11
E	4	and	6
F	5	and	0

Use this table to work these exercises.

1. Explain why this economy cannot produce 2 pounds of fish and 18 pounds of berries.

2. Explain why 3 pounds of fish and 11 pounds of berries achieves production efficiency.

3. Explain why it would be inefficient to produce 4 pounds of fish and 5 pounds of berries.

4. Explain why moving from row A to row B of the table involves a tradeoff.

5. Explain why the citizens of this economy could enjoy a free lunch if they were producing 4 pounds of fish and 5 pounds of berries.

CHECKPOINT 3.2

■ Calculate opportunity cost.

Quick Review

- *Opportunity cost is a ratio* Along a *PPF*, the opportunity cost of one good equals the quantity of the other good forgone divided by the increase in the first good.

Additional Practice Problem 3.2

Possibility	Fish (pounds)		Fruit (pounds)
A	0.0	and	36.0
B	4.0	and	35.0
C	7.5	and	33.0
D	10.5	and	30.0
E	13.0	and	26.0
F	15.0	and	21.0
G	16.5	and	15.0
H	17.5	and	8.0
I	18.0	and	0.0

1. The table above shows Robinson Crusoe's production possibilities. How does Crusoe's op-portunity cost of a pound of fish change as he catches more fish?

Solution to Additional Practice Problem 3.2

Move from	Increase in fish (pounds)	Decrease in fruit (pounds)	Opportunity cost of fish (pounds of fruit)
A to B	4.0	1.0	0.25
B to C	3.5	2.0	0.57
C to D	3.0	3.0	1.00
D to E	2.5	4.0	1.60
E to F	2.0	5.0	2.50
F to G	1.5	6.0	4.00
G to H	1.0	7.0	7.00
H to I	0.5	8.0	16.00

1. The table above shows Crusoe's opportunity cost of a pound of fish. His opportunity cost of a pound of fish increases as he catches more fish. As he moves from point A to point B and catches his first fish, the opportunity cost is only 0.25 pounds of fruit per pound of fish. But as he moves from point H to point I and catches only fish, the opportunity cost has increased to 16.0 pounds of fruit per pound of fish.

■ Self Test 3.2

Fill in the blanks

Along a production possibilities frontier, the opportunity cost of obtaining one more unit of a good is the amount of another good that is ____ (gained; forgone). The opportunity cost is equal to the quantity of the good forgone ____ (plus; divided by) the increase in the quantity of the other good. As more of a good is produced, its opportunity cost ____.

True or false

1. Moving from one point on the *PPF* to another point on the *PPF* has no opportunity cost.

2. When moving along the *PPF*, the quantity of CDs increases by 2 and the quantity of DVDs decreases by 1, so the opportunity cost is 2 CDs minus 1 DVD.

3. Increasing opportunity costs are common.

Multiple choice

1. The opportunity cost of one more slice of pizza in terms of sodas is the
   a. number of pizza slices we have to give up to get one extra soda.
   b. number of sodas we have to give up to get one extra slice of pizza.
   c. total number of sodas that we have divided by the total number of pizza slices that we have.
   d. total number of pizza slices that we have divided by the total number of sodas that we have.
   e. price of a pizza slice minus the price of a soda.

2. Moving between two points on a *PPF*, a country gains 6 automobiles and forgoes 3 trucks. The opportunity cost of 1 automobile is
   a. 3 trucks.
   b. 6 automobiles – 3 trucks.
   c. 2 trucks.
   d. 1/2 of a truck.
   e. 1 automobile.

3. Moving between two points on a *PPF*, a country gains 8 desktop computers and forgoes 4 laptop computers. The opportunity cost of 1 desktop computer is
   a. 4 laptops.
   b. 8 desktops.
   c. 1 desktop.
   d. 2 laptops.
   e. 1/2 of a laptop.

4. A country produces only cans of soup and ink pens. If the country produces on its bowed outward *PPF* and increases the production of cans of soup, the opportunity cost of additional
   a. cans of soup is increasing.
   b. cans of soup is decreasing.
   c. cans of soup remain unchanged.
   d. ink pens is increasing.
   e. More information is needed to determine what happens to the opportunity cost.

5. Moving along a country's *PPF*, a reason opportunity costs increase is that
   a. unemployment decreases as a country produces more and more of one good.
   b. unemployment increases as a country produces more and more of one good.
   c. technology declines as a country produces more and more of one good.
   d. some resources are better suited for producing one good rather than the other.
   e. technology must advance in order to produce more and more of one good.

6. Increasing opportunity costs exist
   a. in the real world.
   b. as long as there is high unemployment.
   c. only in theory but not in real life.
   d. for a country but not for an individual.
   e. inside the *PPF* but not on the *PPF*.

Complete the graph

Production point	MP3 players (millions per year)		DVD players (millions per year)
A	4.0	and	0.0
B	3.0	and	3.0
C	2.0	and	4.0
D	1.0	and	4.7
E	0.0	and	5.0

1. The table shows the production possibilities for a nation.
   a. Placing MP3 players on the vertical axis, label the axes in Figure 3.2 and graph the production possibilities frontier.

■ **FIGURE 3.2**

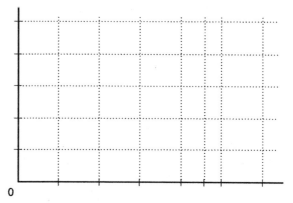

b. What is the opportunity cost per DVD player of moving from point *A* to point *B*? *B* to *C*? *C* to *D*? *D* to *E*? How does the opportunity cost change as more DVD players are produced?

Short answer and numeric questions

Production point	Cans of soda (millions per year)		Candy bars (millions per year)
A	8.0	and	0.0
B	6.0	and	4.0
C	4.0	and	6.0
D	2.0	and	7.0
E	0.0	and	7.5

1. The table above shows the production possibilities for Sweetland.
   a. What is the opportunity cost per candy bar player of moving from point *A* to point *B*? *B* to *C*? *C* to *D*? *D* to *E*?
   b. What is the opportunity cost per can of soda of moving from point *E* to point *D*? *D* to *C*? *C* to *B*? *B* to *A*?
   c. How does the opportunity cost of a candy bar change as more candy bars are produced? How does the opportunity cost of a soda change as more sodas are produced?

2. What is the opportunity cost of increasing the production of a good while moving along a *PPF*? Why does this opportunity cost increase?

3. What does it mean for the opportunity cost to be a ratio?

Additional Exercises (also in MyEconLab Test A)

Possibility	Fish (pounds)		Berries (pounds)
A	0	and	20
B	3.0	and	18
C	5.5	and	15
D	7.5	and	11
E	9.0	and	6
F	10.0	and	0

The table shows Robinson Crusoe's production possibilities in winter. Use the information in this table to work the exercises.
1. If Crusoe currently catches 5.5 pounds of fish and picks 11 pounds of berries a day, what is his opportunity cost of an extra pound of berries? And what is his opportunity cost of an extra pound of fish? Explain your answers.
2. If Crusoe produces efficiently, does his opportunity cost of a pound of berries increase as he spends more time picking berries? Explain.

CHECKPOINT 3.3

■ **Explain what makes production possibilities expand.**

Quick Review

- *Opportunity cost of growth* The opportunity cost of economic growth is the current consumption goods and services forgone.

Additional Practice Problem 3.3
1. Does economic growth eliminate scarcity?

Solution to Additional Practice Problem 3.3
1. Economic growth does not eliminate scarcity. Scarcity exists as long as people's wants exceed what can be produced. Economic growth increases the goods and services that can be produced but people's wants will continue to outstrip the ability to produce. While economic growth means that additional wants can be satisfied, people's wants are infinite and so scarcity will continue to be present even with economic growth.

■ **Self Test 3.3**

Fill in the blanks

A sustained expansion of production possibilities is called ____. Economic growth shifts the *PPF* ____ (inward; outward). The *PPF* shows that economic growth requires ____ (a decrease; an increase) in the current production of consumption goods. The opportunity cost of increasing economic growth is the loss of the ____ (current; future) goods that can be consumed.

True or false
1. Economic growth abolishes scarcity.

2. The opportunity cost of economic growth is less consumption goods in the future.
3. Production possibilities per person in the United States have remained constant during the last 30 years.

Multiple choice

1. To increase its economic growth, a nation should
   a. limit the number of people in college because they produce nothing.
   b. encourage spending on goods and services.
   c. encourage education because that increases the quality of labor.
   d. increase current consumption.
   e. eliminate expenditure on capital goods.

2. Other things equal, if Mexico devotes more resources to train its population than Spain,
   a. Mexico will be able to eliminate opportunity cost faster than Spain.
   b. Mexico will be able to eliminate scarcity faster than Spain.
   c. Spain will grow faster than Mexico.
   d. Mexico will grow faster than Spain.
   e. Mexico will have more current consumption than Spain.

3. If a nation devotes a larger share of its current production to consumption goods, then
   a. its economic growth will slow down.
   b. its *PPF* will shift outward.
   c. its *PPF* will shift inward.
   d. some productive factors will become unemployed.
   e. it must produce at a point within its *PPF*.

4. Which of the following is correct?
   i. As an economy grows, the opportunity costs of economic growth decrease.
   ii. Economic growth has no opportunity cost.
   iii. The opportunity cost of economic growth is current consumption forgone.
   a. i only.
   b. ii only.
   c. iii only.
   d. i and iii.
   e. i and ii.

5. When a country's production possibilities frontier shifts outward over time, the country is experiencing
   a. no opportunity cost.
   b. economic growth.
   c. higher unemployment of resources.
   d. a decrease in unemployment of resources.
   e. an end to opportunity cost.

6. The opportunity cost of economic growth is _____ and the benefit of economic growth is _____.
   a. increased current consumption; increased future consumption
   b. increased current consumption; decreased future consumption
   c. decreased current consumption; increased future consumption
   d. decreased current consumption; decreased future consumption.
   e. nothing; increased future consumption.

Complete the graph

■ **FIGURE 3.3**

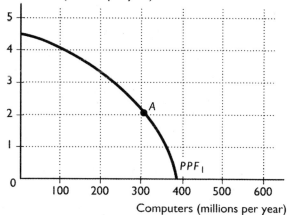

1. In the above figure, illustrate what happens if there is a technological breakthrough in the production of computers but not in the production of automobiles.
   a. Suppose the economy was initially producing at point *A*. After the breakthrough, is it possible for the economy to produce more computers *and* more automobiles?

Short answer and numeric questions

1. What is the opportunity cost of economic growth?

2. What is the benefit of economic growth?

Additional Exercises (also in MyEconLab Test A)

Possibility	Education services (graduates)		Consumption goods (units)
A	1,000	and	0
B	750	and	1,000
C	500	and	2,000
D	0	and	3,000

1. If the nation shown in the table above uses all its resources to produce consumption goods, at what rate will the nation grow? If the nation increases the number of graduates from 0 to 750, will the nation experience economic growth? Explain your answer.

CHECKPOINT 3.4

■ **Explain how people gain from specialization and trade.**

Quick Review

- *Comparative advantage* The ability of a person to perform an activity or produce a good or service at a lower opportunity cost than someone else.

Additional Practice Problem 3.4

1. Tony and Patty produce scooters and snowboards. The figure shows their production possibilities per day. With these production possibilities, the opportunity cost of a snowboard for Patty is 1/2 a scooter and for Tony is 2 scooters. Patty has a lower opportunity cost and therefore she has the comparative advantage in snowboards. The opportunity cost of a scooter for Patty is 2

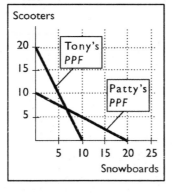

snowboards and for Tony is 1/2 of a snowboard. Tony has a lower opportunity cost and so he has the comparative advantage in scooters.

Suppose Patty acquires new equipment for scooter production that lets her produce a maximum of 60 rather than 10 scooters a day, should Patty and Tony specialize and trade?

Solution to Additional Practice Problem 3.4

1. Once Patty can produce 60 scooters a day, her opportunity costs change. Her opportunity cost of a scooter falls to 1/3 of a snowboard per scooter and her opportunity cost of a snowboard rises to 3 scooters per snowboard. With these opportunity costs, the comparative advantages have switched: Patty now has a comparative advantage in scooters and Tony in snowboards. Patty and Tony should still specialize and trade, only now Patty will specialize in scooters and Tony will specialize in snowboards. Comparative advantage can switch as the production possibilities frontier shifts outward.

■ **Self Test 3.4**

Fill in the blanks

A person (or nation) has ____ (a comparative; an absolute) advantage if they are more productive than another in producing a good. A person has ____ (a comparative; an absolute) advantage in an activity if that person can perform the activity at a lower opportunity cost than someone else. It ____ (is; is not) possible for someone to have a comparative advantage in all activities. It ____ (is; is not) possible for someone to have an absolute advantage in all activities. If people specialize according to ____ (comparative; absolute) advantage and then trade, they can get to a consumption ____ (outside; inside) their production possibilities frontiers.

True or false

1. A person has an absolute advantage in an activity if the person can perform the activity at lower opportunity cost than someone else.

2. To achieve the gains from trade, a producer specializes in the product in which he or she has a comparative advantage and then trades with others.

3. Specialization and trade can make both producers better off even if one of them has an absolute advantage in producing all goods.

Multiple choice

1. "Comparative advantage" is defined as a situation in which one person can produce
   a. more of all goods than another person.
   b. more of a good than another person.
   c. a good for a lower dollar cost than another person.
   d. a good for a lower opportunity cost than another person.
   e. all goods for lower opportunity costs than another person.

For the next three questions, use the following information: Scott and Cindy both produce only pizza and tacos. In one hour, Scott can produce 20 pizzas or 40 tacos. In one hour, Cindy can produce 30 pizzas or 40 tacos.

2. Scott's opportunity cost of producing 1 taco is
   a. 1/2 of a pizza.
   b. 1 pizza.
   c. 2 pizzas.
   d. 20 pizzas.
   e. 2 tacos.

3. Cindy's opportunity cost of producing 1 taco is
   a. 3/4 of a pizza.
   b. 1 pizza.
   c. 30 pizzas.
   d. 40 pizzas.
   e. 1 taco.

4. Based on the data given,
   a. Cindy has a comparative advantage in producing tacos.
   b. Scott has a comparative advantage in producing tacos.
   c. Cindy and Scott have the same comparative advantage in producing tacos.
   d. neither Cindy nor Scott has a comparative advantage in producing tacos.
   e. Cindy and Scott have the same comparative advantage in producing pizzas.

5. In one hour John can produce 20 loaves of bread or 8 cakes. In one hour Phyllis can produce 30 loaves of bread or 15 cakes. Which of the following statements is true?
   a. Phyllis has a comparative advantage in producing bread.
   b. John has a comparative advantage in producing cakes.
   c. Phyllis has an absolute advantage in both goods.
   d. John has an absolute advantage in both goods.
   e. Phyllis has a comparative advantage in producing both cakes and bread.

6. In one hour John can produce 20 loaves of bread or 16 cakes. In one hour Phyllis can produce 30 loaves of bread or 15 cakes. Which of the following statements is true?
   a. Phyllis has a comparative advantage in producing cakes.
   b. John has a comparative advantage in producing cakes.
   c. Phyllis has an absolute advantage in both goods.
   d. John has an absolute advantage in both goods.
   e. Phyllis has a comparative advantage in producing both cakes and bread.

7. In one hour John can produce 20 loaves of bread or 16 cakes. In one hour Phyllis can produce 30 loaves of bread or 15 cakes. John and Phyllis will reap the largest gains from specialization and trade if John produces _____ and Phyllis produces _____.
   a. only bread; only cakes
   b. only cakes; only bread
   c. both bread and cakes; only loaves
   d. only cakes; both bread and cakes
   e. both bread and cake; both bread and cake

Complete the graph

■ **FIGURE 3.4**

Shirts (per day)

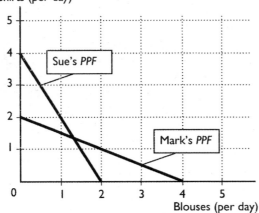

1. Figure 3.4 shows Mark and Sue's *PPFs*.
   a. What is Sue's opportunity cost of producing a shirt? What is Mark's opportunity cost of producing a shirt?
   b. Who has the comparative advantage in producing shirts?
   c. What is Sue's opportunity cost of producing a blouse? What is Mark's opportunity cost of producing a blouse?
   d. Who has the comparative advantage in producing blouses?
   e. Who should specialize in producing blouses and who should specialize in producing shirts?

f. If Mark and Sue specialize according to their comparative advantage, indicate the total production of shirts and blouses by putting a point in Figure 3.4 showing the total production. Label the point *A*.
g. How does point *A* show the gains from trade?

Short answer and numeric questions

1. Why should people specialize according to their comparative advantage?
2. When it comes to trading one good for another, why is comparative advantage crucial and absolute advantage unimportant?

Additional Exercises (also in MyEconLab Test A)

Sara and Fran produce boards and sails for windsurfing. The tables show their production possibilities. Each week Sara produces 6 boards and 6 sails, and Fran produces 24 boards and 24 sails.

Sara's Production Possibilities		
Boards (per week)		Sails (per week)
15	and	0
12	and	2
9	and	4
6	and	6
3	and	8
0	and	10

Fran's Production Possibilities		
Boards (per week)		Sails (per week)
40	and	0
32	and	12
24	and	24
16	and	36
8	and	48
0	and	60

1. Who has a comparative advantage in producing boards? And who has a comparative advantage in producing sails?
2. Can Sara and Fran gain by changing their production and trading 1 board for 1 sail? Explain why or why not.

■ SELF TEST ANSWERS

■ CHECKPOINT 3.1

Fill in the blanks

The <u>production possibilities frontier or *PPF*</u> is the boundary between the combinations of goods and services that can and that cannot be produced given the available <u>factors of production</u> and <u>state of technology</u>. Production points outside the *PPF* <u>are unattainable</u>. Production points <u>on</u> the *PPF* are production efficient. Society has the possibility of a free lunch if production occurs <u>inside</u> the *PPF*. When resources are fully employed we face a <u>tradeoff</u>.

True or false

1. True; page 62
2. True; page 62
3. False; page 63
4. True; pages 62-63

Multiple choice

1. c; page 60
2. b; pages 61-62
3. d; page 62
4. e; pages 62-63
5. a; page 64
6. a; pages 63-64

Complete the graph

■ FIGURE 3.5

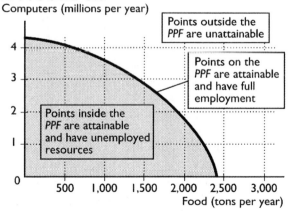

Computers (millions per year)

1. Figure 3.5 shows a *PPF* between computers and food; pages 61-62.

Short answer and numeric questions

1. The factors that limit the amount of production in *any* economy are the available resources and the state of technology; page 60.
2. All points *on* the production possibilities frontier are production efficient. Moving from one point to another incurs an opportunity cost so there is tradeoff; pages 62-64.
3. When the nation is producing at a point with unemployment of a resource, there are free lunches available because the production of some goods and services can be increased without decreasing the production of anything else. When the nation is producing at full employment of all factors of production, the production point is on the *PPF* and so only tradeoffs are available: If the production of one good or service is increased, the production of something else must be decreased; pages 63-64.

Additional Exercises (also in MyEconLab Test A)

1. The combination of 2 pounds of fish and 18 pounds of berries is not attainable. After the economy produces 2 pounds of fish, the maximum amount of berries it can produce is 15 pounds, not 18 pounds; page 62.
2. The combination of 3 pounds of fish and 11 pounds of berries is production efficient because it lies on the nation's production possibilities frontier. After producing 3 pounds of fish, the production possibilities frontier indicates that the maximum amount of berries that can be produced is 11 pounds, which is the amount produced in the question; pages 62-63.
3. It is inefficient to produce 4 pounds of fish and 5 pounds of berries because it is possible to more berries (or more fish). In particular, after producing 4 pounds of fish the production possibilities frontier indicates that it is possible to produce 6 pounds of berries, 1 pound *more* than the (inefficient) amount in the question, 5 pounds of berries; page 63.

4. Moving from row *A* to row *B* involves a tradeoff because the production of more fish is traded off against the production of fewer berries; pages 63-64.

5. The citizens could enjoy a free lunch if they were producing 4 pounds of fish and 5 pounds of berries because this production combination is inefficient. According to the production possibilities frontier, after producing 4 pounds of fish if resource use is rearranged so that it efficient, the nation could produce 6 pounds of berries, 1 pound *more* than the (inefficient) amount in the question, 5 pounds of berries. Hence by using resources more efficiently, the citizens could have more berries and not lose any fish, a free lunch; pages 63-64.

■ CHECKPOINT 3.2

Fill in the blanks

Along a production possibilities frontier, the opportunity cost of obtaining one more unit of a good is the amount of another good that is forgone. The opportunity cost is equal to the quantity of the good forgone divided by the increase in the quantity of the other good. As more of a good is produced, its opportunity cost increases.

True or false

1. False; page 66
2. False; page 67
3. True; page 68

Multiple choice

1. b; page 66
2. d; page 66
3. e; page 66
4. a; page 67
5. d; page 68
6. a; page 68

Complete the graph

1. a. Figure 3.6 illustrates the production possibilities frontier; page 66.
   b. The opportunity cost of moving from point

■ FIGURE 3.6

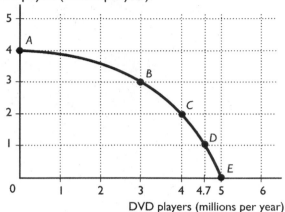

MP3 players (millions per year)

DVD players (millions per year)

A to point *B* to is 0.33 MP3 players per DVD player; from *B* to *C* is 1.00 MP3 player per DVD player; from *C* to *D* is 1.43 MP3 players per DVD player; and, from *D* to *E* is 3.33 MP3 players per DVD player. The opportunity cost increases; page 66.

Short answer and numeric questions

1. a. The opportunity cost of moving from point *A* to point *B* to is 0.5 cans of soda per candy bar; from *B* to *C* is 1.0 can of soda per candy bar; from *C* to *D* is 2.0 cans of soda per candy bar; and, from *D* to *E* is 4.0 cans of soda per candy bar; page 66.
   b. The opportunity cost of moving from point *E* to point *D* to is 0.25 candy bars per can of soda; from *D* to *C* is 0.50 candy bars per can of soda; from *C* to *B* is 1.00 candy bar per can of soda; and, from *B* to *A* is 2.00 candy bars per can of soda; page 66.
   c. As more candy bars are produced, the opportunity cost increases. As more cans of soda are produced, the opportunity cost increases; page 67.

2. The opportunity cost of increasing production of one good is the production of some other good forgone. The opportunity cost increases, so that increasingly large amounts of the other good are forgone, because resources are not equally productive in all activities. When initially increasing the production of one good, resources that are well suit-

ed for its production are used. When still more of the good is produced, resources that are less well suited must be used. Because the resources are ill suited, more are necessary to increase the production of the first good, and the forgone amount of the other good increases; page 68.

3. The opportunity cost is the amount of a good forgone to gain an additional unit another good. We divide the quantity of the good forgone by the increase in the other good. So opportunity cost is a ratio—the change in the quantity of one good divided by the change in the quantity of another good; page 68.

Additional Exercises (also in MyEconLab Test A)

1. His opportunity cost of a pound of berries and a pound of fish are both zero. The opportunity cost is zero because he is operating inside his production possibilities frontier. He could pick 4 more pounds of berries without giving up any fish or catch 2 more fish without giving up any berries; page 64.

Move from	Increase in berries picked (pounds)	Decrease in fish caught (pounds)	Opportunity cost of berries (pounds of fish)
F to E	6.0	1.0	0.17
E to D	5.0	1.5	0.30
D to C	4.0	2.0	0.50
C to B	3.0	2.5	0.83
B to A	2.0	3.0	1.50

2. Crusoe's opportunity cost of a pound of berries is the fish he forgoes. To calculate the opportunity cost, compute the increase in fruit and the decrease in fish as he increases the time he spends picking berries and decreases the time he spends catching fish. Then, divide the decrease in fish by the increase in berries to get the opportunity cost of a pound of berries. The table above shows the opportunity cost of a pound of berries moving along the *PPF*. As Crusoe moves from point *F* to point *E* and then to point *D* and so forth, his opportunity cost of a pound of berries increases. His opportunity cost increases as he picks more berries because initially he picks from the most productive bushes and so must spend a short period of

time picking berries, that is, a short period of time away from fishing. But as he picks more berries, he must pick from less productive bushes and so spends increasing more time away from fishing; pages 66 and 68.

■ CHECKPOINT 3.3

Fill in the blanks

A sustained expansion of production possibilities is called <u>economic growth</u>. Economic growth shifts the *PPF* <u>outward</u>. The *PPF* shows that economic growth requires <u>a decrease</u> in the current production of consumption goods. The opportunity cost of increasing economic growth is the loss of the <u>current</u> goods that can be consumed.

True or false

1. False; page 71
2. False; pages 71-72
3. False; page 72

Multiple choice

1. c; page 71
2. d; pages 71-72
3. a; page 71
4. d; page 71
5. b; page 71
6. c; page 71

Complete the graph

■ FIGURE 3.7

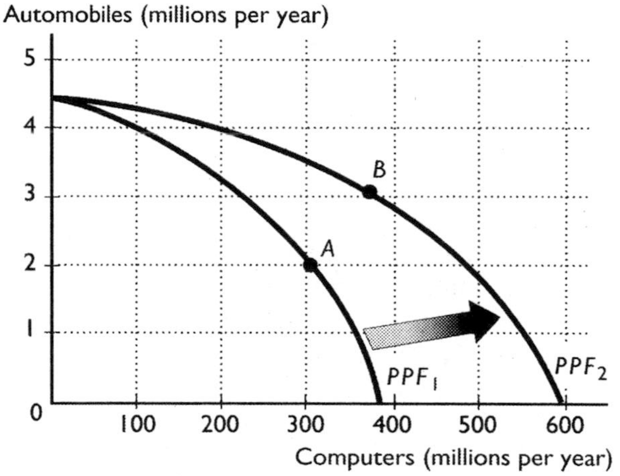

1. Figure 3.7 illustrates the new production

possibilities frontier. Because the technological breakthrough did not affect automobile production, the maximum amount of automobiles that can be produced on the vertical axis does not change; pages 71-72.

1. a. Figure 3.7 shows that it is possible for the production of *both* automobiles and computers to increase, as a movement from the initial point *A* to a possible new point *B* illustrates; page 71.

Short answer and numeric questions

1. Economic growth requires either developing new technologies, accumulating more human capital, or accumulating more capital. All of these avenues require resources, so the opportunity cost of economic growth is the decrease in the current production of goods and services; page 71.

2. The benefit from economic growth is increased consumption per person in the future after the production possibilities frontier has expanded; page 71.

Additional Exercises (also in MyEconLab Test A)

1. If the nation uses all of its resources to produce consumption goods, it will not grow because it does not increase its human capital, which is its only source of economic growth. If the nation increases its graduates from 0 to 750, the nation will experience economic growth because its human capital increases; page 71.

■ CHECKPOINT 3.4

Fill in the blanks

A person (or nation) has an absolute advantage if they are more productive than another in producing a good. A person has a comparative advantage in an activity if that person can perform the activity at a lower opportunity cost than someone else. It is not possible for someone to have a comparative advantage in all activities. It is possible for someone to have an absolute advantage in all activities. If people specialize according to comparative advantage and then trade, they can get to a consumption point outside their production possibilities frontiers.

True or false

1. False; pages 73-74
2. True; page 76
3. True; pages 76-77

Multiple choice

1. d; page 74
2. a; page 74
3. a; page 74
4. b; pages 75-76
5. c; pages 75-76
6. b; pages 75-76
7. a; pages 75-76

Complete the graph

1. a. Sue's opportunity cost of a shirt is 1/2 of a blouse because, when moving along her *PPF* to produce 1 more shirt she gives up 1/2 of a blouse. Mark's opportunity cost of a shirt is 2 blouses; page 75

   b. Sue has the comparative advantage in producing shirts because her opportunity cost is lower; pages 75-76.

   c. Sue's opportunity cost of a blouse is 2 shirts because, when moving along her *PPF*, to produce 1 more blouse she gives up 2 shirts. Mark's opportunity cost of a blouse is 1/2 of a shirt; page 75.

   d. Mark has the comparative advantage in producing blouses because his opportunity cost is lower; pages 75-76.

   e. Mark should specialize in producing blouses and Sue should specialize in producing shirts; page 76.

   f. Mark produces 4 blouses and Sue produces 4 shirts, so a total of 4 shirts and 4 blouses are produced. Figure 3.8 (on the next page) shows this production as point *A*; pages 76-77.

   g. If Mark and Sue agree that the total production at point *A* should be divided evenly, then both Mark and Sue will receive 2 shirts and 2 blouses. When both were producing only for themselves, neither could produce 2 shirts and 2 blouses because this point is beyond both their *PPFs*. By specializing and trading, *both*

Mark and Sue can consume at a point out-side of their *PPFs*; page 77.

■ **FIGURE 3.8**

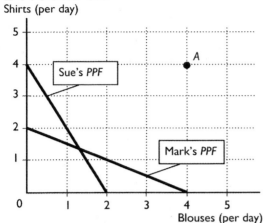

Shirts (per day)

Blouses (per day)

Short answer and numeric questions

1. A person's comparative advantage is the good that the person can produce at a lower opportunity cost than can other people. When this person specializes in the production of the good, it is produced at the lowest cost; page 75.

2. People are willing to trade if they can obtain a good at lower opportunity cost than what it costs them to produce the good. Comparative advantage tells which person has a lower opportunity cost. Even if a person has an absolute advantage in all goods, he or she does not have a comparative advantage in all goods. So comparative advantage determines who produces a product and who does not; page 75.

Additional Exercises (also in MyEconLab Test A)

1. For each board Sara makes, she forgoes 2/3 of a sail, so for her the opportunity cost of 1 board is 2/3 of a sail. For each board Fran makes, she forgoes 1½ sails, so for her the opportunity cost of 1 board is 1½ sails. The opportunity cost of producing a board is lower for Sara, so she has the comparative advantage in producing boards.

   For each sail Sara makes, she forgoes 1½ boards, so for her the opportunity cost of 1 sail is 1½ boards. For each sail Fran makes, she forgoes 2/3 of a board, so for her the opportunity cost of 1 sail is 2/3 of a board. The opportunity cost of producing a sail is lower for Fran, so she has the comparative advantage in producing sails; pages 75-76.

2. Yes, Sara and Fran can gain by changing their production and then trading 1 board for 1 sail. Sara will trade boards with Fran in exchange for sails. With trade, each sail has the opportunity cost for Sara of 1 board, less than her opportunity cost of 1½ boards if she does not trade. Fran will trade sails with Sara in exchange for boards. With trade, each board has the opportunity cost for Fran of 1 sail, less than her opportunity cost of 1½ sails if she does not trade. Sara and Fran can both have more boards and more sails if they specialize and trade; pages 76-77.

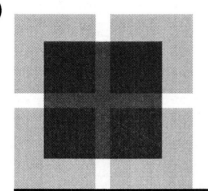

Demand and Supply

Chapter 4

Demand and supply determine the quantities and prices of goods and services.

1 Distinguish between quantity demanded and demand, and explain what determines demand.

The quantity demanded is the amount of any good, service, or resource that people are willing and able to buy during a specified period at a specified price. Demand is the relationship between the quantity demanded and the price of a good when all other influences on buying plans remain the same. The law of demand states: Other things remaining the same, if the price of a good rises, the quantity demanded of that good decreases; and if the price of a good falls, the quantity demanded of that good increases. A demand curve is a graph of the relationship between the quantity demanded of a good and its price when all other influences on buying plans remain the same. The market demand is the sum of the demands of all the buyers in a market. A change in price leads to a *change in the quantity demanded* and a movement along the demand curve. Factors that *change demand* and shift the demand curve are: prices of related goods; expected future prices; income; expected future income and credit; number of buyers; and preferences. If demand increases, the demand curve shifts rightward.

2 Distinguish between quantity supplied and supply, and explain what determines supply.

The quantity supplied is the amount of any good, service, or resource that people are willing and able to sell during a specified period at a specified price. Supply is the relationship between the quantity supplied and the price of a good when all other influences on selling plans remain the same. The law of supply states that other things remaining the same, if the price of a good rises, the quantity supplied of that good increases; and if the price of a good falls, the quantity supplied of that good decreases. A supply curve is a graph of the relationship between the quantity supplied of a good and its price when all other influences on selling plans remain the same. A change in price leads to a *change in the quantity supplied* and a movement along the supply curve. Factors that *change supply* and shift the supply curve are: prices of related goods; prices of resources and other inputs; expected future prices; number of sellers; and productivity. If supply increases, the supply curve shifts rightward.

3 Explain how demand and supply determine price and quantity in a market, and explain the effects of changes in demand and supply.

The equilibrium price and equilibrium quantity occur when the quantity demanded equals the quantity supplied. An increase in demand raises the price and increases the quantity. An increase in supply lowers the price and increases the quantity. An increase in both demand and supply increases the quantity but the price might rise, fall, or not change. An increase in demand and a decrease in supply raises the price but the quantity might increase, decrease, or not change. Changes in demand and supply in the opposite direction to those given above lead to opposite changes in price and quantity.

CHECKPOINT 4.1

■ **Distinguish between quantity demanded and demand, and explain what determines demand.**

Quick Review

- *Change in the quantity demanded* A change in the quantity of a good that people plan to buy that results from a change in the price of the good.
- *Law of demand* If the price of a good rises, the quantity demanded of that good decreases, and if the price of a good falls, the quantity demanded of that good decreases.
- *Change in demand* A change in the quantity that people plan to buy when any influence on buying plans, other than the price of the good, changes. These other influences include: prices of related goods, expected future prices; income, expected future income and credit, number of buyers, and preferences.

Additional Practice Problems 4.1

1. In the market for motor scooters, several events occur, one at a time. Explain the influence of each event on the quantity demanded of scooters and on the demand for scooters. Illustrate the effects of each event either by a movement along the demand curve or a shift in the demand curve for scooters and say which event (or events) illustrates the law of demand in action. These events are:
   a. The price of a scooter falls.
   b. The price of a car falls.
   c. Citing rising injury rates, cities and towns ban scooters from busy streets.
   d. Scooters are a normal good and income increases.
   e. Scooters become unfashionable and the number of buyers decreases.

2. Suppose that each year Anna, Ben, Carol, and Dana are willing and able to buy scooters as shown in the table.

Price (dollars per scooter)	Quantity demanded			
	Anna	Ben	Carol	Dana
100	0	0	0	0
75	1	0	0	0
50	2	1	1	0
25	2	1	2	1

■ **FIGURE 4.1**

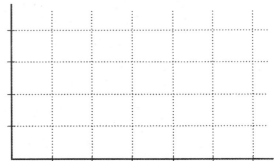

Using the information in the table:
   a. Label the axes in Figure 4.1 above.
   b. Graph the market demand curve.

Solutions to Additional Practice Problems 4.1

1a. This problem emphasizes the distinction between a change in the quantity demanded and a change in demand. A fall in the price of a scooter brings an increase in the quantity demanded of scooters, which is illustrated by a movement down along the demand curve for scooters as shown in the figure. This event illustrates the law of demand in action.

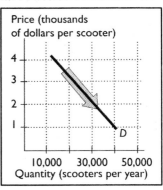

1b. A car is a substitute for a scooter. With the lower price of a car, some people who previously would have bought a scooter will now buy a car instead. So a fall in the price of cars decreases the demand for scooters. The demand curve for scooters shifts leftward, as shown in the figure below.

1c. Rising injury rates and banning scooters from streets changes preferences and makes scooters less desirable. The demand for scooters decreases and the demand curve

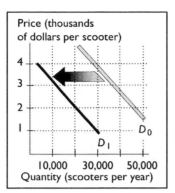

for the scooters shifts leftward as shown in the figure leftward as shown in the figure by the shift from demand curve D_0 to demand curve D_1.

1d. A scooter is a normal good, so people will buy more scooters when their income increases. The demand for scooters increases and the demand curve shifts rightward as illustrated in the figure.

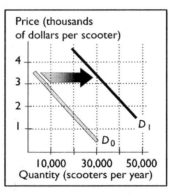

1e. A decrease in the number of buyers decreases the demand for scooters. The demand curve shifts leftward.

■ **FIGURE 4.2**

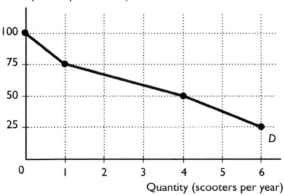

2a. Figure 4.2 labels the axes.

2b. The market demand curve is derived by adding the quantities demanded by Anna, Ben, Carol, and Dana at each price. The market demand curve is illustrated in Figure 4.2.

■ **Self Test 4.1**

Fill in the blanks

The ____ (demand schedule; law of demand) states that other things remaining the same, if the price of a good rises, the ____ (quantity demanded of; demand for) that good decreases. A ____ is a graph of the relationship between the quantity demanded of a good and its price. Demand curves are ____ (downward; upward) sloping. An increase in demand shifts the demand curve ____. Factors that change demand lead to a ____ (shift of; movement along) the demand curve. Factors that change demand are ____, ____, ____, ____, ____, and ____.

True or false

1. The law of demand states that other things remaining the same, if the price of a good rises, the quantity demanded of that good increases.

2. If the quantity of ice cream demanded at each price increases, there is a movement along the demand curve for ice cream.

3. When Sue's income increases, her demand for movies increases. For Sue, movies are a normal good.

4. A rise in the price of a computer increases the demand for computers because a computer is a normal good.

5. If people's incomes fall and all other influences on buying plans remain the same, the demand for computers will decrease and there will be a movement along the demand curve.

Multiple choice

1. The "law of demand" indicates that if the University of Maine increases the tuition, all other things remaining the same,
   a. the demand for classes will decrease at the University of Maine.
   b. the demand for classes will increase at the University of Maine.
   c. the quantity of classes demanded will increase at the University of Maine.
   d. the quantity of classes demanded will decrease at the University of Maine.
   e. both the demand for and the quantity of classes demanded will decrease at the University of Maine.

2. Other things remaining the same, the quantity of a good or service demanded will increase if the price of the good or service
   a. rises.
   b. falls.
   c. does not change.
   d. rises or does not change.
   e. rises or falls.

3. Teenagers demand more soda than other age groups. If the number of teenagers increases, everything else remaining the same,
   a. market demand for soda increases.
   b. market demand for soda decreases.
   c. market demand for soda does not change.
   d. there is a movement along the market demand curve for soda.
   e. None of the above answers is correct because the effect on the demand depends whether the supply curve shifts.

4. One reason the demand for laptop computers might increase is a
   a. fall in the price of a laptop computers.
   b. fall in the price of a desktop computer.
   c. a change in preferences as laptops have become more portable, with faster processors and larger hard drives.
   d. poor quality performance record for laptop computers.
   e. a decrease in income if laptops are a normal good.

5. The number of buyers of sport utility vehicles, SUVs, decreases sharply. So the
   a. demand curve for SUVs shifts leftward.
   b. demand curve for SUVs shifts rightward.
   c. demand curve for SUVs does not shift nor is there a movement along the demand curve.
   d. demand curve for SUVs does not shift but there is a movement downward along it.
   e. the supply curve for SUVs shifts rightward.

■ **FIGURE 4.3**

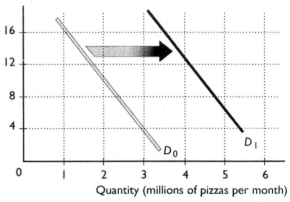

6. The shift of the demand curve for pizza illustrated in Figure 4.3 could be the result of
   a. a rise in income if pizza is a normal good.
   b. a fall in the price of fried chicken, a substitute for pizza.
   c. consumers coming to believe that pizza is unhealthy.
   d. the belief that pizza will fall in price next month.
   e. a fall in the price of a pizza.

7. The shift of the demand curve for pizza illustrated in Figure 4.3 could be the result of
   a. a rise in income if pizza is an inferior good.
   b. a fall in the price of soda, a complement for pizza.
   c. a decrease in the number of college students if college students eat more pizza than other age groups.
   d. a rise in the price of a pizza.
   e. a fall in the price of a pizza.

8. When moving along a demand curve, which of the following changes?
   a. the consumers' incomes
   b. the prices of other goods
   c. the number of buyers
   d. the price of the good
   e. the consumers' preferences

9. If the price of a DVD falls,
   i. the demand curve for DVDs shifts rightward.
   ii. the demand curve for DVDs will not shift.
   iii. there is a movement along the demand curve for DVDs.
   a. i only.
   b. ii only.
   c. iii only.
   d. ii and iii.
   e. i and iii.

10. Pizza and tacos are substitutes and the price of a pizza increases. Which of the following correctly indicates what happens?
   a. The demand for pizzas decreases and the demand for tacos increases.
   b. The demand for both goods decreases.
   c. The quantity of tacos demanded increases and the quantity of pizza demanded decreases.
   d. The quantity of pizza demanded decreases and the demand for tacos increases.
   e. The demand for each decreases because both are normal goods.

Complete the graph

Price (dollars per bundle of cotton candy)	Quantity (bundles of cotton candy per month)
1	10,000
2	8,000
3	7,000
4	4,000

1. The demand schedule for cotton candy is given in the following table. In Figure 4.4, draw the demand curve. Label the axes.

   a. If the price of cotton candy is $2 a bundle, what is the quantity demanded?

■ **FIGURE 4.4**

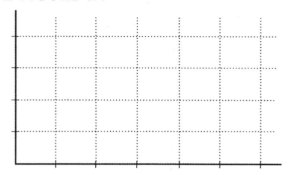

   b. If the price of cotton candy is $3 a bundle, what is the quantity demanded?
   c. Does the demand curve you drew slope upward or downward?

■ **FIGURE 4.5**

Price (dollars per pound of butter)

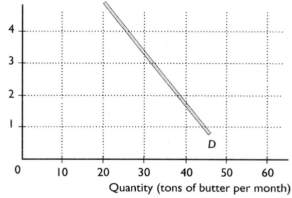

Quantity (tons of butter per month)

2. Butter is a normal good and margarine is substitute for butter. Figure 4.5 shows the demand curve for butter.

   a. In Figure 4.5, show how the demand curve shifts if incomes rise. Label this demand curve D_1.
   b. In Figure 4.5, show how the demand curve shifts if margarine falls in price. Label this demand curve D_2.
   c. If the price of butter falls from $4 a pound to $3 a pound, does the demand curve shift toward demand curve D_1, D_2, or neither? Explain your answer.

Short answer and numeric questions

Price (dollars per gallon)	Quantity demanded (gallons per week)
3.20	316
3.30	310

1. The table above gives the demand schedule for gasoline for a group of students. If the price of gasoline falls from $3.30 to $3.20 per gallon, how much gas will the students buy?

2. Explain the difference between a change in quantity demanded and a change in demand.

3. What is the difference between a movement along a demand curve and a shift in a demand curve?

Additional Exercises (also in MyEconLab Test A)

The following events occur one at a time in the market for Caribbean cruises.

   a. Caribbean cruises become more popular.

   b. The price of a Caribbean cruise rises.

   c. The price of a cruise to Asia falls.

   d. Celebrity Cruises launches its new "students only" Caribbean cruises.

   e. People expect the price of a Caribbean cruise to fall next season.

   f. Cruise companies increase the number of leading rock artists booked for their onboard entertainment.

1. Explain the effect of each event on the demand for Caribbean cruises.

2. Use a graph to illustrate the effect of each event.

3. Does any event (or events) illustrate the law of demand?

CHECKPOINT 4.2

■ **Distinguish between quantity supplied and supply, and explain what determines supply.**

Quick Review

- *Change in quantity supplied* A change in the quantity of a good that suppliers plan to sell that results from a change in the price of the good.

- *Change in supply* A change in the quantity that suppliers plan to sell when any influence on selling plans other than the price of the good changes.

Additional Practice Problems 4.2

1. In the market for motor scooters, several events occur, one at a time. Explain the effect of each on the quantity supplied of scooters and on the supply of scooters. Illustrate the effects of each either by a movement along the supply curve or a shift in the supply curve and say which illustrate the law of supply. These events are:

   a. The price of a scooter rises.

   b. The price of the steel used to make scooters rises.

   c. The number of firms making scooters decreases.

   d. Technological change increases the productivity of the factories making scooters.

Price (dollars per ton of plywood)	Quantity supplied (tons of plywood per month)			
	Eddy	Franco	George	Helen
100	2	2	1	1
75	2	1	1	1
50	1	1	1	0
25	0	0	1	0

■ **FIGURE 4.6**

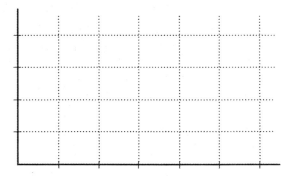

2. Each month Eddy, Franco, George, and Helen are willing and able to sell plywood as shown in the table above.

   a. Label the axes in Figure 4.6.

   b. Graph the market supply curve.

Solutions to Additional Practice Problems 4.2

1a. This problem emphasizes the distinction between a change in the quantity supplied and a change in supply. A rise in the price of a scooter increases the quantity of scooters sup-

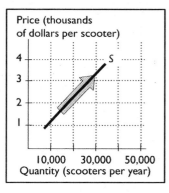

plied, which is illustrated by a movement up along the supply curve as shown in the figure. There is no change in the supply and the supply curve does not shift. This event illustrates the law of supply in action.

1b. When the price of the steel used to make scooters rises, the cost to produce scooters increases, which decreases the supply of scooters. The supply curve shifts leftward as shown.

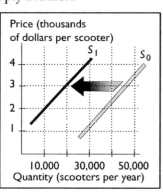

1c. A decrease in the number of firms producing scooters decreases the supply of scooters. The supply curve shifts leftward, as illustrated in the figure above.

1d. An increase in the productivity of the factories making scooters lowers the costs of producing scooters. The supply of scooters increases and the supply curve shifts rightward, as illustrated in the figure.

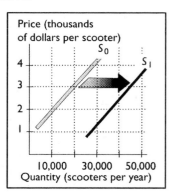

■ **FIGURE 4.7**
Price (dollars per ton of plywood)

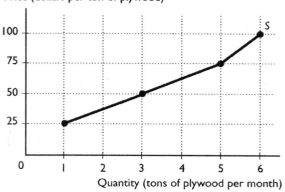

Quantity (tons of plywood per month)

Price (dollars per ton of plywood)	Quantity supplied (tons per month)
100	6
75	5
50	3
25	1

2a. The axes are labeled in Figure 4.7.

2b. The market supply curve is derived by adding the quantities supplied by Eddy, Franco, George, and Helen at each price. The table above gives the resulting sum and the market supply curve is illustrated in Figure 4.7.

■ **Self Test 4.2**

Fill in the blanks

The ____ (quantity supplied; supply) of a good is the amount people are willing and able to sell during a specified period at a specified price. The law of supply states that other things remaining the same, if the price of a good rises, the quantity supplied ____. A supply curve is ____ (upward; downward) sloping. A change in the price of a good changes ____ (supply; the quantity supplied) and is illustrated by a ____ the supply curve. Factors that change supply are ____, ____, ____, ____, and ____.

True or false

1. The law of supply states that other things remaining the same, if the price of a good rises, the supply of the good increases.

2. When new technology for producing computers is used by manufacturers, the supply of computers increases.

3. If the wage rate paid to chefs rises and all other influences on selling plans remain the same, the supply of restaurant meals will increase.

4. If the price of coffee is expected to rise next month, the supply of coffee this month will decrease.

5. The supply of a good will increase and there will be a movement up along the supply curve of the good if the price of one of its substitutes in production falls.

Multiple choice

1. The quantity supplied of a good, service, or resource is ____ during a specified period and at a specified price.
   a. the amount that people are able to sell
   b. the amount that people are willing to sell
   c. the amount that people are able and willing to sell
   d. the amount that people are willing and able to buy
   e. the amount sold

2. One reason supply curves have an upward slope is because
   a. increased supply will require increased technology.
   b. people will pay a higher price when less is supplied.
   c. a higher price brings a greater profit, so firms want to sell more of that good.
   d. to have more of the good supplied requires more firms to open.
   e. None of the above answers is correct because supply curves have a downward slope.

3. Which of the following indicates that the law of supply applies to makers of soda?
   a. An increase in the price of a soda leads to an increase in the demand for soda.
   b. An increase in the price of a soda leads to an increase in the supply of soda.
   c. An increase in the price of a soda leads to an increase in the quantity of soda supplied.
   d. A decrease in the price of a soda leads to an increase in the quantity of soda demanded.
   e. A decrease in the price of a soda leads to an increase in the supply of soda.

4. The market supply curve is the ____ of the ____.
   a. horizontal sum; individual supply curves
   b. vertical sum; individual supply curves
   c. horizontal sum; individual supply curves minus the market demand
   d. vertical sum; individual supply curves minus the market demand
   e. vertical average; individual supply curves

5. If the costs to produce pizza increase, which will occur?
   a. The supply of pizza will decrease.
   b. The quantity of pizzas supplied will increase as sellers try to cover their costs.
   c. Pizza will cease to be produced and sold.
   d. The demand curve for pizza will shift leftward when the price of a pizza increases.
   e. The demand curve for pizza will shift rightward when the price of a pizza increases.

6. A rise in the price of a substitute in production for a good leads to
   a. an increase in the supply of that good.
   b. a decrease in the supply of that good.
   c. no change in the supply of that good.
   d. a decrease in the quantity of that good supplied.
   e. no change in either the supply or the quantity supplied of the good.

7. An increase in the productivity of producing jeans results in
   a. the quantity of jeans supplied increasing.
   b. the supply of jeans increasing.
   c. buyers demanding more jeans because they are now more efficiently produced.
   d. buyers demanding fewer jeans because their price will fall, which signals lower quality.
   e. some change but the impact on the supply of jeans is impossible to predict.

■ **FIGURE 4.8**

Price (dollars per pizza)

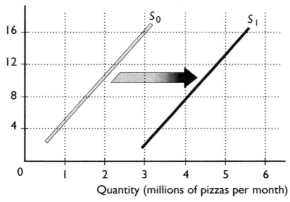

8. The shift of the supply curve of pizza illustrated in Figure 4.8 could be the result of
   a. a rise in the price of cheese used to produce pizza.
   b. a decrease in the number of firms producing pizza.
   c. an increase in the productivity of the firms producing pizza.
   d. a rise in the price of a substitute in production.
   e. a rise in the price of a pizza.

9. The shift of the supply curve of pizza illustrated in Figure 4.8 could be the result of
   a. a rise in income if pizza is a normal good.
   b. a fall in the price of soda, a consumer complement for pizza.
   c. an increase in the number of firms producing pizza.
   d. a rise in the price of a pizza.
   e. a rise in the wage paid the workers who make pizza.

10. The price of leather used to produce shoes rises, so the supply of shoes ____ and the supply curve of shoes ____.
    a. increases; shifts rightward
    b. increases; shifts leftward
    c. decreases; shifts rightward
    d. decreases; shifts leftward
    e. does not change; does not shift

Complete the graph

Price (dollars per bundle of cotton candy)	Quantity (bundles of cotton candy per month)
1	4,000
2	8,000
3	10,000
4	12,000

1. The supply schedule for cotton candy is given in the table above. In Figure 4.4, you previously drew a demand curve for cotton candy. Now use the supply schedule to draw the supply curve in Figure 4.4.
   a. If the price of cotton candy is $2 a bundle, what is the quantity supplied?
   b. If the price of cotton candy is $3 a bundle, what is the quantity supplied?
   c. Does the supply curve you drew slope upward or downward?

■ **FIGURE 4.9**

Price (dollars per ton of rubber bands)

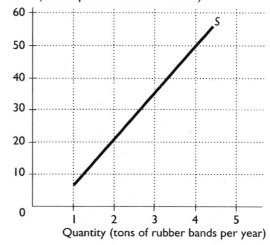

2. Figure 4.9 shows a supply curve for rubber bands. Suppose the productivity of produc-

ing rubber bands increases. In Figure 4.9, illustrate the effect of this event.

Short answer and numeric questions

1. What is the law of supply?
2. What influence(s) lead to a change in the quantity supplied? A change in supply?

Price (dollars per pizza)	Quantity supplied (pizza per day)			
	Tom	Bob	Kate	Market supply
14	20	12	15	____
12	16	10	10	____
10	12	8	5	____
8	8	6	0	____

3. The table gives the supply schedules for the three pizza producers in a small town. Calculate the market supply schedule.

Additional Exercises (also in MyEconLab Test A)

Factories can use their resources to produce either DVDs or CDs. In the market for DVDs, the following events occur one at a time:
   a. The price of a CD falls.
   b. A new robot technology lowers the cost of producing DVDs.
   c. The price of a DVD falls.
   d. The price of a DVD is expected to rise next year.
   e. The wage rate paid to DVD factory workers increases.

1. Explain the effect of each event on the supply of DVDs.
2. Show on a graph the effect of each event.
3. Does any event (or events) illustrate the law of supply?

CHECKPOINT 4.3

■ **Explain how demand and supply determine the price and quantity in a market, and explain the effects of changes in demand and supply.**

Quick Review

• *Market equilibrium* When the quantity demanded equals the quantity supplied.

Additional Practice Problems 4.3

1. Hot dogs are an inferior good and people's incomes rise. What happens to the equilibrium price and quantity of hot dogs?

2. Hot dog producers develop new technology that increases their productivity. What happens to the price and quantity of hot dogs?

3. The price of a hot dog bun falls and, simultaneously, the number of hot dog producers increases. The effect of the fall in the price of a hot dog bun is less than the effect of the increase in the number of producers. What happens to the equilibrium price and quantity of hot dogs?

Solutions to Additional Practice Problems 4.3

1. When income increases, the demand for an inferior good decreases and the demand curve shifts leftward. The supply does not change and the sup-

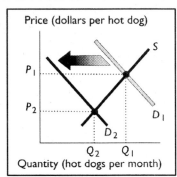

ply curve does not shift. The equilibrium price of a hot dog falls and the equilibrium quantity decreases, as illustrated in the figure.

2. When the productivity of producing a good increases, the supply of the good increases and the supply curve shifts rightward. So the supply

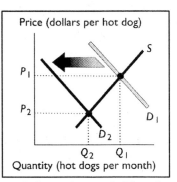

curve of hot dogs shifts rightward. The demand does not change and so the demand curve does not shift. As illustrated, the price of a hot dog falls and the quantity increases.

3. The fall in the price of a complement, hot dog buns, increases the demand for hot dogs and the demand curve for hot dogs shifts rightward. The in-

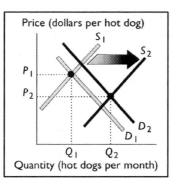

crease in the number of producers increases the supply of hot dogs and the supply curve shifts rightward. Because the increase in supply exceeds the increase in demand, the price of a hot dog falls and the quantity increases, as shown in the figure.

■ Self Test 4.3

Fill in the blanks

The price at which the quantity demanded equals the quantity supplied is the ____. In a diagram, the ____ is determined where the supply and demand curves intersect. If the price exceeds the equilibrium price, the price ____ (rises; falls). An increase in demand ____ (raises; lowers) the equilibrium price and ____ (increases; decreases) the equilibrium quantity. An increase in supply ____ (raises; lowers) the equilibrium price and ____ (increases; decreases) the equilibrium quantity. If both the demand and supply increase, definitely the equilibrium ____ increases but the effect on the equilibrium ____ is ambiguous.

True or false

1. If the price of asparagus is below the equilibrium price, there is a shortage of asparagus and the price of asparagus will rise until the shortage disappears.

2. When the demand for skateboards decreases and the supply of skateboards remains unchanged, the quantity supplied of skateboards decreases as the price rises.

3. Gasoline refiners expect the price of oil will fall next month. If the supply of oil does not change, the equilibrium price of oil today falls and the equilibrium quantity today decreases.

4. As summer comes to an end and winter sets in, the demand for and supply of hamburger buns decrease. The price of a hamburger bun definitely remains the same.

5. The number of buyers of grapefruit juice increases and at the same time severe frost decreases the supply of grapefruit juice. The price of grapefruit juice will rise.

Multiple choice

1. The equilibrium price of a good occurs if the
   a. quantity of the good demanded equals the quantity of the good supplied.
   b. quantity of the good demanded is greater than the quantity of the good supplied.
   c. quantity of the good demanded is less than the quantity of the good supplied.
   d. demand for the good is equal to the supply of the good.
   e. price of the good seems reasonable to most buyers.

2. Which of the following is correct?
   i.   A surplus puts downward pressure on the price of a good.
   ii. A shortage puts upward pressure on the price of a good
   iii. There is no surplus or shortage at equilibrium.
   a. i and ii..
   b. i and iii.
   c. ii and iii.
   d. i, ii, and iii.
   e. only iii.

3. The number of people looking to buy ceiling fans increases, so there is an increase in the
   a. quantity of ceiling fans demanded and a surplus of ceiling fans.
   b. demand for ceiling fans and a rise in the price of a ceiling fan.
   c. demand for ceiling fans and a surplus of ceiling fans.
   d. supply of ceiling fans and no change in the price of a ceiling fan.
   e. demand for ceiling fans and in the supply of ceiling fans.

4. Which of the following is the best explanation for why the price of gasoline increases during the summer months?
   a. Oil producers have higher costs of production in the summer.
   b. Sellers have to earn profits during the summer to cover losses in the winter.
   c. There is increased driving by families going on vacation.
   d. There is less competition among oil refineries in the summer.
   e. The number of gas stations open 24 hours a day rises in the summer months and so the price must rise to cover the higher costs.

5. Suppose that the price of lettuce used to produce tacos increases. This change means that the equilibrium price of a taco ____ and the equilibrium quantity ____.
   a. rises; increases
   b. rises; decreases
   c. falls; increases
   d. falls; decreases
   e. does not change; decreases

6. The technology associated with manufacturing computers has advanced enormously. This change has led to the price of a computer ____ and the quantity ____.
   a. rising; increasing
   b. rising; decreasing
   c. falling; increasing
   d. falling; decreasing
   e. falling; not changing

7. Candy makers accurately anticipate the increase in demand for candy for Halloween so that the supply of candy and the demand for candy increase the same amount. As a result, the price of candy ____ and the quantity of candy ____.
   a. rises; does not change
   b. falls; increases
   c. does not change; increases
   d. does not change; does not change
   e. rises; rises

8. During 2010 the supply of gasoline decreased while at the same time the demand for gasoline increased. If the magnitude of the increase in demand was greater than the magnitude of the decrease in supply, then the equilibrium price of gasoline ____ and the equilibrium quantity ____.
   a. increased; increased
   b. increased; decreased
   c. increased; did not change
   d. decreased; did not change
   e. did not change; increased

Complete the graph

1. In Checkpoint 4.1 you drew a demand curve in Figure 4.4; in Checkpoint 4.2, you drew a supply curve in that figure. Return to Figure 4.4 and answer the following questions.
   a. If the price of cotton candy is $1, what is the situation in the market?
   b. If the price of cotton candy is $3, what is the situation in the market?
   c. What is the equilibrium price and equilibrium quantity of cotton candy?

Price (dollars per sweatshirt)	Quantity demanded (sweatshirts per season) Hockey team	Soccer team	Quantity supplied (sweatshirts per season)
35	5	8	32
30	6	9	25
25	8	11	19
20	12	15	12
15	17	20	8

2. The table gives the demand and supply schedules for sweatshirts. What is the market demand schedule? At what price will the quantity demanded be equal to the quantity supplied? What is the equilibrium quantity?

■ **FIGURE 4.10**

Price (dollars per piece of gold jewelry)

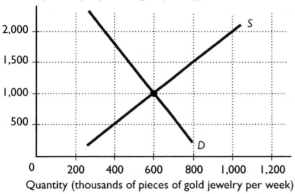

Quantity (thousands of pieces of gold jewelry per week)

3. Figure 4.10 shows the supply and demand for gold jewelry. In the figure, show what happens to the price and quantity if gold jewelry is a normal good and people's incomes rise.

■ **FIGURE 4.11**

Price (dollars per piece of gold jewelry)

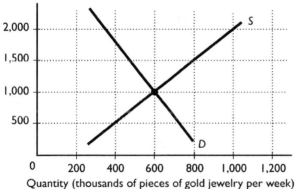

Quantity (thousands of pieces of gold jewelry per week)

4. Figure 4.11 shows the supply and demand for gold jewelry. Suppose that consumers think that silver jewelry is a substitute for gold jewelry. In Figure 4.12, show what happens to the price and quantity if the price of silver jewelry falls.

■ **FIGURE 4.12**

Price (dollars per piece of gold jewelry)

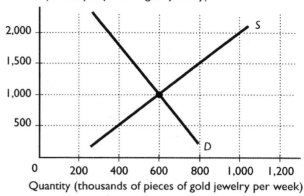

Quantity (thousands of pieces of gold jewelry per week)

5. Figure 4.12 shows the supply and demand for gold jewelry. Suppose the price of the gold that is used to produce gold jewelry rises. In the figure, show what happens to the price and quantity of gold jewelry.

Short answer and numeric questions

1. How is a shortage different from a surplus?

2. People read that drinking orange juice helps prevent heart disease. What is the effect on the equilibrium price and quantity of orange juice?

3. The cost of memory chips used in computers falls. What is the effect on the equilibrium price and quantity of computers?

4. New cars are a normal good and people's incomes increase. Simultaneously, auto manufacturers must pay more for their workers' health insurance. What is the effect on the price and quantity of new cars?

5. The Eye on Your Life on page 103 points out that supply and demand will be a big part of your life. How can you use the model to make day-to-day decisions, such as when to buy gasoline?

Additional Exercises (also in MyEconLab Test A)

Price (dollars per bar)	Quantity demanded	Quantity supplied
	(bars per week)	
1.00	3,000	1,000
1.50	2,500	1,500
2.00	2,000	2,000
2.50	1,500	2,500
3.00	1,000	3,000

The table shows the demand and supply schedules for energy bars.

1. What is the market equilibrium?

2. If the price of bar is $1.50, describe the situation in the energy bar market. Explain how market equilibrium is restored.

3. A rise in income increases the quantity demanded by 1,000 bars a week at each price. Explain how the market adjusts to its new equilibrium.

4. A fire knocks out a large energy-bar factory and a fitness craze sends more people to the gym. How do these events influence demand and supply? Describe how the equilibrium price and equilibrium quantity change.

SELF TEST ANSWERS

■ CHECKPOINT 4.1

Fill in the blanks

The <u>law of demand</u> states that other things remaining the same, if the price of a good rises, the <u>quantity demanded of</u> that good decreases. A <u>demand curve</u> is a graph of the relationship between the quantity demanded of a good and its price. Demand curves are <u>downward</u> sloping. An increase in demand shifts the demand curve <u>rightward</u>. Factors that change demand lead to a <u>shift of</u> the demand curve. Factors that change demand are <u>prices of related goods</u>, <u>expected future prices</u>, <u>income</u>, <u>expected future income and credit</u>, <u>number of buyers</u>, and <u>preferences</u>.

True or false

1. False; page 85
2. False; page 84
3. True; page 89
4. False; page 89
5. False; page 90

Multiple choice

1. d; page 85
2. b; page 85
3. a; page 89
4. c; page 89
5. a; page 89
6. a; page 89
7. b; page 89
8. d; page 90
9. d; page 90
10. d; pages 89-90

Complete the graph

1. Figure 4.13 illustrates the demand curve, labeled *D* in the diagram. (The supply curve is from the first "Complete the Graph" question in Checkpoint 4.2.)
   a. 8,000 bundles per month
   b. 7,000 bundles per month
   c. The demand curve slopes downward; page 90.

■ FIGURE 4.13

Price (dollars per bundle of cotton candy)

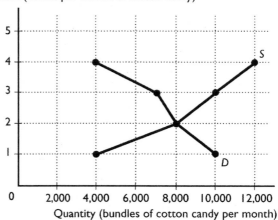

Quantity (bundles of cotton candy per month)

■ FIGURE 4.14

Price (dollars per pound of butter)

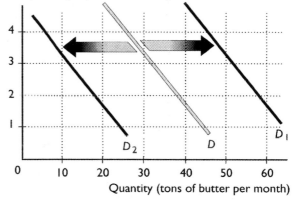

Quantity (tons of butter per month)

2. a. The demand increases and the demand curve shifts rightward, as shown in Figure 4.14 by the shift to *D*₁; page 90
   b. The demand decreases and the demand curve shifts leftward, as shown in Figure 4.14 by the shift to *D*₂; page 90
   c. The demand curve does not shift. The fall in the price of butter leads to an increase in the quantity demanded and a movement along the demand curve, not a shift of the demand curve; page 90.

Short answer and numeric questions

1. When the price falls from $3.30 a gallon to $3.20 a gallon, the quantity of gasoline de-

manded increases from 310 gallons to 316 gallons; page 86.

2. A change in the quantity demanded occurs when the price of the good changes. A change in demand occurs when any other influence on buying plans other than the price of the good changes; page 88.

3. A movement along a demand curve reflects a change in the quantity demanded and is the result of a change in the price of the product. A shift in a demand curve reflects a change in demand and is the result of a change in any factor, other than the price, that affects demand; page 90.

Additional Exercises (also in MyEconLab Test A)

1. a. Caribbean cruises becoming more popular reflects a change in preferences. The demand increases; page 89.

   b. The price of a cruise rising decreases the quantity of cruises demanded; page 90.

   c. Cruises to Asia are substitutes for cruises in the Caribbean. The fall in the price of a cruise to Asia decreases the demand for Caribbean cruises; page 88.

   d. Launching a new "students only" Caribbean cruise makes cruises more attractive to students and so increases the number of demanders. The demand increases; page 89.

   e. People expecting the price of a Caribbean to fall next season decreases the number of people who want to take a cruise this season. The fall in the expected future price decreases the demand today; page 89.

   f. Increasing the number of leading rock artists performing on cruses increases people's preferences to take a cruise. The demand increases; page 89.

2. a. Caribbean cruises becoming more popular increases demand and the demand curve shifts rightward. Figure 4.15 illustrates this change with the rightward shift of the demand curve from D_0 to D_1; page 90.

   b. The price of a cruise rising decreases the quantity of cruises demanded. There is a movement up along the demand curve as

Price (thousands of dollars per cruise)

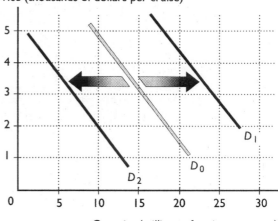

Quantity (millions of cruises per year)

Price (thousands of dollars per cruise)

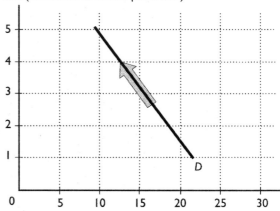

Quantity (millions of cruises per year)

illustrated in Figure 4.16 by the gray arrow. This change reflects the law of demand; page 90.

   c. The fall in the price of a cruise to Asia decreases the demand for Caribbean cruises and the demand curve shifts leftward. Figure 4.15 illustrates this change with the leftward shift of the demand curve from D_0 to D_2; page 89.

   d. Launching a new "students only" Caribbean cruise makes cruises more attractive to students so demand increases and the demand curve shifts rightward. Figure 4.15 illustrates this change with the rightward shift of the demand curve from D_0 to D_1; page 90.

   e. People expecting the price of a Caribbean to fall next season decreases demand today so the demand curve shifts leftward, from D_0 to D_2 in Figure 4.15; page 90.

   f. Increasing the number of leading rock artists performing on cruses increases demand so the demand curve shifts rightward, as illustrated in Figure 4.15 by the shift from D_0 to D_1; page 90.

3. Only the second event, the rise in the price of a Caribbean cruise, reflects the law of demand. All the other events reflect a change in demand; page 90.

■ CHECKPOINT 4.2

Fill in the blanks

The <u>quantity supplied</u> of a good is the amount people are willing and able to sell during a specified period at a specified price. The law of supply states that other things remaining the same, if the price of a good rises, the quantity supplied <u>increases</u>. A supply curve is <u>upward</u> sloping. A change in the price of a good changes <u>the quantity supplied</u> and is illustrated by a <u>movement along</u> the supply curve. Factors that change supply are <u>prices of related goods</u>, <u>prices of resources and other inputs</u>, <u>expected future prices</u>, <u>number of sellers</u>, and <u>productivity</u>.

True or false

   1. False; page 92
   2. True; page 96
   3. False; page 96
   4. True; page 96
   5. False; page 96

Multiple choice

   1. c; page 92
   2. c; page 92
   3. c; page 92
   4. a; page 94
   5. a; page 96
   6. b; page 96
   7. b; page 96

   8. c; page 96
   9. c; page 96
 10. d; page 97

Complete the graph

1. The supply curve is illustrated in Figure 4.13, labeled S in the diagram.
   a. 8,000 bundles per month.
   b. 10,000 bundles per month.
   c. The supply curve slopes upward; page 93.

■ FIGURE 4.17

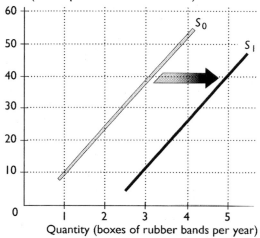

2. Figure 4.17 illustrates the shift; pages 96-97.

Short answer and numeric questions

1. If other things remain the same, when the price of a good falls (rises), sellers decrease (increase) the quantity supplied; page 92.

2. A change in the price of the product leads to a change in the quantity supplied. Changes in: prices of related goods; prices of resources and other inputs; expectations; number of sellers; and productivity lead to changes in supply; page 97.

Price (dollars per pizza)	Market supply (pizzas per day)
14	47
12	36
10	25
8	14

3. The market supply schedule is in the table above; page 94.

Additional Exercises (also in MyEconLab Test A)

1. a. CDs and DVDs are substitutes in production. When the price of a CD falls, the supply of DVDs increases; page 95.

   b. The new robot technology lowers the cost of producing DVDs and increases the supply of DVDs; page 96.

   c. When the price of a DVD falls, the quantity of DVDs supplied decreases and there is a movement down along the supply curve of DVDs; page 97.

   d. If the price of a DVD is expected to rise next year, supply decreases now; page 96.

   e. If the wage rate paid to DVD factory workers increases, the supply of DVDs decreases because the price of a resource used to produce DVDs has risen; page 96.

2. a. When the price of a CD falls, the supply of DVDs increases and the supply curve of DVDs shifts rightward. In Figure 4.18 the supply curve shifts from S_0 to S_1; page 97.

   b. The new robot technology lowers the cost of producing DVDs and shifts the supply curve of DVDs rightward. In Figure 4.18 this shift is illustrated by the shift from S_0 to S_1; page 97.

   c. When the price of a DVD falls, the quantity of DVDs supplied decreases and there is a movement down along the supply curve of DVDs. In Figure 4.19 as the price falls from $20 per DVD to $10 per DVD the arrow shows that quantity supplied decreases from 200 million to 100 million; page 97.

   d. If the price of a DVD is expected to rise next year, the supply curve shifts leftward, as illustrated in Figure 4.18 by the shift from S_0 to S_2; page 97.

   e. If the wage rate paid to DVD factory workers increases, the supply curve shifts leftward, as illustrated in Figure 4.18 by the shift from S_0 to S_2; page 97.

3. Only the third event, the fall in the price of a DVD, reflects the law of supply. All the other events reflect a change in supply; page 97.

■ **FIGURE 4.18**

Price (dollars per DVD)

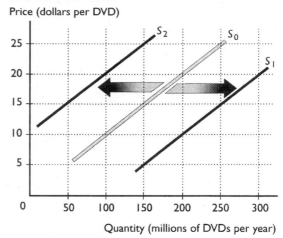

Quantity (millions of DVDs per year)

■ **FIGURE 4.19**

Price (dollars per DVD)

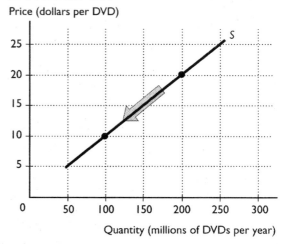

Quantity (millions of DVDs per year)

■ **CHECKPOINT 4.3**

Fill in the blanks

The price at which the quantity demanded equals the quantity supplied is the <u>equilibrium price</u>. In a diagram, the <u>equilibrium price</u> is determined where the supply and demand curves intersect. If the price exceeds the equilibrium price, the price <u>falls</u>. An increase in demand <u>raises</u> the equilibrium price and <u>increases</u> the equilibrium quantity. An increase in supply <u>lowers</u> the equilibrium price and <u>increases</u> the equilibrium quantity. If both the demand and supply increase, definitely the equilibrium <u>quantity</u> increases but the effect on the equilibrium <u>price</u> is ambiguous.

True or false

1. True; page 99
2. False; page 101
3. True; page 102
4. False; page 104
5. True; page 104

Multiple choice

1. a; page 99
2. d; page 100
3. b; page 101
4. c; page 101
5. b; page 102
6. c; page 102
7. c; page 104
8. a; page 104

Complete the graph

1. a. A shortage of 6,000 bundles a month; page 100.
   b. A surplus of 3,000 bundles a month; page 100.
   c. The equilibrium price is $2 a bundle of cotton candy and the equilibrium quantity is 8,000 bundles a month; page 100.

Price (dollars per sweatshirt)	Quantity demanded (sweatshirts per season)
35	13
30	15
25	19
20	27
15	37

2. In the table, the market demand schedule is obtained by summing the Hockey team's demand and the Soccer team's demand. The equilibrium price is $25 and the equilibrium quantity is 19 sweatshirts; page 100.

3. Figure 4.20 shows the effect of the increase in income. The increase in income increases the demand for normal goods, such as gold jewelry. The demand curve shifts rightward and the supply curve does not shift. The price of gold jewelry rises, to $1,500 in the figure, and the quantity increases, to 800,000 pieces per week in the figure; page 101.

■ **FIGURE 4.20**
Price (dollars per piece of gold jewelry)

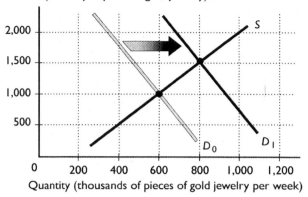

Quantity (thousands of pieces of gold jewelry per week)

■ **FIGURE 4.21**
Price (dollars per piece of gold jewelry)

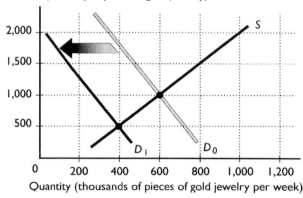

Quantity (thousands of pieces of gold jewelry per week)

4. Figure 4.21 shows the effect of the fall in price of silver jewelry. A fall in the price of a substitute decreases the demand gold jewelry. The demand curve shifts leftward and the supply curve does not shift. The price of gold jewelry falls, to $500 in the figure, and the quantity decreases, to 400,000 pieces per week in the figure; page 101.

5. Figure 4.22 (on the next page) shows the effect of the fall in the price of gold. The price of gold is a cost to the producers of gold jewelry. A rise in the cost decreases the supply of the good. The supply curve shifts leftward and the demand curve does not shift. The price of gold jewelry rises, to $1,750 in the figure, and the quantity decreases, to 400,000 pieces per week in the figure; page 102.

■ **FIGURE 4.22**

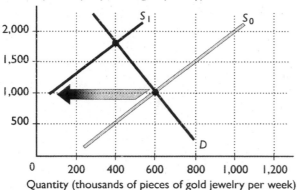

Price (dollars per piece of gold jewelry)

Quantity (thousands of pieces of gold jewelry per week)

Short answer and numeric questions

1. When a shortage exists, the price of the good is below the equilibrium price. The quantity demanded is greater than the quantity supplied. When a surplus exists, the price of the good is above the equilibrium price. The quantity demanded is less than the quantity supplied; page 100.

2. The increase in preferences increases the demand for orange juice and the demand curve shifts rightward. The price of orange juice rises and the quantity increases; page 101.

3. The fall in cost increases the supply of computers. The supply curve of computers shifts rightward. The price falls and the quantity increases; page 102.

4. The increase in income increases the demand for normal goods and shifts the demand curve for new cars rightward. The increase in health insurance premiums decreases the supply of new cars and shifts the supply curve of new cars leftward. The price of a new car definitely rises. The effect on the quantity is ambiguous: it rises if the demand effect is larger, falls if the supply effect is larger, and does not change if the two effects are the same size; page 104.

5. You can use supply and demand to determine if you want to buy gasoline immediately or perhaps hold off for a few days. For in-stance, if you read that a hurricane threatens oil derricks in the Gulf of Mexico, you can reason that if the hurricane actually strikes, the supply of oil will decrease and price of oil will soar. In this case, you ought to fill up your car today to avoid the possibility of paying a higher price next week.

Additional Exercises (also in MyEconLab Test A)

1. The market equilibrium is a price of $2.00 a bar and a quantity of 2,000 bars a week; page 99.

2. If the price of an energy bar is $1.50, the quantity demanded, 2,500 bars, is greater than the quantity supplied, 1,500 bars, so there is a shortage of 1,000 bars a week and the price rises. As the price rises, the quantity demanded decreases, the quantity supplied increases, and the shortage decreases. The price rises until it reaches $2.00, when the shortage disappears; page 99.

3. If the demand for energy bars increases by 1,000 bars at each price, the new equilibrium price is $2.50 a roll of film and the new equilibrium quantity is 2,500 bars a week. There is a shortage of energy bars at the original equilibrium price of $2.00 a bar, after the increase in demand. The shortage leads to the price rising. As the price rises, the quantity demanded decreases, the quantity supplied increases, and the shortage decreases. The price rises until the shortage disappears at a price of $2.50 a bar; page 101.

4. The fire decreases the supply and shifts the supply curve leftward. The fitness craze increases demand and shifts the demand curve rightward. At the initial equilibrium price, there is a shortage of energy bars and the price rises. If the magnitude of the decrease in supply is greater than the magnitude of the increase in demand, the equilibrium quantity decreases. If the magnitude of the decrease in supply is less than the magnitude of the increase in demand, the equilibrium quantity increases. In both cases the price rises; page 102.

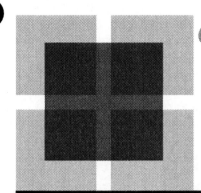

GDP: A Measure of Total Production and Income

Chapter 5

1 **Define GDP and explain why the value of production, income, and expenditure are the same for an economy.**

Gross Domestic Product, GDP, is the market value of all the final goods and services produced within a country in a given time period. Only final goods and services are included in GDP; intermediate goods and services are not included. Expenditures are consumption expenditure (*C*), investment (*I*), government expenditure on goods and services (*G*), and net exports of goods and services (*NX*). Investment is the purchase of new capital goods and additions to inventories. Total expenditure is equal to $C + I + G + NX$. Firms pay out the revenue they receive to households as payment for labor, capital, land, and entrepreneurship. These payments are households' income. We call total income *Y*. The circular flow shows that total expenditure equals total income so that $Y = C + I + G + NX$.

2 **Describe how economic statisticians measure GDP and distinguish between nominal GDP and real GDP.**

GDP is measured using the expenditure approach and the income approach. The expenditure approach adds the four sources of expenditure: consumption expenditure, investment, government expenditure on goods and services, and net exports of goods and services. Expenditures on used goods and financial assets are not in GDP. The income approach adds two categories of income (wage income plus interest, rent, and profit income). This sum is net domestic product at factor cost. To get to GDP, subsidies are subtracted, and indirect taxes and depreciation are added. A statistical discrepancy is added or subtracted to the income approach GDP so that GDP using the income approach equals GDP using the expenditure approach. Disposable personal income is income received by households minus personal income taxes paid. Real GDP is the value of final goods and services produced in a given year expressed in the prices of a base year; nominal GDP is the value of final goods and services produced in a given year using prices of that year.

3 **Describe the uses of real GDP and explain its limitations as a measure of the standard of living.**

The standard of living is the level of the consumption of the goods and services that people enjoy. Average income per person determines the standard of living so real GDP per person is used to compare the standard of living over time or across nations. Real GDP fluctuates around potential GDP in a business cycle, going from an expansion to a peak to a recession to a trough. Potential GDP is the value of real GDP when all factors of production are fully employed. A recession is commonly defined as a time when real GDP decreases for at least two successive quarters. Real GDP per person is an imperfect measure of the standard of living because it excludes household production, underground production, the value of leisure time, environmental quality, health and life expectancy, and political freedom and justice.

CHECKPOINT 5.1

■ **Define GDP and explain why the value of production, income, and expenditure are the same for an economy.**

Quick Review

- *Total expenditure* Total expenditure is the total amount received by producers of final goods and services and equals $C + I + G + NX$.

- *Total income* Total income is the income paid to all factors of production and equals total expenditure.

Additional Practice Problems 5.1

1. Last year in a small country to the South, consumption expenditure was $70 billion, investment was $16 billion, government purchases of goods and services were $12 billion, exports were $4 billion, and imports were $3 billion.
   a. What did GDP last year equal?
   b. This year imports increased to $5 billion. If all the other types of expenditure stay the same, what does GDP this year equal?

2. Suppose that GDP equals $12 trillion, consumption expenditure equals $7 trillion, investment equals $3.5 trillion, and government expenditure on goods and services equals $2.5 trillion. What does net exports equal?

3. One of the four expenditure categories is net exports. How can net exports be negative?

Solutions to Additional Practice Problems 5.1

1a. To solve this problem use the equality between GDP and expenditure, GDP = $C + I + G + NX$. Last year's GDP = $70 billion + $16 billion + $12 billion + ($4 billion − $3 billion) = $99 billion.

1b. This year, imports increased from $3 billion to $5 billion, so replace the $3 billion in the calculation with $5 billion and GDP for this year is $97 billion. The $2 billion increase in imports results in a $2 billion decrease in GDP.

2. GDP = $C + I + G + NX$. So NX = GDP − $C − I − G$. In this case, NX = $12 trillion − $7 trillion − $3.5 trillion − $2.5 trillion, which equals −$1 trillion.

3. Net exports equals the value of exports of goods and services minus the value of imports of goods and services. If, as is the case in the United States, the value of imports exceeds the value of exports, net exports is negative.

■ **Self Test 5.1**

Fill in the blanks

The market value of all the final goods and services produced within a country in a given time period is _____ (GDP; investment). _____ (Two; Three; Four) groups buy the final goods and services produced. Net exports of goods and services equals the value of _____ (imports; exports) minus the value of _____ (imports; exports). $C + I + G + NX$ equals _____ and _____.

True or false

1. The computer chip that Dell Corp. buys from Intel Corp. is a final good.
2. Expenditure on a bulldozer is consumption expenditure.
3. The value of net exports of goods and services can be negative.
4. The value of production equals income, which equals expenditure.

Multiple choice

1. The abbreviation "GDP" stands for
   a. Gross Domestic Product.
   b. Gross Domestic Prices.
   c. General Domestic Prices.
   d. Great Domestic Prices.
   e. Government's Domestic Politics.

2. GDP is equal to the _____ value of all the final goods and services produced within a country in a given period of time.
   a. production
   b. market
   c. wholesale
   d. retail
   e. typical

3. The following are all *final* goods except
   a. flour used by the baker to make cupcakes.
   b. bread eaten by a family for lunch.
   c. pencils used by a 6th grader in class.
   d. Nike shoes used by a basketball player.
   e. a computer used by Intel to design new computer chips.

4. Investment is defined as
   a. the purchase of a stock or bond.
   b. financial capital.
   c. what consumers do with their savings.
   d. the purchase of new capital goods by firms.
   e. spending on capital goods by governments.

5. In one year, a firm increases its production by $9 million and increases sales by $8 million. All other things in the economy remaining the same, which of the following is true?
   a. GDP increases by $8 million and inventory investment decreases by $1 million.
   b. GDP increases by $9 million and inventory investment increases by $1 million.
   c. Inventory investment decreases by $1 million.
   d. GDP increases by $8 million and investment increases by $1 million.
   e. GDP increases by $17 million.

6. Total expenditure equals
   a. $C + I + G + NX$.
   b. $C + I + G - NX$.
   c. $C + I - G + NX$.
   d. $C \ I + G + NX$.
   e. $C - I - G - NX$.

Short answer and numeric questions

1. Why aren't intermediate goods or services counted in GDP?

2. Classify each of the following into the components of U.S. GDP: consumption expenditure, investment, government purchases of goods and services, exports, or imports.
   a. The purchase in Portland of a Sony DVD player made in Japan.

   b. A family's purchase of a birthday cake at the local Safeway grocery store.
   c. Microsoft's purchase of 100 Dell servers.
   d. The purchase of a new pizza oven by a Pizza Hut in Houston.
   e. The U.S. government's purchase of 15 stealth fighters.

3. Why does total expenditure equal total income?

Additional Exercises (also in MyEconLab Test A)

1. Classify the following items as a final good or an intermediate good and expenditure on final goods as consumption expenditure or investment:
   a. The fertilizer bought by a Florida tomato grower.
   b. The ringtone you bought today.
   c. New computers bought by PepsiCo.
   d. The aircraft bought by Southwest Airlines.

■ **FIGURE 5.1**

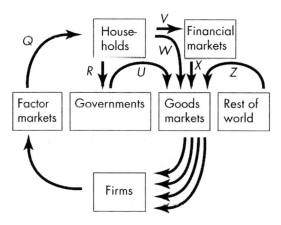

2. Figure 5.1 shows the flows of expenditure and income on Big Foot Island. In 2007, W was $60 million; V was $20 million; U was $15 million; X was $25 million; and Z was zero. Calculate total income and net taxes.

CHECKPOINT 5.2

■ **Describe how economic statisticians measure GDP and distinguish between nominal GDP and real GDP.**

Quick Review

- *Expenditure approach* GDP equals the sum of consumption expenditure, investment, government expenditure on goods and services and net exports of goods and services.
- *Income approach* GDP equals the sum of wage income plus interest, rent, and profit income minus subsidies plus indirect taxes and depreciation plus or minus any statistical discrepancy.

Additional Practice Problem 5.2

Item	Amount (billions of dollars)
Wages	5,875
Consumption expenditure	6,987
Indirect taxes less subsidies	630
Interest, rent, and profit	2,248
Depreciation	1,329
Investment	1,586
Statistical discrepancy	0
Net exports	–349

1. The table above gives some of the items in the U.S. National Income and Product Accounts in 2001.

  a. Calculate U.S. GDP in 2001.

  b. Did you use the expenditure approach or the income approach for this calculation?

  c. What was the government's expenditure on goods and services in 2001?

Solutions to Additional Practice Problem 5.2

1a. This question focuses on calculating GDP. To solve problems such as this, you need to know how to use the expenditure approach and the income approach. The expenditure approach adds four categories of expenditure while the income approach adds the two income categories and then makes a few additional adjustments.

To calculate GDP using the expenditure approach the four categories of expenditure you need to know are: consumption, investment, government expenditure on goods and services, and net exports. The table does not give the value of government expenditures on goods and services, so you cannot find GDP using the expenditure approach.

To calculate GDP using the income approach you need to know the values of wage income and of interest, rent, and profit income. Adding these two income streams together yields net domestic income at factor cost. To adjust to GDP, you need also indirect taxes less subsidies, depreciation, and any statistical discrepancy. All these items are listed in the table, so GDP can be calculated using the income approach. In this case, GDP = $5,875 billion + $2,248 + $630 billion + $1,329 billion + $0, which is $10,082 billion.

1b The only way GDP can be calculated in part (a) is by the income approach, which is the approach used.

1c. GDP was calculated in part (a) using the income approach. The expenditure approach notes that GDP = $C + I + G + NX$. Subtract C, I, and NX from both sides of the equation to show that $G = GDP - C - I - NX$. Using the values of GDP, C, I, and NX yields $G =$ $10,082 billion − $6,987 billion − $1,586 billion + $349 billion = $1,858 billion. (The net exports were negative, so −(−$349 billion) equals + $349 billion).

■ **Self Test 5.2**

Fill in the blanks

The ____ approach and the ____ approach are two methods used to calculate GDP. Expenditure on used goods ____ (is; is not) included in GDP. Wages is part of the ____ (expenditure; income) approach to calculating GDP. To calculate GDP, depreciation is ____ (added to; subtracted from) net domestic product at factor cost. GNP equals GDP ____ (plus; minus) net factor income from abroad. For the United States, the difference between GDP and GNP is

____ (large; small). ____ (Real; Nominal) GDP values production during the year using constant prices; ____ (real; nominal) GDP values production using prices that prevailed during the year.

True or false

1. The expenditure approach measures GDP by using data on consumption expenditure, investment, government expenditures on goods and services, and net exports of goods and services.

2. In the United States, expenditure on used goods is becoming an increasingly large fraction of GDP.

3. The income approach uses data on consumption expenditure, investment, government purchases of goods and services, and net exports of goods and services to calculate GDP.

4. Disposable personal income is usually larger than GDP.

Multiple choice

1. In calculating GDP, economists
   a. use only total expenditure.
   b. can use either total expenditure or total income.
   c. use only total income.
   d. measure total income minus total expenditure.
   e. measure total income plus total expenditure.

2. The expenditure approach to measuring GDP is based on summing
   a. wages, interest, rent, and profit.
   b. each industry's production.
   c. the values of final goods, intermediate goods, used goods, and financial assets.
   d. consumption expenditure, investment, government expenditure on goods and services, and net exports of goods and services.
   e. consumption expenditure, investment, government expenditure on goods and services, and net exports minus wages, interest, rent, and profit.

3. Suppose GDP is $10 billion, consumption expenditure is $7 billion, investment is $2 billion, and government expenditure on goods and services is $2 billion. Net exports of goods and services must be
   a. $1 billion.
   b. −$1 billion.
   c. $2 billion.
   d. −$2 billion.
   e. $10 billion.

4. According to the expenditure approach to measuring GDP, in the United States the largest component of GDP is
   a. consumption expenditure.
   b. investment.
   c. government expenditure.
   d. net exports of goods and services.
   e. wages.

5. Which of the following is <u>NOT</u> one of the income categories used in the income approach to measuring GDP?
   a. wages
   b. rent
   c. interest
   d. taxes paid by persons
   e. profit

6. Nominal GDP can change
   a. only if prices change.
   b. only if the quantities of goods and services change.
   c. only if prices increase.
   d. if either prices *or* the quantities of goods and services change.
   e. only if prices *and* the quantities of the goods and services change.

7. The difference between nominal GDP and real GDP is
   a. the indirect taxes used in their calculations.
   b. the prices used in their calculations.
   c. that nominal GDP includes the depreciation of capital and real GDP does not.
   d. that nominal GDP includes net exports and real GDP includes net imports.
   e. that real GDP includes the depreciation of capital and nominal GDP does not.

Short answer and numeric questions

Item	Amount (dollars)
Wages	3,900
Consumption expenditure	4,000
Indirect taxes minus subsidies	400
Interest, rent, and profit	1,400
Government expenditure	1,000
Investment	1,100
Net exports	300
Statistical discrepancy	300

1. The table above gives data for a small nation:
   a. What is the nation's GDP? Did you use the expenditure or income approach to calculate GDP?
   b. What is the net domestic product at factor cost?
   c. What does depreciation equal?

2. What adjustments must be made to net domestic product at factor cost to convert it to GDP? Why must these adjustments be made?

3. What adjustments must be made to GDP to calculate GNP? To calculate disposable personal income?

4. What is the difference between real GDP and nominal GDP? Are the two ever equal?

5. To measure changes in production, why do we use real GDP rather than nominal GDP?

Additional Exercises (also in MyEconLab Test A)

Item	Amount (trillions of dollars)
Wages	6.0
Government expenditure	2.0
Interest, rent, and profit	2.4
Consumption expenditure	7.4
Investment	1.6
Net exports	0
Indirect taxes minus subsidies	0.7
Retained profits	1.6
Transfer payments	1.3
Personal income taxes	1.1
GNP	10.5
Depreciation	1.3

The table above shows some of the items in the U.S. National Income and Product Accounts in 2005. Use the table to answer Exercises 1, 2, and 3.

1. Use the income approach to calculate net domestic product at factor cost and the statistical discrepancy.

2. Calculate the differences between GDP, GNP, and U.S. national income.

3. Calculate disposable personal income. What percentage of total income is disposable personal income and what percentage of disposable personal income is consumption expenditure?

GDP data for 2010		
Item	Quantity	Price
Apples	60	$0.50
Oranges	80	$0.25

GDP data for 2012		
Item	Quantity	Price
Apples	160	$1.00
Oranges	220	$2.00

4. The two tables show some data for an economy. If the base year is 2012, calculate the economy's nominal GDP and real GDP in 2010.

CHECKPOINT 5.3

■ **Describe the uses of real GDP and explain its limitations as a measure of the standard of living.**

Quick Review

- *Potential GDP* The value of real GDP when all factors of production—labor, capital, land, and entrepreneurial ability—are fully employed.

- *Standard of living* The standard of living among different nations or over a period of time can be compared using real GDP per person.

- *Goods and services omitted from GDP* Household production, underground production, leisure time, and environmental quality are omitted from GDP.

Additional Practice Problems 5.3

1. How has real GDP per person changed in the United States since 1961?

2. How do you think the standard of living in the United States today compares with the standard of living 150 years ago?

Solutions to Additional Practice Problems 5.3

1. Real GDP per person has increased substantially since 1961. In fact, real GDP per person has more than doubled since 1961. In the United States for the past 100 years real GDP per person has doubled about every 30 years.

2. The standard of living now is dramatically higher than it was 150 years ago. First, even though totally accurate data for real GDP per person from 150 years ago is not available, it is certain that real GDP per person is much higher today even after taking account of the fact that household production was more common 150 years ago when many more people grew their own food. People today enjoy significantly more leisure time, which significantly boosts today's standard of living. Perhaps the edge on environment quality goes to the past or perhaps not because solid waste pollution (from horses) was a major issue 150 years ago. Considering health and life expectancy, and political freedom and social justice, people today are much better off than people 150 years ago.

■ Self Test 5.3

Fill in the blanks

Real GDP ____ (can; cannot) exceed potential GDP. The value of household production ____ (is; is not) included in GDP. The value of people's leisure time ____ (is; is not) included in GDP. As it is calculated, GDP ____ (does; does not) subtract the value of environmental degradation resulting from production. Real GDP ____ (takes; does not take) into account the extent of a country's political freedom.

True or false

1. A recession follows a business cycle peak.

2. As currently measured, real GDP does not include the value of household production.

3. Production in the underground economy is part of the "investment" component of GDP.

4. The production of anti-pollution devices installed by electric utilities is not counted in GDP because the devices are designed only to eliminate pollution.

5. A country's real GDP does not take into account the extent of political freedom in the country.

Multiple choice

1. In the years after 1998, the most severe recession occurred during
   a. 1998.
   b. 2000-2001.
   c. 2008-2009.
   d. 1999-2001.
   e. 2005.

2. Which of the following is <u>NOT</u> part of the business cycle?
   a. recession
   b. peak
   c. inflation
   d. trough
   e. expansion

3. In the business cycle, what immediately precedes the time when real GDP is falling?
   a. recession
   b. peak
   c. depression
   d. trough
   e. expansion

4. GDP handles household production by
   a. estimating a dollar value of the goods purchased to do housework.
   b. estimating a dollar value of the services provided.
   c. ignoring it.
   d. including it in exactly the same way that all other production is included.
   e. including it in real GDP but not in nominal GDP because there are no prices paid for the work.

5. You hire some of your friends to help you move to a new house. You pay them $200 and buy them dinner at Pizza Hut. Which of the following is true?
   a. The $200 should be counted as part of GDP but not the dinner at Pizza Hut.
   b. If your friends do not report the $200 on their tax forms, it becomes part of the underground economy.
   c. The dinner at Pizza Hut should be counted as part of GDP but not the $200.
   d. Hiring your friends is an illegal activity and should not be counted in GDP.
   e. Neither the $200 nor the dinner should be counted in GDP because both are household production.

6. The value of leisure time is
   a. included in GDP and, in recent years, has become an increasing large part of GDP.
   b. excluded from GDP.
   c. zero.
   d. directly included in GDP but, in recent years, has become a decreasing large part of GDP.
   e. directly included in GDP and, in recent years, has not changed much as a fraction of GDP.

7. A new technology is discovered that results in all new cars producing 50 percent less pollution. The technology costs nothing to produce and cars do not change in price. As a result of the technology, there is a reduction in the number of visits people make to the doctor to complain of breathing difficulties. Which of the following is true?
   a. real GDP decreases as a result of fewer doctor services being provided.
   b. real GDP is not affected.
   c. nominal GDP increases to reflect the improvement in the health of the population.
   d. real GDP decreases to reflect the decrease in pollution.
   e. nominal GDP does not change and real GDP increases.

Short answer and numeric questions
1. What is the relationship between real GDP and potential GDP?
2. What are the parts of a business cycle? What is their order?
3. What general categories of goods and services are omitted from GDP? Why is each omitted?
4. If you cook a hamburger at home, what happens to GDP? If you go to Burger King and purchase a hamburger, what happens to GDP?

Additional Exercises (also in MyEconLab Test A)
1. The United Nations Human Development Report gives the following data for real GDP per person in 2002: China, $4,580; Russia, $8,230; Canada, $29,480; United States, $35,750. Life expectancy at birth is 79.3 in Canada, 77.0 in the United States, 70.5 in China, and 66.7 in Russia. Freedom House rates political freedom as follows: Canada and the United States, 1.1 (1.0 is the most free); Russia, 4.5; and China, 7.6 (ratings in the 7+ range are the least free). How do life expectancy at birth and political freedom change the relative ranking of living standards that real GDP per person indicate?

SELF TEST ANSWERS

■ CHECKPOINT 5.1

Fill in the blanks

The market value of all the final goods and services produced within a country in a given time period is <u>GDP</u>. <u>Four</u> groups buy the final goods and services produced. Net exports equals the value of <u>exports</u> minus the value of <u>imports</u>. $C + I + G + NX$ equals <u>total expenditure</u> and <u>total income</u>.

True or false

1. False; page 112
2. False; page 113
3. True; page 114
4. True; page 115

Multiple choice

1. a; page 112
2. b; page 112
3. a; page 112
4. d; page 113
5. b; page 113
6. a; page 114

Short answer and numeric questions

1. Intermediate goods or services are not counted in GDP because if they were, they would be double counted. A computer produced by Dell Corp. is included in GDP. But if the Intel chip that is part of the computer is also included in GDP, then the Intel chip is counted twice: once when it is produced by Intel, and again when it is included in the computer produced by Dell; page 112.

2. a. Import; page 114.
   b. Consumption expenditure; page 113.
   c. Investment; page 113.
   d. Investment; page 113.
   e. Government expenditure on goods and services; page 114.

3. Total expenditure is the amount received by producers of final goods and services from the sales of these goods and services

Because firms pay all the revenue they receive to households in payment for the factors of production, total expenditure equals total income. From the viewpoint of firms, the value of production is the cost of production, and the cost of production is equal to income. From the viewpoint of consumers of goods and services, the value of production is the cost of buying the production, which equals expenditure; pages 114-115.

Additional Exercises (also in MyEconLab Test A)

1. a. The fertilizer is an intermediate good because it will be used to grow tomatoes; page 112.
   b. The ringtone is a final good because you are the final user. It is part of consumption expenditure; pages 112-113.
   c. The computers are a final good. Because they are purchased by Pepsi, they are investment; pages 112-113.
   d. The aircraft bought by Southwest Airlines are a final good. Because they are purchased by Southwest Airlines, they are investment; pages 112-113.

■ FIGURE 5.2

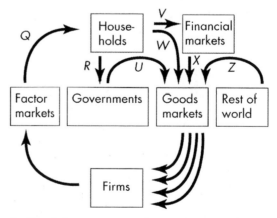

2. Total income equals total expenditure and total expenditure equals the sum of consumption expenditure, investment, government expenditure on goods and services, and net exports of goods and services. In Figure

5.2, consumption expenditure equals flow W and is $60 million; investment is X and is $25 million; government expenditure on goods and services is flow U and is $15 million; and, net exports of goods and services is flow Z and is $0. Total expenditure equals the sum of these flows, $100 million. Total income equals total expenditure, so total income equals $100 million. To calculate net taxes, subtract from households' total income their consumption expenditure and their saving. Total income equals total expenditure, so total income equals $100 million. Consumption expenditure is $60 million and saving, which is flow V, is $20 million, so net taxes equals $20 million; pages 114-115.

■ CHECKPOINT 5.2

Fill in the blanks

The <u>expenditure</u> approach and the <u>income</u> approach are two methods used to calculate GDP. Expenditure on used goods <u>is not</u> included in GDP. Wages is part of the <u>income</u> approach to calculating GDP. To calculate GDP, depreciation is <u>added to</u> net domestic product at factor cost. GNP equals GDP <u>plus</u> net factor income from abroad. For the United States, the difference between GDP and GNP is <u>small</u>. <u>Real</u> GDP values production during the year using constant prices; <u>nominal</u> GDP values production using prices that prevailed during the year.

True or false

1. True; page 117
2. False; page 118
3. False; page 119
4. False; page 121

Multiple choice

1. b; page 117
2. d; page 117
3. b; page 117
4. a; page 117
5. d; page 119
6. d; page 122
7. b; page 122

Short answer and numeric questions

1. a. GDP = $6,400, which is the sum of consumption expenditure, investment, government expenditures on goods and services, and net exports of goods and services. The expenditure approach was used; page 117.

   b. Net domestic product at factor cost equals $5,300, the sum of wage income plus interest, rent, and profit income; page 119.

   c. The difference between GDP and net domestic product at factor cost, which is $1,100, equals indirect taxes minus subsidies plus depreciation plus any statistical discrepancy. The statistical discrepancy equals zero. Indirect taxes minus subsidies equals $400, so depreciation equals $700; pages 119-120.

2. To change net domestic product at factor cost to GDP, three sets of adjustments must be made. First, net domestic product at factor cost is measured at firms' costs; to convert costs to equal the market prices paid, taxes must be added and subsidies subtracted. Second, net domestic product does not include depreciation but GDP does. So, depreciation must be added. Finally, any statistical discrepancy must be added or subtracted; pages 119-120.

3. To calculate GNP, net factor income from abroad must be added (or subtracted, if it is negative) from GDP. Then, to calculate disposable personal income, from GNP depreciation and retained profits must be subtracted, transfer payments must be added, and then any statistical discrepancy must be either added or subtracted; page 121.

4. The difference between real GDP and nominal GDP lies in the prices used to value the final goods and services. Real GDP uses prices from a fixed base year. Nominal GDP uses prices from the current year for which GDP is being calculated. Real GDP equals nominal GDP in the base year; page 122.

5. Nominal GDP is computed using prices and quantities from the given year. From one

year to the next, both prices and quantities can change, so nominal GDP will change if either the prices change or the quantities—production—change. Real GDP uses prices from a base year. So from one year to the next changes in real GDP reflect changes in the quantities, that is, changes in production; page 122.

Additional Exercises (also in MyEconLab Test A)
1. Using the income approach, net domestic product at factor cost = Wages + Interest, rent, and profit = $6.0 trillion + $2.4 trillion = $8.4 trillion.

   The statistical discrepancy equals the GDP expenditure total minus the GDP income total. GDP calculated using the expenditure approach is $11.0 trillion. To calculate GDP using the income approach, we add net domestic product at factor cost, indirect taxes less subsidies, and depreciation. So GDP using the income approach equals $8.4 trillion + $0.7 trillion + $1.3 trillion = $10.4 trillion. So the statistical discrepancy equals $11.0 trillion – $10.4 trillion = $600 billion; pages 119-120.

2. GNP equals GDP plus net factor income from other countries, so the difference between the two is net factor income from other countries. Net factor income from other countries = GNP – GDP, so using the data in the problem, net factor income from other countries = $11.0 trillion – $10.5 trillion = $500 billion.

   U.S. national income = GNP – depreciation – statistical discrepancy = $10.5 trillion – $1.3 trillion – $600 billion = $7.6 trillion; page 121.

3. Disposable personal income = national income – retained profits plus transfer payments – personal income taxes = $7.6 trillion – $1.6 trillion + $1.3 trillion – $1.1 trillion = $6.2 trillion.

   As a percentage of U.S. national income, disposable personal income is ($6.2 trillion ÷ $7.6 trillion) × 100 = 81.6 percent. As a percentage of disposable personal income, con-

sumption is ($7.4 trillion ÷ $6.2 trillion) × 100 = 119 percent; page 121.

4. Nominal GDP equals (60 apples × $0.50 per apple) + (80 oranges × $0.25 per orange) = $50. Real GDP in 2010 is calculated using the 2010 quantities and the 2012 prices. Real GDP equals (60 apples × $1.00 per apple) + (80 oranges × $2.00 per orange) = $220; pages 122-123.

■ CHECKPOINT 5.3
Fill in the blanks
Real GDP <u>can</u> exceed potential GDP. The value of household production <u>is not</u> included in GDP. The value of people's leisure time <u>is not</u> included in GDP. As it is calculated, GDP <u>does not</u> subtract the value of environmental degradation resulting from production. Real GDP <u>does not take</u> into account the extent of a country's political freedom.

True or false
1. True; pages 126-127
2. True; page 129
3. False; page 129
4. False; page 129
5. True; page 130

Multiple choice
1. c; page 127
2. c; pages 127-128
3. b; pages 127-128
4. c; page 129
5. b; page 129
6. b; page 129
7. a; page 129

Short answer and numeric questions
1. Potential GDP is the value of real GDP when all factors of production are fully employed. Over time potential GDP grows. Real GDP fluctuates around the growth path of potential GDP. These fluctuations reflect the business cycle; pages 125-126.

2. The business cycle is made up of the expansion phase, when real GDP is growing; the peak, when real GDP reaches its highest level; the recession phase, when real GDP is falling for at least 6 months; and the trough, when real GDP is at its lowest level. The order of the business cycle is from expansion to peak to recession to trough, and then back to expansion; pages 126-127.

3. Goods and services omitted from GDP are household production, underground production, leisure time, and environmental quality. GDP measures the value of goods and services that are bought in markets. Because household production, leisure time, and environmental quality are not purchased in markets, they are excluded from GDP. Even though underground production frequently is bought in markets, the activity is unreported and is not included in GDP; page 129.

4. If you cook a hamburger at home, the meat you purchased is included in GDP but the production of the hamburger is not included in GDP because it is household production. If you buy a hamburger at Burger King, the production of the hamburger is included in GDP; page 129.

Additional Exercises (also in MyEconLab Test A)

1. The relatively high life expectancy and political freedom means Canada's and the United States' relative rankings rise. The low life expectancy and political freedom decrease China's and Russia's rankings; page 131.

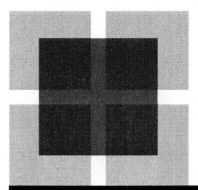

Appendix: Measuring Real GDP

APPENDIX CHECKLIST

The appendix shows how the Bureau of Economic Analysis calculates real GDP.

❶ Measuring Real GDP

Real GDP depends on the prices used to value the production of goods and services. The Bureau of Economic Analysis (BEA) uses prices from adjacent years to value the production and thereby creates a chained-dollar real GDP. For instance, between 2011 and 2012, first, prices from 2011 are used to value the goods and services produced in 2011 and the goods and services produced in 2012. Then the growth rate between these two years is calculated. Second, prices from 2012 are used to value the production in 2011 and the production in 2012. Then the (second) growth rate between these two years is calculated. These two growth rates are averaged to give the final growth rate between these two years. This growth rate is applied to real GDP for 2011 to calculate real GDP for 2012. The real GDPs for all the years are chained back to the base year real GDP by the growth rates between years.

CHECKPOINT I

■ Measuring Real GDP

Quick Review

- *Real GDP* The value of the final goods and services produced in a given year valued at the prices of a base year.

- *Nominal GDP* The value of the final goods and services produced in a given year valued at the prices that prevailed in that year.

Additional Practice Problem I

1. In a small, tropical nation suppose real GDP in 2011 is $5 billion and nominal GDP in 2011 is $10 billion. In 2012, nominal GDP is $12 billion. If GDP in 2012, measured using 2011 prices is $11.5 billion and GDP in 2011, measured using 2012 prices, is $11 billion, what does real GDP in 2012 equal?

Solution to Additional Practice Problem I

1. This question gives you practice you need in how real GDP is calculated. Take each part step-by-step:

   First we need the growth rate of GDP from 2011 to 2012 measured using 2011 prices. Nominal GDP in 2011 (which is GDP in 2011 measured using 2011 prices) is $10 billion and GDP in 2012 measured using 2011 prices is $11.5 billion. So the growth rate of GDP using 2011 prices is [($11.5 billion − $10.0 billion) ÷ $10 billion] × 100, which is 11.5 percent.

   Next we need the growth rate of GDP from 2011 to 2012 measured using 2012 prices. GDP in 2011 measured with 2012 prices is $11 billion and nominal GDP in 2012 (which is GDP in 2012 measured using 2012 prices) is $12 billion. So the growth rate of GDP using 2012 prices is [($12 billion − $11 billion) ÷ $11 billion] × 100, which is 9.1 percent.

Finally, we average the two growth rates to give a growth rate of 10.3 percent between 2011 and 2012. This percentage change is applied to real GDP in 2011, $5 billion, to give real GDP in 2012. This procedure means that real GDP in 2012 equals ($5 billion × 1.103) which is $5.52 billion.

■ Self Test 1

Fill in the blanks

The BEA calculates real GDP in a given year using prices from ____ (that year only; that year and the previous year). Real GDP in any given year ____ (is; is not) chained back to the base year.

True or false

1. Real GDP is just a more precise name for GDP.

2. Real GDP equals nominal GDP in the base year.

3. The base year for real GDP changes each year.

Multiple choice

1. Real GDP measures the value of goods and services produced in a given year valued using
   a. base year prices.
   b. prices of that same year.
   c. no prices.
   d. future prices.
   e. government approved prices.

2. In a small country, using prices of 2011, GDP in 2011 was $100 and GDP in 2012 was $110. Using prices of 2012, GDP in 2011 was $200 and GDP in 2012 was $210. The country's

BEA will calculate ____ percent as the growth in real GDP between those years.
   a. 10
   b. 5
   c. 15
   d. 7.5
   e. None of the above answers is correct.

3. Using prices from 2011, GDP grew 10 percent between 2011 and 2012; using prices from 2012, GDP grew 8 percent between 2011 and 2012. For its link back to the base year, the BEA will use ____ percent as the growth in real GDP between 2011 and 2012.
   a. 10
   b. 8
   c. 2
   d. 18
   e. 9

Short answer and numeric questions

Item	Data for 2011 Quantity	Data for 2011 Price	Data for 2012 Quantity	Data for 2012 Price
Pizza	100	$10.00	150	$20.00
Soda	50	$2.00	75	$4.00

1. An economy produces only pizza and soda. The table above gives the quantities produced and prices in 2011 and 2012. The base year is 2011.

   a. What is nominal GDP in 2011?
   b. What is real GDP in 2011?
   c. What is nominal GDP in 2012?
   d. What is real GDP in 2012?

2. How does the chained-dollar method of calculating real GDP link the current year's real GDP to the base year's real GDP?

SELF TEST ANSWERS

■ CHECKPOINT I

Fill in the blanks

The BEA calculates real GDP in a given year using prices from <u>that year and the previous year</u>. Real GDP in any given year <u>is</u> chained back to the base year.

True or false

1. False; page 137
2. True; page 137
3. False; page 139

Multiple choice

1. a; page 137
2. d; pages 138-139
3. e; page 139

Short answer and numeric questions

1. a. Nominal GDP = (100 pizzas × $10 per pizza) + (50 sodas × $2 per soda) = $1,100, the sum of expenditure on pizza and expenditure on soda; pages 137-138.
   b. Because 2011 is the base year, real GDP = nominal GDP, so real GDP = $1,100; pages 137-139.
   c. Nominal GDP = (150 pizzas × $20 per pizza) + (75 sodas × $4 per soda) = $3,300, the sum of expenditure on pizza and expenditure on soda; pages 137-139.
   d. Using 2011 prices, GDP grew from $1,100 in 2011 to $1,650 in 2012, a percentage increase of 50 percent. Using 2012 prices, GDP grew 50 percent between 2011 and 2012. The average growth is 50 percent, so real GDP in 2012 is 50 percent higher than in 2011, which means that real GDP in 2012 is $1,650; pages 138-139.

2. From one year to the next, real GDP is scaled by the growth rate (which is the percentage change) from the first year to the next. For instance, real GDP in 2011 is linked to real GDP in 2010 using the growth rate from 2010. Next in turn, real GDP in 2012 is linked to real GDP in 2011 using the growth rate from 2011, and so on. These links are like the links in a chain. They link real GDP in the current year back to the base year and the base year prices; page 139.

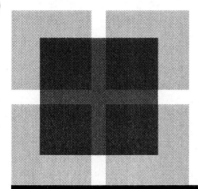

Jobs and Unemployment

Chapter 6

1 Define the unemployment rate and other labor market indicators.

The Current Population Survey is a monthly survey of 60,000 households across the country that is the basis for the nation's labor market statistics. The working-age population is non-institutionalized people aged 16 and over who are not in the U.S. Armed Forces. The labor force is the sum of the number of people employed and the number unemployed. To be unemployed, a person must have no employment, be available for work, and either have made an effort to find a job during the previous four weeks or be waiting to be recalled to a job from which he or she was laid off. The unemployment rate is the percentage of people in the labor force who are unemployed. The labor force participation rate is the percentage of the working-age population who are members of the labor force. A marginally attached worker is a person who is available and willing to work but has not made specific efforts to find a job within the previous four weeks but has looked for work sometime in the recent past. A discouraged worker is a marginally attached worker who is not searching for work because previous attempts to find a job within the past four weeks were unsuccessful. Full-time workers are those who usually work 35 hours or more a week. Some part-time workers are looking for full-time work but cannot find it because of unfavorable economic conditions and are called "part time for economic reasons".

2 Describe the trends and fluctuations in the indicators of labor market performance in the United States.

Since 1948, the average U.S. unemployment rate has been 5.8 percent. In the Great Depression of the 1930s, the U.S. unemployment rate reached 25 percent. From 1960 to 2011, the labor force participation rate increased. The labor force participation rate for men decreased and for women increased. A broad measure of the unemployment rate, called U-6, includes discouraged workers, marginally attached workers, and part time for economic reason workers. The number of workers who are part time for economic reasons rises during recessions and falls during expansions.

3 Describe the types of unemployment, define full employment, and explain the link between unemployment and real GDP.

Unemployment is classified into three types: frictional (normal labor turnover), structural (changes in necessary job skills or job locations), or cyclical (changes in the business cycle). The duration of unemployment increases in recessions. Full employment occurs when there is no cyclical unemployment. At full employment, the unemployment rate is the natural unemployment rate and GDP equals potential GDP. The natural unemployment rate increases when: the number of young workers increases; there is a rapid pace of technological change; the real wage exceeds the equilibrium real wage; and, unemployment benefits increase. The output gap is real GDP minus potential GDP expressed as a percentage of potential GDP. In recessions, the GDP gap becomes negative and unemployment rises.

CHECKPOINT 6.1

■ Define the unemployment rate and other labor market indicators.

Quick Review

- *Unemployment rate* The unemployment rate is the percentage of the people in the labor force who are unemployed. That is,

$$\text{Unemployment rate} = \frac{(\text{Unemployed people})}{(\text{Labor force})} \times 100$$

- *Labor force participation rate* The labor force participation rate is the percentage of the working-age population who are members of the labor force. It equals

$$\text{Participation rate} = \frac{(\text{Labor force})}{(\text{Working - age people})} \times 100$$

Additional Practice Problems 6.1

1. Determine the labor market status of each of the following people:
   a. Don is 21 and a full-time college student.
   b. Shirley works for 20 hours a week as an administrative assistant and is looking for a full-time job.
   c. Clarence was laid off from his job selling keyboards to computer manufacturers and is actively seeking a new job.
   d. Pat quit her job as an account executive 6 months ago but, unable to find a new position, has stopped actively searching.

2. The Bureau of Labor Statistics reported that in June 2005, the labor force was 149.1 million, employment was 141.6 million, and the working-age population was 225.9 million. Calculate for that month the:
   a. Unemployment rate.
   b. Labor force participation rate.

Solutions to Additional Practice Problems 6.1

1a. Don is neither working nor looking for work, so he is not in the labor force.

1b. Shirley is working for pay for more than 1 hour a week, so she is employed and part of the labor force. She is working less than 35 hours a week, so she is a part-time worker. Because she is looking for a full-time job, Shirley is an involuntary part-time worker.

1c. Clarence is actively seeking a new job, so he is unemployed. Clarence is part of the labor force.

1d. Pat is neither working nor actively looking for work, so she is not in the labor force. Pat is a discouraged worker.

2a. The labor force equals the sum of the number of people employed and the number of people unemployed. Subtracting the number employed from the labor force gives the number of unemployed. The labor force is 149.1 million and the number of employed is 141.6 million, so the number unemployed is 149.1 million − 141.6 million, which is 7.5 million. To calculate the unemployment rate, divide the number of unemployed by the labor force and multiply by 100. The unemployment rate equals (7.5 million ÷ 149.1 million) × 100, which is 5.0 percent.

2b. The labor force participation rate is the percentage of the working-age population who are members of the labor force. The labor force participation rate equals the labor force divided by the working-age population all multiplied by 100, which is (149.1 million ÷ 225.9 million) × 100 = 66.0 percent.

■ Self Test 6.1

Fill in the blanks

The ____ (working-age population; labor force) is the total number of people aged 16 years and over and who are not in jail, hospital, or some other form of institutional care. The unemployment rate equals the ____ divided by the ____ and then multiplied by 100. The labor force participation rate equals the ____ divided by the ____ and then multiplied by 100. Discouraged workers ____ (are; are not) counted as being unemployed while other marginally attached workers ____ (are; are not) counted as being unemployed. Workers who are part time for economic reasons ____ (are; are not) counted as being unemployed.

True or false

1. If Bob has been laid off by Ford, but expects to be recalled within the next three weeks, he is part of the labor force.

2. People are counted as unemployed if they work less than 40 hours per week.

3. The unemployment rate decreases when unemployed workers find jobs.

4. The labor force participation rate measures the percentage of the labor force that is employed.

5. Marginally attached workers have jobs.

Multiple choice

1. Assume the U.S. population is 300 million. If the working age population is 240 million, 150 million are employed, and 6 million are unemployed, what is the labor force?
   a. 300 million
   b. 240 million
   c. 156 million
   d. 150 million
   e. 144 million

2. To be counted as employed by the BLS, in the week before the survey the person must have worked for pay for _____.
   a. at least 1 hour
   b. at least 5 hours
   c. more than 20 hours
   d. 40 hours
   e. None of the above are right because the BLS counts as employed anyone who works volunteer hours at a non-profit institution.

3. Bo is available and willing to work but has not actively looked for work in the past month. Bo is ____ of the labor force and is ____.
   a. part; counted as being unemployed
   b. part; not counted as being unemployed
   c. not part; not counted as being unemployed
   d. not part; counted as being unemployed only if he has had a job within the last 12 months
   e. not part; counted as being unemployed regardless of whether or not he has had a job within the last 12 months

4. Which of the following statements about the United States is (are) correct?
   i. The labor force is larger than the number of employed people.
   ii. The labor force is larger than the number of unemployed people.
   iii. The number of unemployed people is larger than the number of employed people.
   a. ii only.
   b. iii only.
   c. ii and iii.
   d. i and ii.
   e. i, ii, and iii.

5. The unemployment rate equals
   a. (number of people without a job ÷ population) × 100.
   b. (number of people unemployed ÷ labor force) × 100.
   c. (number of people without a job ÷ working-age population) × 100.
   d. (number of people unemployed ÷ population) × 100.
   e. [(working-age population − number of people employed) ÷ labor force] × 100.

6. If the working age population is 200 million, 150 million are employed, and 6 million are unemployed, the unemployment rate is ____.
   a. 3.0 percent
   b. 25.0 percent
   c. 4.0 percent
   d. 12.0 percent
   e. 3.8 percent

7. Discouraged workers and marginally attached workers are
   a. counted as being employed by the BLS but are not part of the labor force.
   b. counted as being employed by the BLS and are part of the labor force.
   c. counted as being unemployed by the BLS and are part of the labor force.
   d. not part of the labor force.
   e. counted as being unemployed by the BLS but are not part of the labor force.

8. While in school, Kiki spends 20 hours a week as a computer programmer for Microsoft and studies 30 hours a week.
   a. Kiki is classified as a full-time worker, working 50 hours a week.
   b. Kiki is classified as a part-time worker, working 30 hours a week.
   c. Kiki is classified as a part-time worker, working 20 hours a week.
   d. Because Kiki is a student, she is not classified as working.
   e. Because Kiki is a student, she is classified as a full-time worker, working 20 hours a week at a paid job.

9. Part-time workers for noneconomic reasons are people who
   a. work less than 35 hours a week but would like to work more than 35 hours a week.
   b. work more than 35 hours a week but would like to work less than 35 hours a week.
   c. have lost their jobs within the last four weeks and are seeking another job.
   d. do not want to work full time.
   e. are discouraged workers.

Short answer and numeric questions

Category	Number of people
Total population	2,600
Working-age population	2,000
Not in the labor force	500
Employed	1,300

1. The table above gives the status of the population of a (small!) nation.
   a. What is the size of the labor force?
   b. What is the number of unemployed workers?
   c. What is the unemployment rate?
   d. What is the labor force participation rate?

Category	Number of people
Working-age population	3,000
Unemployed	100
Employed	1,900

2. The table above gives the status of the population of another (small!) nation.
   a. What is the size of the labor force?
   b. What is the unemployment rate?
   c. What is the labor force participation rate?

3. What criteria must a person meet to be counted as being unemployed?

4. How does a discouraged worker relate to a marginally attached worker? Explain why a discouraged worker is not counted as part of the labor force.

5. Are part-time workers who are part time for economic reasons counted as being employed, underemployed, or unemployed?

Additional Exercises (also in MyEconLab Test A)

1. The Bureau of Labor Statistics reported that in June 2005, the labor force was 151.1 million, employment was 143.3 million, and the working-age population was 226.2 million. Calculate the unemployment rate and the labor force participation rate in June 2005.

2. Statistics Canada reported that in June 2005, the Canadian labor force was 17.1 million, employment was 15.7 million, and the working-age population was 25.1 million. Calculate the Canadian unemployment rate and the labor force participation rate in June 2005.

3. In June 2005, the U.S. labor force was 151.1 million, U.S. employment was 143.3 million, and the U.S. working-age population was 226.2 million In June 2005, in Canada, the labor force was 17.1 million, employment was 15.7 million, and the working-age population was 25.1 million. Do you think jobs are harder to find in Canada or in the United States? Why?

Item	MA	U.S.
	(thousands)	
Working-age population	5,000	226,000
Labor force	3,400	149,300
Employment	3,200	141,700
Unemployment	200	7,600

4. The table above sets out data on the labor force in Massachusetts (MA) and in the United States in 2005. Calculate the unemployment rate and the labor force participation

rate in Massachusetts. Compare these two labor market indicators in Massachusetts with the U.S. averages.

CHECKPOINT 6.2

■ **Describe the trends and fluctuations in the indicators of labor market performance in the United States.**

Quick Review

- *Labor force participation rate* The percentage of the working-age population who are members of the labor force.

- *U-6* An alternative measure of the unemployment rate which counts discouraged workers, marginally attached workers, and people employed part time for economic reasons as unemployed members of the labor force.

Additional Practice Problems 6.2

1. How does the unemployment rate change in a recession? Since 1929, in what time period was the unemployment rate the highest and what did it equal?

2. Are workers employed part time for economic reasons counted as unemployed when calculating the official U-3 unemployment rate? If they are, how do they affect the unemployment rate; if they are not, how would their inclusion affect the unemployment rate?

Solutions to Additional Practice Problems 6.2

1. The unemployment rate rises during recessions. Since 1929, the unemployment rate reached its peak of approximately 25 percent in 1932 during the Great Depression.

2. Workers employed part time for economic reasons are *not* counted as unemployed in the official U-3 unemployment rate. Indeed, they are counted as employed when computing that unemployment rate. If they were counted as unemployed, the unemployment rate would increase. As Figure 6.5 in the textbook shows,

the increase would be larger during recessions because the number of workers employed part time for economic reasons increases during recessions.

■ Self Test 6.2

Fill in the blanks

The unemployment rate in 2011 was ____ (higher; lower) than the average over the last six decades. Since 1960, the male labor force participation rate ____ and the female participation rate ____. Counting both discouraged workers and marginally attached workers as unemployed ____ (raises; lowers) the unemployment rate. The number of workers who are part time for noneconomic reasons ____ (rises; does not change; falls) during recessions and the number of workers who are part time for economic reasons ____ (rises; does not change; falls) during recessions.

True or false

1. The unemployment rate during the 2008-2009 recession was lower than the unemployment rate during the Great Depression.

2. Although the female labor force participation rate increased over the last 40 years, it is still less than the male labor force participation rate.

3. During the 2008-2009 recession, the unemployment rate that included marginally attached workers and discouraged workers as unemployed was double the unemployment rate that did not include these workers.

4. The number of workers employed part-time for economic reasons rises during recessions.

Multiple choice

1. From 1948 to 2011, the average unemployment rate in the United States was approximately
   a. 3.1 percent.
   b. 5.8 percent.
   c. 12.0 percent.
   d. 24.4 percent.
   d. 9.6 percent.

2. From 1981 to 2011, the unemployment rate in the United States
   a. was always lower than the unemployment rate in Japan.
   b. almost always equaled the unemployment rate in Canada.
   c. generally rose while the unemployment rate in the Eurozone fell.
   d. was usually lower than the unemployment rate in the Eurozone.
   e. was usually higher than the unemployment rate in Canada.

3. Between 1960 and 2011,
   a. both the male and female labor force participation rates increased.
   b. the male labor force participation rate decreased rapidly, the female labor force participation rate decreased slowly, and the two rates are now equal.
   c. the male labor force participation rate decreased and the female labor force participation rate increased.
   d. both the male and female labor force participation rates decreased slowly.
   e. the male labor force participation rate did not change and the female labor force participation rate increased.

4. The women's labor force participation rate is
   a. higher in Japan than in the United States.
   b. higher in the United States than in France.
   c. higher in Italy than in the United States.
   d. higher in Spain than in Iceland.
   e. higher in the United States than in Iceland or Norway.

5. In a recession, which unemployment rate is the highest?
   a. The U-1 unemployment rate.
   b. The U-6 unemployment rate.
   c. The U-2 unemployment rate.
   d. The U-3 unemployment rate.
   e. None of the above answers are correct because the highest unemployment rate changes from one recession to the next.

6. In 2011, part-time workers for noneconomic reasons were about ____ of total employment

and part-time workers for economic reasons were about ____ of total employment.
   a. 3 percent; 25 percent
   b. 17 percent; 17 percent
   c. 2 percent; 12 percent
   d. 13 percent; 20 percent
   e. 13 percent; 6 percent

7. The number of part-time workers for economic reasons ____ during recessions and the number of part-time workers for noneconomic reasons ____ during recessions.
   a. increases; increases
   b. increases; decreases
   c. increases; does not change
   d. does not change; does not change
   e. decreases; increases

Short answer and numeric questions

1. During a recession, what happens to:
   a. the unemployment rate?
   b. the number of part-time workers for economic reasons?
   c. the number of part-time workers for noneconomic reasons?

2. How does the unemployment rate during the Great Depression compare with more recent unemployment rates?

3. How do the U-3, U-5, and U-6 measures of the unemployment rate differ? What happens to them when the economy enters a recession?

Additional Exercises (also in MyEconLab Test A)

1. During which decade—the 1970s, 1980s, or 1990s—did the labor force participation rate of women increase most? Suggest some reasons why this rapid increase occurred during that decade.

2. In which decade did the labor force participation rate of men decrease most? Why do you think this rapid decrease occurred in that decade?

3. Describe the trends in the unemployment rate, the labor force participation rates of men and women, part-time workers for noneconomic reasons, and part-time workers for economic reasons from 1994 to 2011. Why did these trends occur?

CHECKPOINT 6.3

■ **Describe the types of unemployment, define full employment, and explain the link between unemployment and real GDP.**

Quick Review

- *Frictional unemployment* Unemployment that arises from normal labor market turnover.
- *Structural unemployment* Unemployment that arises when changes in technology or international competition change the skills needed to perform jobs or change the location of jobs.
- *Cyclical unemployment* Unemployment that fluctuates over the business cycle, rising during a recession and falling during an expansion.
- *Full employment* When there is no cyclical unemployment.
- *Natural unemployment rate* The unemployment rate at full employment.
- *Potential GDP* The value of real GDP when all the economy's factors of production are employed.
- *Output gap* Real GDP minus potential GDP, expressed as a percentage of potential GDP.

Additional Practice Problems 6.3

1. Each of the following people is actively seeking work. Classify each as either frictionally, structurally, or cyclically unemployed:
   a. Perry lost his job when foreign competition bankrupted his company.
   b. Sam did not like his boss and so he quit his job.
   c. Sherry just graduated from college.
   d. Jose was fired when his company downsized in response to a recession.
   e. Pat was laid off from her job at the Gap because customers liked the fashions at JCPenney better.

2. In a recession, what happens to the output gap?

Solutions to Additional Practice Problems 6.3
1a. Perry is structurally unemployed.
1b. Sam is frictionally unemployed.
1c. Sherry is frictionally unemployed.
1d. Jose is cyclically unemployed.
1e. Pat is frictionally unemployed.
2. In a recession, real GDP is less than potential GDP, so the output gap is negative.

■ **Self Test 6.3**

Fill in the blanks
The normal unemployment from labor market turnover is called ____ unemployment, and the unemployment that fluctuates over the business cycle is called ____ unemployment. When ____ (frictional; structural; cyclical) unemployment equals zero, the economy is experiencing ____ employment and the unemployment rate is the ____. When potential GDP exceeds real GDP, the output gap is ____ (positive; negative) and the unemployment rate ____ (is higher than; is lower than) the natural unemployment rate.

True or false
1. There can easily be times when there is no unemployment.
2. The unemployment that arises when technology changes is termed technological unemployment.
3. When the U.S. economy is at full employment, the unemployment rate is zero.
4. Increasing unemployment benefits increase the natural unemployment rate.
5. Potential GDP is the amount of real GDP when the economy is at full employment.

Multiple choice
1. Tommy graduates from college and starts to look for a job. Tommy is
   a. frictionally unemployed.
   b. structurally unemployed.
   c. cyclically unemployed.
   d. unnecessarily unemployed.
   e. employed because he is looking for work.

2. If an entire industry relocates to a foreign country, the relocation leads to a higher rate of ____ unemployment.
   a. frictional
   b. structural
   c. structural and cyclical
   d. cyclical
   e. None of the above answers are correct because there is no unemployment created.

3. Who is cyclically unemployed?
   a. Casey, who lost his job because the technology changed so that he was no longer needed.
   b. Katrina, an office manager who quit her job to search for a better job closer to home.
   c. Kathy, a steelworker who was laid off but has stopped looking for a new job because she can't find one.
   d. David, a new car salesman who lost his job because of a recession.
   e. Samantha, who quit her job to return to college to earn her MBA.

4. An increase in unemployment benefits ____ unemployment and an increase in international competition that changes the location of jobs ____ unemployment.
   a. increases structural; decreases frictional
   b. decreases structural; decreases cyclical
   c. decreases cyclical; decreases cyclical
   d. increases frictional; increases structural
   e. decreases cyclical; increases cyclical

5. Which of the following *lowers* frictional unemployment?
   a. more young people in the economy.
   b. decreasing unemployment benefits.
   c. increasing the pace of technological change.
   d. increasing the minimum wage.
   e. None of the above answers are correct because all of the answers raise frictional unemployment.

6. When the economy is at full employment,
   a. the natural unemployment rate equals zero.
   b. the amount of cyclical unemployment equals zero.
   c. the amount of structural unemployment equals zero.
   d. there is no unemployment.
   e. the amount of frictional unemployment equals zero.

7. When the unemployment rate is less than the natural unemployment rate, real GDP is ____ potential GDP.
   a. greater than
   b. less than
   c. unrelated to
   d. equal to
   e. not comparable to

Short answer and numeric questions
1. What are the three types of unemployment?
2. How does the average time a worker spends as unemployed change during a recession?
3. What is the relationship between full employment, the natural unemployment rate, and potential GDP?
4. If the unemployment rate exceeds the natural unemployment rate, what is the relationship between real GDP and potential GDP? Is the output gap at this time positive or negative?

SELF TEST ANSWERS

■ CHECKPOINT 6.1

Fill in the blanks

The <u>working-age population</u> is the total number of people aged 16 years and over and who are not in jail, hospital, or some other form of institutional care. The unemployment rate equals the <u>number of people unemployed</u> divided by the <u>labor force</u> and then multiplied by 100. The labor force participation rate equals the <u>labor force</u> divided by the <u>working-age population</u> and then multiplied by 100. Discouraged workers <u>are not</u> counted as unemployed while other marginally attached workers <u>are not</u> counted as unemployed. Workers who are part time for economic reasons <u>are not</u> counted as unemployed.

True or false

1. True; page 142
2. False; page 142
3. True; page 143
4. False; page 144
5. False; page 144

Multiple choice

1. c; page 142
2. a; page 142
3. c; page 142
4. d; page 142
5. b; page 143
6. e; page 143
7. d; page 144
8. c; page 145
9. d; page 145

Short answer and numeric questions

1. a. 1,500; page 142.
   b. 200; page 142.
   c. 13.3 percent; page 143.
   d. 75.0 percent; page 144.
2. a. 2,000; page 143.
   b. 5.0 percent; page 143.
   c. 66.7 percent; page 144.

3. The person must be without employment, available for work, and actively searching or waiting to be recalled to a job from which he or she was laid off; page 142.

4. A marginally attached worker is a person without a job, who is not looking for work at the present but has looked for work in the recent past. A discouraged worker is marginally attached worker who is not looking for work because previous job searches were unsuccessful.. A discouraged worker is not counted as unemployed because the worker is not actively seeking a job; page 144.

5. Underemployed; page 145.

Additional Exercises (also in MyEconLab Test A)

1. Unemployment rate = (151.1 million − 143.3 million) ÷ 151.1 million × 100 = 5.2 percent.
   Labor force participation rate = (151.1 million ÷ 226.2 million) × 100 = 66.8 percent; pages 143-144.

2. Unemployment rate = (17.1 million − 15.7 million) ÷ 17.1 million × 100 = 8.2 percent.
   Labor force participation rate = (17.1 million ÷ 25.1 million) × 100 = 68.1 percent; pages 143-144.

3. Probably it is more difficult to find a job in the nation with the higher unemployment rate. In that case, jobs were harder to find in Canada because Canada's unemployment at that time exceeded the U.S. unemployment rate; page 143.

4. In Massachusetts the unemployment rate equals 200 thousand ÷ 3,400 thousand × 100 = 5.9 percent and the labor force participation rate equals (3,400 thousand ÷ 5,000 thousand) × 100 = 68.0 percent. In the United States, the unemployment rate equals 7,600 thousand ÷ 149,300 thousand × 100 = 5.1 percent and the labor force participation rate equals (149,300 thousand ÷ 226,000 thousand) × 100 = 66.1 percent. The unemployment rate is higher in Massachusetts and so is the labor force participation rate; pages 143-144.

■ CHECKPOINT 6.2

Fill in the blanks

The unemployment rate in 2011 was <u>higher</u> than the average over the last six decades. Since 1960, the male labor force participation rate <u>fell</u> and the female participation rate <u>rose</u>. Counting both discouraged workers and marginally attached workers as unemployed <u>raises</u> the unemployment rate. The number of workers who are part time for noneconomic reasons <u>does not change</u> during recessions and the number of workers who are part time for economic reasons <u>rises</u> during recessions.

True or false

1. True; page 147
2. True; pages 148-149
3. False; page 150
4. True; page 151

Multiple choice

1. b; page 147
2. d; page 148
3. c; pages 148-149
4. b; page 149
5. b; page 150
6. e; page 151
7. c; page 151

Short answer and numeric questions

1. a. The unemployment rate rises; pages 147-148.
   b. The number of part-time workers for economic reasons increases; page 151.
   c. The number of part-time workers for non-economic reasons does not change; page 151.

2. The unemployment rate during the Great Depression was *much* higher, reaching near 25 percent, than recent unemployment rates, which reached approximately 10 percent in 1982 and 2009; pages 147-148.

3. The U-3 measure of the unemployment rate is the "official measure;" it counts as unemployed only unemployed workers. The U-5 measure of the unemployment rate counts discouraged workers and marginally attached workers as unemployed members of the labor force. The U-6 measure of the unemployment modifies the U-5 measure by also counting part-time workers for economic reasons as unemployed. All three measures rise when the economy enters a recession; page 150.

Additional Exercises (also in MyEconLab Test A)

1. The 1970s was the decade in which the labor force participation rate of women increased the most. Women generally increased their labor force participation rate throughout the last 50 years for four reasons: They pursued a college education and so increased their earning power; technological change created a large number of white-collar jobs with flexible work hours that a large number of women found attractive; technological change in the home increased time available for paid employment; and more families wanted two income earners. Because the 1970s had relatively high unemployment rates, the major reason for the large increase in women's participation rate during the 1970s was the last of the four reasons—specifically more families wanted two income earners to help with their budgets; pages 148-149.

2. The labor force participation rate of men decreased most in the 1960s. The 1960s were generally a time of prosperity. So the reduction in men's labor force participation rate during this decade might be attributable to a large number of men retiring at an early age because of increases in wealth; page 150.

3. Between 1994 and 2011, the unemployment rate fell, rose, fell again, and then rose much higher than before in the 2008-2009 recession; the labor force participation rates for men generally fell and for women leveled off with only a slight fall after 2000; the percentage of part-time workers for noneconomic reasons in the labor force has slightly declined over these years; and the percentage of part-time workers for economic reasons declined, rose, fell a bit and rose very substantially in the

2008-2009 recession. The main cause of the rise in the unemployment rate was the deep recession of 2008-2009. The fall in the labor force participation rate of men continues a long-term trend while the relatively constant and slight fall labor force participation rate of women seems to have brought an end to the longer-term trend of increases in this rate. The declines and then strong rise in the percentage of part-time workers for economic reasons indicates the economy's greater reliance on full-time workers during expansions and greater reliance on part-time workers during recessions, especially those who are working part time for economic reasons; pages 148-151.

■ CHECKPOINT 6.3

Fill in the blanks

The normal unemployment from labor market turnover is called <u>frictional</u> unemployment, and the unemployment that fluctuates over the business cycle is called <u>cyclical</u> unemployment. When <u>cyclical</u> unemployment equals zero, the economy is experiencing <u>full</u> employment and the unemployment rate is the <u>natural unemployment rate</u>. When potential GDP exceeds real GDP, the output gap is <u>negative</u> and the unemployment rate <u>is higher than</u> the natural unemployment rate.

True or false
1. False; page 153
2. False; page 153
3. False; page 154
4. True; page 155
5. True; page 156

Multiple choice
1. a; page 153
2. b; page 153
3. d; page 154
4. d; pages 155
5. b; page 155
6. b; page 154
7. a; pages 155-156

Short answer and numeric questions
1. Unemployment is either frictional, structural, or cyclical; pages 153.
2. The average duration of unemployment (the length of time a person is unemployed) rises in a recession; pages 154.
3. When the economy is at full employment, the unemployment rate is the natural unemployment rate. When the economy is at full employment, the amount of GDP produced is potential GDP; pages 154-156.
4. If the unemployment rate exceeds the natural unemployment rate, real GDP is less than potential GDP. The output gap is negative; pages 155-156.

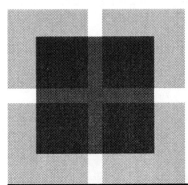

The CPI and the Cost of Living

Chapter 7

Chapter 7 explores how the CPI and other price level indices are measured.

1   Explain what the Consumer Price Index (CPI) is and how it is calculated.

The Consumer Price Index (CPI) measures the average of the prices paid by urban consumers for a fixed market basket of consumer goods and services. The CPI compares the cost of the fixed market basket of goods and services at one time with the cost of the fixed market basket in the reference base period, currently 1982–1984. The CPI in the base period is 100. If the CPI is now 150, it costs 50 percent more to buy the same goods and services than it cost in the base period. To construct the CPI market basket, households are surveyed on what they buy. Then each month the Bureau of Labor Statistics checks the prices of the 80,000 goods and services in the basket. To calculate the CPI, the cost of the market basket using current prices is divided by the cost of the basket using base period prices and the result is multiplied by 100. The inflation rate is the percentage change in the price level from one year to the next and is equal to [(CPI in current year − CPI in previous year) ÷ (CPI in previous year)] × 100.

2   Explain the limitations of the CPI and describe other measures of the price level.

The CPI has four sources of bias that lead to an inaccurate measure of the cost of living. These biases are the new goods bias (new goods replace old goods), the quality change bias (goods and services increase in quality), the commodity substitution bias (changes in relative prices lead consumers to change the items they buy), and the outlet substitution bias (consumers switch to shopping more often in discount stores). The overall CPI bias has been estimated to overstate inflation by 1.1 percentage points per year. The CPI bias distorts private contracts, increases government outlays and decreases government tax revenues. The GDP price index is an average of current prices of all the goods and services included in GDP expressed as a percentage of base-year prices. The GDP price index uses the prices of all goods and services in GDP and weights each item using information about current quantities. The PCE (Personal Consumption Expenditure) price index is an average of the current prices of the goods and services included in the consumption expenditure component of GDP expressed as a percentage of base year prices. The core inflation rate is the percentage change in the PCE index excluding the prices of food and energy. The CPI inflation rate generally exceeds the PCE inflation rate.

3   Adjust money values for inflation and calculate real wage rates and real interest rates.

To compare values measured in dollars in different years, the nominal values must be converted to real values. Real GDP equals nominal GDP divided by the price level and multiplied by 100. The real wage rate measures the quantity of goods and services that an hour's work can buy. It equals the nominal wage rate divided by the CPI and multiplied by 100. The real interest rate equals the nominal interest rate minus the inflation rate.

CHECKPOINT 7.1

■ **Explain what the Consumer Price Index (CPI) is and how it is calculated.**

Quick Review

- *CPI market basket* The goods and services in the CPI and the relative importance attached to each of them.
- *CPI formula* The CPI equals:

$$\frac{\text{Cost of CPI basket at current period prices}}{\text{Cost of CPI basket at base period prices}} \times 100.$$

- *Inflation rate* The inflation rate equals:

$$\frac{(\text{CPI in current year} - \text{CPI in previous year})}{\text{CPI in previous year}} \times 100.$$

Additional Practice Problem 7.1

Item	Quantity (2011)	Price (2011)	Quantity (2012)	Price (2012)
Limes	20	$1.00	15	$1.00
Biscuits	30	$1.00	45	$0.75
Rum	10	$10.00	8	$11.00

1. A Consumer Expenditure Survey in Scurvy shows that people consume only limes, biscuits, and rum. The Consumer Expenditure Survey for both 2011 and 2012 are in the table above. The base year is 2011.

   a. What and how much is in the CPI market basket?

   b. What did the CPI market basket cost in 2011? What was the CPI in 2011?

   c. What did the CPI market basket cost in 2012? What was the CPI in 2012?

   d. What was the inflation rate between 2011 and 2012?

Solution to Additional Practice Problem 7.1

1a. The market basket is 20 limes, 30 biscuits, and 10 rums, the quantities consumed in the base year of 2011.

1b. In 2011 the market basket cost $(20 \times \$1.00) + (30 \times \$1.00) + (10 \times \$10.00) = \$150$. Because 2009 is the base year, the CPI = 100.0.

1c. In 2012 the market basket cost $(20 \times \$1.00) + (30 \times \$0.75) + (10 \times \$11.00) = \$152.50$. The CPI in 2012 is equal to $(\$152.50) \div (\$150.00) \times 100$, which is 101.7.

1d. The inflation rate equals $[(101.7 - 100.0) \div 100] \times 100 = 1.7$ percent.

■ **Self Test 7.1**

Fill in the blanks

The ____, also called the CPI, is a measure of the average of the prices paid by urban consumers for a fixed market basket of consumer goods and services. In the reference base period, the CPI equals ____. Each ____ (month; year) the Bureau of Labor Statistics checks the prices of the goods and services in the CPI basket. The CPI equals the cost of the CPI basket at current prices ____ (plus; minus; divided by) the cost of the CPI basket at base period prices, all multiplied by 100. To measure changes in the cost of living, the ____ (inflation rate; CPI in the reference base period) is used.

True or false

1. In the reference base period, the CPI equals 1.0.
2. The CPI market basket is changed from one month to the next.
3. If the cost of the CPI basket at current period prices equals $320, then the CPI equals 320.
4. If the cost of the CPI market basket at current period prices exceeds the cost of the CPI market basket at base period prices, the inflation rate between these two periods is positive.
5. If the CPI increases from 110 to 121, the inflation rate is 11 percent.

Multiple choice

1. The CPI is reported once every
   a. year.
   b. quarter.
   c. month.
   d. week.
   e. other year.

2. The Consumer Price Index (CPI) measures
   a. the prices of a few consumer goods and services.
   b. the prices of those consumer goods and services that increased in price.
   c. the average of the prices paid by urban consumers for a fixed market basket of goods and services.
   d. consumer confidence in the economy.
   e. the average of the costs paid by businesses to produce a fixed market basket of consumer goods and services.

3. If a country had a CPI of 105.0 last year and a CPI of 102.0 this year, then
   a. the average prices of goods and services increased between last year and this year.
   b. the average prices of goods and services decreased between last year and this year.
   c. the average quality of goods and services decreased between last year and this year.
   d. there was an error when calculating the CPI this year.
   e. the quantity of consumer goods and services produced decreased between last year and this year.

4. The period for which the Consumer Price Index is defined to equal 100 is called the
   a. reference base period.
   b. base year.
   c. starting point.
   d. zero period.
   e. beginning period.

5. In the United States, the good or service given the most weight in the CPI basket when calculating the CPI is
   a. food and beverages.
   b. taxes.
   c. housing.
   d. medical care.
   e. recreation.

6. Suppose the market basket of consumer goods and services costs $180 using the base period prices, and the same market basket of goods and services costs $300 using the cur-

rent period prices. The CPI for the current period equals
   a. 166.7.
   b. 66.7.
   c. 160.0.
   d. 60.0.
   e. 300.0.

7. Suppose the CPI last year was 82.3 and this year is 90.9. Based on this information, we can calculate that the inflation rate between these years is
   a. 10.4 percent.
   b. 8.6 percent.
   c. 90.9 percent.
   d. 82.3 percent.
   e. 9.09 percent.

8. In the United States, the inflation rate since 1999 generally was
   a. higher than between 1979 to 1981.
   b. much higher than in the 1980s.
   c. lower than between 1979 to 1981.
   d. much higher than between 1989 to 1999.
   e. negative.

Short answer and numeric questions

Item	Quantity (2011)	Price (2011)	Quantity (2012)	Price (2012)
Pizza	10	$10.00	15	$10.00
Burritos	20	$1.00	25	$0.75
Rice	30	$0.50	20	$1.00

1. The table above gives the expenditures of households in the small nation of Studenvia. 2011 is the reference base period.
   a. What is the cost of the CPI market basket in 2011?
   b. What is the cost of the CPI market basket in 2012?
   c. What is the CPI in 2011?
   d. What is the CPI in 2012?
   e. What is the inflation rate in 2012?

2. Suppose the CPI was 100.0 in 2011, 110.0 in 2012, 121.0 in 2013, and 133.1 in 2014. What is the inflation rate in 2012, 2013, and 2014?

3. If the price level rises slowly, is the inflation rate positive or negative? Why?

Additional Exercises (also in MyEconLab Test A)
The people of Firestorm City buy only firecrackers and bandages. A Consumer Expenditure Survey in 2011 shows that the average household spent $150 on firecrackers and $15 on bandages. In 2007, the reference base year, the price of a firecracker was $2, and the price of bandages was $1 a pack. In the current year, 2012, firecrackers are $3 each and bandages are $1.25 a pack.

1. Calculate the CPI market basket and the percentage of a household's budget spent on firecrackers in the base year.

2. Calculate the CPI in 2012 and the inflation rate in 2012.

CHECKPOINT 7.2

■ **Explain the limitations of the CPI and describe other measures of the price level.**

Quick Review

- *Commodity substitution bias* People cut back on their purchases of items that become relatively more costly and increase their consumption of items that become relatively less costly.

Additional Practice Problems 7.2

1. When households buy broccoli, they discard some of it because it is bruised. Say 20 percent is discarded. Now suppose that new, genetically engineered broccoli is developed that does not bruise so that all the broccoli that is purchased can be used. People prefer the new broccoli, so they switch to buying the new broccoli. If the price of the new broccoli is 10 percent higher than the old, what actually happens to the CPI and what should happen to the CPI?

2. When the price of textbook is $105 a book, Anthony buys his books at the bookstore closest to him. When textbooks rise in price to $145 a book at that store, Anthony drives several miles away to a store where the books are sold

for only $125. How does Anthony's decision affect the CPI?

Solutions to Additional Practice Problems 7.2

1. With the introduction of the new broccoli, the CPI rises because the new broccoli's price is higher (10 percent) than the old broccoli. But, the CPI should actually decrease because people pay only 10 percent more for 20 percent more (useable) broccoli. This problem illustrates how the quality change bias can bias the CPI upwards.

2. Anthony's decision reflects outlet substitution. When the price of a good rises, consumers, such as Anthony, switch the stores from which they buy goods and services to less expensive outlets. But the CPI, as constructed, does not take into account this point. The CPI will record that the price of textbooks rose by $40, from $105 to $145. This outlet substitution bias means that the CPI overstates the true rise in the cost of living.

■ **Self Test 7.2**

Fill in the blanks

The sources of bias in the CPI as a measure of the cost of living are the ____, ____, ____, and ____. The Boskin Commission concluded that the CPI ____ (overstates; understates) inflation by ____ (1.1; 2.2; 3.3) percentage points a year. The CPI bias leads to ____ (an increase; a decrease) in government outlays.

True or false

1. The CPI is a biased measure of the cost of living.

2. Commodity substitution bias refers to the ongoing replacement of old goods by new goods.

3. The bias in the CPI is estimated to overstate inflation by approximately 1.1 percentage points a year.

4. The CPI bias can distort private contracts.

5. The GDP price index is influenced by the prices of investment goods as well as the prices of exported goods and services.

6. The core inflation rate is the inflation rate of energy and food prices.

7. Inflation measured using the GDP price index is generally lower than inflation measured using the CPI.

Multiple choice

1. All of the following are a bias in the CPI <u>EXCEPT</u> the
   a. new goods bias.
   b. outlet substitution bias.
   c. commodity substitution bias.
   d. GDP price index bias.
   e. quality change bias.

2. An example of the new goods bias in the calculation of the CPI is a price increase in
   a. butter relative to margarine.
   b. an iPod player relative to a Walkman.
   c. a 2012 Honda Civic Si Coupe relative to a 2012 Honda Civic Si Sedan.
   d. textbooks bought through the campus bookstore relative to textbooks bought through Amazon.com.
   e. a Caribbean cruise for a couple who has never been on a cruise before.

3. The price of dishwashers has remained constant while the quality of dishwashers has improved. The CPI
   a. is adjusted monthly to reflect the improvement in quality.
   b. is increased monthly to reflect the increased quality of dishwashers.
   c. has an upward bias if it is not adjusted to take account of the higher quality.
   d. has an upward bias because it does not reflect the increased production of dishwashers.
   e. does not take account of any quality changes because it is a price index not a quality index.

4. Joe buys chicken and beef. If the price of beef rises and the price of chicken does not change, Joe will buy _____ for the CPI.
   a. more beef and create a new goods bias
   b. more chicken and create a commodity substitution bias
   c. the same quantity of beef and chicken and create a commodity substitution bias
   d. less chicken and beef and create a quality change bias
   e. more chicken and eliminate the commodity substitution bias

5. The CPI bias was estimated by the Congressional Advisory Commission on the Consumer Price Index as
   a. understating the actual inflation rate by about 5 percentage points a year.
   b. understating the actual inflation rate by more than 5 percentage points a year.
   c. overstating the actual inflation rate by about 1 percentage point a year.
   d. overstating the actual inflation rate by more than 5 percentage points a year.
   e. understating the actual inflation rate by about 1 percentage point a year.

6. A consequence of the CPI bias is that it
   a. decreases government outlays.
   b. increases international trade.
   c. reduces outlet substitution bias.
   d. distorts private contracts.
   e. means that it is impossible to measure the inflation rate.

7. Because the CPI is a biased measure of the inflation rate, government outlays will
   a. increase at a faster rate than the actual inflation rate.
   b. increase at the same rate as the actual inflation rate.
   c. increase at a slower rate than the actual inflation rate.
   d. sometimes increase faster and sometimes increase slower than the actual inflation rate depending on whether the actual inflation rate exceeds 1.1 percent per year or is less than 1.1 percent per year.
   e. None of the above because the bias in the CPI does not affect government outlays.

Short answer and numeric questions

1. What are the sources of bias in the CPI? Briefly explain each.

2. Once you graduate, you move to a new town and sign a long-term lease on a townhouse. You agree to pay $1,000 a month rent and to change the monthly rent annually by the percentage change in the CPI. For the next 4 years, the CPI increases 5 percent each year. What will you pay in monthly rent for the second, third, and fourth years of your lease? Suppose the CPI overstates the inflation rate by 1 percentage point a year. If the CPI bias was eliminated, what would you pay in rent for the second, third, and fourth years?

3. How is the core inflation rate calculated?

Additional Exercises (also in MyEconLab Test A)

Item	3005		3006	
	Quantity	Price	Quantity	Price
Games	20	$60	10	$70
Time travel	0	--	20	$8,000

1. In Virtual Reality, time travel became possible only in 3006. Economists in the Statistics Bureau decided to conduct a Consumer Expenditure Survey in both 3005 and 3006 to check the substitution bias of the CPI. The table shows the results of the survey. It shows the items that consumers buy and their prices. The Statistics Bureau fixes the reference base year as 3005. Calculate the CPI in 3006 and the inflation rate measured by the CPI in 3006.

CHECKPOINT 7.3

■ **Adjust money values for inflation and calculate real wage rates and real interest rates.**

Quick Review

- *Real wage rate* The real wage rate equals the nominal wage rate divided by the CPI and multiplied by 100.
- *Real interest rate* The real interest rate equals the nominal interest rate minus the inflation rate.

Additional Practice Problems 7.3

Year	Minimum wage (dollars per hour)	CPI
1955	0.75	26.7
1965	1.25	31.6
1975	2.10	56.7
1985	3.35	107.5
1995	4.25	152.4
2005	5.15	194.1

1. The table above shows the minimum wage and the CPI for six different years. The reference base period is 1982–1984.
   a. Calculate the real minimum wage in each year in 1982–1984 dollars.
   b. In which year was the minimum wage the highest in real terms?
   c. In which year was the minimum wage the lowest in real terms?

2. Nominal GDP = $10 trillion, real GDP = $9 trillion. What is the GDP price index?

3. Suppose Sally has saved $1,000 dollars. Sally wants a 3 percent real interest rate on her savings. What nominal interest rate would she need to receive if the inflation rate is 7 percent?

Solutions to Additional Practice Problems 7.3

Year	Real minimum wage (1982-1984 dollars per hour)
1955	2.81
1965	3.96
1975	3.70
1985	3.12
1995	2.79
2005	2.65

1a. Using the CPI to adjust nominal values to real values is a key use of the CPI. Keep in mind that to convert a nominal price (such as the nominal wage rate) into a real price (such as the real wage rate), you divide by the CPI and multiply by 100, but to convert the nominal interest rate into the real interest rate, you subtract the inflation rate. To convert the nominal minimum wages in the table to real prices, divide the price by the CPI in that year and then multiply by 100. In 1955, the nominal minimum wage gas was $0.75 an hour and the CPI was 26.7, so the real minimum wage is ($0.75 ÷ 26.7) × 100 = $2.81. The rest of the real minimum wages in the table above are calculated similarly.

1b. In real terms, the minimum wage was highest in 1965 when it equaled $3.96.

1c. In real terms, the minimum wage was the lowest in 2005 when it equaled $2.65.

2. GDP price index = (Nominal GDP ÷ Real GDP) × 100 = ($10 trillion ÷ $9 trillion) × 100 = 111.1.

3. The real interest rate equals the nominal interest rate minus the inflation rate. Rearranging this formula shows that the nominal interest rate equals the real interest rate plus the inflation rate. To get a 3 percent real interest rate with a 7 percent inflation rate, Sally needs the nominal interest rate to be equal to 3 percent plus 7 percent, or 10 percent.

■ Self Test 7.3

Fill in the blanks

The GDP price index equals 100 times _____ (real; nominal) GDP divided by _____ (real; nominal) GDP. The nominal wage rate is the average hourly wage rate measured in _____ (current; reference base year) dollars. The real wage rate is the average hourly wage rate measured in dollars of the _____ (current; given base) year. The real wage rate equals the nominal wage rate _____ (plus; times; divided by) the CPI multiplied by 100. The real interest rate equals the nominal interest rate _____ (plus; minus; divided by) the _____ (CPI; inflation rate).

True or false

1. Real prices and nominal prices are unrelated.

2. Real GDP equals nominal GDP divided by the CPI, multiplied by 100.

3. A change in the real wage rate measures the change in the goods and services that an hour's work can buy.

4. The nominal interest rate is the percentage return on a loan expressed in dollars; the real interest rate is the percentage return on a loan expressed in purchasing power.

5. If the nominal interest rate is 8 percent a year and the inflation rate is 5 percent a year, then the real interest rate is 3 percent a year.

Multiple choice

1. In 2011 apples cost $1.49 a pound. The CPI was 120 in 2011 and 140 in 2012. If there is no change in the real price of an apple in 2012, what is the price of a pound of apples in 2012?
   a. $2.74
   b. $1.69
   c. $1.66
   d. $1.74
   e. $1.28

2. In 1970, the CPI was 39 and in 2000 it was 172. A local phone call cost $0.10 in 1970. What is the price of this phone call in 2000 dollars?
   a. $1.42
   b. $0.39
   c. $1.72
   d. $0.44
   e. $0.23

3. Nominal GDP is $12.1 trillion and real GDP is $11.0 trillion. The GDP price index is
   a. 90.1.
   b. 121.0
   c. 1.10.
   d. 91.0.
   e. 110.0

4. The nominal wage rate is the
   a. minimum hourly wage that a company can legally pay a worker.
   b. average hourly wage rate measured in the dollars of a given base year.
   c. minimum hourly wage rate measured in the dollars of a given reference base year.
   d. average hourly wage rate measured in current dollars.
   e. wage rate after inflation has been adjusted out of it.

5. The average starting salary for a history major is $29,500. If the CPI is 147.5, the real salary is
   a. $200.00 an hour.
   b. $20,000.
   c. $35,000.
   d. $43,513.
   e. $14,750.

6. Since 1981, the
   a. real wage rate increased steadily.
   b. nominal wage rate increased and the real wage rate did not change by very much.
   c. real wage rate increased more than the nominal wage rate.
   d. nominal wage rate increased at an uneven pace whereas the increase in the real wage rate was steady and constant.
   e. nominal wage rate and real wage rate both decreased.

7. The real interest rate is equal to the
   a. nominal interest rate plus the inflation rate.
   b. nominal interest rate minus the inflation rate.
   c. nominal interest rate times the inflation rate.
   d. nominal interest rate divided by the inflation rate.
   e. inflation rate minus the nominal interest rate.

8. You borrow at a nominal interest rate of 10 percent. If the inflation rate is 4 percent, then the real interest rate is
   a. the $10 in interest you have to pay.
   b. 16 percent.
   c. 2.5 percent.
   d. 6 percent.
   e. 14 percent.

9. In the United States for the last 40 years, the nominal interest rate
   a. and the real interest rate both decreased in almost every year.
   b. and the real interest rate were both constant in almost every year.
   c. was constant in most years and the real interest rate fluctuated.
   d. exceeded the real interest rate in virtually all the years.
   e. exceeded the real interest rate in about half of the years and the real interest rate was greater than the nominal interest rate in the other half of the years.

Short answer and numeric questions

1. For each of the following pairs of real GDP and nominal GDP, calculate the price level.
   a. Nominal GDP = $12 trillion, real GDP = $10 trillion.
   b. Nominal GDP = $12 trillion, real GDP $16 trillion.
   c. Nominal GDP = $8 trillion, real GDP = $4 trillion.

Job	Salary (dollars per year)	CPI
Job A	20,000	105
Job B	25,000	120
Job C	34,000	170

2. Often the cost of living varies from state to state or from large city to small city. After you graduate, suppose you have job offers in 3 locales. The nominal salary and the CPI for each job is given in the table above.
   a. Which job offers the highest real salary?
   b. Which job offers the lowest real salary?

c. In determining which job to accept, what is more important: the real salary or the nominal salary? Why?

Year	Real interest rate (percent per year)	Nominal interest rate (percent per year)	Inflation rate (percent per year)
2010	____	10	5
2011	____	6	1
2012	4	6	____
2013	5	____	3

3. The table above gives the real interest rate, nominal interest rate, and inflation rate for various years in a foreign country. Complete the table.

4. In 1980, the nominal interest rate was 12 percent. In 2011, the nominal interest rate was 4 percent. From this information, can you determine if you would rather have saved $1,000 in 1980 or 2011? Explain your answer.

Additional Exercises (also in MyEconLab Test A)

1. In 2005, the GDP price index was 105 and real GDP was $4 trillion (2000 dollars). In 2006, nominal GDP was $5.4 trillion and real GDP was $4.5 trillion (2000 dollars). Calculate the increase in nominal GDP and the increase in the GDP price index in 2006.

Year	Nominal interest rate (percent per year)	Inflation rate (percent per year)
1992	4.6	1.7
1993	3.0	1.2
1994	2.1	0.7
1995	1.2	−0.1
1996	0.4	0.1

2. The table shows the nominal interest rate and inflation rate in Japan for several years. In which year was the real interest rate the highest and in which year was the real interest rate the lowest?

3. In 1986, 1996, and 2006, average weekly earnings in the United States were $310, $413, and $567 respectively. The CPI was 110, 157, and 202 respectively. In which of these three years was the real average weekly earnings highest and in which year was it lowest?

SELF TEST ANSWERS

■ CHECKPOINT 7.1

Fill in the blanks

The <u>Consumer Price Index</u>, also called the CPI, is a measure of the average of the prices paid by urban consumers for a fixed market basket of consumer goods and services. In the reference base period, the CPI equals <u>100</u>. Each <u>month</u> the Bureau of Labor Statistics checks the prices of the goods and services in the CPI basket. The CPI equals the cost of the CPI basket at current prices <u>divided by</u> the cost of the CPI basket at base period prices, all multiplied by 100. To measure changes in the cost of living, the <u>inflation rate</u> is used.

True or false

1. False; page 164
2. False; page 164
3. False; page 167
4. True; page 167
5. False; page 167

Multiple choice

1. c; page 164
2. c; page 164
3. b; page 164
4. a; page 164
5. c; page 165
6. a; page 167
7. a; page 167
8. c; page 168

Short answer and numeric questions

1. a. The cost is $135; page 166.
   b. The cost is $145. The quantities used to calculate this cost are the base period, 2009, quantities; page 166.
   c. The CPI is 100; page 167.
   d. The CPI is 107.4; page 167.
   e. The inflation rate is 7.4 percent; page 167.
2. The inflation rate for each year is 10 percent; page 167.
3. Whenever the price level rises, the infla-tion rate is positive. If the price level rises slowly, the inflation rate is small; if the price level rises rapidly, the inflation rate is large; page 167.

Additional Exercises (also in MyEconLab Test A)

1. The CPI market basket is the quantities bought during the Expenditure Survey year, 2011. Households spend $150 on firecrackers at $2 a firecracker so the quantity of fire-crackers bought was 75. Households spend $15 on bandages at $1 a pack so the quantity of bandages bought was 15 packs. The CPI market basket is 75 firecrackers and 15 packs of bandages.

   In the base year, expenditure on firecrackers was $150 and expenditure on bandages was $15, so the household budget was $165. Ex-penditure on firecrackers was ($150 ÷ $165) × 100, which is 90.9 percent of the household budget; pages 166-167.

2. To calculate the CPI in 2012, find the cost of the CPI market basket in 2012 and 2011. In 2011, the CPI market basket costs $165 ($150 for firecrackers and $15 for bandages). In 2012, the CPI basket costs $225 for firecrack-ers (75 × $3 a firecracker) plus $18.75 (15 packs of bandages × $1.25 a pack), which sums to $243.75. The CPI in 2012 equals ($243.75 ÷ $165) × 100 = 147.7.

   The inflation rate in 2012 is [(147.7 − 100.0) ÷ 100.0] × 100, which is 47.7 percent; pages 166-167.

■ CHECKPOINT 7.2

Fill in the blanks

The sources of bias in the CPI as a measure of the cost of living are the <u>new goods bias</u>, <u>quality change bias</u>, <u>commodity substitution bias</u>, and <u>outlet substitution bias</u>. The Boskin Com-mission concluded that the CPI <u>overstates</u> infla-tion by <u>1.1</u> percentage points a year. The CPI bias leads to <u>an increase</u> in government outlays.

True or false

1. True; page 170
2. False; page 171
3. True; page 171
4. True; page 172
5. True; page 173
6. False; page 173
7. True; page 174

Multiple choice

1. d; page 170
2. b; page 170
3. c; page 171
4. b; page 171
5. c; page 171
6. d; page 172
7. a; page 172

Short answer and numeric questions

1. There are four sources of bias in the CPI: the new goods bias, the quality change bias, the commodity substitution bias, and the outlet substitution bias. The new goods bias refers to the fact that new goods replace old goods. The quality change bias occurs because at times price increases in existing goods are the result of increased quality. The commodity substitution bias occurs because consumers buy fewer goods and services when their prices rise compared to other, comparable products. Finally, the outlet substitution bias refers to the fact that when prices rise, people shop more frequently at discount stores to take advantage of the lower prices in these stores; pages 170-171.

2. The monthly rent increases by 5 percent each year. For the second year the monthly rent equals $1,000 × 1.05, which is $1,050. For the third year the monthly rent equals $1,050 × 1.05, which is $1,102.50. And for the fourth year the monthly rent equals $1,102.50 × 1.05, which is $1,157.63. If the CPI bias was eliminated, the monthly rent would increase by 4 percent each year. The monthly rent would be $1,040

for the second year, $1,081.60 for the third year, and $1,124.86 for the third year; page 172.

3. The core inflation rate is the inflation rate calculated using the PCE price level excluding the prices of energy and food; page 173.

Additional Exercises (also in MyEconLab Test A)

1. Using the 3005 CPI market basket, the cost of the basket in 3005 is $1,200 and the cost of the basket in 3006 is $1,400. (Note that time travel does not enter into the cost in 3006 because it is not in the CPI market basket.) So the CPI in 3006 is ($1,400 ÷ $1,200) × 100, which is 116.7. The change in the CPI from 3005 to 3006 is 16.7. The initial CPI in 3005 is 100.0 (since it is a base year). So the inflation rate is equal to (16.7 ÷ 100) × 100, or 16.7 percent; pages 166-167, 170.

■ CHECKPOINT 7.3

Fill in the blanks

The GDP price index equals 100 times nominal GDP divided by real GDP. The nominal wage rate is the average hourly wage rate measured in current dollars. The real wage rate is the average wage rate measured in dollars of the given base year. The real wage rate equals the nominal wage rate divided by the CPI multiplied by 100. The real interest rate equals the nominal interest rate minus the inflation rate.

True or false

1. False; page 176
2. False; page 178
3. True; pages 178-179
4. True; page 180
5. True; page 180

Multiple choice

1. d; page 176
2. d; page 176
3. e; page 178
4. d; page 178

5. b; page 178
6. b; pages 178-179
7. b; page 180
8. d; page 180
9. d; page 181

Short answer and numeric questions

1. a. GDP price index = ($12 trillion ÷ $10 trillion) × 100 = 120; page 178.
   b. GDP price index = ($12 trillion ÷ $16 trillion) × 100 = 75; page 178.
   c. GDP price index = ($8 trillion ÷ $4 trillion) × 100 = 200; page 178.

2. a. The real salary equals (nominal salary ÷ CPI) × 100. The real salary is $19,048 for Job A, $20,833 for Job B, and $20,000 for Job C. The real salary is highest for Job B; page 178.
   b. The real salary is lowest for Job A; page 178.
   c. The real salary is more important than the nominal salary because the real salary measures the quantity of goods and services you can buy; pages 178-179.

Year	Real interest rate (percent per year)	Nominal interest rate (percent per year)	Inflation rate (percent per year)
2010	5	10	5
2011	5	6	1
2012	4	6	2
2013	5	8	3

3. The completed table is above; page 176.

4. You cannot determine when you would rather have been a saver. Savers are interested in the real interest rate because the real interest rate is the percentage return expressed in purchasing power. Without knowing the inflation rate, there are not enough data given to compute the real interest rate; page 180.

Additional Exercises (also in MyEconLab Test A)

1. Nominal GDP = real GDP × P ÷ 100, where P is the GDP price index. So in 2005 nominal GDP equals $4 trillion × 105 ÷ 100, which is $4.2 trillion. Between 2005 and 2006, nominal GDP has increased by $1.2 trillion, which is 28.6 percent.

   The equality Nominal GDP = real GDP × P ÷ 100 can be rearranged to give P = nominal GDP ÷ real GDP × 100. So in 2006, the GDP price index equals $5.4 trillion ÷ $4.5 trillion × 100, which is 120. Between 2005 and 2006, the GDP price index has increased by 15, which is 14.3 percent; pages 177-178.

2. The real interest rate for each year is equal to the nominal interest rate minus the inflation rate. Using this formula yields:

   1992 4.6 percent – 1.7 percent = 2.9 percent
   1993 3.0 percent – 1.2 percent = 1.8 percent
   1994 2.1 percent – 0.7 percent = 1.4 percent
   1995 1.2 percent – (–0.1) percent = 1.3 percent
   1996 0.4 percent – 0.1 percent = 0.3 percent

   The real interest rate was the highest in 1992 and lowest in 1996; page 180.

3. The real wage rate is equal to the nominal wage rate divided by the CPI and then multiplied by 100. So the 1986 real wage rate equals $310 ÷ 110 × 100, or $281.82. The 1996 real wage rate equals $413 ÷ 157 × 100, or $263.06. And the 2006 real wage rate equals $567 ÷ 202 × 100, or $280.69. The real wage rate was the highest in 1986 and was the lowest in 1996; page 178.

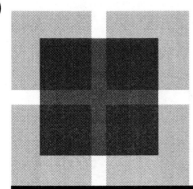

Potential GDP and the Natural Unemployment Rate

Chapter 8

Chapter 8 begins by introducing different macroeconomic schools of thought. The three main schools of thought are classical macroeconomics, Keynesian macroeconomics, and monetarist macroeconomics. Classical macroeconomics asserts that markets work well and, although the economy will fluctuate, no government intervention is needed. But classical macroeconomics couldn't explain why the Great Depression lasted so long. Keynesian economics was borne during the Great Depression and asserted that depressions were the result of too little spending. Keynesian economics calls for government intervention to assist the economy. Monetarist macroeconomics says that the classical approach is generally correct but that fluctuations in the quantity of money also create business cycles. The consensus view is that classical economics explains the economy when it is at or close to full employment and Keynesian economics applies in recessions and depressions. Monetarist economics explains inflation and also adds to the Keynesian view by suggesting other causes of recessions. The consensus view emphasizes that maintaining economic growth is more important than eliminating business cycle fluctuations because the Lucas wedge (the cost of slower economic growth) is much larger than Okun gaps (the cost of business cycle recessions).

1 Explain what determines potential GDP.

Potential GDP is the value of real GDP when all the economy's factors of production—labor, capital, land, and entrepreneurial ability—are fully employed. The production function shows the maximum quantity of real GDP that can be produced as the quantity of labor employed changes and all other influences on production remain the same. Its shape reflects diminishing returns, so that each additional hour of labor employed produces a successively smaller addition of real GDP. The quantity of labor employed is determined in the labor market. The quantity of labor demanded increases when the real wage rate falls and decreases when the real wage rate rises. The quantity of labor supplied increases when the real wage rate rises and decreases when the real wage rate falls. Labor market equilibrium occurs at the intersection of the labor supply curve and the labor demand curve. When the labor market is in equilibrium, the economy is at full employment. At this point real GDP, determined using equilibrium employment and the production function, equals potential GDP.

2 Explain what determines the natural unemployment rate.

The natural unemployment rate is the unemployment rate at full employment and consists of frictional and structural unemployment. The two fundamental causes of unemployment at full employment are job search, which is the activity of looking for an acceptable job, and job rationing, which occurs when the real wage rate exceeds the equilibrium wage rate creating a surplus of labor. The amount of job search depends on demographic change, unemployment benefits, and structural change. Job rationing occurs when there is an efficiency wage, a minimum wage, or a union wage because all of these factors force the real wage above the equilibrium real wage.

CHECKPOINT 8.1

■ **Explain what determines potential GDP.**

Quick Review

- *Production function* The production function shows the maximum quantity of real GDP that can be produced as the quantity of labor employed changes and all other influences on production remain constant.

- *Equilibrium in a market* The equilibrium in a market occurs at the intersection of the demand and supply curves.

Additional Practice Problem 8.1

Quantity of labor demanded (billions of hours per year)	Real GDP (hundreds of billions of 2005 dollars)	Real wage rate (2005 dollars per hour)
0	0	50
10	5	40
20	9	30
30	12	20
40	14	10

1. The table above describes a small economy's production function and its demand for labor. The table below describes the supply of labor in this economy.

Quantity of labor supplied (billions of hours per year)	Real wage rate (2005 dollars per hour)
0	10
10	20
20	30
30	40
40	50

a. Make graphs of the production function and the labor market.

b. Does the production function show diminishing returns?

c. What is the equilibrium employment, real wage rate, and potential GDP?

d. Suppose that the population grows so that the quantity of labor supplied increases by 20 billion hours at every real wage rate.

What is the effect on the real wage rate and on potential GDP?

Solutions to Additional Practice Problem 8.1

1a. The production function is a graph of the first two columns of the first table. The figure to the right shows the relationship between labor and real GDP.

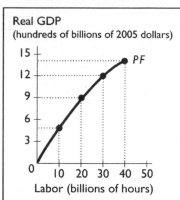

The second figure to the right shows the labor market. The labor demand curve is the first and third columns in the first table. It shows

the relationship between the real wage rate and the quantity of labor demanded. The labor supply curve is from the second table and shows the relationship between the real wage rate and the quantity of labor supplied.

1b. The production function shows diminishing returns because every additional 10 billion hours of labor employed increases real GDP by less.

1c. Find the equilibrium in the labor market. Then use the production function to determine how much GDP this full-employment quantity of labor produces, which is the potential GDP. Equilibrium employment is where the labor demand curve and the labor supply curve intersect. The second figure in part (a) shows that the equilibrium real wage rate is $30 an hour and the equilibrium employment is 20 billion hours per year. The production function, in the first figure in part (a), shows that when 20 billion hours of labor are employed, GDP is $900 billion, so potential GDP equals $900 billion.

Quantity of labor supplied (billions of hours per year)	Real wage rate (2005 dollars per hour)
20	10
30	20
40	30
50	40
60	50

1d. The new labor supply schedule is given in the table above and shown in the figure. In the figure, the labor supply curve shifts rightward from LS_1 to LS_2.

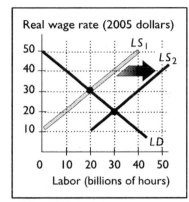

The equilibrium quantity of labor increases to 30 billion hours and the equilibrium real wage rate falls to $20. The production function in the first table in the practice problem shows that when employment is 30 billion hours, real GDP is $1,200 billion. So, the increase in the population increases potential GDP to $1,200 billion.

■ Self Test 8.1

Fill in the blanks

_____ (Classical; Keynesian) macroeconomics asserts that government intervention is needed to achieve full employment. The consensus view believes that _____ (classical; Keynesian; monetarist) macroeconomics best describes the economy at full employment. The relationship that shows the maximum quantity of real GDP that can be produced as the quantity of labor employed changes is _____ (the production func-

tion; potential GDP). The quantity of labor demanded _____ (increases; decreases) as the real wage rate falls and the quantity of labor supplied _____ (increases; decreases) as the real wage rate falls. If the real wage rate exceeds the equilibrium real wage rate, there is a _____ (shortage; surplus) of labor. When the labor market is in equilibrium, there is _____ and real GDP equals _____.

True or false

1. Classical macroeconomics says that markets work well and government intervention cannot improve on the performance of markets.

2. The consensus view asserts that the problem of business cycle fluctuations is much more important than the problem of sustaining economic growth.

3. Real GDP can exceed potential GDP permanently.

4. The production function shows how the quantity of labor hired depends on the real wage rate.

5. The nominal wage rate influences the quantity of labor demanded because what matters to firms is the number of dollars they pay for an hour of labor.

6. At the labor market equilibrium the real wage rate sets the quantity of labor demanded equal to the quantity of labor supplied.

7. When the labor market is in equilibrium, the economy is at full employment and real GDP equals potential GDP.

Multiple choice

1. _____ adopts the view that aggregate fluctuations are a natural consequence of an expanding economy.
   a. Classical macroeconomics
   b. Keynesian economics
   c. Monetarist macroeconomics
   d. The Lucas wedge
   e. The Okun gap

2. Potential GDP
   a. is the quantity of GDP produced when the economy is at full employment of all resources.
   b. can never be exceeded.
   c. can never be attained.
   d. is another name for real GDP.
   e. is another name for nominal GDP.

3. With fixed quantities of capital, land, and entrepreneurship and fixed technology, the amount of real GDP produced increases when ____ increases.
   i.   the quantity of labor employed
   ii. the inflation rate
   iii. the price level
   a. i only.
   b. ii only.
   c. iii only.
   d. ii and iii.
   e. i, ii, and iii.

4. The production function graphs the relationship between
   a. nominal GDP and real GDP.
   b. real GDP and the quantity of labor employed.
   c. real GDP and capital.
   d. nominal GDP and the quantity of labor employed.
   e. real GDP and the supply of labor.

5. The quantity of labor demanded definitely increases if the
   a. real wage rate rises.
   b. real wage rate falls.
   c. nominal wage rate rises.
   d. nominal wage rate falls.
   e. supply of labor decreases.

6. The labor supply curve has a ____ slope because as the real wage rate rises, ____.
   a. negative; firms hire fewer workers
   b. positive; the opportunity cost of leisure rises
   c. positive; the opportunity cost of leisure falls
   d. negative; households work more hours
   e. positive; firms offer more jobs

7. The real wage rate is $35 an hour. At this wage rate there are 100 billion labor hours supplied and 200 billion labor hours demanded. There is a
   a. shortage of 300 billion hours of labor.
   b. shortage of 100 billion hours of labor.
   c. surplus of 100 billion hours of labor.
   d. surplus of 300 billion hours of labor.
   e. shortage of 200 billion hours of labor.

■ **FIGURE 8.1**

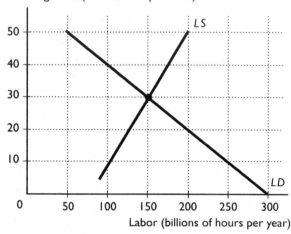

8. In Figure 8.1, the equilibrium real wage rate is ____ per hour and equilibrium employment is ____ billions of hours per year.
   a. $50; 200
   b. $10; 100
   c. $30; more than 300
   d. $20; 125
   e. $30; 150

9. In Figure 8.1, full employment is reached when employment is ____ billions of hours a year.
   a. 150
   b. 200
   c. 250
   d. more than 300
   e. More information is needed about the nation's production function to answer the question.

10. When the labor market is in equilibrium, real GDP _____ potential GDP.
    a. is greater than
    b. is equal to
    c. is less than
    d. might be greater than, less than, or equal to
    e. is not comparable to

11. Compared to the U.S. production function, the European production function is
    a. higher.
    b. lower.
    c. the same.
    d. lower than the U.S. production function at low levels of employment and higher than the U.S. production function at high levels of employment.
    e. higher than the U.S. production function at low levels of employment and lower than the U.S. production function at high levels of employment.

Complete the graph

Quantity of labor (billions of hours per year)	Real GDP (billions of 2005 dollars)
0	0
10	400
20	725
30	900
40	960
50	1,000

1. The above table gives data for a nation's production function. In Figure 8.2, draw the production function. Label the axes. How are diminishing returns reflected?

2. Figure 8.3 illustrates the labor market for the nation with the production function given in the previous problem. In the figure, identify the equilibrium real wage rate and employment. Using the production function in Figure 8.2, what is the nation's potential GDP?

3. Using the data in Problems 1 and 2, suppose that both the labor supply and labor demand curves shift rightward by 10 billion labor hours and the production function does not change. What is the nation's potential GDP?

■ **FIGURE 8.2**

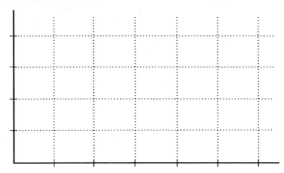

■ **FIGURE 8.3**

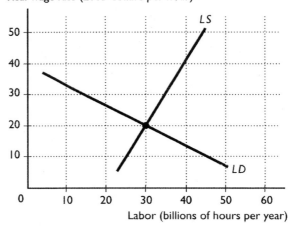

Short answer and numeric questions

1. What are the differences between classical macroeconomics and Keynesian macroeconomics?

2. What is the relationship between equilibrium in the labor market and potential GDP? Be sure to explain the role played by the production function.

3. Suppose a nation's production function shifts upward. If the equilibrium quantity of labor does not change, what is the effect on the nation's potential GDP?

4. Suppose a nation's production function shifts upward and the equilibrium quantity of labor increases. What is the effect on the nation's potential GDP?

Additional Exercises (also in MyEconLab Test A)

Quantity of labor demanded (billions of hours per year)	Real GDP (billions of 2005 dollars)	Real wage (2005 dollars per hour)
0	0	
1	5	5
2	9	4
3	12	3
4	14	2
5	15	1

Quantity of labor supplied (billions of hours per year)	Real wage (2005 dollars per hour)
0	1.50
1	2.00
2	2.50
3	3.00
4	3.50
5	4.00

1. This first table above describes an economy's production function and demand for labor. The second table above describes the supply of labor in this economy.

   Use the data in the tables to make graphs of the labor market and production function. What are equilibrium employment, real wage rate, and potential GDP?

CHECKPOINT 8.2

■ **Explain what determines the natural unemployment rate.**

Quick Review

- *Job search* Job search is the activity of looking for an acceptable vacant job. Job search is influenced by demographic changes, unemployment benefits, and structural change.
- *Job rationing* Job rationing is a situation that arises when the real wage rate is above the full-employment equilibrium level. An efficiency wage, a minimum wage, or a union wage can lead to job rationing.

Additional Practice Problems 8.2

1. Why do demographic changes affect the amount of job search?
2. What factors can keep the real wage rate above the full-employment level? How do these factors affect the amount of employment?
3. Since 1969, how has the real minimum wage generally changed in the United States? What effect would this trend have on the natural unemployment rate?

Solutions to Additional Practice Problems 8.2

1. Demographic changes affect the amount of job search because younger workers conduct more job search than do older workers. In particular, older workers generally have already settled into a career, whereas younger workers are often entering the labor market for the first time. As new entrants, younger workers must search for a job. In addition, younger workers often switch between jobs before settling upon their career and while they are switching, they are searching for a new job.

2. Job rationing, when the real wage rate is above the full-employment equilibrium level, is the result of efficiency wages, the minimum wage, and union wages. An efficiency wage is a real wage that a firm sets above the full-employment equilibrium level in order to motivate its workers to work harder. A minimum wage is a government regulation that sets the lowest wage legal to pay. A union wage is a wage rate negotiated between a labor union and a firm. Because these wage rates are above the full-employment level, the quantity of labor employed is less than it otherwise would be.

3. Since 1969 there has been a general downward trend in the real minimum wage. The drop was most prolonged between 1979 and 1989, after which the real minimum wage has generally hovered near $6 an hour. The general downward trend in the real minimum wage reduces the amount of job rationing, thereby decreasing the natural unemployment rate.

■ Self Test 8.2

Fill in the blanks

The unemployment rate at full employment is the ____. The activity of looking for an acceptable vacant job is called ____ (job search; job rationing). An increase in unemployment benefits ____ (decreases; increases) job search. Job rationing occurs when the real wage rate is ____ (above; below) the equilibrium level. A minimum wage set above the equilibrium wage rate ____ (creates; does not create) unemployment. If the real wage rate is above the full-employment equilibrium level, the natural unemployment rate ____ (increases; decreases).

True or false

1. The amount of job search depends on a number of factors including demographic change.
2. An increase in unemployment benefits, other things remaining the same, will increase the amount of time spent on job search.
3. Job rationing has no effect on the natural unemployment rate.
4. Job rationing results in a shortage of labor.
5. Teenage labor is not affected by the minimum wage.

Multiple choice

1. In the United States since 1960, the average unemployment rate was highest during the decade of the
   a. 1960s.
   b. 1970s.
   c. 1980s.
   d. 1990s.
   e. 2000s.

2. The two fundamental causes of unemployment at full employment are
   a. seasonal jobs and technological change.
   b. foreign competition and financial bankruptcies.
   c. job search and job rationing.
   d. decreases in labor productivity and more generous retirement benefits.
   e. demographic change and decreases in the demand for labor.

3. Job search is defined as
   a. the activity of looking for an acceptable, vacant job.
   b. saying you are looking for a job when you are actually not looking.
   c. attending school to increase your employability.
   d. equivalent to job rationing.
   e. being paid an efficiency wage.

4. The more generous the amount of unemployment benefits, the
   a. higher the opportunity cost of job search.
   b. lower the opportunity cost of job search.
   c. shorter the time spent searching until accepting a suitable job.
   d. shorter the time spent searching for a suitable job and the higher the opportunity cost of being unemployed.
   e. lower the natural unemployment rate.

5. Job rationing occurs if
   a. the minimum wage is set below the equilibrium wage rate.
   b. an efficiency wage is set below the equilibrium wage rate.
   c. a union wage is set below the equilibrium wage rate.
   d. the real wage rate is pushed above the equilibrium wage rate.
   e. the Lucas wedge is positive.

6. Intel wants to attract the most productive and knowledgeable workers. To achieve this goal it could pay ____ wage.
   a. an efficiency
   b. a minimum
   c. a nominal
   d. an equilibrium
   e. a Lucas wedge

7. Collective bargaining by unions can result in a union wage rate that is ____ the equilibrium real wage rate and creates a ____ of labor.
   a. above; surplus
   b. above; shortage
   c. below; surplus
   d. below; shortage
   e. equal to; surplus

■ **FIGURE 8.4**

Real wage rate (2005 dollars per hour)

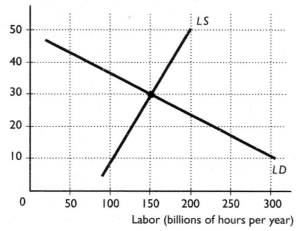

8. In Figure 8.4, of the wages listed below, there is the most job rationing and unemployment if the real wage rate equals
   a. $10 per hour.
   b. $20 per hour.
   c. $30 per hour.
   d. $40 per hour.
   e. None of the above is correct because at any real wage rate there is never any job rationing.

9. In Figure 8.4, if there is any job rationing, the real wage rate must be ____ per hour and employment is ____ billion hours.
   a. less than $30; more than 150
   b. equal to $30; equal to 150
   c. less than $30; less than 150
   d. more than $30; less than 150
   e. less than $20; less than 150

Complete the graph

■ **FIGURE 8.5**

Real wage rate (2005 dollars per hour)

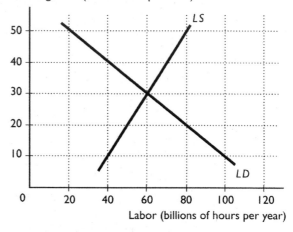

1. Figure 8.5 illustrates the labor market.
   a. What is the equilibrium wage rate? Equilibrium employment?
   b. What must a firm do to set an efficiency wage?
   c. Suppose the government imposes a minimum wage that creates a surplus of 60 billion hours of labor a year. What is the minimum wage?
   d. If a union negotiates on behalf of its members, what can you say about the range of wage rates the union will try to obtain?
   e. In your answers to (b), (c), and (d), is there any unemployment? Compare your answers to parts (b), (c), and (d). How does the employment that results in these situations compare with that in part (a)?

Short answer and numeric questions

Real wage rate (2005 dollars per hour)	Quantity of labor demanded (billions of hours per year)	Quantity of labor supplied (billions of hours per year)
10	180	150
20	160	160
30	140	170
40	120	180

1. The above table gives the labor demand and labor supply schedules for a nation.
   a. What is the equilibrium wage rate?
   b. Suppose firms set an efficiency wage of $30 an hour. What is the effect of this wage rate?
   c. Suppose the government sets a minimum wage of $30 an hour. What is the effect of the minimum wage?
   d. Suppose unions negotiate a wage of $30 an hour. What is the effect of the union wage?
   e. How do your answers to parts (b), (c), and (d) compare?

2. The demographics of the United States are such that there will be an increase in young people entering the labor force between 2009 and 2014. What do you predict will be the effect on the U.S. unemployment rate?

3. Why do unemployment benefits affect the natural unemployment rate?

4. An efficiency wage is a wage that exceeds the equilibrium wage rate. Why would a firm pay an efficiency wage?

Additional Exercises (also in MyEconLab Test A)
The economy of Sweden has seen changes during the past 50 years, but the change has been steady and population growth has been modest. Sweden has high unemployment benefits, a high minimum wage, and strong labor unions. Use this information to answer Exercises **1** and **2**.

1. Does the unemployment that Sweden experiences arise primarily from job search or job rationing?

2. Which of the factors listed suggest that Sweden has a higher natural unemployment rate than the United States and which suggest that Sweden has a lower natural unemployment rate than the United States?

■ **FIGURE 8.6**

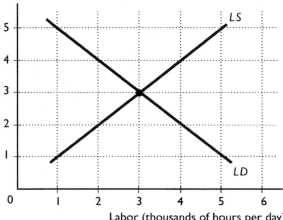

Figure 8.6 illustrates the labor market on Sandy Island. In addition (not shown in the figure), a survey tells us that when Sandy Island is at full employment, people spend 1,000 hours a day in job search. Use this information to answer Exercises 3 and 4.

3. Find the full-employment equilibrium real wage rate and quantity of labor employed and calculate the natural unemployment rate.

4. If the government introduces a minimum wage of $4 an hour, how much unemployment is created?

■ SELF TEST ANSWERS

■ CHECKPOINT 8.1

Fill in the blanks

<u>Keynesian</u> macroeconomics asserts that government intervention is needed to achieve full employment. The consensus view believes that <u>classical</u> macroeconomics best describes the economy at full employment. The relationship that shows the maximum quantity of real GDP that can be produced as the quantity of labor employed changes is <u>the production function</u>. The quantity of labor demanded <u>increases</u> as the real wage rate falls and the quantity of labor supplied <u>decreases</u> as the real wage rate falls. If the real wage rate exceeds the equilibrium real wage rate, there is a <u>surplus</u> of labor. When the labor market is in equilibrium, there is <u>full employment of labor</u> and real GDP equals <u>potential GDP</u>.

True or false

1. True; page 188
2. False; pages 189-190
3. False; page 191
4. False; page 192
5. False; page 193
6. True; pages 196-197
7. True; page 197

Multiple choice

1. a; page 188
2. a; page 191
3. a; pages 191-192
4. b; page 192
5. b; pages 193-194
6. b; pages 195-196
7. b; pages 196-197
8. e; pages 196-197
9. a; page 197
10. b; page 197
11. b; page 198

Complete the graph

1. Figure 8.7 illustrates the production function. In the table, diminishing returns are

■ FIGURE 8.7

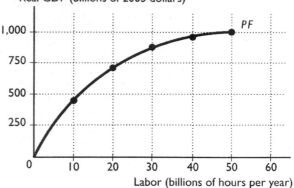

Real GDP (billions of 2005 dollars)

demonstrated by the fact that each additional 10 billion hours of labor increases real GDP by a smaller amount. In the figure, diminishing returns are illustrated by the slope of the production function, which becomes less steep as the quantity of labor increases; pages 192-193.

2. The equilibrium real wage rate is $20 an hour and the equilibrium employment is 30 billion hours. Potential GDP is $900 billion; page 197.

3. If both the labor demand and labor supply curves shift rightward by 10 billion labor hours, then equilibrium employment increases by 10 billion hours to 40 billion hours. Potential GDP increases to $960 billion; page 197.

Short answer and numeric questions

1. Classical macroeconomics believes that markets work well and government intervention cannot improve the economy. Keynesian economics believes that a market economy is unstable and needs government intervention to help it reach full employment and sustained economic growth; pages 188-189.

2. The equilibrium quantity of labor is the amount of full employment. The production function shows how much GDP this full-employment quantity of labor produces and this quantity of GDP is potential GDP; page 197.

3. If the production function shifts upward, the amount of real GDP produced by every quantity of labor increases. The nation's potential GDP increases; pages 192, 197.

4. On both counts, the upward shift of the production function and the increase in employment, potential GDP increases; pages 192, 197.

Additional Exercises (also in MyEconLab Test A)

■ **FIGURE 8.8**

Real wage rate (2005 dollars per hour)

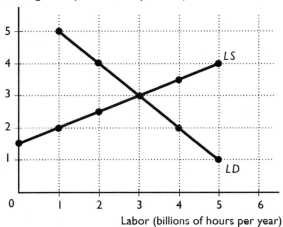

Labor (billions of hours per year)

■ **FIGURE 8.9**

Real GDP (billions of 2005 dollars per year)

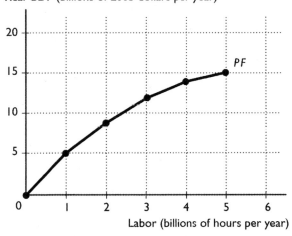

Labor (billions of hours per year)

1. The demand for labor curve and supply of labor curve are illustrated in Figure 8.8. The production function is illustrated in Figure 8.9.

The equilibrium wage rate and employment is determined in the labor market, illustrated in Figure 8.8. The equilibrium quantity of labor is 3 billion hours and the equilibrium real wage rate is $3 an hour. This is the real wage rate at which the quantity of labor demanded equals the quantity of labor supplied.

Potential GDP is the real GDP produced by the equilibrium quantity of labor. The production function in Figure 8.9 shows that 3 billion hours of labor produces potential GDP of $12 billion; pages 196-197.

■ **CHECKPOINT 8.2**

Fill in the blanks

The unemployment rate at full employment is the natural unemployment rate. The activity of looking for an acceptable, vacant job is called job search. An increase in unemployment benefits increases job search. Job rationing occurs when the real wage rate is above the equilibrium level. A minimum wage set above the equilibrium wage rate creates unemployment. If the real wage rate is above the full-employment equilibrium level, the natural unemployment rate increases.

True or false
1. True; page 201
2. True; page 201
3. False; pages 202-203
4. False; pages 203-204
5. False; page 203

Multiple choice
1. c; page 200
2. c; page 201
3. a; page 201
4. b; page 201
5. d; pages 202-203
6. a; page 203
7. a; page 203
8. d; page 204
9. d; pages 201-204

Complete the graph

1. a. The equilibrium wage rate is $30 and employment is 60 billion hours; page 197.
   b. An efficiency wage is set higher than the equilibrium wage rate, so the firm must set the wage rate above $30; page 203.
   c. A minimum wage of $50 an hour creates a labor surplus of 60 billion hours a year; pages 203-204.
   d. The union will strive to set a wage rate that is higher than the competitive wage, so the union will try to set a wage that is higher than $30; pages 203-204.
   e. In each of the answers to parts (a), (b), and (c), unemployment occurs. And in each of the answers, employment is less than 60 billion hours; page 204.

Short answer and numeric questions

1. a. The equilibrium wage rate is $20 an hour because that is the wage rate at which the quantity of labor demanded equals the quantity supplied. Employment is 60 billion hours; page 197.
   b. If firms set an efficiency wage of $30 an hour, there is a labor surplus of 30 billion hours a year (170 billion hours supplied minus 140 billion hours demanded); pages 203-204.
   c. If the government sets a minimum wage of $30 an hour, there is a labor surplus of 30 billion hour a year; pages 203-204.
   d. If unions negotiate a wage of $30 an hour, there is a labor surplus of 30 billion hours a year; pages 203-204.
   e. In each of the answers to parts (b), (c), and (d) there is a labor surplus of 30 billion hours a year. All three of the events raise the wage rate above its equilibrium and create unemployment. All three of the events lower employment; page 204.

2. The natural unemployment rate increases as more young people enter the labor force and search for jobs. The natural unemployment rate in the United States likely will increase between 2009 and 2014; page 201.

3. If unemployment benefits increase, the opportunity cost of job search decreases. Workers spend more time unemployed, searching for jobs and so the natural unemployment rate increases; page 201.

4. A firm pays an efficiency wage rate to motivate its employees to work hard. The employees work hard to avoid being let go because they know that if they have to take another job, they would probably be paid the lower equilibrium wage rate; page 203.

Additional Exercises (also in MyEconLab Test A)

1. Of the factors mentioned, high unemployment benefits lead to increased job search. But a high minimum wage and strong labor unions lead to job rationing. So it is not possible to determine if Sweden's unemployment arises primarily from job rationing or job search; pages 201-203.

2. Of the factors mentioned, the only one that points toward Sweden having a lower natural unemployment rate than the United States is the modest population growth. All of the other factors—high unemployment benefits, high minimum wage, and strong labor force unions—point toward Sweden having a higher natural unemployment rate than the United States; pages 201-203.

3. The full-employment equilibrium real wage rate is $3 per hour and the full-employment quantity of labor is 3,000 hours per day.
   There are 1,000 hours per day of unemployed people searching for jobs, so the total labor force is 3,000 hours + 1,000 hours, which is 4,000 hours per day. The unemployment rate is (1,000 hours) ÷ (4,000 hours) × 100, or 25 percent; page 204.

4. If the government introduces a minimum wage of $4.00 an hour, 4,000 hours of labor are supplied by households but only 2,000 hours of labor are demanded by firms. So the resulting unemployment is 4,000 hours – 2,000 hours, or 2,000 hours per day; pages 203-204.

Economic Growth

Chapter 9

Chapter 9 discusses the factors that determine economic growth, studies different theories that explain economic growth, and examines possible government polices to speed economic growth.

1 Define and calculate the economic growth rate, and explain the implications of sustained growth.

Economic growth is a sustained expansion of production possibilities and is measured as the increase in real GDP over a given time period. The economic growth rate is the annual percentage change of real GDP. The standard of living depends on real GDP per person, which equals real GDP divided by the population. The Rule of 70 says that the number of years it takes for the level of a variable to double approximately equals 70 divided by the annual percentage growth rate of the variable.

2 Explain the sources of labor productivity growth.

Labor productivity is the quantity of real GDP produced by one hour of labor. When labor productivity grows, real GDP per person grows. Growth of labor productivity depends on saving and investment in more physical capital, and expansion of human capital and discovery of better technologies. Capital is subject to the law of diminishing returns. The productivity curve is the relationship that shows how real GDP per hour of labor changes as the quantity of capital per hour of labor changes. As the quantity of capital per hour of labor increases, additional capital raises labor productivity by less. Expansion of human capital and discovery of better technologies shift the productivity curve upward, increasing labor productivity. Real GDP equals labor productivity multiplied by aggregate hours of labor.

3 Review the theories of economic growth.

Old growth theory, called the classical theory, predicts that labor productivity growth is temporary. If real GDP rises above the subsistence level, a population explosion occurs. Labor productivity falls and real GDP per person returns to the subsistence level. New growth theory predicts that our unlimited wants will lead us to ever greater labor productivity and perpetual economic growth. It emphasizes that human capital growth and discoveries are the result of choices. It also says that technological discoveries bring profit and competition destroys profit, thereby creating the incentive for more technological discoveries. Additionally as capital increases, although a *firm* experiences diminishing returns, the *economy* does not which means that labor productivity can grow indefinitely.

4 Describe policies that speed economic growth.

The preconditions for economic growth are economic freedom, property rights, and markets. Economic freedom occurs when people are able to make personal choices, their private property is protected by rule of law, and they are free to buy and sell in markets. Governments can increase economic growth by creating incentives to save, invest, and innovate; by encouraging saving; by encouraging research and development; by encouraging international trade; and by improving the quality of education.

CHECKPOINT 9.1

■ **Define and calculate the economic growth rate, and explain the implications of sustained growth.**

Quick Review

- *Growth rate* The growth rate of real GDP equals

$$\frac{\left(\begin{array}{c}\text{Real GDP in}\\\text{current year}\end{array}\right)-\left(\begin{array}{c}\text{Real GDP in}\\\text{previous year}\end{array}\right)}{\left(\text{Real GDP in previous year}\right)}\times100$$

- *Growth rate of real GDP per person* The growth rate of real GDP per person equals (growth rate of real GDP)–(growth rate of population).

- *Rule of 70* The number of years it takes for the level of any variable to double is approximately 70 divided by the annual percentage growth rate of the variable.

Additional Practice Problem 9.1

1. In the nation of Transylvania in 2009, real GDP was $3.0 million and the population was 1,000. In 2010, real GDP was $3.3 million and the population was 1,050.
   a. What is Transylvania's economic growth rate in 2010?
   b. What is the population growth rate?
   c. What is Transylvania's growth rate of real GDP per person?
   d. Did Transylvania's standard of living rise?
   e. Approximately how long will it take for real GDP per person to double?

Solution to Additional Practice Problem 9.1

1. This question uses three growth rate formulas. The first is the formula that calculates the economic growth rate; the second is the formula that calculates the growth rate of real GDP per person; the third is the Rule of 70.
1a. The economic growth rate is the growth rate of real GDP. Transylvania's economic growth rate equals [($3.3 million – $3.0 million) ÷ $3.0 million] × 100 = 10 percent.

1b. Transylvania's population growth rate equals [(1,050 – 1,000) ÷ 1,000] × 100 = 5 percent.
1c. Transylvania's real GDP per person growth rate equals the growth rate of real GDP minus the growth rate of the population, or 10 percent – 5 percent = 5 percent.
1d. Transylvania's real GDP per person rose, so Transylvania's standard of living increased.
1e. The number of years it takes for real GDP per person to double is given by the Rule of 70. Transylvania's real GDP per person is growing at 5 percent per year, so it will take approximately 70 ÷ 5 or 14 years for Transylvania's real GDP per person to double.

■ Self Test 9.1

Fill in the blanks

The growth rate of real GDP equals real GDP in the current year minus real GDP in the previous year divided by real GDP ____ in the (current; previous) year, then multiplied by 100. The growth rate of real GDP per person equals the growth rate of real GDP ____ (minus; plus) the growth rate of the population. The number of years it takes for the level of any variable to double is approximately ____ divided by the annual percentage growth rate of the variable.

True or false

1. If real GDP last year was $1.00 trillion and real GDP this year is $1.05 trillion, the growth rate of real GDP this year is 5 percent.

2. Real GDP per person equals real GDP divided by the population.

3. If a nation's population grows at 2 percent and its real GDP grows at 4 percent, then the growth rate of real GDP per person is 2 percent.

4. If real GDP is growing at 2 percent a year, it will take 50 years for real GDP to double.

Multiple choice

1. The economic growth rate is measured as the
   a. annual percentage change of real GDP.
   b. annual percentage change of employment.
   c. level of real GDP.
   d. annual percentage change of the population.
   e. amount of population.

2. Real GDP is $9 trillion in the current year and $8.6 trillion in the previous year. The economic growth rate between these years has been
   a. 10.31 percent.
   b. 4.65 percent.
   c. 5.67 percent.
   d. 7.67 percent.
   e. $0.4 trillion.

3. The standard of living is measured by
   a. real GDP.
   b. employment.
   c. employment per person.
   d. real GDP per person.
   e. the population.

4. If the population growth rate is greater than the growth rate of real GDP, then real GDP per person
   a. falls.
   b. rises.
   c. does not change.
   d. might rise or fall.
   e. cannot be measured.

5. If real GDP increases by 6 percent and at the same time the population increases by 2 percent, then real GDP per person grows by
   a. 6 percent.
   b. 4 percent.
   c. 2 percent.
   d. 8 percent.
   e. 3 percent.

6. If a country's real GDP is growing at 4 percent a year, its real GDP will double in
   a. 14 years.
   b. 17.5 years.
   c. 23.3 years.
   d. 35 years.
   e. 25 years.

Short answer and numeric questions

Year	Real GDP (billions of 2005 dollars)
2010	100.0
2011	110.0
2012	121.0
2013	133.1

1. The above table gives a nation's real GDP. What is the growth rate of real GDP in 2011? In 2012? In 2013?

Year	Real GDP growth rate (percent)	Population growth rate (percent)
2010	3	2
2011	4	2
2012	1	2
2013	4	4

2. The table above has a nation's real GDP growth rate and its population growth rate.
   a. What is the growth rate of real GDP per person for each year?
   b. In what years did the standard of living improve?

3. If a nation's real GDP grows at 3 percent a year, how long does it take for real GDP to double? If the growth rate is 4 percent, how long does it take for real GDP to double? If the growth rate is 5 percent, how long does it take real GDP to double?

Additional Exercises (also in MyEconLab Test A)

1. In Canada, real GDP was $1,012 billion in 2000 and $1,028 billion in 2001. The population was 30.8 million in 2000 and 31.1 million in 2001. Calculate Canada's economic growth rate in 2001, the growth rate of real GDP per person in Canada in 2001, and the approximate number of years it will take for real GDP per person in Canada to double if the 2001 economic growth and population growth rates are maintained.

2. Calculate the change in the number of years it will take for real GDP per person in China to double if its economic growth rate increases from 10.6 percent to 12 percent a year and its population growth rate rises from 1 percent to 2 percent a year.

CHECKPOINT 9.2

■ Explain the sources of labor productivity growth.

Quick Review

- *Labor productivity* Labor productivity equals real GDP divided by aggregate hours. When labor productivity grows, real GDP per person grows.

Additional Practice Problem 9.2

Item	2003	2004
Aggregate hours (billions)	232.2	234.5
Real GDP (trillions of 2005 dollars)	10.32	10.76

1. The table above provides some data for the U.S. economy in 2003 and 2004.
   a. What is the growth rate of real GDP in 2004?
   b. What is labor productivity in 2003 and 2004?
   c. Calculate the growth rate of labor productivity in 2004.
   d. How does the growth rate of labor productivity you calculated compare with the typical growth in the United States since 1960?

Solution to Additional Practice Problem 9.2

1a. The growth rate of real GDP in 2004 is [($10.76 trillion − $10.32 trillion) ÷ $10.32 trillion] × 100, which is 4.3 percent.

1b. Labor productivity is real GDP divided by aggregate hours. So labor productivity in 2003 is $10.32 trillion ÷ 232.2 billion hours, which is $44.44 per hour of labor. In 2004 labor productivity is $10.76 trillion ÷ 234.5 billion hours, which is $45.88 per hour of labor.

1c. The growth rate of labor productivity is labor productivity in 2004 minus the labor productivity in 2003, divided by labor productivity in 2003, all multiplied by 100. The growth rate of labor productivity equals [($45.88 per hour − $44.44 per hour) ÷ $44.44 per hour] × 100, which is 3.24 percent.

1d. The increase in labor productivity in 2004 was lower than in the early 1960s but was higher than the average since then.

■ Self Test 9.2

Fill in the blanks

Labor productivity equals real GDP ____ (multiplied by; divided by) aggregate hours. Saving and investment in physical capital ____ (increase; decrease) labor productivity. If the quantity of capital is small, an increase in capital brings a ____ (large; small) increase in production. The productivity curve shows that if the quantity of capital per hour of labor is small, an increase in capital brings a ____ (large; small) increase in labor productivity. Education, training, and job experience increase ____ (investment in physical capital; human capital). Advances in technology result in ____ (a movement upward along the productivity curve; an upward shift of the productivity curve). Real GDP grows when ____ and ____ grow.

True or false

1. Real GDP increases if aggregate hours increase or labor productivity increases.

2. If labor productivity increases and aggregate hours do not change, then real GDP per person increases.

3. Capital is not subject to the law of diminishing returns.

4. The productivity curve shows that an increase in capital decreases labor productivity.

5. The discovery and applications of new technology has increased labor productivity.

6. Growth of human capital increases labor productivity and shifts the productivity curve upward.

Multiple choice

1. If real GDP is $1,200 billion, the population is 60 million, and aggregate hours are 80 billion, labor productivity is
   a. $5.00 an hour.
   b. $6.67 an hour.
   c. $15.00 an hour.
   d. $20,000.
   e. $150 an hour.

2. If aggregate hours are 100 billion hours and labor productivity is $40 an hour, than real GDP equals
   a. $100 billion.
   b. $40 billion.
   c. $100 trillion.
   d. $2.5 trillion.
   e. $4 trillion.

3. Which of the following lists gives factors that increase labor productivity?
   a. saving and investment in physical capital, and wage increases
   b. expansion of human capital, labor force increases, and discovery of new technologies
   c. expansion of human capital, population growth, and discovery of new technologies
   d. saving and investment in physical capital, expansion of human capital, and discovery of new technologies
   e. labor force increases and wage increases

4. Growth in physical capital depends most directly upon the
   a. amount of saving and investment.
   b. number of firms in the nation.
   c. rate of population growth.
   d. amount of government expenditures.
   e. level of human capital.

5. Human capital is
   a. the same as labor productivity.
   b. a measure of the number of labor hours available.
   c. the accumulated skills and knowledge of workers.
   d. the average number of years of schooling of the labor force.
   e. is what people are born with and cannot be changed.

6. The productivity curve shifts upward when
   a. physical capital increases.
   b. human capital decreases.
   c. hours of labor increase.
   d. hours of labor decrease.
   e. technology advances.

Complete the graph

■ **FIGURE 9.1**

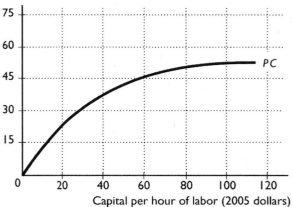

Real GDP per hour of labor (2005 dollars)

1. Figure 9.1 shows a productivity curve.
   a. How does this figure show diminishing marginal returns?
   b. In the figure, show the effect of an increase in human capital.
   c. In the figure, show the effect of an advance in technology

Short answer and numeric questions

Year	Real GDP (trillion of 2005 dollars)	Aggregate hours (billions)
1964	3.00	133.6
1974	4.32	158.7
1984	5.81	185.3
1994	7.84	211.5
2004	10.76	234.5

1. The table above has data from the United States. For each year, calculate labor productivity.

2. Real GDP is $9 trillion and aggregate hours are 200 billion. What is labor productivity?

3. Aggregate hours are 200 billion and labor productivity is $45 an hour. What is real GDP?

4. What three factors increase labor productivity?

Additional Exercises (also in MyEconLab Test A)

Year	Aggregate hours (billions)	Real GDP (billions of 2005 dollars)	Capital per hour of labor (2005 dollars)
2010	240.0	9,500	105.0
2011	249.6	10,070	107.1

The table provides some data on an economy in 2010 and 2011.

1. Calculate the growth rate of real GDP in 2011.

2. Calculate labor productivity in 2010 and 2011.

3. Calculate the growth rate of labor productivity in 2011.

4. Compare the growth rate of labor productivity and the growth rate of capital per hour of labor in 2011. Why might they differ?

CHECKPOINT 9.3

■ **Review the theories of economic growth.**

Quick Review

- *Old growth theory* The clash between an exploding population and limited resources will eventually bring economic growth to an end. Income is driven to the subsistence level. Old growth theory is called the "classical growth theory" or "Malthusian theory" or the "Doomsday theory."

- *New growth theory* Unlimited wants will lead us to ever greater productivity and perpetual economic growth.

Additional Practice Problems 9.3

1. In the classical theory, why is an increase in labor productivity only temporary?

2. Some economic advisors urge less developed nations to restrict their birth rate. These economists claim that a high birth rate impoverishes a nation.

   a. What growth theory are these advisors following?

   b. What would a new growth theory proponent say about this recommendation?

Solutions to Additional Practice Problems 9.3

1. An increase in labor productivity lifts real GDP per person above the subsistence level, the minimum amount necessary to sustain life. People respond by increasing the birth rate so a population explosion occurs. The population grows so large that capital per worker and hence labor productivity falls. The fall in labor productivity forces real GDP per person back to the subsistence level, after which population growth ends.

2a. These advisors are following the classical theory of economic growth. They believe that if real GDP per person rises in these nations, then the birth rate will increase and drive real GDP per person back to the subsistence level. They identify the low real GDP per person in these nations with a high birth rate and resulting high population growth rate.

2b. A new growth theory proponent likely would disagree with the suggestion to limit the birth rate. According to this theory, the pace at which new discoveries are made and at which technology advances depends on how many people are looking for a new technology and how intensively they are looking. In this case, limiting the population leads to a reduction in the discovery of new technologies and a decrease in the growth rate of real GDP per person.

■ **Self Test 9.3**

Fill in the blanks

The classical growth theory is the same as the _____ (Malthusian; new growth) theory. Classical growth theory says an increase in real GDP per person leads to more rapid growth in _____. New growth theory says that economic growth will persist _____ (temporarily; indefinitely). According to new growth theory, technological advances are the result of _____ (chance; people's pursuit of profit). New growth theory concludes that _____ (the economy; a firm) does not experience diminishing returns. The description that growth is like a perpetual motion machine best fits the _____ (old; new) growth theory.

True or false

1. The classical growth theory concludes that eventually real GDP per person returns to the subsistence level.

2. Malthusian theory is another name for the new growth theory.

3. The new growth theory emphasizes that people make choices about how long to remain in school, developing their human capital.

4. The new growth theory points out that because production activities can be replicated, the economy does not experience diminishing returns.

5. The new growth theory predicts that economic growth can persist indefinitely.

Multiple choice

1. If real GDP per person is above the subsistence level, the according to classical growth theory,
   a. the population will increase.
   b. the population will decrease.
   c. the standard of living continues to improve.
   d. labor productivity will increase.
   e. more technological advances occur.

2. Classical growth theory predicts that increases in
   a. real GDP per person are permanent and sustainable.
   b. real GDP per person are temporary and not sustainable.
   c. resources permanently increase labor productivity.
   d. resources permanently increase real GDP per person.
   e. competition increase economic growth.

3. The theory that suggests that our unlimited wants will lead to perpetual economic growth is the
   a. classical growth theory.
   b. sustained growth theory.
   c. old growth theory.
   d. new growth theory.
   e. Malthusian growth theory.

4. The new growth theory states that
   a. technological advances are the result of random chance.
   b. technological advances result from choices.
   c. technological advances are the responsibility of the government.
   d. the subsistence income level leads to technological advances.
   e. it is impossible to replicate production activities.

5. According to the new growth theory _____ is the factor that motivates technological change.
   a. random chance
   b. profit
   c. diminishing returns
   d. the replication of activities
   e. decisions about how much human capital to acquire

Short answer and numeric questions

1. What role do technological advances play in each of the three growth theories?

2. In which of the two growth theories does population growth play a critical role and what is its role?

3. What role do diminishing returns play in the new growth theory?

4. Which growth theory is most pessimistic about the prospects for persistent economic growth? Which is most optimistic?

Additional Exercises (also in MyEconLab Test A)

1. What are the three facts about market economies that new growth theory emphasizes and how do those facts influence the economic growth rate? Provide examples.

2. Why don't diminishing returns limit growth in new growth theory?

3. Families in China are permitted to have only one child. Predict the effects of this policy on economic growth according to classical, neoclassical, and new growth theories.

CHECKPOINT 9.4

■ **Describe policies that speed economic growth.**

Quick Review

- *Preconditions for economic growth* The three preconditions are economic freedom, property rights, and markets.
- *Policies to achieve growth* Five policies are to create incentive mechanisms, encourage saving, encourage research and development, encourage international trade, and improve the quality of education.

Additional Practice Problem 9.4

1. In 1949 East and West Germany had about the same real GDP per person. By 1989, when East Germany collapsed, West Germany had a real GDP per person more than twice the level of East Germany's. Why did East Germany grow so much more slowly than West Germany over those 40 years?

Solution to Additional Practice Problem 9.4

1. In 1949, East Germany was formed with state ownership of capital and land, and virtually no economic freedom. West Germany was formed with private ownership of most capital and land, and significant economic freedom.

   West Germany had the preconditions for economic growth; East Germany did not. When East Germany collapsed in 1989, West Germany had more human capital, more capital per hour of labor, and better technology. The different incentives had given West German workers the incentive to acquire human capital, West German investors the incentive to acquire physical capital, and West German entrepreneurs the incentive to innovate new and better technology.

■ Self Test 9.4

Fill in the blanks

_____, _____, and _____ are preconditions for economic growth. Policies the government can take to encourage faster economic growth are to _____ (create; discourage) incentive mechanisms; _____ (encourage; discourage) saving; _____ (encourage; discourage) research and development; _____ (encourage; discourage) international trade; and improve the quality of _____ (education; pollution control).

True or false

1. To achieve economic growth, economic freedom must be coupled with a democratic political system.

2. Markets slow specialization and hence slow economic growth.

3. Encouraging saving can increase the growth of capital and stimulate economic growth.

4. Limiting international trade will increase economic growth.

Multiple choice

1. Economic freedom means that
   a. firms are regulated by the government.
   b. some goods and services are free.
   c. people are able to make personal choices and their property is protected.
   d. the rule of law does not apply.
   e. the nation's government is a democracy.

2. Property rights protect
   a. only the rights to physical property.
   b. only the rights to financial property.
   c. all rights except rights to intellectual property.
   d. rights to physical property, financial property, and intellectual property.
   e. the government's right to impose taxes.

3. Which of the following statements is FALSE?
   a. Saving helps create economic growth.
   b. Improvements in the quality of education are important for economic growth.
   c. Free international trade helps create economic growth.
   d. Faster population growth is the key to growth in real GDP per person.
   e. Economic freedom requires property rights.

4. Saving
   a. slows growth because it decreases consumption.
   b. finances investment which brings capital accumulation.
   c. has no impact on economic growth.
   d. is very low in most East Asian nations.
   e. is important for a country to gain the benefits of international trade.

5. The fastest growing nations today are those with
   a. barriers that significantly limit international trade.
   b. the fastest growing exports and imports.
   c. government intervention in markets to ensure high prices.
   d. few funds spent on research and development.
   e. the least saving.

6. Economic growth is enhanced by
   a. free international trade.
   b. limiting international trade so that the domestic economy can prosper.
   c. discouraging saving, because increased saving means less spending.
   d. ignoring incentive systems.
   e. increasing welfare payments to the poor so they can afford to buy goods.

Short answer and numeric questions

1. Does persistent economic growth necessarily occur when a nation meets all the preconditions for growth?

2. What role do specialization and trade play in determining economic growth?

3. Is it possible for the government to create a large increase in the economic growth rate, say from 3 percent to 10 percent in a year?

4. The Eye on Your Life discussed the roles played by economic growth in your life. How important do you think the technological advances that have lead to economic growth are in determining the quality of your life?

Additional Exercises (also in MyEconLab Test A)

1. What is the key reason why economic growth is either absent or slow in some societies?

2. Is economic freedom the same as democracy? Can you think of a country that enjoys economic freedom and achieves rapid economic growth but does not have democracy?

3. Why are markets a necessary precondition for economic growth?

4. Explain why, other things remaining the same, a country or region that adopts free international trade (for example, Hong Kong) has a faster economic growth rate than a country that restricts international trade (for example, Myanmar).

SELF TEST ANSWERS

■ CHECKPOINT 9.1

Fill in the blanks

The growth rate of real GDP equals real GDP in the current year minus real GDP in the previous year divided by real GDP in the <u>previous</u> year, then multiplied by 100. The growth rate of real GDP per person equals the growth rate of real GDP <u>minus</u> the growth rate of the population. The number of years it takes for the level of any variable to double is approximately <u>70</u> divided by the annual percentage growth rate of the variable.

True or false

1. True; page 212
2. True; page 212
3. True; page 213
4. False; page 213

Multiple choice

1. a; page 212
2. b; page 212
3. d; page 212
4. a; page 213
5. b; page 213
6. b; page 213

Short answer and numeric questions

1. 10 percent; 10 percent; 10 percent; page 212.

2. a. 1 percent; 2 percent; −1 percent; 0 percent; page 212.

   b. 2005 and 2006; page 212.

3. Use the Rule of 70. So, 70 ÷ 3 = 23.3 years; 70 ÷ 4 = 17.5 years; 70 ÷ 5 = 14 years; page 213.

Additional Exercises (also in MyEconLab Test A)

1. Canada's economic growth rate = [($1,028 billion − $1,012 billion) ÷ $1,012] billion × 100 = 1.6 percent. The growth rate of Canada's population is [(31.1 million − 30.8 million) ÷ 30.8 million] × 100, which is 1.0 percent. Canada's growth rate of real GDP per person = 1.6 percent − 1.0 percent = 0.6 percent. Real

GDP per person doubles in approximately 70 ÷ 0.6 = 116.7 years; pages 212-213.

2. Before the changes, real GDP per person is growing at 10.6 percent − 1 percent = 9.6 percent per year. At this rate, real GDP per person will double in approximately 70 ÷ 9.6 = 7.3 years. After the changes, real GDP per person is growing at 12.0 percent − 2 percent = 10.0 percent per year. At this rate, real GDP per person will double in approximately 70 ÷ 10.0 = 7.0 years. So these changes shave 0.3 of a year off of the time it takes for real GDP to double; page 213.

■ CHECKPOINT 9.2

Fill in the blanks

Labor productivity equals real GDP <u>divided by</u> aggregate hours. Saving and investment in physical capital <u>increase</u> labor productivity. If the quantity of capital is small, an increase in capital brings a <u>large</u> increase in production. The productivity curve shows that if the quantity of capital per hour of labor is small, an increase in capital brings a <u>large</u> increase in labor productivity. Education, training, and job experience increase <u>human capital</u>. Advances in technology result in <u>an upward shift of the productivity curve</u>. Real GDP grows when <u>the quantity of labor</u> and <u>labor productivity</u> grow.

True or false

1. True; pages 216, 221
2. True; page 216
3. False; page 217
4. False; page 218
5. True; pages 219-220
6. True; page 220

Multiple choice

1. c; page 216
2. e; page 216
3. d; page 216
4. a; page 216

5. c; page 218

6. e; page 220

Complete the graph

■ FIGURE 9.2

Real GDP per hour of labor (2005 dollars)

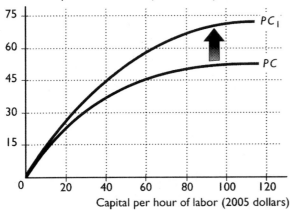

Capital per hour of labor (2005 dollars)

1. a. Diminishing marginal returns mean that when capital per hour of labor is small, an increase brings a larger increase in real GDP per hour of labor than when capital per hour of labor is large. This law is shown by the shape of the productivity curve. In the figure, along productivity curve *PC* an increase in capital per hour of labor from $20 to $40 raises real GDP per hour of labor by $15 while an increase from $60 to $80 increases real GDP per hour of labor by only $5; page 218.

   b. An increase in human capital shifts the productivity curve upward, in Figure 9.2 to a curve such as *PC₁*; page 220.

   c. Similar to an increase in human capital, an advance in technology shifts the productivity curve upward, in Figure 9.2 again to a curve such as *PC₁*; page 220.

Short answer and numeric questions

1. Labor productivity equals real GDP ÷ aggregate hours. So labor productivity in 1964 was $22.45 an hour; in 1974 was $27.22 an hour; in 1984 was $31.35 an hour; in 1994 was $37.07 an hour; and in 2004 was $45.88 an hour; page 216.

2. Labor productivity is $45 an hour; page 216.

3. Real GDP is $9 trillion; page 216.

4. Three factors increase labor productivity. First, increasing saving and investment in physical capital gives workers more capital with which to work, which increases labor productivity. Second, increasing the amount of human capital makes workers more productive and increases labor productivity. Human capital can increase either through formal schooling or on-the-job experience. Finally, discovering new technologies makes workers more productive and increases labor productivity. Often these new technologies are embedded in new capital equipment; pages 216-220.

Additional Exercises (also in MyEconLab Test A)

1. Growth rate of real GDP in 2011 = [($10,070 billion − $9,500 billion) ÷ $9,500 billion]× 100 = 6.0 percent; page 212.

2. Labor productivity in 2010 = $9,500 billion ÷ 240 billion hours = $39.58 an hour. Labor productivity in 2011 = $10,070 billion ÷ 249.6 billion hours = $40.34 an hour; page 216.

3. The growth rate of labor productivity equals the change in labor productivity divided by the initial level and then multiplied by 100, which is [($40.34 − $39.58) ÷ $39.58] × 100 = 1.92 percent; page 212.

4. The growth rate of capital per hour of labor equals the change in capital per hour of labor divided by the initial level and then multiplied by 100, which equals [($107.1 − $105.0) ÷ $105.0] × 100 = 2.00 percent. The growth of labor productivity grew by almost the same amount, 1.92 percent. The fact that these two growth rates were so close is random chance because factors other than the capital per hour of labor influence labor productivity. In particular, if human capital expands or technology advances, labor productivity will grow more rapidly. Additionally, there is no necessary reason why growth in capital per hour of labor should translate one-to-one into growth in labor productivity; pages 216-220.

■ CHECKPOINT 9.3

Fill in the blanks

The classical growth theory is the same as the <u>Malthusian</u> theory. Classical growth theory says an increase in real GDP per person leads to more rapid growth in <u>the population</u>. New growth theory says that economic growth will persist <u>indefinitely</u>. According to new growth theory, technological advances are the result of <u>people's pursuit of profit</u>. New growth theory concludes that <u>the economy</u> does not experience diminishing returns. The description that growth is like a perpetual motion machine best fits the <u>new</u> growth theory.

True or false

1. True; page 224
2. False; page 224
3. True; page 225
4. True; page 225
5. True; page 225

Multiple choice

1. a; page 224
2. b; page 224
3. d; page 224
4. b; pages 224-225
5. b; pages 224-225

Short answer and numeric questions

1. In the classical growth theory, advances in technology start a temporary period of economic growth. Ultimately, however, economic growth stops. In the new growth theory, economic growth continues indefinitely, in part because technology grows indefinitely; page 224.

2. Population growth plays a crucial role only in the classical growth theory. In the classical, or "Malthusian theory," population growth after a technological advance forces the economy back to a subsistence real income; page 224.

3. The new growth theory assumes that although a *firm* is subject to diminishing returns, the *economy* is not subject to dimin-

ishing returns. So as capital accumulates, economy-wide labor productivity grows indefinitely; page 225.

4. The most optimistic theory is the new growth theory, which concludes that economic growth can continue forever. The most pessimistic theory is the old growth theory, which concludes that the economy will return to a subsistence level of real income; pages 224-225.

Additional Exercises (also in MyEconLab Test A)

1. First, human capital grows because of choices. Second, discoveries result from choices. Lastly, discoveries bring profit and competition destroys profit. With respect to the first factor, human capital growth depends, in part, on how long people remain in school, what they study, and how hard they study. Discoveries result from choices, which depend on how many people are looking for new technology and how intensively they are looking, not mere luck. And, competition serves to squeeze profits. People are constantly seeking lower-cost methods of production or new and better products, which leads to economic growth; pages 224-225.

2. New growth theory suggests that diminishing returns are not growth limiting. According to the new growth theory, as capital accumulates, labor productivity grows indefinitely as long as people devote resources to expanding human capital and introducing new technologies. In addition, new growth theory points out that even though there might be diminishing returns to a *firm*, there are not necessarily diminishing returns to the *economy* as a whole because activities can be replicated. In other words, it is possible for the economy as a whole to add another, say, computer chip factory identical to a first factory. Because the second factory is identical to the first, the output should be identical to the first and so the economy as whole does not experience diminishing returns; page 225.

3. According to the old growth theory, that is

the classical theory of growth, an effort by China to slow population growth by limiting the number of children in each family initially would have the effect of increasing the amount of capital per hour of labor. So, labor productivity and real GDP per person increase. As GDP per person rises, real GDP per person rises above the subsistence level and population should increase yet again. The overall effect is unclear: If China can successfully limit population growth in face of the tendency for it to increase when real GDP per person rises, then real GDP per person can remain above the subsistence level. However, if China's best efforts are insufficient, then the rise in GDP per person serves to increase population growth and real GDP per person returns to the subsistence level.

According to new growth theory, the pace at which new discoveries are made and at which technology advances depends on how many people are looking for a new technology and how intensively they are looking. This assumption leads to the conclusion that efforts to limit population through regulating the number of children that people are allowed to have will lead to a reduction in the discovery of new technologies and a decrease in the rate of labor productivity growth. So, China's growth policy slows the growth in real GDP per person; pages 224-225.

■ CHECKPOINT 9.4

Fill in the blanks

Economic freedom, property rights, and markets are preconditions for economic growth. Policies the government can take to encourage faster economic growth are to create incentive mechanisms; encourage saving; encourage research and development; encourage international trade; and improve the quality of education.

True or false
1. False; page 228
2. False; page 228

3. True; page 229
4. False; page 230

Multiple choice
1. c; page 228
2. d; page 228
3. d; pages 228-229
4. b; pages 228-229
5. b; page 230
6. a; page 230

Short answer and numeric questions
1. No, economic growth does not necessarily occur when all preconditions for growth are satisfied. Without the preconditions, economic growth will not occur but simply having them is not enough to guarantee economic growth. For growth to occur and be persistent, people must have incentives that encourage saving and investment, expansion of human capital, and the discovery and application of new technologies. With these incentives and the preconditions, economic persisting growth will occur; pages 228-229.

2. Growth begins when people can specialize in the activities in which they have a comparative advantage and trade with each other. As an economy reaps the benefits from specialization and trade, production and consumption grow, real GDP per person increases, and the standard of living rises; page 229.

3. No, the government cannot create a huge increase in the economic growth rate. The government can pursue policies that will nudge the growth rate upward. And, over time, policies that create even small increases in the economic growth rate will have large benefits; page 230.

4. The importance of these technological advances is hard to overstate. For instance, the next time you watch a movie from the 1930s, the 1940s, the 1950s, the 1960s, 1970s, or even the 1980s look carefully at what is *not* present. Do you see portable

computers? Smart phones? iPads? Elaborate life-saving equipment in hospitals? Cars with enhanced safety features and incredible durability? GPS? The answers are, of course, no. All of these technological advances came in response to people's insatiable desire for a higher standard of living and other people's equally insatiable pursuit of profit.

Additional Exercises (also in MyEconLab Test A)

1. The key reason why economic growth is either absent or slow is that some societies lack the incentive system that encourages growth-producing activities. And economic freedom is the fundamental precondition for creating the incentives that lead to economic growth; page 228.

2. Economic freedom is not the same as democracy. The rule of law is the key requirement to economic freedom, not democracy. Several non-democratic countries enjoy economic freedom and achieve rapid economic growth. China is an example of a non-democratic but rapidly growing nation; page 228.

3. Markets enable people to trade and to save and invest. Markets are where buyers and sellers get information and do business with each other; pages 228-229.

4. Free trade stimulates growth by extracting all the available gains from specialization and exchange. Countries that have substantial trade barriers often have slower economic growth because the restrictions they impose on their countries promote inefficient industries and punish potentially efficient industries that could find markets beyond their borders; page 230.

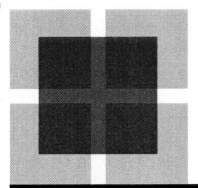

Chapter

Finance, Saving, and Investment

10

1 Describe the financial markets and the key financial institutions.

Finance is the lending and borrowing that moves funds from savers to spenders. Physical capital is the tools, machines, buildings, and other items that have been produced in the past and are used to produce additional goods and services. Financial capital is the funds firms use to buy and operate physical capital. Gross investment is the total amount spent on new capital goods; net investment equals gross investment minus depreciation. Net investment is the change in the quantity of capital. Saving is the amount of income that is not paid in taxes or spent on consumption. Saving is the source of financial capital. Borrowers and savers interact in the markets for financial capital: the loan markets, the bond markets, and the stock markets. Financial institutions, such as investment banks, commercial banks, government-sponsored mortgage lenders, pension funds, and insurance companies, are firms that operate on both sides of the markets for financial capital. A financial institution's net worth is the market value of what it has lent minus the market value of what it has borrowed. If net worth is negative, the firm is insolvent; if a firm is faced with a sudden demand to repay more of what it has borrowed than the amount of cash it has on hand, the firm is illiquid. There is an inverse relationship between the interest rate and the price of an asset; if the asset price rises, the interest rate falls.

2 Explain how borrowing and lending decisions are made and how these decisions interact in the loanable funds market.

The main source of the demand for loanable funds is firms demand for loanable funds to finance investment. Other things remaining the same, the higher the real interest rate, the smaller the quantity of loanable funds demanded so that the demand for loanable funds curve slopes downward. The demand for loanable funds changes when the expected profit changes; if the expected profit increases, the demand for loanable funds increases. The main source of the supply of loanable funds is households supply of savings. Other things remaining the same, the higher the real interest rate, the greater the quantity of loanable funds supplied so that the supply of loanable funds curve slopes upward. Factors that change the supply of loanable funds are: disposable income, wealth, expected future income, and default risk. The loanable funds market equilibrium occurs at the real interest rate at which the quantity of loanable funds demanded equals the quantity supplied.

3 Explain how a government budget surplus or deficit influences the real interest rate, investment, and saving.

A government budget surplus adds to the supply of loanable funds, thereby lowering the real interest rate and increasing the quantity of investment. A government budget deficit adds to the demand for loanable funds, raising the real interest rate and decreasing (crowding out) investment. The Ricardo-Barro effect says that private saving increases to offset a government budget deficit so no crowding out occurs.

CHECKPOINT 10.1

■ **Describe the financial markets and the key financial institutions.**

Quick Review

- *Net investment* Net investment is the change in the quantity of capital and equals gross investment minus depreciation.

- *Interest rates and asset prices* The interest rate on an asset is a percentage of the asset's price. So if the asset's price rises, then the interest rate on the asset falls and if the asset's price falls, then the interest rate on the asset rises.

Additional Practice Problems 10.1

1. On December 31, 2008 CSX railroad had capital of $19.5 billion dollars. During 2009 CSX made investments of $1.0 billion and had $0.4 billion of capital depreciate.
   a. What was CSX's gross investment?
   b. What was CSX's net investment?
   c. What was the amount of CSX's capital stock on December 31, 2009? By how much did the capital stock change? How does this answer compare to the answer to part (b)?

2. Nvidia, the 3-D graphics accelerator company, wanted to raise $200 million to build a new headquarters building and buy other physical capital. What methods could Nvidia have used to obtain the financial capital to purchase the physical capital it needed?

3. For a financial institution, what is the relationship between net wealth, solvency, and insolvency?

Solutions to Additional Practice Problems 10.1

1a. CSX's gross investment is equal to their total investment, $1.0 billion.

1b. CSX's net investment is equal to its gross investment minus its depreciation, or $1.0 billion minus $0.4 billion, which is $0.6 billion.

1c. CSX's capital stock on December 31, 2009 equals its capital stock on December 31, 2008 plus its (gross) investment minus its depreciation, or $19.5 billion + $1.0 billion − $0.4 billion, which is $20.1 billion. CSX's capital increased by $0.6 billion, which is the same as CSX's net investment. It is the case that the change in the capital stock equals net investment.

2. Nvidia had a number of choices in the markets for financial capital. It could have sold new shares of stock, so the current stockholders would share future profits with new stockholders. It could have sold bonds, which means it would be borrowing the funds from the buyers of the bonds. Or it could have arranged a bank loan. If Nvidia sold bonds or borrowed from a bank, Nvidia would have increased its debt and would be required at some time to repay whoever loaned it the funds. As it happens, Nvidia actually financed its new capital by selling bonds.

3. A financial institution's net worth is the market value of what it has lent (which are its assets) minus the market value of what it has borrowed (which are its liabilities). If the net worth is positive, the firm is solvent but if the net worth is negative, then the firm is insolvent.

■ **Self Test 10.1**

Fill in the blanks

Finance and money ____ (are; are not) essentially the same thing. ____ (Physical; Financial) capital consists of tools, instruments, machines, buildings, and other items that have been produced in the past and that are used to produce goods and services. Net investment equals ____ (gross investment; depreciation) minus ____ (gross investment; depreciation). A ____ (bond; stock) is a certificate of ownership and claim to the profit that a firm makes. Fannie Mae is an example of ____ (an investment bank, a government-sponsored mortgage lender). If other things remain the same, an increase in the price of an asset ____ (raises; lowers) the interest rate on the asset.

True or false

1. Financial capital and physical capital are two different names for the same thing.

2. Net investment equals gross investment minus depreciation.

3. The loan market is one of the nation's financial capital markets.

4. A bond issued by a firm is a certificate of ownership and claim to the profits that the firm makes.

5. Investment banks and commercial banks are both examples of financial institutions.

6. A firm that is insolvent must also be illiquid.

Multiple choice

1. Which of the following is *not* an example of physical capital?
   a. a building
   b. a bond
   c. a dump truck
   d. a lawn mower
   e. a computer

2. The decrease in the value of capital that results from its use and obsolescence is
   a. appreciation.
   b. deconstruction.
   c. depreciation.
   d. gross investment.
   e. net investment.

3. Which of the following formulas is correct?
   a. Net investment = gross investment + depreciation
   b. Net investment = gross investment + capital
   c. Net investment = gross investment – depreciation
   d. Net investment = gross investment – saving
   e. Net investment = gross investment – wealth

4. Intel's capital at the end of the year equals Intel's capital at the beginning of the year
   a. minus its stock dividends.
   b. plus net investment.
   c. minus depreciation.
   d. plus gross investment.
   e. plus depreciation.

5. Economists use the term "financial markets" to mean the markets in which
   a. firms purchase their physical capital.
   b. firms supply their goods and services.
   c. households supply their labor services.
   d. firms get the funds that they use to buy physical capital.
   e. the government borrows to fund any budget surplus.

6. When a student uses a credit card to buy an iPod, the student is
   a. borrowing in the bond market.
   b. lending in the bond market.
   c. lending in the loan market.
   d. borrowing in the loan market.
   e. lending in the stock market.

7. Which of the following is *not* a financial institution?
   a. an insurance company
   b. a pension fund
   c. Freddie Mac
   d. a commercial bank
   e. None of the above is correct because they are all financial institutions.

8. If the market value of what it has lent is less than the market value of it has borrowed, a financial institution's net worth is ____ and it is ____.
   a. negative; illiquid but not necessarily insolvent
   b. negative; insolvent but not necessarily illiquid
   c. positive; illiquid and insolvent
   d. negative; illiquid and insolvent
   e. positive; insolvent but not necessarily illiquid

9. A bond's price is $80 and the bond pays $8 in interest every year. The bond's interest rate is ____.
   a. 8 percent
   b. 10 percent
   c. 4 percent
   d. 80 percent
   e. None of the above are correct.

Short answer and numeric questions

1. What is the relationship between physical capital and financial capital?

2. What is the difference between gross investment and capital?

3. In 2012, Regis Hair purchased 10 hair dryers for $3,300 each. During the year, depreciation was $13,000. What was the amount of Regis' gross investment and net investment?

4. What are Fannie Mae and Freddie Mac? How do they operate on both sides of the financial markets?

5. Suppose a bond pays interest of $40 per year and its price is $600. What is the interest rate on the bond? If the price rises to $800, what now is the bond's interest rate?

Additional Exercises (also in MyEconLab Test A)

1. Annie runs a fitness center. On December 31, 2011, she bought an existing business with exercise equipment and a building worth $300,000. During 2012, business was poor, so she sold some of her equipment for $100,000. What was Annie's gross investment, depreciation, and net investment during 2012? What was the value of Annie's capital at the end of 2012?

2. Karrie is a golf pro, and after she paid taxes, her income from golf and from stocks and bonds was $1,500,000 in 2012. At the beginning of 2012, she owned $900,000 worth of stocks and bonds. At the end of 2012, Karrie's stocks and bonds were worth $1,900,000. How much did Karrie save during 2012 and how much did she spend on consumption goods and services?

CHECKPOINT 10.2

■ **Explain how borrowing and lending decisions are made and how these decisions interact in the loanable funds market.**

Quick Review

- *Demand for loanable funds* The relation-ship between the quantity of loanable funds demanded and the real interest rate, other things remaining the same.

- *Supply of loanable funds* The relationship between the quantity of loanable funds supplied and the real interest rate, other things remaining the same.

Additional Practice Problems 10.2

1. Over the past decade or so, the development of ever more powerful computers has increased the profit from investing in new personal computers. This effect has affected all firms in the economy. The initial demand for

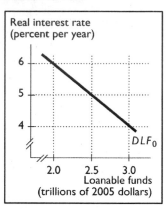

loanable funds is shown in the figure. Use the figure to show the effect the higher expected profit has on the demand for loanable funds.

2. In 2013, in the United States at a real interest rate of 4 percent a year, the quantity of loanable funds supplied is $2.0 trillion; at a real interest rate of 6 percent a year, the quantity of loanable funds supplied is $2.5 trillion; and at a real interest rate of 8 percent a year, the quantity of loanable funds supplied is $3.0 trillion.

a. In the figure, draw a graph of the U.S. supply of loanable funds curve.

b. In 2013 a large number of households start to believe that their future disposable income

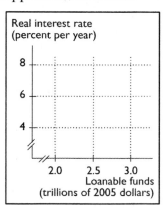

will be higher than they had previously thought. Explain how this belief influences the supply of loanable funds. Illustrate the effect of this change on the supply of loanable funds curve.

c. In 2014, the housing market recovers so that house prices soar and U.S. households' wealth increases. If other things remain the same, explain how this change influences the supply of loanable funds. What is the effect on the supply of loanable funds curve?

3. Draw a graph illustrating the effect on the equilibrium real interest rate and equilibrium saving and investment when the supply of loanable funds increases and the demand for loanable funds increases by more.

Solutions to Additional Practice Problems 10.2

1. An increase in the expected profit from investing in personal computers increases investment demand and shifts the demand for loanable funds curve rightward. In the figure, the demand for loanable funds curve

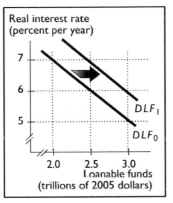

shifts rightward from DLF_0 to DLF_1. At any real interest rate firms have increased the quantity of investment they demand.

2a. The figure illustrates the U.S. supply of loanable funds curve. The supply curve, SLF_0, slopes upward because an increase in the real interest rate increases saving, which increases the quantity of loanable funds supplied.

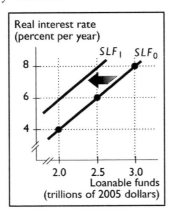

2b. An increase in expected future income decreases the amount people's saving and thereby decreases the supply of loanable funds. The U.S. supply of loanable funds decreases and the supply of loanable funds curve shifts leftward. In the above figure, the supply of loanable funds curve shifts leftward from SLF_0 to SLF_1. At any real interest rate, households have decreased the quantity of loanable funds they supply.

2c. The increase in people's wealth decreases the amount they save at each real interest rate. Saving decreases so the supply of loanable funds decreases and the supply of loanable funds curve shifts leftward. In the above figure, the supply of loanable funds curve shifts leftward from SLF_0 to SLF_1.

3. The figure that shows the demand for loanable funds curve and the supply of loanable funds curve illustrates how the real interest rate is determined. Use this diagram the same way you use the supply and demand figures you studied in Chapter 4. Equilibrium occurs where the demand for loanable funds curve intersects the supply of loanable funds curve and a shift in either curve changes the equilibrium real interest rate and the equilibrium quantity of loanable funds.

In this case, the increase in the supply of loanable funds shifts the supply of loanable funds curve rightward. The increase in the demand for loanable funds shifts the demand for loanable funds curve rightward.

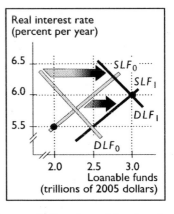

The shift of the demand for loanable funds curve exceeds the shift of the supply of loanable funds curve, so, as illustrated in the figure, the real interest rate rises, from 5.5 percent to 6.0 percent, and the quantity of loanable funds increases, from $2 trillion to $3 trillion.

■ Self Test 10.2

Fill in the blanks

Other things remaining the same, the higher the real interest rate, the _____ (greater; smaller) the quantity of loanable funds demanded. An increase in expected profit _____ (increases; decreases) the demand for loanable funds. Other things remaining the same, the higher the real interest rate, the _____ (greater; smaller) the quantity of loanable funds supplied. An increase in saving _____ (increases; decreases) loanable funds. The financial market is in equilibrium when the quantity of loanable funds supplied _____ the quantity of loanable funds demanded.

True or false

1. Other things remaining the same, the higher the real interest rate, the smaller the quantity of loanable funds demanded.

2. When the expected profit changes, there is a movement along the demand for loanable funds curve.

3. The real interest rate is the opportunity cost of consumption expenditure.

4. An increase in wealth leads to a decrease in saving.

5. If the real interest rate is greater than the equilibrium real interest rate, there is a shortage of loanable funds in the financial market.

Multiple choice

1. If the real interest rate falls, other things being the same, the quantity of loanable funds demanded _____ and the quantity of loanable funds supplied _____.
   a. increases; decreases
   b. increases; increases
   c. decreases; does not change
   d. does not change; decreases
   e. decreases; decreases

2. The demand for loanable funds
   a. increases in a recession.
   b. decreases in an expansion.
   c. increases when firms are optimistic about the profit from investing in capital.
   d. increases when wealth increases.
   e. decreases when wealth increases.

■ FIGURE 10.1

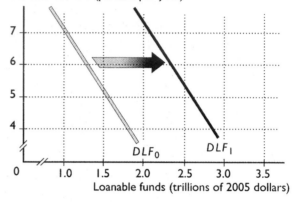
Real interest rate (percent per year)

Loanable funds (trillions of 2005 dollars)

3. The shift of the demand for loanable funds curve in Figure 10.1 could reflect _____ in investment and might be the result of _____.
   a. an increase; an increase in households' wealth
   b. an increase; a decrease in households' wealth
   c. a decrease; a fall in expected profit
   d. a decrease; a fall in the default risk
   e. an increase; a rise in expected profit

4. Other things remaining the same, a _____ in the real interest rate _____ the quantity of saving and _____ the quantity of loanable funds supplied.
   a. fall; increases; increases
   b. rise; increases; increases
   c. fall; increases; decreases
   d. fall; decreases; increases
   e. rise; increases; decreases

5. If the real interest rate falls, there is
   a. an upward movement along the supply of loanable funds curve.
   b. a downward movement along the supply of loanable funds curve.
   c. a rightward shift of the supply of loanable funds curve and no shift in the demand for loanable funds curve.
   d. a leftward shift of the supply of loanable funds curve and no shift in the demand for loanable funds curve.
   e. a leftward shift of the supply of loanable funds curve and a rightward shift in the demand for loanable funds curve.

6. An increase in wealth leads to ____ loanable funds.
   a. an increase in the supply of
   b. an increase in the demand for
   c. a decrease in the supply of
   d. a decrease in the demand for
   e. no change in either the supply of loanable funds or the demand for

7. If, at the current interest rate, the quantity of loanable funds supplied is less than the quantity of loanable funds demanded, then
   a. the supply of loanable funds curve shifts rightward and the real interest rate rises.
   b. the supply of loanable funds curve shifts leftward and the real interest rate falls.
   c. the real interest rate falls.
   d. the real interest rate rises.
   e. the supply of loanable funds curve shifts leftward and the real interest rate rises.

8. If expected profit falls, the demand for loanable funds curve shifts ____ and the real interest rate ____.
   a. rightward; rises
   b. rightward; falls
   c. leftward; rises
   d. leftward; falls
   e. leftward; does not change

■ **FIGURE 10.2**
Real interest rate (percent per year)

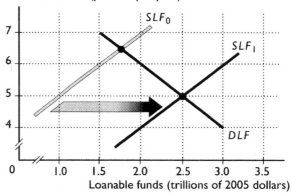

9. In Figure 10.2, ____ has increased and the equilibrium quantity of loanable funds ____.
   a. wealth; increases
   b. default risk; increases
   c. expected profit; decreases
   d. expected future income; decreases
   e. disposable income; increases

Complete the graph

■ **FIGURE 10.3**
Real interest rate (percent per year)

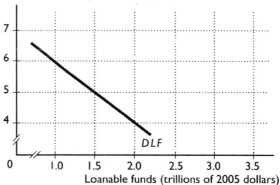

1. Figure 10.3 shows a demand for loanable funds curve.
   a. Because the economy enters an expansion, the expected profit increases. Show the effect of this change on the demand for loanable funds curve in Figure 10.3.

■ **FIGURE 10.4**

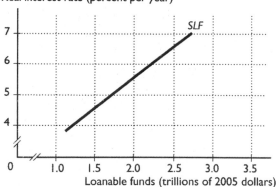
Real interest rate (percent per year)

2. Figure 10.4 shows a supply of loanable funds curve.
   a. Suppose disposable income increases. Show the effect of this change on the supply of loanable funds curve in Figure 10.4.
   b. Suppose wealth increases. Show the effect of this change on the supply of loanable funds curve in Figure 10.4.

Real interest rate (percent per year)	Demand for loanable funds (trillions of 2005 dollars)	Supply of loanable funds (trillions of 2005 dollars)
4	2.5	1.5
5	2.0	2.0
6	1.5	2.5
7	1.0	3.0

■ **FIGURE 10.5**

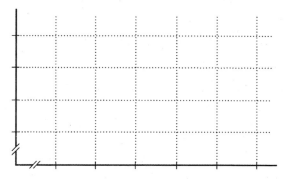

3. The table above gives a supply of loanable funds schedule and a demand for loanable funds schedule.
   a. Label the axes and draw the supply of loanable funds curve and the demand for

loanable funds curve in Figure 10.5.
   b. What is the equilibrium real interest rate? What is the equilibrium quantity of loanable funds?
   c. Suppose that firms become more optimistic about their expected profit. In Figure 10.5, show this change. What is the effect on the real interest rate and quantity of loanable funds and investment?

Short answer and numeric questions
1. What is the relationship between investment and the demand for loanable funds?

2. Why does an increase in the real interest rate decrease the quantity of loanable funds demanded?

3. What factors shift the demand for loanable funds curve? The supply of loanable funds curve?

4. If the real interest rate is less than its equilibrium value, what forces drive it to its equilibrium?

Additional Exercises (also in MyEconLab Test A)
In 2013, the Lee family had a disposable income of $80,000, wealth of $140,000, and an expected future income of $80,000 a year. At a real interest rate of 4 percent a year, the Lee family saves $15,000 a year; at a real interest rate of 6 percent a year, they save $20,000 a year; and at a real interest rate of 8 percent, they save $25,000 a year. Use this information to answer Exercises 1 and 2.

1. Draw a graph of the Lee family's supply of loanable funds curve.

2. In 2014, suppose that the stock market crashes and the Lee family's wealth decreases by 50 percent. Explain how this decrease in wealth influences the Lee family's supply of loanable funds curve.

3. Draw graphs that illustrate the effect of an increase in the demand for loanable funds and an even larger increase in the supply of loanable funds on the real interest rate and the equilibrium quantity of loanable funds.

CHECKPOINT 10.3

■ **Explain how a government budget surplus or deficit influences the real interest rate, investment, and saving.**

Quick Review

• *Crowding-out effect* The tendency for a government budget deficit to raise the real interest rate and decrease investment.

Additional Practice Problems 10.3

1. The table shows the demand for loanable funds schedule and the private supply of loanable funds schedule.

Real interest rate (percent per year)	Demand for loanable funds	Supply of loanable funds
	(trillions of 2005 dollars per year)	
4	2.7	2.1
5	2.6	2.2
6	2.5	2.3
7	2.4	2.4
8	2.3	2.5
9	2.2	2.6
10	2.1	2.7

a. If the government's budget is balanced (so there is no budget deficit nor budget surplus), what is the equilibrium real interest rate, the equilibrium the quantity of loanable funds, and the quantity of investment?

b. If the government budget surplus is $200 billion, and there is no Ricardo-Barro effect, what are the equilibrium real interest rate, the quantity of private saving, and the quantity of investment?

c. If the government budget deficit is $200 billion, and there is no Ricardo-Barro effect, what are the equilibrium real interest rate, the quantity of private saving, and the quantity of investment? Is there any crowding out?

d. If the Ricardo-Barro effect occurs, how do your answers to part (b) and part (c) change? How does the equilibrium real interest rate and quantity of investment in these two cases compare to your answer to part (a)?

2. With a Ricardo-Barro effect, what is the impact of a government budget deficit or surplus? Does the size of the deficit or surplus matter?

Solutions to Additional Practice Problems 10.3

1a. With no budget deficit or surplus, private saving is the total supply of loanable funds and private investment is the total demand for loanable funds. The equilibrium real interest rate is 7 percent a year. The equilibrium quantity of loanable funds is $2.4 trillion. Investment also is $2.4 trillion.

1b. When the government has a $200 billion budget surplus, it is adding that amount to private saving. At the initial real interest rate of 7 percent, there is a surplus of loanable funds. The real interest rate falls. When the real interest rate falls to 6 percent, the quantity of private saving is $2.3 trillion and the total quantity of loanable funds is $2.5 trillion. The quantity of loanable funds demanded is also $2.5 trillion so this real interest is the equilibrium. The equilibrium real interest rate is 6 percent, the equilibrium quantity of private saving is $2.3 trillion, and the equilibrium quantity of investment is $2.5 trillion.

1c. If the government has a $200 billion deficit, the demand for loanable funds at every real interest rate is $200 billion more than the private demand for loanable funds shown in the table. The equilibrium real interest rate is 8 percent because at this interest rate, the total quantity of loanable funds supplied, $2.5 trillion, equals the total quantity of loanable funds demanded. Private saving is $2.5 trillion and investment is $2.3 trillion. In comparison to the situation with no government deficit, $100 billion of investment has been crowded out.

1d. If the Ricardo-Barro effect occurs, then when the government has a $200 billion surplus in part (b), private saving decreases by $200 billion. As a result, the supply of loanable funds does not change. In this case, the equilibrium real interest rate is 7 percent, the quantity of private saving is $2.2 trillion, and the quantity of investment remains $2.4 trillion.

When the government has a deficit of $200 billion in part (c), private saving increases by $200 billion so the supply of loanable funds increases. The equilibrium real interest rate is

7 percent, the quantity of private saving is $2.6 trillion, and the quantity of investment remains $2.4 trillion.

2. The Ricardo-Barro effect says that government deficits and surpluses do not matter. Private saving changes to offset the budget deficit or surplus. Whether a deficit or surplus is large or small is inconsequential because it does not change the real interest rate or the quantity of investment.

■ Self Test 10.3

Fill in the blanks

Total saving equals private saving ____ (plus; minus) government saving. A government budget surplus ____ (increases; decreases) government saving. The crowding-out effect is the tendency for a government budget deficit to ____ (increase; decrease) private investment. The Ricardo-Barro effect says that an increase in the government deficit will lead to ____ (an increase; a decrease) in private saving.

True or false

1. Governments do not participate in the loanable funds market.

2. With no Barro-Ricardo effect, an increase in government saving leads to a fall in the real interest rate.

3. With no Barro-Ricardo effect, an increase in government saving leads to an increase in the quantity of investment.

4. The crowding-out effect is the tendency of a government budget surplus to crowd out private saving.

5. The Ricardo-Barro effect holds that the government budget deficit has no effect on the real interest rate or investment.

Multiple choice

1. With no Ricardo-Barro effect, a government budget surplus
   a. increases the supply of loanable funds.
   b. increases the demand for loanable funds.
   c. decreases the supply of loanable funds.
   d. decreases the demand for loanable funds.
   e. has no effect on either the supply or the demand for loanable funds.

2. Suppose the government has a budget surplus. Then
   a. private saving is equal to investment.
   b. private saving is greater than investment and government saving is positive.
   c. private saving is less than investment and government saving is positive.
   d. private saving is greater than investment and government saving is positive.
   e. private saving is greater than investment and government saving is negative.

3. With no Ricardo-Barro effect, a government budget surplus ____ the real interest rate because the ____ loanable funds increases.
   a. raises; demand for
   b. lowers; demand for
   c. raises; supply of
   d. lowers; supply of
   e. None of the above answers are correct because the real interest rate does not change.

4. If there is no Ricardo-Barro effect, a government budget deficit will ____ the real interest rate and ____ the quantity of investment.
   a. raise; increase
   b. raise; decrease
   c. lower; increase
   d. lower; decrease
   e. not change; not change

5. The "crowding-out effect" refers to how a government budget deficit
   a. shifts only the supply of loanable funds curve leftward.
   b. shifts only the demand for loanable funds curve leftward.
   c. shifts both the demand for and the supply of loanable funds curves leftward.
   d. decreases the equilibrium quantity of investment.
   e. increases the equilibrium quantity of investment.

6. The Ricardo-Barro effect says that a government budget deficit leads to
   a. a higher real interest rate.
   b. a lower real interest rate.
   c. no change in the real interest rate.
   d. an increase in demand for loanable funds.
   e. an increase in the quantity of investment.

Complete the graph

Real interest rate (percent per year)	Demand for loanable funds (trillions of 2005 dollars)	Supply of loanable funds (trillions of 2005 dollars)
4	2.5	1.5
5	2.0	2.0
6	1.5	2.5
7	1.0	3.0

1. The above table has a supply of loanable funds schedule and a demand for loanable funds schedule.
   a. In Figure 10.6 label the axes. Assuming there is no government saving, draw the supply of loanable funds curve and the demand for loanable funds curve.
   b. If the government has no budget deficit or surplus, what is the equilibrium real interest rate and quantity of investment?
   c. If the government has a $1.0 trillion deficit, and there is no Ricardo-Barro effect, draw the demand for loanable funds curve in Figure 10.6. What is the equilibrium real interest rate and quantity of investment?
   d. If the government has a $1.0 trillion defi-

■ FIGURE 10.6

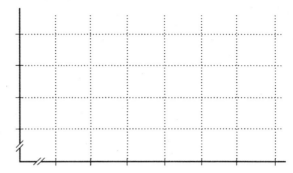

cit, and there is a Ricardo-Barro effect, draw the demand for loanable funds curve in Figure 10.6. What is the equilibrium real interest rate and quantity of investment?

Short answer and numeric questions

1. What is the crowding-out effect?

2. How does the Ricardo-Barro effect modify the conclusion of the crowding-out effect?

3. The Eye on Your Life discussed some of the many transactions you will make in the loanable funds markets. Many students are financing part or all of their college educations by using student loans. How does the decision to finance a college education using student loans compare to a firm's decision to finance a new piece of capital equipment by using loans?

Additional Exercises (also in MyEconLab Test A)

Real interest rate (percent per year)	Loanable funds demanded	Loanable funds supplied
	(trillions of 2005 dollars per year)	
4	8.5	5.5
5	8.0	6.0
6	7.5	6.5
7	7.0	7.0
8	6.5	7.5
9	6.0	8.0
10	5.5	8.5

In the loanable funds market set out in the table above, the demand for loanable funds increases by $1 trillion at each real interest rate and the supply of loanable funds increases by $2 trillion at each interest rate. Suppose there is no Ricardo-Barro effect.

1. If the government budget is balanced, what are the real interest rate, the quantity of loanable funds, investment, and private saving? Is there any crowding out in this situation?

2. If the government budget deficit is $1 trillion, what are the real interest rate, the quantity of loanable funds, investment, and private saving? (Recall that there is no Ricardo-Barro effect.) Is there any crowding out in this situation?

3. If the government wants to stimulate the quantity of investment and increase it to $9 trillion, what must it do?

SELF TEST ANSWERS

■ CHECKPOINT 10.1

Fill in the blanks

Finance and money <u>are not</u> essentially the same thing. <u>Physical</u> capital consists of tools, instruments, machines, buildings, and other items that have been produced in the past and that are used to produce goods and services. Net investment equals <u>gross investment</u> minus <u>depreciation</u>. A <u>stock</u> is a certificate of ownership and claim to the profit that a firm makes. Fannie Mae is an example of <u>a government-sponsored mortgage lender</u>. If other things remain the same, an increase in the price of an asset <u>lowers</u> the interest rate on the asset.

True or false

1. False; page 238
2. True; page 238
3. True; page 239
4. False; page 240
5. True; page 241
6. False; page 242

Multiple choice

1. b; page 238
2. c; page 238
3. c; page 238
4. b; page 238
5. d; page 239
6. d; page 239
7. e; page 241
8. b; page 242
9. b; page 242

Short answer and numeric questions

1. Physical capital is the tools, machines, buildings, and other items that have been produced in the past and are used to produce additional goods and services. Financial capital is the funds firms use to buy and operate physical capital. Hence a firm needs financial capital in order to buy a piece of physical capital; page 238.
2. Capital is the tools, machines, buildings, and other items that have been produced in the past and are used to produce additional goods and services. Investment is the purchase of new capital, so investment *adds* to the total amount of capital. Gross investment is the total amount of investment spent on new capital goods; page 238.
3. Regis' gross investment was $33,000, and net investment, which equals gross investment minus depreciation, was $20,000; page 238.
4. Fannie Mae and Freddie Mac are government-sponsored enterprises. They both buy and sell in financial markets. On the buying side, they buy mortgages from banks. They then package these mortgages into mortgage-backed securities and sell them to others, such as pension funds; page 241.
5. The interest rate equals the (amount paid) ÷ (price of the asset) × 100. In the first case in the problem, the interest rate is ($40) ÷ ($600) × 100, which is 6.67 percent. When the price rises to $800, the interest rate falls to ($40) ÷ ($800) × 100, or 5.00 percent.; page 242.

Additional Exercises (also in MyEconLab Test A)

1. Annie's gross investment during 2012 was −$100,000 because she sold some of her capital. Annie's depreciation during 2012 was $0. Annie's net investment during 2012 was −$100,000, which equals gross investment (−$100,000) minus depreciation ($0). Anne's capital equals her capital at the beginning of 2012, $300,000, plus her net investment in 2012, −$100,000, so her capital at the end of 2012 was $200,000; pages 238-239.
2. Karrie's wealth increased by $1,000,000 in 2012. So her saving in 2012 was $1,000,000. (This point assumes no capital gains or losses on her stocks and bonds.) Her income after taxes was $1,500,000. Her consumption equals her income minus her saving, which is $1,500,000 − $1,000,000 = $500,000; pages 238-239.

■ CHECKPOINT 10.2

Fill in the blanks

Other things remaining the same, the higher the real interest rate, the <u>smaller</u> the quantity of loanable funds demanded. An increase in expected profit <u>increases</u> the demand for loanable funds. Other things remaining the same, the higher the real interest rate, the <u>greater</u> the quantity of loanable funds supplied. An increase in saving <u>increases</u> loanable funds. The financial market is in equilibrium when the quantity of loanable funds supplied <u>equals</u> the quantity of loanable funds demanded.

True or false

1. True; page 245
2. False; page 246
3. True; page 247
4. True; page 248
5. False; page 250

Multiple choice

1. a; pages 245, 247
2. c; page 246
3. e; page 246
4. b; page 247
5. b; pages 247-248
6. c; page 248
7. d; page 250
8. d; pages 246, 251
9. e; pages 248, 251

Complete the graph

1. a. The increase in expected profit increases investment and thereby increases the demand for loanable funds. The demand for loanable funds curve shifts rightward, from DLF_0 to DLF_1 in Figure 10.7; page 246.

2. a. An increase in disposable income increases saving and the supply of loanable funds curve shifts rightward, from SLF_0 to SLF_1 in Figure 10.8; pages 248-249.

   b. An increase in wealth decreases saving and thereby decreases the supply of loan-

■ FIGURE 10.7

Real interest rate (percent per year)

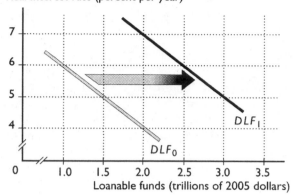

Loanable funds (trillions of 2005 dollars)

■ FIGURE 10.8

Real interest rate (percent per year)

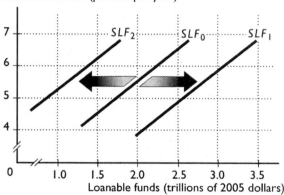

Loanable funds (trillions of 2005 dollars)

■ FIGURE 10.9

Real interest rate (percent per year)

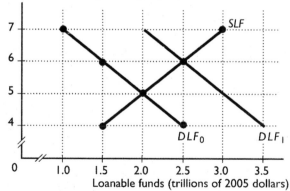

Loanable funds (trillions of 2005 dollars)

able funds. The supply of loanable funds curve shifts leftward, in Figure 10.8 from SLF_0 to SLF_2; pages 248-249.

3. a. The axes are labeled and the curves are drawn in Figure 10.9. The supply of loan-

able funds curve is *SLF* and the demand for loanable funds curve is *DLF0*; pages 245, 248.

b. The equilibrium real interest rate is 5 percent a year. The equilibrium quantity of loanable funds is $2.0 trillion; page 250.

c. The increase in the expected profit increases investment and shifts the demand for loanable funds curve rightward from *DLF0* to *DLF1*. The real interest rate rises and the quantity of investment and loanable funds increase; page 251.

Short answer and numeric questions

1. The demand for loanable funds comes from business investment, a government budget deficit, and international investment or lending. Of these three sources of demand, the largest is business investment, so it is the largest part of the demand for loanable funds; page 244.

2. The real interest rate is the opportunity cost of the funds used for investment. These funds might be borrowed or they might be the financial resources of the firm's owners. The opportunity cost of *both* sources is the real interest rate. In the case of borrowed funds, the real interest rate is the opportunity cost because it is what is really paid to the lender. In the case of the owners' funds, the real interest rate is the opportunity cost because the funds could be loaned and earn the real interest rate. An increase in the real interest rate increases the opportunity cost of financing investment so the quantity of loanable funds demanded decreases; page 245.

3. The demand for loanable funds curve shifts when the expected profit changes. Technological change, changes in the phase of the business cycle, population growth, and subjective influences, that is, swings of optimism and pessimism, all change the expected profit and shift the demand for loanable funds curve. The supply of loanable funds curve shifts when disposable income, wealth, expected future disposable income; and default risk change; pages 246-247.

4. If the real interest rate is less than the equilibrium real interest rate, the quantity of loanable funds demanded exceeds the quantity of loanable funds supplied. Borrowers can't find all the loans they want, but lenders are able to lend all the funds they have available. So the real interest rate rises and the quantity of loanable funds demanded decreases, while the quantity of loanable funds supplied increases. The equilibrium occurs when the interest rate is such that quantity of loanable funds demanded equals the quantity of loanable funds supplied; page 250.

Additional Exercises (also in MyEconLab Test A)

■ FIGURE 10.10

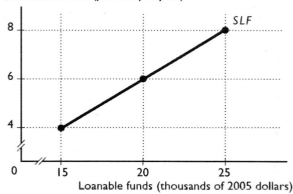
Real interest rate (percent per year)

1. The graph showing the Lee family's supply of loanable funds curve is in Figure 10.10; page 248.

2. A stock market crash decreases the Lee family's wealth, so the Lee family increases its saving. The Lee family's supply of loanable funds increases and its supply of loanable funds curve shifts rightward; page 249.

3. The increase in the demand for loanable funds raises the real interest rate and increases the equilibrium quantity of loanable funds. The increase in the supply of loanable funds lowers the real interest rate and increases the equilibrium quantity of loanable funds. If the change in the supply of loanable funds exceeds the change in the demand for loanable funds, the real interest rate falls. Both changes increase the equilibrium quan-

■ **FIGURE 10.11**

Real interest rate (percent per year)

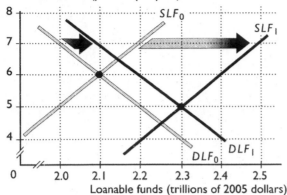

tity of loanable funds, so the equilibrium quantity of loanable funds increases.

Figure 10.11 illustrates this situation. The increase in the demand for loanable funds shifts the demand for loanable funds curve rightward from DLF_0 to DLF_1. The increase in the supply of loanable funds shifts the supply of loanable funds curve rightward from SLF_0 to SLF_1. As Figure 10.11 shows, the real interest rate falls, from 6 percent a year to 5 percent a year. The equilibrium quantity of loanable funds increases, from $2.1 trillion to $2.3 trillion; page 251.

■ **CHECKPOINT 10.3**

Fill in the blanks

Total saving equals private saving <u>plus</u> government saving. A government budget surplus <u>increases</u> government saving. The crowding-out effect is the tendency for a government budget deficit to <u>decrease</u> private investment. The Ricardo-Barro effect says that an increase in the government deficit will lead to <u>an increase</u> in private saving supply.

True or false

1. False; page 254
2. True; pages 254-255
3. True; pages 254-255
4. False; page 256
5. True; page 256

Multiple choice

1. a; page 254
2. c; pages 254-255
3. d; pages 254-255
4. b; pages 255-256
5. d; page 256
6. c; page 256

Complete the graph

■ **FIGURE 10.12**

Real interest rate (percent per year)

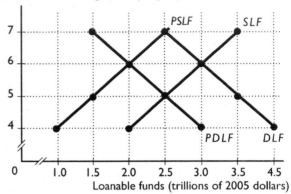

1. a. Figure 10.12 labels the axes and plots the curves. The supply of loanable funds curve is labeled *PSLF*. With no government budget surplus, this curve is the same as the overall supply of loanable funds curve. The demand for loanable funds curve is labeled *PDLF*. With no government budget deficit, this curve is the same as the overall demand for loanable funds curve; page 255.

   b. If the government has no budget deficit or surplus, then in Figure 10.12 the supply of loanable funds curve is the same as the supply of loanable funds curve labeled *PSLF* and the demand for loanable funds curve is the same as the demand for loanable funds curve labeled *PDLF*. The equilibrium real interest rate is 6 percent a year and the equilibrium quantity of loanable funds, which is the equilibrium quantity of investment, is $2.0 trillion; page 255.

c. With the government budget deficit and no Ricardo-Barro effect, the total quantity of loanable funds demanded equals the quantity of investment plus the government budget deficit of $1.0 trillion. Using this result, the total demand for loanable funds is labeled *DLF* in Figure 10.12. This curve equals the private demand for loanable funds curve plus an additional $1.0 trillion at every real interest rate. The equilibrium real interest rate is 7 percent, the equilibrium quantity of loanable funds is $2.5 trillion, and the quantity of investment decreases to $1.5 trillion; pages 255-256.

d. With a $1.0 trillion government deficit, the Ricardo-Barro effect asserts that private saving increases by the amount of the deficit. So at every interest rate, the quantity of loanable funds is $1 trillion more than the amount given in the table. The total supply of loanable funds curve with the Ricardo-Barro effect is *SLF* in Figure 10.12. The equilibrium real interest rate is 5 percent, the equilibrium quantity of loanable funds is $3.0 trillion, and investment is $2.0 trillion. This amount of investment is the same as in part (a); page 256.

Short answer and numeric questions

1. The crowding-out effect is the tendency for a government budget deficit to decrease private investment. It occurs because a government deficit increases the demand for loanable funds, thereby raising the real interest rate and decreasing investment; pages 255-256.

2. The Ricardo-Barro effect says that private savers increase their saving in response to a government budget deficit. Private saving offsets any change in government saving. In this case, a government budget deficit has no effect on the equilibrium quantity of loanable funds, investment, or the equilibrium real interest rate; page 254.

3. The decision to finance a college education using loans is very similar to a firm's decision to finance a piece of capital equipment using loans. In both cases, the payoff from the purchase occurs throughout the future and the payments for the purchase are also made throughout the future. A business, of course, looks at the expected future profit from the capital before the business buys it. Similarly, one of the benefits from a college education is higher future income. These are reasons why a college education is said to help develop a person's "human capital."

Additional Exercises (also in MyEconLab Test A)

1. The real interest rate is 6 percent, and the quantity of loanable funds, private saving, and investment are all $8.5 trillion. There is no crowding out; page 250.

2. The equilibrium real interest rate becomes 7 percent. The equilibrium quantity of loanable funds is $9.0 trillion, the equilibrium quantity of investment is $8.0 trillion, and the equilibrium quantity of private saving is $9.0 trillion. There is crowding out of $500 billion of investment; pages 255-256.

3. Assuming no Ricardo-Barro effect, the government needs to have a budget surplus of $1 trillion. In this case, the new equilibrium real interest rate is 5 percent, the quantity of investment is $9 trillion, and the quantity of private saving is $8 trillion; pages 254-255.

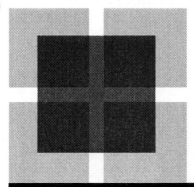

The Monetary System

Chapter 11

1 Define money and describe its functions.

Money is any commodity or token that is generally accepted as a means of payment. Money serves as a medium of exchange, a unit of account, and a store of value. Money consists of currency (dollar bills and coins outside of banks) and deposits at banks and other financial institutions. Currency in a bank, credit cards, debit cards, and electronic checks are not money. M1 (currency, traveler's checks, and checkable deposits owned by individuals and businesses) and M2 (M1 plus savings and small time deposits, money market funds and other deposits) are two measures of money.

2 Describe the functions of banks.

Banks (and other financial institutions) accept deposits and provide services that enable payments to be made and received. Banks profit by making loans at a higher interest rate than the interest rate paid on deposits. A bank's reserves are the currency in its vault and the balance in its reserve account at a Federal Reserve Bank. The Fed sets the required reserve ratio, the minimum percentage of deposits that must be held as reserves. The federal funds rate is the interest rate on interbank loans.

3 Describe the functions of the Federal Reserve System (the Fed).

The Federal Reserve System is the U.S. central bank. The Federal Open Market Committee is the Fed's main policy-making committee. The Fed has four policy tools: required reserve ratios, discount rate (the interest rate at which the Fed stands ready to lend reserves to commercial banks), open market operations (purchase or sale of government securities by the Fed in the open market), and extraordinary crisis measures (quantitative easing, credit easing [the Fed buys private securities], and operation twist). The monetary base is the sum of coins, Federal Reserve notes, and banks' reserves held at the Fed.

4 Explain how the banking system creates money and how the Fed controls the quantity of money.

When a bank makes a loan, it deposits the loan in the borrower's checkable deposit, thereby creating money. To spend the loan, the borrower writes a check. The loaning bank loses deposits and reserves when the check clears. The bank in which the check is deposited gains the reserves and deposits. It now has excess reserves, which it lends. This process eventually concludes because at each round the change in excess reserves shrinks. Open market operations change the quantity of money. If the Fed buys government securities, banks' excess reserves increase, banks lend the excess reserves, new deposits are created, and the quantity of money increases. If the Fed sells government securities, the reverse occurs. The monetary base changes by the amount of the open market operation. The money multiplier is the number by which a change in the monetary base is multiplied to find the change in the quantity of money; it equals $(1 + C/D) \div (R/D + C/D)$ where C is currency, D is deposits and R is reserves so C/D is the currency drain ratio and R/D is the desired reserve ratio.

CHECKPOINT 11.1

■ Define money and describe its functions.

Quick Review

- *M1* M1 consists of currency held by individuals and businesses, traveler's checks, and checkable deposits owned by individuals and businesses. Currency inside banks is not counted as part of M1.
- *M2* M2 consists of M1 plus savings deposits and small time deposits, money market funds, and other deposits.

Additional Practice Problems 11.1

1. You go to the bank and withdraw $200 from your checking account. You keep $100 in cash and deposit the other $100 in your savings account. What is the change in M1? What is the change in M2?

2. Janice goes to her bank's website and transfers $300 from her checking account to her savings account. What is the change in M1? What is the change in M2

3. In January 2001, currency held by individuals and businesses was $534.9 billion; traveler's checks were $8.1 billion; checkable deposits owned by individuals and businesses were $559.3 billion; savings deposits were $1,889.7 billion; small time deposits were $1,052.6 billion; and money market funds and other deposits were $952 billion.
   a. What was M1 in January 2001?
   b. What was M2 in January 2001?

Solutions to Additional Practice Problems 11.1

1. Your checking account decreased by $200, your currency increased by $100, and your savings account increased by $100. M1, which includes your currency and your checkable deposit, is changed by the decrease in the checking account and the increase in currency. The net effect on M1 is −$200 + $100 = −$100, that is, M1 decreases by $100. M2, which includes your currency, your checkable deposits, and your savings account, does not change. The change

in your checkable deposits, −$200, is balanced by the change in your currency, +$100, and the change in your savings account, +100. There was no change in M2.

2. M1 decreases by $300. While the funds were in Janice's checking account, they were part of M1. But once they are transferred to her savings account, they are no longer part of M1. M2 does not change. The $300 was part of M2 when it was in Janice's checking account because funds in checking accounts are part of M1 and all of M1 is in M2. And, funds in savings accounts are also part of M2. So switching funds from a checking account to a savings account does not change M2.

3a. M1 is the sum of currency, traveler's checks, and checkable deposits owned by individuals and businesses. So, M1 equals $534.9 billion + $8.1 billion + $559.3 billion, which is $1,102.3 billion.

3b. M2 equals M1 plus savings deposits, small time deposits, and money market funds and other deposits. So M2 equals $1,102.3 billion + $1,889.7 billion + $1,052.6 billion + $952 billion, which is $4,996.6 billion.

■ Self Test 11.1

Fill in the blanks

Any commodity or token that is generally accepted as a means of payment is ____. A ____ (unit of account; store of value; medium of exchange) is an object that is generally accepted in return for goods and services. A ____ (unit of account; store of value; medium of exchange) is an agreed-upon measure for stating prices of goods and services. A ____ (unit of account; store of value; medium of exchange) is any commodity or token that can be held and exchanged later for goods and services. Currency inside the banks ____ (is; is not) money and currency outside the banks ____ (is; is not) money. A credit card ____ (is; is not) money. M1 is ____ (more; less) than M2. Checkable deposits ____ (are; are not) part of M1 and savings deposits ____ (are; are not) part of M1.

True or false

1. Using money as a medium of exchange is called barter.
2. Prices in terms of money reflect money's role as a unit of account.
3. Currency is money but checkable deposits at banks are not money.
4. M1 and M2 are official measures of money.
5. A debit card is not money.

Multiple choice

1. Which of the following best defines what money is now and what it has been in the past?
   a. currency
   b. currency plus checking deposits
   c. currency plus credit cards
   d. anything accepted as a means of payment
   d. anything used as a store of value

2. Which of the following is not a function of money?
   i. unit of account
   ii. store of value
   iii. unit of debt
      a. i only.
      b. ii only.
      c. iii only.
      d. Both ii and iii.
      e. Both i and ii.

3. Barter is
   a. the exchange of goods and services for money.
   b. the pricing of goods and services with one agreed upon standard.
   c. the exchange of goods and services directly for other goods and services.
   d. a generally accepted means of payment.
   e. storing money for use at a later date.

4. If someone buries money in a tin can beneath a tree, the money is functioning as a
   a. medium of exchange.
   b. unit of account.
   c. means of payment.
   d. store of value.
   e. bartering tool.

5. Which of the following counts as part of M1?
   a. $5,000 worth of gold
   b. $5,000 worth of government bonds
   c. $5,000 in a checking account
   d. $5,000 credit line on a credit card
   e. $5,000 of real estate

6. M2 equals
   a. M1 and is just another name for currency outside of banks.
   b. M1 plus savings deposits, small time deposits, and money market fund deposits.
   c. M1 minus traveler's checks because they are not really money.
   d. currency plus savings deposits, all time deposits, and money market funds and other deposits.
   e. M1 plus savings deposits and small time deposits minus money market fund deposits.

7. If currency outside of banks is $800 billion; traveler's checks are $10 billion; checkable deposits owned by individuals and businesses are $700 billion; savings deposits are $4,000 billion; small time deposits are $1,000 billion; and money market funds and other deposits are $800 billion, then M1 equals ____ billion.
   a. $7,310
   b. $5,800
   c. $2,510
   d. $1,510
   e. $710

8. Credit cards, debit cards, and e-checks are
   a. always counted as money.
   b. not money.
   c. sometimes counted as money, depending on how they are used.
   d. sometimes counted as money, depending on what is purchased.
   e. sometimes counted as money, depending on what measure of money is being used.

Short answer and numeric questions

1. Why was it possible at one time to use whale's teeth as money?
2. What are the functions of money?
3. Why is currency money?

4. In January 2005, currency held outside of banks was $699.6 billion; traveler's checks were $7.5 billion; checkable deposits owned by individuals and businesses were $649.2 billion; savings deposits were $3,544.7 billion; small time deposits were $824.5 billion; and money market funds and other deposits were $711.4 billion.

a. What was M1 in January 2005?

b. What was M2 in January 2005?

5. Some parts of M2 are not money. Why are these parts included in M2?

6. Why are e-checks not money?

Additional Exercises (also in MyEconLab Test A)

1. Which of the following items are money in the United States today?

a. Checkable deposits at First Boston Bank

b. General Motors stock held by individuals

c. A Sacagawea dollar coin

d. U.S. government securities

e. Money market funds

2. Sara withdraws $2,000 from her time deposit account at Bank of America, keeps $100 in cash, and deposits the balance in her checking account at Citibank. What are the immediate changes in M1 and M2?

3. In March 2004, currency outside of banks was $666.8 billion; traveler's checks in circulation were $7.8 billion; checkable deposits owned by individuals and businesses were $651.1 billion; savings deposits were $3,279.1 billion; time deposits were $802.7 billion; and money market funds and other deposits were $760.5 billion. Calculate M1 and M2 in March 2004.

CHECKPOINT 11.2

■ **Describe the functions of banks.**

Quick Review

- *Reserves* A bank's reserves consist of the currency in its vault plus the balance on its reserve account at a Federal Reserve Bank.

Additional Practice Problems 11.2

1. The Acme Bank just sold $100 in securities in exchange for a $100 bill. It made a $50 loan, and the borrower left with the cash. It also accepted a $60 cash deposit.

a. How have the bank's reserves changed as a result of all these actions?

b. How have its deposits changed?

2. A bank has the following deposits and assets: $300 in checkable deposits, $800 in savings deposits, $900 in small time deposits, $1,000 in loans to businesses, $950 in government securities, $20 in currency, and $30 in its reserve account at the Fed. Calculate the bank's:

a. Total deposits

b. Deposits that are part of M1

c. Deposits that are part of M2

d. Reserves

e. What is the ratio of the bank's reserves to its deposits?

Solutions to Additional Practice Problems 11.2

1a. The $100 sale of securities adds $100 to reserves. The $50 loan which the borrower then withdrew as cash removes $50 from the bank and out of its reserves, and the $60 deposit adds to reserves. The net result is +$100 − $50 + $60, which is +$110. Acme has $110 more in reserves.

1b. The $60 deposit is the only transaction that affects its deposits, so deposits rise by $60.

2a. Total deposits are the sum of checkable deposits, $300, savings deposits, $800, and small time deposits, $900, which equals a total of $2,000.

2b. The only deposits that are part of M1 are checkable deposits, $300.

2c. All of the bank's deposits are part of M2, so deposits that are part of M2 are $2,000.

2d. Reserves are the currency in the bank's vault plus the balance on its reserve account at a Federal Reserve Bank. Reserves are $20 + $30, which equals $50.

2e. The ratio of reserves to deposits is $50 ÷ $2,000, which equals 2.5 percent.

■ Self Test 11.2

Fill in the blanks

The currency in a bank's vault is part of the bank's ____ (reserves; loans). Banks can borrow or lend reserves in the ____ (reserves; federal funds) market. At commercial banks in the United States, the majority of deposits ____ (are; are not) checkable deposits.

True or false

1. A commercial bank accepts checkable deposits, savings deposits, and time deposits.

2. A commercial bank maximizes its stockholders' wealth by refusing to make any risky loans.

3. When a credit union has excess reserves, it makes loans to its members at an interest rate called the federal funds rate.

Multiple choice

1. A commercial bank's main goal is to
   a. provide loans to its customers.
   b. maximize the wealth of its stockholders.
   c. help the government when it needs money.
   d. lend money to the Federal Reserve banks.
   e. open checking and savings accounts.

2. A commercial bank's reserves are
   a. bonds issued by the U.S. government that are very safe.
   b. the provision of funds to businesses and individuals.
   c. currency in its vault plus the balance on its reserve account at a Federal Reserve Bank.
   d. savings and time deposits.
   e. its loans.

3. Which of the flowing lists includes only banks' assets?
   a. liquid assets, loans, securities, and reserves.
   b. reserves, savings deposits, securities, and loans.
   c. reserves, securities, and savings deposits
   d. securities, reserves, checkable deposits, and liquid assets.
   e. reserves, checkable deposits, and loans.

4. A bank has $400 in checkable deposits, $800 in savings deposits, $700 in time deposits, $900 in loans to businesses, $300 in outstanding credit card balances, $500 in government securities, $10 in currency in its vault, and $20 in deposits at the Fed. The bank's deposits that are part of M1 equal
   a. $1,900.
   b. $400.
   c. $1,210.
   d. $530.
   e. $410.

5. Which of the following accepts deposits from and/or sell shares to the general public?
   i. money market funds
   ii. thrift institutions
   iii. commercial banks
   a. i only.
   b. ii only.
   c. iii only.
   d. ii and iii.
   e. i, ii, and iii.

6. Which of the following is a thrift institution?
   a. a savings and loan association
   b. a money market fund
   c. a commercial bank
   d. a loan institution
   e. the Federal Reserve

Short answer and numeric questions

1. What are a bank's reserves? How does a bank use its account at the Federal Reserve Bank?

Additional Exercises (also in MyEconLab Test A)

1. Explain how a bank makes a profit.

A savings and loan association (S&L) has $550 in checkable deposits, $1,600 in home loans, $900 in savings deposits, $600 in government securities, $800 in time deposits, $50 in currency, and no deposit at the Fed. Use this information to answer Exercises 2, 3, and 4.

2. Calculate the S&L's total deposits, deposits that are part of M1, and deposits that are part of M2.

3. Calculate the S&L's loans and reserves.

4. On which items does the S&L pay interest and on which items does it receive interest?

CHECKPOINT 11.3

■ **Describe the functions of the Federal Reserve System (the Fed).**

Quick Review

- *Federal Reserve System* The Federal Reserve System is the central bank of the United States.

Additional Practice Problems 11.3

1. What are required reserve ratios?

2. What is the discount rate?

3. In August, 2005 Federal Reserve notes and coins were $785 billion, and banks' reserves at the Fed were $9 billion, the gold stock was $11 billion, and the Fed owned $742 billion of government securities. What did the monetary base equal?

Solutions to Additional Practice Problems 11.3

1. Banks are required by law to hold a certain fraction of their deposits as reserves. The Federal Reserve determines what fraction banks must hold as reserves. These fractions are called the banks' required reserve ratios.

2. Banks can borrow reserves from the Federal Reserve. The interest rate they pay on these loans is the discount rate.

3. The monetary base is the sum of the coins and Federal Reserve notes plus banks' reserves at the Fed. In this case the monetary base equals $785 billion + $9 billion, which is $794 billion.

■ **Self Test 11.3**

Fill in the blanks

There are _____ (2; 6; 12) Federal Reserve Banks. The Fed's main policy-making committee is the _____ (Board of Governors; Federal Open Market Committee). The Fed sets the minimum percentage of deposits that must be held as reserves, which is called the _____ (discount rate; required reserve ratio). The interest rate at which the Fed stands ready to lend reserves to commercial banks is the _____ (discount; open market operation) rate. Quantitative easing is an example of _____. The purchase or sale of government securities by the Federal Reserve is an _____.

True or false

1. The Federal Reserve System is the central bank of the United States.

2. An open market operation is the purchase or sale of government securities by the Federal Reserve from the U.S. government.

3. If banks use $1 million of reserves to buy $1 million worth of newly printed bank notes from the Fed, the monetary base does not change.

Multiple choice

1. Regulating the amount of money in the United States is one of the most important responsibilities of the
   a. State Department.
   b. state governments.
   c. Treasury Department.
   d. Federal Reserve.
   e. U.S. Mint.

2. The Board of Governors of the Federal Reserve System has
   a. 12 members appointed by the president of the United States.
   b. 12 members elected by the public.
   c. seven members appointed by the president of the United States.
   d. seven members elected by the public.
   e. seven members appointed to life terms.

3. The Fed's policy tools include
   a. required reserve ratios, the discount rate, open market operations, and extraordinary crisis measures.
   b. holding deposits for the U.S. government, reserve requirements, and the discount rate.
   c. setting regulations for lending standards and extraordinary crisis measures.
   d. supervision of the banking system and buying and selling commercial banks.
   e. required reserve ratios, income tax rates, and open market operations.

4. The Fed's policy is determined by the
   a. Federal Open Market Committee.
   b. Executive Council to the Governor.
   c. Regional Federal Reserve Banks.
   d. Board of Governors.
   e. Federal Monetary Policy Committee.

5. The minimum percent of deposits that banks must hold and cannot loan is determined by the
   a. interest rate.
   b. discount rate.
   c. required reserve ratio.
   d. federal funds rate.
   e. ratio of M2 to M1.

6. The discount rate is the interest rate that
   a. commercial banks charge their customers.
   b. commercial banks charge each other for the loan of reserves.
   c. the Fed charges the government for loans.
   d. the Fed charges commercial banks when it loans reserves to the banks.
   e. the Fed pays commercial banks on their reserves held at the Fed.

7. The monetary base is the
   a. minimum reserves banks must hold to cover any losses from unpaid loans.
   b. sum of coins, Federal Reserve notes, and banks' reserves at the Fed.
   c. sum of gold and foreign exchange held by the Fed.
   d. sum of government securities and loans to banks held by the Fed.
   e. sum of coins, required reserves, and bank loans.

8. If Federal Reserve notes and coins are $765 billion, and banks' reserves at the Fed are $8 billion, the gold stock is $11 billion, and the Fed owns $725 billion of government securities, what does the monetary base equal?
   a. $765 billion
   b. $773 billion
   c. $776 billion
   d. $744 billion
   e. $1,509 billion

9. If the Federal Reserve ____ the required reserve ratio, the interest rate ____.
   a. lowers; rises
   b. lowers; falls
   c. raises; does not change
   d. raises; falls
   e. Not enough information is given because the effect depends also on the size of the monetary base.

Short answer and numeric questions

1. How many people are on the Board of Governors of the Federal Reserve System? How are they selected?

2. What is the FOMC and who are its members?

3. Suppose that banks' deposits are $600 billion and that the required reserve ratio is 10 percent.
   a. What is the minimum amount of reserves banks must hold?
   b. Suppose the Federal Reserve lowers the required reserve ratio to 8 percent. Now what is the minimum amount of reserves banks must hold?
   c. Suppose the Federal Reserve raises the required reserve ratio to 12 percent. Now what is the minimum amount of reserves banks must hold?

4. What is the monetary base?

Additional Exercises (also in MyEconLab Test A)

1. What is a central bank and what is the central bank in the United States?

2. Suppose that in September 2019, the monetary base in the United States was $750 billion, Federal Reserve notes were $630 billion, and the quantity of coins was $40 billion. What were the commercial banks' deposits at the Fed?

3. Suppose that in December 2019, the monetary base in Canada was $85 billion, Bank of Canada notes were $75 billion, and the quantity of coins was $3 billion. What were the reserve deposits of the Canadian banks at the Bank of Canada?

CHECKPOINT 11.4

■ **Explain how the bank system creates money and how the Fed controls the quantity of money.**

Quick Review

- *Excess reserves* Excess reserves equal actual reserves minus desired reserves.
- *Money multiplier* The number by which a change in the monetary base is multiplied to find the resulting change in the quantity of money.

Additional Practice Problems 11.4

1. The desired reserve ratio is 0.05 and banks have no excess reserves. Katie deposits $500 in currency in her bank. Calculate:
    a. The change in the bank's reserves as soon as Katie makes the deposit.
    b. The bank's excess reserves as soon as Katie makes the deposit.
    c. The maximum amount that Katie's bank can loan.

2. If the desired reserve ratio is 10 percent and the currency drain ratio is 30 percent of deposits, what is the size of the money multiplier? By how much will a $10 billion increase in the monetary base change the quantity of money?

3. If the desired reserve ratio is 20 percent and the currency drain ratio is 30 percent of deposits, what is the size of the money multiplier? By how much will a $10 billion increase in the monetary base change the quantity of money?

4. Using problems 2 and 3, what is the effect on the money multiplier when the desired reserve ratio rises?

Solutions to Additional Practice Problems 11.4

1a. The new deposit of $500 increases the bank's actual reserves by $500.

1b. The bank wants to keep 5 percent of deposits as reserves. So desired reserves increase by 5 percent of the deposit, or ($500) × (0.05), which is $25. As a result, excess reserves,

which are actual reserves minus desired reserves, increase by $500 − $25, which is $475.

1c. The crucial point to keep in mind is that banks can loan their excess reserves in order to boost their revenue and profit. So Katie's bank can loan a maximum of $475.

2. The money multiplier = $(1 + C/D) \div (R/D + C/D)$ where C/D is the currency drain ratio and R/D is the desired reserve ratio. So the money multiplier equals $(1 + 0.3) \div (0.1 + 0.3)$, which is 3.25. With this money multiplier, a $10 billion increase in the monetary base increases the quantity of money by 3.25 × $10 billion, or $32.5 billion.

3. The money multiplier = $(1 + C/D) \div (R/D + C/D)$ where C/D is the currency drain ratio and R/D is the desired reserve ratio. The money multiplier equals $(1 + 0.3) \div (0.2 + 0.3)$, which is 2.6. A $10 billion increase in the monetary base increases the quantity of money by 2.6 × $10 billion, or $26 billion.

4. An increase in the desired reserve ratio shrinks the size of the money multiplier.

■ Self Test 11.4

Fill in the blanks

When the Fed purchases government securities, it _____ (decreases; increases) the quantity of money. An open market sale of government securities by the Fed _____ (decreases; increases) the monetary base and _____ (decreases; increases) banks' excess reserves. An increase in currency held outside the banks is called _____ (an excess currency removal; a currency drain; a multiplier reserve). If the money multiplier is 2.0, a $4 million increase in the monetary base will create an increase of _____ ($2; $8) million in the quantity of money. The larger the desired reserve ratio, the _____ (larger; smaller) is the _____ (currency drain; money multiplier).

True or false

1. When a bank increases its loans, it creates money.

2. The desired reserve ratio has no effect on the amount of money banks can create.

3. When the Fed buys securities in an open market operation, it pays for them with newly created bank reserves.

4. When the Fed buys government securities, the effect on the money supply depends on whether the Fed buys the securities from a bank or the general public.

5. When the Fed sells government securities, it decreases the quantity of banks' reserves.

6. If the Fed increases the monetary base by $1 billion, the ultimate increase in the quantity of money will be less than $1 billion.

7. The larger the currency drain ratio, the larger the money multiplier.

8. If the currency drain ratio is 20 percent and the desired reserve ratio is 10 percent, the money multiplier is 1.675.

Multiple choice

1. Excess reserves are the
   a. same as the required reserves.
   b. amount of reserves the Fed requires banks to hold.
   c. amount of reserves held above what is desired.
   d. amount of reserves a bank holds at the Fed.
   e. amount of reserves banks keep in their vaults.

2. Banks can make loans up to an amount equal to their
   a. total deposits.
   b. total reserves.
   c. required reserves.
   d. excess reserves.
   e. total government securities.

3. If the Fed buys government securities, then
   a. the quantity of money is not changed, just its composition.
   b. new bank reserves are created.
   c. the quantity of money decreases.
   d. bank reserves are destroyed.
   e. banks' excess reserves decrease.

4. The Citizens First Bank sells $100,000 of government securities to the Fed. This sale immediately
   a. decreases the quantity of money.
   b. decreases the bank's checkable deposits.
   c. increases the bank's reserves.
   d. decreases the bank's assets.
   e. increases the bank's required reserves.

5. When the Fed sells securities in an open market operation
   a. the monetary base increases and the quantity of money increases.
   b. the monetary base does not change.
   c. only commercial banks can be buyers.
   d. the monetary base does not change.
   e. buyers pay for the securities with money and bank reserves.

6. When the Fed conducts an open market purchase, the first round changes in the money creation process are that excess reserves ____, bank deposits ____, and the quantity of money ____.
   a. decreases; decreases; decrease
   b. increases; do not change; increase
   c. decreases; increases; does not change
   d. do not change; increases; increase
   e. increase; increase; increases

7. The money multiplier is used to determine how much the
   a. monetary base increases when the Fed purchases government securities.
   b. quantity of money increases when the monetary base increases.
   c. monetary base increases when the quantity of money increases.
   d. quantity of money increases when the required reserve ratio increases.
   e. monetary base increases when the Fed sells government securities.

8. A currency drain is cash ____ and has ____ effect on the money multiplier.
   a. draining into the banks; no
   b. draining into the banks; an
   c. held outside the banks; an
   d. held at the Fed; an
   e. held as reserves; no

9. The Fed makes an open market operation purchase of $200,000. The currency drain ratio is 30 percent of deposits and the desired reserve ratio is 10 percent. By how much does the quantity of money increase?
   a. $800,000
   b. $333,333
   c. $2,000,000
   d. $650,000
   e. $465,116

Short answer and numeric questions

Round	Increase in deposits (dollars)	Increase in currency (dollars)	Increase in reserves (dollars)	Increase in excess reserves (dollars)
A			1,000	1,000
B	____	____	____	____
C	____	____	____	____
D	____	____	____	____

1. Suppose the Fed buys $1,000 of government securities from Hayward National Bank. The desired reserve ratio is 10 percent and the currency drain ratio is 25 percent of deposits. Suppose that all banks loan all of their excess reserves. Complete the above table. Calculate the total increase in deposits and currency following the first four rounds of the multiplier process.

Round	Increase in deposits (dollars)	Increase in currency (dollars)	Increase in reserves (dollars)	Increase in excess reserves (dollars)
A			1,000	1,000
B	____	____	____	____
C	____	____	____	____
D	____	____	____	____

2. Suppose the Fed buys $1,000 of government securities from Fremont National Bank. The desired reserve ratio is 10 percent and the currency drain ratio is 100 percent of deposits. Suppose that all banks loan all of their excess reserves. Complete the above table. Calculate the total increase in deposits and currency following the first four rounds of the multiplier process.

3. In which question, 1 or 2, was the increase in the quantity of money largest after four rounds?

4. Calculate the money multiplier when the desired reserve ratio is 10 percent and the currency drain ratio is 20 percent of deposits. Calculate the money multiplier when the desired reserve ratio is 10 percent and the currency drain ratio is 60 percent of deposits. As the currency drain ratio increases, what happens to the magnitude of the money multiplier?

5. Calculate the money multiplier when the desired reserve ratio is 10 percent and the currency drain ratio is 20 percent of deposits. Calculate the money multiplier when the desired reserve ratio is 20 percent and the currency drain ratio is 20 percent of deposits. As the desired reserve ratio increases, what happens to the magnitude of the money multiplier?

6. Why does an increase in the desired reserve ratio or in the currency drain ratio decrease the magnitude of the money multiplier?

7. The Eye on Your Life talks about your role in creating money. Money also will play a role in your life if you travel because nations often have different moneys. But the U.S. dollar is often accepted, especially in less developed nations. If you take some dollars with you when you travel and then spend a U.S. dollar bill in another nation, how does that affect the amount of U.S. M1?

Additional Exercises (also in MyEconLab Test A)

1. Your bank manager tells you that she doesn't create money: she just lends what is deposited. Explain why she is wrong and how she creates money.

2. If the Fed makes an open market sale of $1

million of securities, what initial changes occur in the economy and what is the process by which the quantity of money in the economy changes?

3. If the Fed makes an open market sale of $1 million of securities, by how much does the quantity of money change and what is the magnitude of the money multiplier?

SELF TEST ANSWERS

■ CHECKPOINT 11.1

Fill in the blanks

Any commodity or token that is generally accepted as a means of payment is <u>money</u>. A <u>medium of exchange</u> is an object that is generally accepted in return for goods and services. A <u>unit of account</u> is an agreed-upon measure for stating prices of goods and services. A <u>store of value</u> is any commodity or token that can be held and exchanged later for goods and services. Currency inside the banks <u>is not</u> money and currency outside the banks <u>is</u> money. A credit card <u>is not</u> money. M1 is <u>less</u> than M2. Checkable deposits <u>are</u> part of M1 and savings deposits <u>are not</u> part of M1.

True or false
1. False; page 265
2. True; page 265
3. False; page 266
4. True; page 266
5. True; page 268

Multiple choice
1. d; page 264
2. c; page 264
3. c; page 265
4. d; page 265
5. c; page 266
6. b; page 266
7. d; page 267
8. b; pages 267-268

Short answer and numeric questions
1. It was possible to use whale's teeth as money because whale's teeth were generally accepted as a means of payment. At one time, most people were willing to trade goods and services in exchange for whale's teeth; pages 264-265.
2. Money has three functions. It is a medium of exchange, an object that is generally accepted in return for goods and services. It is a unit of account, an agreed-upon measure for stating the prices of goods and services. And it is a store of value, a commodity or token that can be held and exchanged at a later date for goods and services; pages 264-265.

3. Currency is money because it is generally accepted as a means of payment. It is generally accepted because the government has declared that currency is money, so that currency is fiat money; page 266.

4. a. M1 is the sum of currency, traveler's checks, and checkable deposits owned by individuals and businesses. So, M1 equals $699.6 billion + $7.5 billion + $649.2 billion, which is $1,356.3 billion; pages 266-267.

   b. M2 equals M1 plus savings deposits, small time deposits, and money market funds and other deposits. So M2 equals $1,356.3 billion + $3,544.7 billion + $824.5 billion + $711.4 billion, which is $6,436.9 billion; pages 266-267.

5. Time deposits, money market funds, and some of the savings deposits included in M2 are not money. They are not money because they are not a means of payment. They are included in M2 because they are very easily converted into money; page 267.

6. E-checks are not money because they are instructions to transfer money from one person's deposit account to another person's deposit account; page 268.

Additional Exercises (also in MyEconLab Test A)
1. a. Checkable deposits are money; page 266.
   b. General Motors stock is not money because it is not a medium of exchange; page 265.
   c. The Sacagawea dollar coin is money; page 266.
   d. U.S. government securities are not money because they are not a medium of exchange; page 265.
   e. Money market funds are not money. They are not a means of payment; page 265.

2. M1 immediately rises by the full amount of the $2,000 withdrawal. The reason is that before, this $2,000 was only a part of M2 not

M1. Now because both cash and checkable accounts are part of M1, M1 rises by $2,000. However, because M2 includes everything that is a part of M1, M2 is left unchanged; page 266.

3. M1 = currency + traveler's checks + checkable deposits = $666.8 billion + $7.8 billion + $651.1 billion = $1,325.7 billion; page 266.

M2 = M1 + saving deposits + time deposits + money market funds = $1,325.7 billion + $3,279.1 billion + $802.7 billion + $760.5 billion = $6,168.0 billion; page 266.

■ CHECKPOINT 11.2

Fill in the blanks

The currency in a bank's vault is part of the bank's <u>reserves</u>. Banks can borrow or lend reserves in the <u>federal funds</u> market. At commercial banks in the United States, the majority of deposits <u>are not</u> checkable deposits.

True or false
1. True; page 270
2. False; page 271
3. False; page 272

Multiple choice
1. b; page 271
2. c; page 271
3. a; page 272
4. b; page 272
5. e; pages 270, 273
6. a; page 273

Short answer and numeric questions
1. A bank's reserves are the currency in its vault plus the balance on its reserve account at a Federal Reserve Bank. A bank uses its account at the Fed to receive and make payments to other banks and to obtain currency; page 271.

Additional Exercises (also in MyEconLab Test A)
1. A bank makes a profit by making loans at a higher interest rate than the interest rate it pays on its deposits; page 271.

2. Total deposits = checkable deposits + savings deposits + time deposits = $550 + $900 + $800 = $2,250. The only deposits that are part of M1 are the checking deposits of $550. The entire $2,250 of deposits are part of M2; page 266.

3. Total loans are $1,600. Reserves are deposits at the Fed plus currency. Because there are no reserves at the Fed, the reserves equal currency, which is $50; page 271.

4. The S&L pays interest on checking deposits, on savings deposits, and on time deposits. It receives interest on the home loans and government securities; pages 272-273.

■ CHECKPOINT 11.3

Fill in the blanks

There are <u>12</u> Federal Reserve Banks. The Fed's main policy-making committee is the <u>Federal Open Market Committee</u>. The Fed sets the minimum percentage of deposits that must be held as reserves, which is called the <u>required reserve ratio</u>. The interest rate at which the Fed stands ready to lend reserves to commercial banks is the <u>discount</u> rate. Quantitative easing is an example of <u>an extraordinary crisis measure</u>. The purchase or sale of government securities by the Federal Reserve is an <u>open market operation</u>.

True or false
1. True; page 275
2. False; page 277
3. True; page 277

Multiple choice
1. d; page 275
2. c; page 276
3. a; page 276
4. a; page 276
5. c; page 276
6. d; page 277
7. b; page 277
8. b; page 277
9. b; page 277

Short answer and numeric questions

1. There are seven members on the Board of Governors of the Federal Reserve System. They are appointed by the president of the United States and confirmed by the U.S. Senate; page 276.

2. The FOMC is the Federal Open Market Committee and it is the main policy-making committee of the Federal Reserve. The members are the seven members of the Board of Governors, the president of the Federal Reserve Bank of New York, and, on an annual rotating basis, four presidents of the other regional Federal Reserve banks; page 276.

3. a. If the required reserve ratio is 10 percent, banks must keep ($600 billion × 0.10) = $60 billion as reserves; page 276.

   b. If the required reserve ratio is lowered to 8 percent, banks must keep ($600 billion × 0.08) = $48 billion as reserves. A decrease in the required reserve ratio decreases the total amount of reserves banks must keep; page 275.

   c. If the required reserve ratio is raised to 12 percent, banks must keep ($600 billion × 0.12) = $72 billion as reserves. An increase in the required reserve ratio increases the total amount of reserves banks must keep page 276.

4. The monetary base is the sum of coins, Federal Reserve notes, and banks' reserves at the Federal Reserve; page 277.

Additional Exercises (also in MyEconLab Test A)

1. A central bank is a public authority that provides banking services to banks and regulates financial institutions and markets. The central bank of the United States is the Federal Reserve System; page 275.

2. The monetary base is the sum of coins, Federal Reserve notes, and banks' reserves at the Federal Reserve. In the question, the monetary base is $750 billion, Federal Reserve notes are $630 billion, and coins are $40 billion. Banks' deposits at the Fed equal $80 billion, which is the monetary base minus Federal Reserve notes and coins; page 277.

3. Similar to the previous exercise, reserves of the Canadian banks at the Bank of Canada equal $7 billion, the monetary base minus Bank of Canada notes and coins; page 277.

■ CHECKPOINT 11.4

Fill in the blanks

When the Fed purchases government securities, it increases the quantity of money. An open market sale of government securities by the Fed decreases the monetary base and decreases banks' excess reserves. An increase in currency held outside the banks is called a currency drain. If the money multiplier is 2.0, a $4 million increase in the monetary base will create an increase of $8 million in the quantity of money. The larger the desired reserve ratio, the smaller is the money multiplier.

True or false

1. True; page 279
2. False; page 280
3. True; pages 281-284
4. False; pages 282-283
5. True; page 284
6. False; pages 284-285
7. False; page 287
8. False; page 287

Multiple choice

1. c; page 280
2. d; page 280
3. b; page 282
4. c; page 282
5. e; page 284
6. e; page 284
7. b; page 285
8. c; pages 285-287
9. d; pages 285-287

Short answer and numeric questions

Round	Increase in deposits (dollars)	Increase in currency (dollars)	Increase in reserves (dollars)	Increase in excess reserves (dollars)
A			1,000.00	1,000.00
B	800.00	200.00	800.00	720.00
C	576.00	144.00	576.00	518.40
D	414.72	103.68	414.72	373.25

1. The completed table is above. After four rounds, currency increases by $447.68, deposits increase by $1,790.72, and the quantity of money increases by the sum of the increase in currency and the increase in deposits, which is $2,238.40; page 284.

Round	Increase in deposits (dollars)	Increase in currency (dollars)	Increase in reserves (dollars)	Increase in excess reserves (dollars)
A			1,000	1,000
B	500.00	500.00	500.00	450.00
C	225.00	225.00	225.00	202.50
D	101.25	101.25	101.25	91.13

2. The completed table is above. After four rounds, currency increases by $826.25, deposits increase by $826.25, and the quantity of money increases by the sum of the increase in currency and the increase in deposits, which is $1,652.50; page 284.

3. The increase in the quantity of money is greater when the currency drain is smaller, in question 1; page 287.

4. The money multiplier = $(1 + C/D) \div (R/D + C/D)$ where C/D is the currency drain ratio and R/D is the desired reserve ratio. The money multiplier for the first part of the question equals $(1 + 0.20) \div (0.20 + 0.10)$, or $(1.20) \div (0.30)$ which is 4.00. The money multiplier for the second part of the question is $(1 + 0.60) \div (0.60 + 0.10)$, or $(1.60) \div (0.70)$, which is 2.29. As the currency drain ratio increases, the magnitude of the money multiplier decreases; pages 286-287.

5. The money multiplier = $(1 + C/D) \div (R/D + C/D)$ where C/D is the currency drain ratio and R/D is the desired reserve ratio. The money multiplier for the first part of the question equals $(1 + 0.20) \div (0.20 + 0.10)$, or $(1.20) \div (0.30)$ which is 4.00. The money multiplier for the second part of the question is $(1 + 0.20) \div (0.20 + 0.20)$, or $(1.20) \div (0.40)$, which is 3.00. As the desired reserve ratio increases, the magnitude of the money multiplier decreases; pages 286-287.

6. The money multiplier exists because of the repeating process of loaning, depositing the proceeds in another bank, and then making another loan. The more each bank loans, the greater the final increase in the quantity of money and the larger the money multiplier. If the desired reserve ratio increases in size, banks will be able to loan less of any additional deposit they receive. And if the currency drain ratio increases, less is deposited in a bank and the bank will be able to loan less. Because an increase in the desired reserve ratio and an increase in the currency drain ratio decrease the amount that can be loaned, both decrease the size of the money multiplier; pages 284-285.

7. If you spend a U.S. dollar bill in another country, there is no effect on the amount of U.S. M1. Indeed, there are estimates that upwards of one half of all U.S. currency is abroad, being used by foreign residents. But the precise amount of U.S. currency abroad is very difficult to measure because often the currency is used for illegal purposes and hence the users are not terribly eager to line up to have their holdings counted by their government!

Additional Exercises (also in MyEconLab Test A)

1. Explain to the bank manager that when the bank makes a loan, it creates a checkable deposit that previously did not exist. Because checkable deposits are part of M1, then we can safely say that making a loan is the equivalent of creating money; page 279.

2. When the Fed sells securities to banks, the Fed receives payment for the securities. If banks directly buy the securities, the payment will be by decreasing the reserves of the banks from to which it sells the securities.

If members of the non-bank buy the securities, the Fed will receive payment in the form of a check drawn on the purchaser's bank and the Fed will "cash" the check by decreasing that bank's reserves. In either case, banks have fewer reserves to loan. Banks' excess reserves fall, so banks call in loans, refuse to renew loans, and make fewer new loans. Bank deposits decrease so that the quantity of money decreases. The initial decrease in the quantity of money spreads as people cut back on their purchases so that firms receive less money in exchange. These firms' banks then have fewer reserves, so they must cut loans, and the process circles into another round; page 284.

3. If the Fed makes an open market sale of $1 million of securities, the quantity of money will decrease by more than $1 million. The quantity of money decreases by an amount equal to the initial decrease in reserves ($1 million) multiplied by the money multiplier. The magnitude of the money multiplier is inversely related to the size of the desired reserve ratio and to the currency drain ratio; that is, an increase in either the desired reserve ratio or the currency drain ratio decreases the magnitude of the money multiplier; pages 284, 286.

Money, Interest, and Inflation

Chapter 12

Chapter 12 discusses how the quantity of money determines the equilibrium nominal interest rate and then studies the relationship between money and the price level. The effects of money on the economy differ in the short run and the long run. This chapter looks at the short run and long run but not at how the long run is reached—examining these ripple effects is the task of the next two chapters.

1 **Explain what determines the demand for money and how the demand for money and the supply of money determine the *nominal* interest rate.**

The amount of money that households and firms choose to hold is the quantity of money demanded. The nominal interest rate is the opportunity cost of holding money. The demand for money curve shows the quantity of money demanded at each nominal interest rate. The supply of money is a fixed quantity. Equilibrium in the money market determines the nominal interest rate. In the short run, the Fed changes the nominal interest rate by changing the quantity of money. When the Fed increases the quantity of money, the nominal interest rate falls

2 **Explain how in the long run, the quantity of money determines the price level and money growth brings inflation.**

In the long run, the value of money adjusts to make the quantity of money demanded equal to the quantity supplied. The price level equals the GDP price index divided by 100, so the value of money is the inverse of the price level, $1/P$. If the price level rises, the value of money falls. The long-run demand for money curve shows the quantity of money demanded at each value of money. In the long run, a change in the quantity of money brings an equal percentage change in the price level. The quantity theory of money is the proposition that when real GDP equals potential GDP, an increase in the quantity of money brings an equal percentage increase in the price level. The equation of exchange shows that the quantity of money multiplied by the velocity of circulation equals nominal GDP. In rates of change, the equation of exchange is money growth + velocity growth equals inflation + real GDP growth. In the long run, other things remaining the same, a change in the growth rate of the quantity of money brings an equal change in the inflation rate. A hyperinflation is inflation at a rate that exceeds 50 percent a month.

3 **Identify the costs of inflation and the benefits of a stable value of money.**

The four costs of inflation are tax costs, shoe-leather costs, confusion costs, and uncertainty costs. Inflation is a tax. With inflation, households and business lose purchasing power, which is the tax on holding money. Inflation interacts with the income tax to lower saving and investment. Shoe-leather costs are costs that arise from an increase in the amount of running around that people do to try to avoid the losses from the falling value of money. Confusion costs are costs of making errors because of rapidly changing prices. Uncertainty costs arise because long-term planning is difficult, so people have a shorter-term focus. Investment falls and the growth rate slows.

CHECKPOINT 12.1

■ **Explain what determines the demand for money and how the demand for money and the supply of money determine the *nominal* interest rate.**

Quick Review

* *Shifts in the demand for money curve* When real GDP, the price level, or financial technology change, the demand for money curve shifts.

* *Equilibrium nominal interest rate* The equilibrium nominal interest rate occurs where the demand for money curve intersects the supply curve because at this interest rate the quantity of money demanded equals the quantity supplied.

Additional Practice Problems 12.1

1. The figure shows the money market.

    a. What is the equilibrium nominal interest rate and quantity of money?

    b. Use the figure to show what happens to the interest rate if the Fed increases the quantity of money from $4.0 trillion to $4.1 trillion.

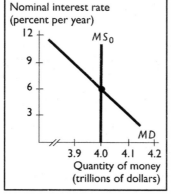

2. Tomorrow all stores will install retinal scanner identification machines, which allow people to make a purchase without having to carry a credit card. What effect will this technological advance have on the demand for money and on the nominal interest rate?

Solutions to Additional Practice Problems 12.1

1a. This problem shows how the nominal interest rate is determined in the money market. As the figure shows, the equilibrium interest rate is 6 percent because this is the interest rate at which the quantity of money demanded equals the quantity of money supplied. The equilibrium quantity of money is $4.0 trillion.

1b. The increase in the quantity of money shifts the supply of money curve rightward, from MS_0 to MS_1. The equilibrium nominal interest rate falls from 6 percent to 3 percent.

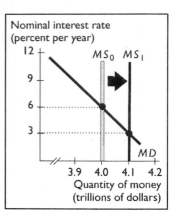

2. This change in technology makes credit purchases more attractive for consumers and merchants. There is an increase in credit purchases and a decrease in the purchases made with money. The demand for money decreases. People want to hold less money than they are actually holding. They buy bonds. The price of a bond rises and the nominal interest rate falls.

■ **Self Test 12.1**

Fill in the blanks

The nominal interest rate equals the real interest rate _____ (plus; minus; divided by) the inflation rate. The opportunity cost of holding money is the _____ (price level; nominal interest rate). An increase in real GDP _____ (increases; decreases) the demand for money and shifts the demand for money curve _____ (rightward; leftward). An increase in the price level _____ (increases; decreases) the demand for money. If the nominal interest rate is above the equilibrium level, people _____ (buy; sell) bonds, the price of a bond _____ (rises; falls), and the interest rate _____ (rises; falls). If the Fed decreases the quantity of money, _____ (supply of; demand for) money curve shifts and the nominal interest rate _____ (rises; falls).

True or false

1. The real interest rate is the opportunity cost of holding money.

2. An increase in real GDP decreases the demand for money.

3. If the price of a government bond rises, the interest rate on the bond rises.

4. When the interest rate is above its equilibrium level, people buy bonds and the interest rate falls.

5. An increase in the quantity of money lowers the interest rate.

Multiple choice

1. The quantity of money demanded
   a. is infinite.
   b. has no opportunity cost.
   c. is the quantity that balances the benefit of holding an additional dollar of money against the opportunity cost of doing so.
   d. is directly controlled by the Fed.
   e. changes very infrequently.

2. Which of the following statements is correct?
   a. Real interest rate – Inflation rate = Nominal interest rate
   b. Real interest rate + Inflation rate = Nominal interest rate
   c. Inflation rate – Real interest rate = Nominal interest rate
   d. Inflation rate + Price index = Nominal interest rate
   e. Inflation rate ÷ Real interest rate = Nominal interest rate

3. The opportunity cost of holding money is the
   a. real interest rate.
   b. nominal interest rate.
   c. inflation rate.
   d. time it takes to go to the ATM or bank.
   e. growth rate of real GDP.

4. The demand for money curve shows the relationship between the quantity of money demanded and
   a. the nominal interest rate.
   b. the real interest rate.
   c. the inflation rate.
   d. real GDP.
   e. nominal GDP.

5. The demand for money ____ when the ____.
   a. increases; price level rises
   b. decreases; price level rises
   c. remains constant; price level rises
   d. increases; nominal interest rate rises
   e. increases; supply of money decreases

6. Every day ____ adjusts to make the quantity of money demanded equal the quantity of money supplied.
   a. the inflation rate
   b. the nominal interest rate
   c. the quantity of money
   d. potential GDP
   e. real GDP

7. If the nominal interest rate is above its equilibrium level, then
   a. people sell financial assets and the interest rate falls.
   b. people buy financial assets and the interest rate falls.
   c. the demand for money curve shifts rightward and the interest rate rises.
   d. the supply of money curve shifts leftward and the interest rate rises.
   e. the demand curve for money shifts leftward and the interest rate falls.

8. When the Fed increases the quantity of money, the
   a. equilibrium nominal interest rate falls.
   b. equilibrium nominal interest rate rises.
   c. demand for money curve shifts rightward.
   d. supply of money curve shifts leftward.
   e. demand for money curve shifts leftward.

Nominal interest rate (percent per year)	Quantity of money, (trillions dollars)
5	3.1
6	3.0
7	2.9
8	2.8
9	2.7
10	2.6

9. The table above gives the demand for money schedule. When the Fed increases the quantity of money from $2.7 trillion to $2.9 trillion, the nominal interest rate ____ from ____.
   a. falls; 9 percent to 5 percent
   b. falls; 7 percent to 6 percent
   c. rises; 5 percent to 8 percent
   d. rises; 6 percent to 8 percent
   e. falls; 9 percent to 7 percent

■ **FIGURE 12.1**

Nominal interest rate (percent per year)

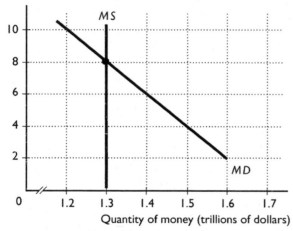

10. The figure above shows the money market. If the Fed increases the quantity of money from $1.3 trillion to $1.4 trillion, the nominal interest rate ____ from ____.
    a. falls; 9 percent to 7 percent
    b. falls; 8 percent to 6 percent
    c. rises; 5 percent to 8 percent
    d. rises; 6 percent to 8 percent
    e. falls; 12 percent to 7 percent

Complete the graph

Nominal interest rate (percent per year)	Quantity of money, (trillions dollars)
5	1.2
6	1.0
7	0.8
8	0.6
9	0.4
10	0.2

1. The table above has data on the nominal interest rate and the quantity of money demanded.

■ **FIGURE 12.2**

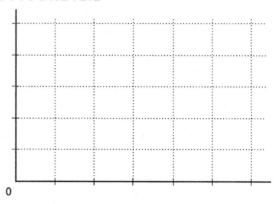

a. Using the data, label the axes and plot the demand for money curve in Figure 12.2.
b. Suppose the Fed sets the quantity of money at $0.6 trillion. Plot this quantity in Figure 12.2. What is the equilibrium nominal interest rate?
c. Suppose the Fed wants to change the nominal interest rate to 6 percent a year. What action must the Fed take?

2. Figure 12.3 (on the next page) shows a demand for money curve and a supply of money curve.
   a. What is the equilibrium nominal interest rate?
   b. Suppose the price level rises so that the demand for money changes by $0.2 trillion at every interest rate. Which direction does the demand for money curve shift? Draw the new demand for money curve in the figure. What is the equilibrium nominal interest rate?

■ **FIGURE 12.3**

Nominal interest rate (percent per year)

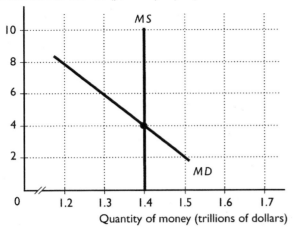

■ **FIGURE 12.4**

Nominal interest rate (percent per year)

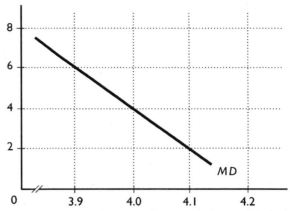

Short answer and numeric questions

1. What are the benefits from holding money?

2. What is the opportunity cost of holding money and why is this the opportunity cost?

3. What effect does an increase in real GDP have on the demand for money?

4. Suppose a government bond pays $100 in interest each year. If the price of the bond is $1,000, what is the interest rate? If the price of the bond is $2,000 dollars, what is the interest rate? As the price of the bond increases, what happens to the interest rate?

5. How can the Fed lower the nominal interest rate?

Additional Exercises (also in MyEconLab Test A)

1. Figure 12.4 shows the demand for money curve. The quantity of money supplied is $3.9 trillion. What is the nominal interest rate?

2. Figure 12.4 shows the demand for money curve. If real GDP decreases, how will the interest rate change? Explain what happens in the market for bonds as the money market returns to equilibrium.

3. Figure 12.4 shows the demand for money curve. If the Fed increases the quantity of money from $3.9 trillion to $4.0 trillion, what is the change in the nominal interest rate? What happens to the price of bonds?

4. Suppose that banks launch an aggressive marketing campaign to get everyone to use credit cards for every conceivable transaction. They offer prizes to new cardholders and slash the interest rate on outstanding credit card balances. How would the demand for money and the nominal interest rate change?

CHECKPOINT 12.2

■ **Explain how in the long run, the quantity of money determines the price level and money growth brings inflation.**

Quick Review

- *Value of money* The value of money is the inverse of the price level.

- *Inflation rate in the long run* In the long run and other things remaining the same, a given percentage change in the quantity of money brings an equal percentage change in the price level.

- *Quantity theory of money* The proposition that when real GDP equals potential GDP, an increase in the quantity of money brings an equal percentage increase in the price level.

- *Equation of exchange* States that the quantity of money multiplied by the velocity of circulation equals the price level multiplied by real GDP, that is $M \times V = P \times Y$.

Additional Practice Problems 12.2

1. How does an increase in the price level affect the value of money?

2. In the long run, how does an increase in the quantity of money affect the price level?

3. In the long run, according to the quantity theory of money, how does an increase in the growth rate of the quantity of money affect the inflation rate?

4. The quantity of money is $90 billion, real GDP is $900 billion, and the price level is 110. What is the velocity of circulation?

Solutions to Additional Practice Problems 12.2

1. An increase in the price level decreases the value of money because with the higher price level a given quantity of money can buyer fewer goods and services.

2. In the long run, the price level rises by the same proportion as the increase in the quantity of money.

3. In the long run, an increase in the growth rate of the quantity of money raises the inflation rate by the same percentage. For instance, if the growth rate of the quantity of money increases by 3 percentage points, in the long run the inflation rate increases by 3 percentage points.

4. The velocity of circulation is the number of times in a year that the average dollar of money gets used to buy final goods and services. The velocity of circulation is calculated using the formula $V = (P \times Y) \div M$. Nominal GDP, which equals $P \times Y$, is $990 billion. So velocity equals ($990 billion) ÷ $90 billion = 11.

■ Self Test 12.2

Fill in the blanks

The higher the price level, the ____ (higher; lower) the value of money. In the long run, an increase in the quantity of money ____ (raises; lowers) the value of money. Other things remaining the same, a given percentage increase in the quantity of money brings an equal per-

centage ____ (increase; decrease) in the price level in the long run. The proposition that when real GDP equals potential GDP, an increase in the quantity of money brings an equal percentage increase in the price level is the ____ (quality; inflation; quantity) theory of money. If the velocity of circulation does not change, the inflation rate equals the growth rate of the ____ (quantity of money; nominal interest rate) ____ (minus; divided by) the growth rate of real GDP. A hyperinflation occurs when ____ (potential GDP; the quantity of money; velocity) grows at a rapid pace.

True or false

1. The value of money is the inverse of the nominal interest rate.

2. The long-run demand for money curve is a vertical line.

3. In the long run, an increase in the quantity of money raises the price level.

4. $M \times P = V \times Y$ is the formula for the equation of exchange.

5. According to the quantity theory of money, in the long run with other things remaining the same, a 5 percent increase in the quantity of money brings a 5 percent increase in the price level.

6. According to the quantity theory of money, if the quantity of money grows 2 percent a year faster than before, the inflation rate falls 2 percentage points from what it had been before the increase in the growth rate of the quantity of money.

Multiple choice

1. In the long run, the price level adjusts
   a. so that the real interest rate equals the nominal interest rate.
   b. so that the inflation rate equals zero.
   c. to achieve money market equilibrium.
   d. so that the inflation rate equals the growth rate of real GDP.
   e. so that the inflation rate is moderate.

2. In the long run, an increase in the quantity of money _____ the value of money and _____ the price level.
   a. raises; raises
   b. does not change; raises
   c. raises; lowers
   d. lowers; raises
   e. lowers; lowers

3. Other things remaining the same, if the quantity of money increases by a given percentage, then in the long run the _____ by the same percentage.
   a. price level rises
   b. price level falls
   c. real interest rate rises
   d. real interest rate falls
   e. nominal interest rate falls

4. The quantity theory of money is a proposition about
   a. the Fed's methods used to change the quantity of money.
   b. nominal and real interest rate.
   c. the relationship between a change in the quantity of money and the price level.
   d. the relationship between financial assets and currency demanded.
   e. the nominal interest rate and the quantity of money demanded.

5. Suppose that $P \times Y$ is $5,000 million a year and the quantity of money is $500 million. Then the velocity of circulation is
   a. 50.
   b. 500.
   c. 10.
   d. 20.
   e. 2,500,000.

6. If the quantity of money grows at 3 percent a year, velocity does not grow, and real GDP grows at 2 percent a year, then the inflation rate equals
   a. 6 percent.
   b. 5 percent.
   c. 1 percent.
   d. −1 percent.
   e. 12 percent.

7. If the quantity of money grows at 4 percent a year, velocity grows at 2 percent, and real GDP grows at 2 percent a year, then the inflation rate equals
   a. 6 percent.
   b. 2 percent.
   c. 0 percent.
   d. 8 percent.
   e. 4 percent.

8. Hyperinflation is
   a. inflation caused by negative growth in the quantity of money.
   b. inflation at a rate that exceeds 50 percent a month.
   c. inflation caused by excessive growth in the demand for money.
   d. inflation at a rate that exceeds 5 percent a month.
   e. only theoretical and has never occurred in the real world.

Short answer and numeric questions
1. Why is $1/P$ equal to the value of money?
2. In the long run, what is the effect of a 5 percent increase in the quantity of money, other things remaining the same?

Year	Quantity of money (billions of dollars)	Velocity of circulation	Price level (2005 = 100)	Real GDP (billions of 2005 dollars)
2011	100	11	___	1,000
2012	110	11	___	1,000
2013	121	11	___	1,000

3. The table above gives data for the nation of Quantoland, a small nation to the south. In 2011, 2012, and 2013, real GDP equals potential GDP.
   a. Complete the table.
   b. Calculate the percentage change in the quantity of money in 2011 and 2012. Then calculate the percentage change in the price level in 2012 and 2013.
   c. What key proposition is illustrated in your answer to part (b)?

Year	Growth in quantity of money (percent)	Growth in velocity of circulation (percent)	Inflation rate (percent)	Growth in Real GDP (percent)
2011	4	2	___	3
2012	7	2	___	3
2013	___	1	4	3

4. The table above gives data for the nation of Velocoland, a small nation to the north. In 2011, 2012, and 2013, real GDP equals potential GDP.

   a. Complete the table.

   b. Between 2011 and 2012, by how much does the growth rate of the quantity of money change? By how much does the inflation rate change?

5. In the long run, if real GDP grows at 3 percent a year, velocity does not change, and the quantity of money grows at 5 percent a year, what is the inflation rate?

6. What is a hyperinflation? What leads to hyperinflation?

Additional Exercises (also in MyEconLab Test A)

1. In 2002, the United Kingdom was at full employment. Nominal GDP was £850 billion, the real interest rate was 5 percent per year, the inflation rate was 6 percent a year, and the price level was 120. Calculate the nominal interest rate. If the real interest rate remains unchanged when the inflation rate in the long run decreases to 3 percent a year, explain how the nominal interest rate changes.

2. In 2003, the United Kingdom was at full employment. Nominal GDP was £900 billion, the nominal interest rate was 8 percent per year, the price level was 130, and the velocity of circulation was constant at 2. What was the quantity of money in the United Kingdom?

3. In exercise 2, if the velocity of circulation remains at 2, money grows at 8 percent a year, and real GDP grows at 5 percent a year in the long run, what is the inflation rate in the long run?

■ **Identify the costs of inflation and the benefits of a stable value of money.**

Quick Review

- *The inflation rate and income tax* Inflation increases the nominal interest rate, and because income taxes are paid on nominal interest income, the true income tax rate rises with inflation.

Additional Practice Problem 12.3

1. In the island of Atlantis where you live, the inflation rate has been varying between 3 percent a year and 10 percent a year in recent years. You are willing to lend money if you are guaranteed a real interest rate of at least 2 percent a year. There are potential borrowers, but they will borrow only if they are guaranteed a real interest rate of not more than 5 percent a year.

   a. Can you successfully make a loan if everyone can accurately predict the inflation rate?

   b. Can you successfully make a loan if neither you nor the borrowers can accurately predict the inflation rate?

   c. What bearing does your answer to part b have on the cost of inflation?

Solution to Additional Practice Problem 12.3

1a. If you and potential borrowers can accurately predict the inflation rate, it is possible to make a loan. If everyone knows the inflation rate is 10 percent a year, you are willing to lend as long as you receive a nominal interest rate of at least 12 percent a year. Borrowers are willing to pay a real interest rate of no more than 5 percent a year, so borrowers are willing to agree to a loan as long as the nominal interest rate is no more than 15 percent a year. Because they are willing to pay up to 15 percent a year and you are willing to take as little as 12 percent a year, it is possible to make a loan with a nominal interest rate between 12 percent a year and 15 percent a year. Similarly, if everyone knows the inflation rate is 3 percent a year, a loan can be made with a nominal interest rate between 5 percent a year and 8 percent a year.

1b. To receive a real interest rate of at least 2 percent a year you must receive a nominal interest rate of at least 12 percent a year in case inflation is 10 percent a year. If borrowers pay a nominal interest rate of 12 percent a year and inflation is 3 percent a year, they are paying a real interest rate of 9 percent a year, well above their maximum real interest rate of 5 percent a year. Because of the uncertainty about the inflation rate, you don't make the loan.

1c. When inflation is uncertain, the loan is not made. Presumably the loan would benefit both the lender and the borrower. The fact it is not made means that both are worse off and reflects the uncertainty costs of inflation.

■ Self Test 12.3

Fill in the blanks

Inflation ____ (is; is not) a tax. The higher the inflation rate, the ____ (lower; higher) the true income tax rate on income from capital. During an inflation, the costs that arise from an increase in the velocity of circulation of money and an increase in the amount of running around to avoid incurring losses from the falling value of money are ____ (shoe-leather; confusion) costs. Increased uncertainty about inflation leads to a ____ (rise; fall) in investment.

True or false

1. Inflation is a tax.

2. The "shoe-leather costs" of inflation are the result of the increase in the velocity of circulation when inflation increases.

3. One of the benefits of inflation is that it makes the value of money change, which benefits both borrowers and lenders.

4. When there is a high inflation rate, the growth rate slows.

Multiple choice

1. Which of the following is <u>NOT</u> a cost of inflation?
   a. tax costs.
   b. confusion costs.
   c. uncertainty costs.
   d. government spending costs.
   e. shoe-leather costs.

2. Becky holds $30,000 as money. After a year during which inflation was 5 percent a year, the inflation tax over that year was
   a. $500.
   b. $1,000.
   c. $1,500.
   d. $3,000.
   e. $5.

3. Suppose a country has a real interest rate of 4 percent and an inflation rate of 3 percent. If the income tax rate is 20 percent, then the after-tax real interest rate is
   a. 2.6 percent a year.
   b. 4.0 percent a year.
   c. 5.6 percent a year.
   d. 7.0 percent a year.
   e. 1.4 percent a year.

4. Shoe-leather costs arise from inflation because the velocity of circulation of money ____ as the inflation rate ____.
   a. increases; falls
   b. decreases; rises
   c. increases; rises
   d. does not change; rises
   e. does not change; falls

5. A consequence of hyperinflation is that people
   a. who make fixed-payment loans to others receive higher payments as inflation increases.
   b. spend time trying to keep their money holdings near zero.
   c. receive higher real wage hikes, which increases their purchasing power for goods and services.
   d. want to lend funds because interest rates are so high.
   e. increase the quantity of money demanded.

6. The uncertainty costs of inflation cause people to
   a. increase their demand for money.
   b. increase investment causing growth to decrease.
   c. focus on the short run, which decreases investment and slows growth.
   d. focus on the long run, which increases investment and speeds growth.
   e. incur more shoe leather costs.

7. The costs of inflation ____ when inflation is more rapid and ____ when inflation is more unpredictable.
   a. increase; increase
   b. increase; decrease
   c. decrease; increase
   d. increase; do not change
   e. do not change; increase

8. It is estimated that if the inflation rate is lowered from 3 percent a year to 0 percent a year, the growth rate of real GDP will rise by ____ percentage points a year.
   a. 0.06 to 0.09
   b. 1 to 3
   c. 2.3
   d. 3.2
   e. 0

Short answer and numeric questions

1. Jose holds $600 of money. If the inflation rate is 5 percent a year, what is Jose's inflation tax?

2. The real interest rate is 2 percent a year and the inflation rate is zero percent a year. If the income tax rate is 25 percent, what is the real after-tax interest rate? If the inflation rate rises to 6 percent a year, what is the real after-tax interest rate? If the inflation rate rises to 10 percent a year, what is the real after-tax interest rate?

3. Why does the velocity of circulation increase in a hyperinflation?

4. On what factors does the cost of inflation depend?

5. The Eye on "What Causes Inflation?" on page 311 shows how the quantity theory can be used to predict inflation trends. How might this help you make decisions on your job?

Additional Exercises (also in MyEconLab Test A)
Sally has a credit card balance of $4,000. The credit card company charges a nominal interest rate of 18 percent a year on unpaid balances. The inflation rate is 3 percent a year.

1. Calculate the real interest rate that Sally pays the credit card company.

2. If the inflation rate falls to 2 percent a year and the nominal interest rate remains the same, calculate the real interest rate that Sally pays.

SELF TEST ANSWERS

■ CHECKPOINT 12.1

Fill in the blanks

The nominal interest rate equals the real interest rate <u>plus</u> the inflation rate. The opportunity cost of holding money is the <u>nominal interest rate</u>. An increase in real GDP <u>increases</u> the demand for money. An increase in the price level <u>increases</u> the demand for money and shifts the demand for money curve <u>rightward</u>. If the nominal interest rate is above the equilibrium level, people <u>buy</u> bonds, the price of a bond <u>rises</u>, and the interest rate <u>falls</u>. If the Fed decreases the quantity of money, <u>supply of</u> money curve shifts and the nominal interest rate <u>rises</u>.

True or false

1. False; pages 295-296
2. False; page 298
3. False; page 299
4. True; page 299
5. True; pages 300-301

Multiple choice

1. c; page 295
2. b; page 296
3. b; page 296
4. a; pages 296-297
5. a; page 297
6. b; page 298
7. b; page 299
8. a; pages 300-301
9. c; pages 300-301
10. b; pages 300-301

Complete the graph

1. a. Figure 12.5 plots the demand for money curve; page 297.
   b. Figure 12.5 shows the supply of money curve when the Fed sets the quantity of money at $0.6 trillion. The equilibrium nominal interest rate is 8 percent a year at the intersection of the *MD* and *MS* curves; pages 298-299.

■ FIGURE 12.5

Nominal interest rate (percent per year)

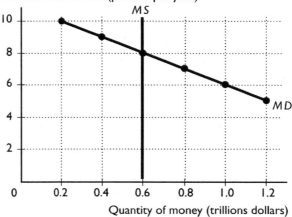

c. To lower the nominal interest rate to 6 percent a year, the Fed increases the quantity of money to $1.0 trillion; page 301.

■ FIGURE 12.6

Nominal interest rate (percent per year)

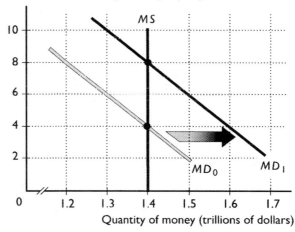

2. a. The equilibrium nominal interest rate is 4 percent; pages 298-299.
   b. The demand for money increases and the demand for money curve shifts rightward. Figure 12.6 shows the new equilibrium interest rate is 8 percent; pages 297, 300-301.

Short answer and numeric questions

1. The benefit from holding money is that a

person can use the money to make payments and do transactions; page 295.

2. The opportunity cost of holding money is the nominal interest rate. By holding money rather than a financial asset, the nominal interest rate is forgone. If Seemi can earn 5 percent a year on a bond, then holding $1,000 in money costs her $50 a year; pages 295-296.

3. An increase in real GDP increases the demand for money; page 297.

4. When the price of the bond is $1,000, the interest rate equals ($100 ÷ $1,000) × 100, which is 10 percent. When the price of the bond is $2,000, the interest rate equals ($100 ÷ $2,000) × 100, which is 5 percent. When the price of the bond increases, the interest rate falls; page 299.

5. To lower the interest rate, the Fed increases the quantity of money; pages 300-301.

Additional Exercises (also in MyEconLab Test A)
1. The nominal interest rate is 6 percent a year because that is the nominal interest rate at which the quantity of money demanded equals the quantity of money supplied; pages 298-299.

2. If real GDP decreases, the nominal interest rate falls. When real GDP decreases, the demand for money curve shifts leftward. At the original nominal interest rate, people want to hold less money than they are actually holding. So they spend the money by buying other financial assets such as bonds. The demand for financial assets increases, the prices of these assets rise, and the nominal interest rate falls. The nominal interest rate keeps falling until the quantity of money that people want to hold increases to equal the quantity of money supplied; pages 297, 299.

3. If the Fed increases the quantity of money to $4.0 trillion, the nominal interest rate falls to 4 percent a year. At the original interest rate, people would like to hold less money then they are actually holding. So they try to get rid of money by buying other financial assets such as bonds. The demand for financial assets increases, the prices of these assets rise,

and the nominal interest rate falls. The nominal interest rate keeps falling until the quantity of money that people want to hold increases to equal the quantity of money supplied; pages 298-299 .

4. The demand for money decreases as people use their credit cards more often and use money less often for transactions.
Because the demand for money decreases, the nominal interest rate falls; pages 298-299.

■ CHECKPOINT 12.2

Fill in the blanks
The higher the price level, the lower the value of money. In the long run, an increase in the quantity of money lowers the value of money. Other things remaining the same, a given percentage increase in the quantity of money brings an equal percentage increase in the price level in the long run. The proposition that when real GDP equals potential GDP, an increase in the quantity of money brings an equal percentage increase in the price level is the quantity theory of money. If the velocity of circulation does not change, the inflation rate equals the growth rate of the quantity of money minus the growth rate of real GDP. A hyperinflation occurs when the quantity of money grows at a rapid pace.

True or false
1. False; pages 303-304
2. False; page 304
3. True; page 305
4. False; page 307
5. True; pages 307-308
6. False; page 309

Multiple choice
1. c; page 303
2. d; page 305
3. a; page 305
4. c; page 306
5. c; pages 306-307
6. c; pages 308-309

7. e; pages 308-309

8. b; page 310

Short answer and numeric questions

1. The value of money equals $1/P$ (where P is the price level, which equals the price index divided by 100) because $1/P$ tells how many goods and services can be purchased with one dollar. If this number falls, then the dollar has lost value because a dollar buys fewer goods and services; pages 303-304.

2. Other things remaining the same, in the long run a 5 percent increase in the quantity of money leads to a 5 percent increase in the price level; pages 305, 308.

Year	Quantity of money (billions of dollars)	Velocity of circulation	Price level (2005 = 100)	Real GDP (billions of 2005 dollars)
2011	100	11	110.0	1,000
2012	110	11	121.0	1,000
2013	121	11	133.1	1,000

3. a. The completed table is above. Use the equation of exchange to solve for the price level; pages 307-308.

   b. In 2012, the percentage change in the quantity of money is [($110 billion – $100 billion) ÷ $100 billion] × 100, which is 10 percent.

   In 2013, the percentage change in the quantity of money is [($121 billion – $110 billion) ÷ $110 billion] × 100, which also is 10 percent.

   In 2012, the percentage change in the price level is [(121.0 – 110.0) ÷ 110.0] × 100, which is 10 percent.

   In 2013, the percentage change in the price level is [(133.1 – 121.0) ÷ 121.0] × 100, which also is 10 percent.

   c. The answer to part (b) illustrates the quantity theory of money, the proposition that, when real GDP equals potential GDP, an increase in the quantity of money brings an equal percentage increase in the price level; pages 305, 308.

Year	Growth in quantity of money (percent)	Growth in velocity of circulation (percent)	Inflation rate (percent)	Growth in Real GDP (percent)
2011	4	2	3	3
2012	7	2	6	3
2013	6	1	4	3

4. a. The completed table is above. Use the equation of exchange in growth rates to solve for the unknowns; page 308.

   b. Between 2011 and 2012, the growth rate of the quantity of money increased by 3 percentage points. Between these two years the inflation rate also increased by 3 percentage points; page 308.

5. The inflation rate equals money growth plus velocity growth minus real GDP growth. Velocity does not grow, so the inflation rate equals 5 percent a year minus 3 percent a year, which is 2 percent a year; page 308.

6. A hyperinflation is inflation at a rate that exceeds 50 percent a month. A hyperinflation is the result of extraordinarily rapid growth in the quantity of money; page 310.

Additional Exercises (also in MyEconLab Test A)

1. The nominal interest rate equals the real interest rate plus the inflation rate. So the nominal interest rate equals the real interest rate, 5 percent a year, plus the inflation rate, 6 percent a year, which is 11 percent a year.

   When the inflation rate decreases by 3 percentage points, the nominal interest rate falls by 3 percentage points, in this case from 11 percent a year to 8 percent a year; pages 296, 308.

2. The equation of exchange is $M \times V = P \times Y$. Rearranging this equation to solve for M gives $M = (P \times Y) \div V$. $P \times Y$ equals nominal GDP, which is given in the problem as £900 billion. Velocity was given as 2. So the quantity of money, M, is (£900 billion) ÷ 2, which is £450 billion; page 307.

3. In growth rates, the equation of exchange is (Money growth) + (Velocity growth) = (Inflation) + (Real GDP growth). Rearranging this equation gives Inflation = (Money growth) +

(Velocity growth) − (Real GDP growth). The velocity of circulation is constant (at 2) so its growth equals 0 percent. Real GDP grows at 5 percent a year and money grows at 8 percent a year, so inflation equals (8 percent a year) + (0 percent a year) − (5 percent a year), which is 3 percent a year; page 308.

■ CHECKPOINT 12.3

Fill in the blanks

Inflation <u>is</u> a tax. The higher the inflation rate, the <u>higher</u> the true income tax rate on income from capital. During an inflation, the costs that arise from an increase in the velocity of circulation of money and an increase in the amount of running around to avoid incurring losses from the falling value of money are <u>shoe-leather</u> costs. Increased uncertainty about inflation leads to a <u>fall</u> in investment.

True or false

1. True; page 313
2. True; page 314
3. False; page 315
4. True; pages 315-320

Multiple choice

1. d; page 313
2. c; page 313
3. a; page 314
4. c; page 314
5. b; page 315
6. c; page 315
7. a; page 315
8. a; pages 315-316

Short answer and numeric questions

1. With an inflation rate of 5 percent a year, Jose losses ($600 × 0.05) = $30 in purchasing power. His money will buy only $570 worth of goods and services. Jose is paying an inflation tax of $30; page 313.

2. The real after-tax interest rate equals the nominal after-tax interest rate minus the inflation rate. When inflation is zero percent a year, the nominal interest rate equals the real interest rate, which is 2 percent a year. With a 25 percent income tax, the nominal after-tax interest rate equals 1.5 percent a year, so the real after-tax interest rate is 1.5 percent a year. When the inflation rate is 6 percent a year, the nominal interest rate equals the real interest rate, 2 percent a year, plus the inflation rate, 6 percent, or 8 percent a year. The tax rate of 25 percent means that the nominal after-tax interest rate is 6 percent a year. In this case the real after-tax interest rate equals 6 percent a year minus the inflation rate, 6 percent a year, which is zero percent a year. When the inflation rate equals 10 percent a year, the nominal interest rate is 12 percent a year so the nominal after-tax interest rate is 9 percent a year. As a result, the real after-tax interest rate is 9 percent a year − 10 percent a year, which is −1 percent a year. In this case, the real after-tax interest rate is negative; page 314.

3. The velocity of circulation increases because people try to spend their money as rapidly as possible to avoid incurring losses from the falling value of money. When people spend their money more rapidly, the velocity of circulation increases, thereby creating more shoe-leather costs; page 314.

4. The costs of an inflation depend on its rate and its predictability. The higher the rate, the greater is the cost and the more unpredictable the rate, the greater is the cost; page 315.

5. The use of the quantity theory illustrated in the Eye on the Cause of Inflation might help you on your job if you are sometimes required to predict or surmise what the inflation rate will be over the next few years. For instance, if you have a job in which you must help your company determine whether to make an investment in a new factory, predicting the inflation rate might be useful information in helping to determine the profitability of the new factory. You could then use the procedure outlined in the Eye on the Cause of Inflation to guide your prediction by focusing on the predicted growth rate of

the quantity of money and the growth rate of real GDP. While the quantity theory won't precisely predict each year's inflation rate, nonetheless it does give a good indicator of what the inflation rate will tend to be over several years.

Additional Exercises (also in MyEconLab Test A)

1. The real interest rate is the nominal interest rate minus the inflation rate, which is 18 percent a year minus 3 percent a year = 15 percent; pages 296, 314.

2. The real interest rate rises to 16 percent a year (18 percent a year minus 2 percent a year); pages 296, 314.

Aggregate Supply and Aggregate Demand

Chapter 13

1 Define and explain the influences on aggregate supply.

Aggregate supply is the output from all firms. Other things remaining the same, the higher the price level, the greater is the quantity of real GDP supplied and the lower the price level, the smaller is the quantity of real GDP supplied. The aggregate supply curve is upward sloping and the potential GDP line is vertical. Moving along the aggregate supply curve, the only influence on production plans that changes is the price level. All other influences on production plans, such as the money wage rate and the money prices of other resources, remain constant. Moving along the potential GDP line, when the price level changes, the money wage rate and the money prices of other resources change by the same percentage as the price level. Aggregate supply changes and the aggregate supply curve shifts when potential GDP changes, the money wage rate changes, or the money prices of other resources change. When the money wage rate or the money prices of other resources rise, aggregate supply decreases.

2 Define and explain the influences on aggregate demand.

Aggregate demand is the relationship between the quantity of real GDP demanded and the price level. Other things the same, the higher the price level, the smaller is the quantity of real GDP demanded and the lower the price level, the greater the quantity of real GDP demanded. A change in the price level changes in the buying power of money, the real interest rate, and the real prices of exports and imports, all of which influence the quantity of real GDP demanded. Factors that change aggregate demand and shift the aggregate demand curve are: expectations about the future; fiscal policy and monetary policy; and the state of the world economy. The aggregate demand multiplier is an effect that magnifies changes in expenditure plans and brings potentially large fluctuations in aggregate demand.

3 Explain how trends and fluctuations in aggregate demand and aggregate supply bring economic growth, inflation, and the business cycle.

Macroeconomic equilibrium occurs at the intersection of the aggregate supply and aggregate demand curves. The macroeconomic equilibrium can be a full-employment equilibrium (real GDP equals potential GDP), an equilibrium with an inflationary gap (real GDP exceeds potential GDP), or an equilibrium with a recessionary gap (real GDP is less than potential GDP). In a recessionary gap, the money wage rate falls so aggregate supply increases and the economy adjusts back to full employment. In an inflationary gap, the money wage rate rises so aggregate supply decreases and the economy adjusts back to full employment. Economic growth is the result of growth in potential GDP; inflation is the result of more rapid growth in aggregate demand than in potential GDP. Fluctuations in aggregate demand and aggregate supply lead to the business cycle. Demand pull inflation starts with an increase in aggregate demand, followed by persisting increases in the quantity of money. Cost-push inflation starts with a decrease in aggregate supply, followed by persisting increases in the quantity of money.

CHECKPOINT 13.1

■ Define and explain the influences on aggregate supply.

Quick Review

- *Aggregate supply* The relationship between the quantity of real GDP supplied and the price level when all other influences on production plans remain the same.
- *Factors that change aggregate supply* Aggregate supply decreases and the aggregate supply curve shifts leftward when potential GDP decreases, when the money wage rate rises, and when the money prices of other resources rise.

Additional Practice Problem 13.1

1. The table shows the aggregate supply schedule for the United Kingdom.
   a. Plot the aggregate supply curve in the figure.

Price level (GDP price index)	Real GDP supplied (billions of 2005 pounds)
90	650
100	700
110	750
120	800
130	850

   b. In the figure, show the effect on the aggregate supply curve of an increase in the U.K. money wage rate. Is there a movement along the curve or a shift of the curve?

Price level (GDP price index)

130
120
110
100
90

0   650 700 750 800 850
Real GDP
(billions of 2005 pounds)

Solution to Additional Practice Problem 13.1

1a. The aggregate supply curve is plotted in the figure in the next column above as AS_0. The aggregate supply curve has a positive slope, so as the price level rises, the quantity of real GDP supplied increases.

1b. Changes in the price level change in the aggregate quantity supplied and result in movements along the aggregate supply curve. Aggregate supply changes and the aggregate supply curve shifts when any influence on production plans other than the price level changes. An increase in the money wage rate decreases aggregate supply and shifts the aggregate supply curve leftward, as illustrated by the shift to AS_1. A change in the money wage rate shifts the aggregate supply curve.

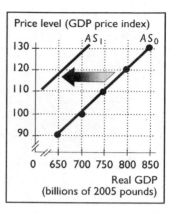

Price level (GDP price index)

130
120
110
100
90

0   650 700 750 800 850
Real GDP
(billions of 2005 pounds)

■ Self Test 13.1

Fill in the blanks

Moving along the aggregate supply curve, as the price level rises, the quantity of real GDP supplied ____ (decreases; does not change; increases) because the real wage rate ____ (falls; rises). Moving along the potential GDP line, the money wage rate ____ (changes; does not change) when the price level changes. When potential GDP increases, a ____ (movement along; shift of) the *AS* curve occurs. When the money wage rate changes, a ____ (movement along; shift of) the *AS* curve occurs.

True or false

1. Along the aggregate supply curve, a rise in the price level decreases the quantity of real GDP supplied.

2. A rise in the price level decreases potential GDP.

3. Anything that changes potential GDP shifts the aggregate supply curve.

4. An increase in potential GDP shifts the aggregate supply curve rightward.

Multiple choice

1. Moving along the potential GDP line, the money wage rate changes by the same percentage as the change in the price level so that the real wage rate
   a. increases.
   b. decreases.
   c. stays at the full-employment equilibrium level.
   d. might either increase or decrease.
   e. stays the same, though not necessarily at the full-employment equilibrium level.

2. The aggregate supply curve is
   a. upward sloping.
   b. downward sloping.
   c. a vertical line.
   d. a horizontal line.
   e. U-shaped.

3. When the price level falls,
   a. the AS curve shifts rightward but the potential GDP line does not shift.
   b. there is a movement upward along the AS curve.
   c. the AS curve shifts leftward but the potential GDP line does not shift.
   d. there is a movement downward along the AS curve.
   e. both the potential GDP line and the AS curve shift leftward.

4. As the price level rises relative to costs and the real wage rate falls, profits ____ and the number of firms in business ____.
   a. increase; increases
   b. increase; decreases
   c. decrease; increases
   d. decrease; decreases
   e. do not change; do not change

■ **FIGURE 13.1**

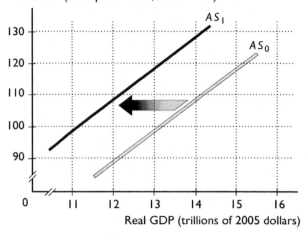

Price level (GDP price index, 2005 = 100)

5. In Figure 13.1, which of the following might be the reason for the shift of the aggregate supply curve from AS_0 to AS_1?
   a. a fall in the money wage rate
   b. an increase in potential GDP
   c. an increase in investment
   d. a fall in the price of oil
   e. a rise in the money wage rate

6. When potential GDP increases,
   a. the AS curve shifts rightward.
   b. there is a movement up along the AS curve.
   c. the AS curve shifts leftward.
   d. there is a movement down along the AS curve.
   e. there is neither a movement along or a shift in the AS curve.

7. If the money wage rate rises,
   a. the AS curve shifts rightward.
   b. there is a movement up along the AS curve.
   c. the AS curve shifts leftward.
   d. there is a movement down along the AS curve.
   e. there is neither a movement along nor a shift in the AS curve.

Complete the graph

Price level (GDP price index 2005 = 100)	Quantity of real GDP supplied (trillions of 2005 dollars)	Potential GDP (trillions of 2005 dollars)
140	17	13
130	15	13
120	13	13
110	11	13
100	9	13

■ **FIGURE 13.2**

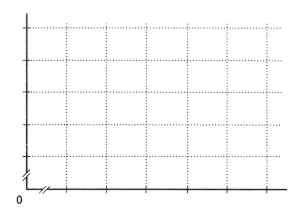

1. The table above gives the aggregate supply schedule and potential GDP schedule for a nation.
   a. Label the axes and then plot the *AS* curve and potential GDP line in Figure 13.2.
   b. Suppose the money wage rate falls. Show the effect of this change on aggregate supply and potential GDP in Figure 13.2.
   c. Use the data in the table to again plot the *AS* curve and potential GDP line in Figure 13.3. Be sure to label the axes.
   d. Potential GDP increases by $2 trillion. Show the effect of this change on aggregate supply and potential GDP in Figure 13.3.

Short answer and numeric questions

1. Why does the *AS* curve slope upward?

2. Why does the aggregate supply curve shift when the money wage rate rises? Why doesn't the potential GDP line also shift?

3. What is the effect on aggregate supply if the money price of oil rises?

■ **FIGURE 13.3**

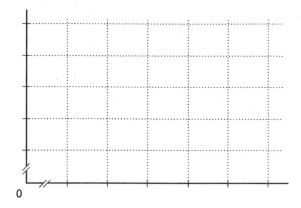

Additional Exercises (also in MyEconLab Test A)

1. Many events have followed the ending of apartheid in South Africa. Explain the effect of each of the following events on South Africa's aggregate supply.
   a. U.S. businesses have established branches in South Africa.
   b. The price level has increased.
   c. Unemployment decreased.
   d. Money wage rates have increased.
   e. Tourism increased, and many new hotels were built.
   f. AIDS became more prevalent.

CHECKPOINT 13.2

■ **Define and explain the influences on aggregate demand.**

Quick Review

- *Factors that change aggregate demand* Aggregate demand changes and the aggregate demand curve shifts if expected future income, expected future inflation, or expected future profit change; if the government or the Federal Reserve take steps that change expenditure plans, such as changes in taxes or in the quantity of money; or the state of the world economy changes.

Additional Practice Problem 13.2

1. Draw aggregate demand curves and illustrate the effects of each event listed below either by a movement along the aggregate demand curve or a shift in the aggregate demand curve. These events are:

   a. The price level falls.

   b. Firms increase their investment because the expected profit increases.

   c. The government cuts its taxes.

Solution to Additional Practice Problem 13.2

1a. To answer this Practice Problem, remember that a change in any factor that influences expenditure plans other than the price level brings a change in aggregate demand and a shift in the *AD* curve. In this part, it *is* the price level that changes, so there is a change in the quantity of real GDP demanded and a movement along the aggregate demand curve. Because the price level falls, there is a downward movement along the aggregate demand curve, as illustrated by the grey arrow in the figure.

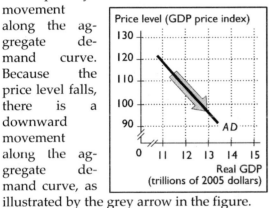

1b. An increase in firms' investment increases aggregate demand. The aggregate demand curve shifts rightward, as shown in the figure by the shift from AD_0 to AD_1.

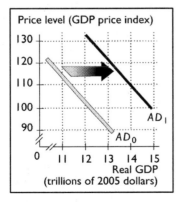

1c. When the government cuts its taxes, households' incomes rise and so they increase their consumption expenditure. Aggregate demand increases and the aggregate demand curve shifts rightward, as illustrated in the previous answer.

■ Self Test 13.2

Fill in the blanks

An increase in the price level ____ (decreases; increases) the quantity of real GDP demanded and a ____ (movement along; shift of) the aggregate demand curve occurs. An increase in expected future income shifts the *AD* curve ____ (leftward; rightward). A tax cut shifts the *AD* curve ____ (leftward; rightward). A decrease in foreign income shifts the *AD* curve ____ (leftward; rightward).

True or false

1. As the price level falls, other things remaining the same, the quantity of real GDP demanded increases.

2. An increase in expected future income will not increase aggregate demand until the income actually increases.

3. A decrease in government expenditure shifts the aggregate demand curve rightward.

4. An increase in Mexican income decreases aggregate demand in the United States because Mexicans will buy more Mexican-produced goods.

Multiple choice

1. When the price level rises there is a ____ the aggregate demand curve.

   a. rightward shift of

   b. movement down along

   c. leftward shift of

   d. movement up along

   e. rotation of

2. A rise in the price level

   a. raises the buying power of money.

   b. decreases the prices of exports.

   c. lowers the buying power of money.

   d. increases aggregate demand.

   e. makes the aggregate demand curve steeper.

3. When the price level rises, the real interest rate ____ and the quantity of real GDP demanded ____.
   a. rises; increases
   b. rises; decreases
   c. falls; increases
   d. falls; decreases
   e. does not change; does not change

■ **FIGURE 13.4**

Price level (GDP price index, 2005 = 100)

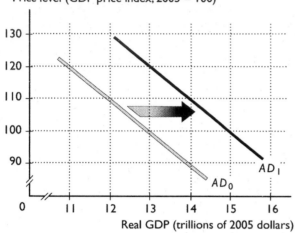

4. In Figure 13.4, the shift in the aggregate demand curve could be the result of
   a. an increase in the quantity of money
   b. a decrease in foreign incomes.
   c. a tax hike.
   d. a fall in the price level.
   e. a decrease in the expected future rate of profit.

5. A change in any of the following factors, <u>EXCEPT</u> ____, shifts the aggregate demand curve.
   a. expectations about the future
   b. the money wage rate
   c. monetary and fiscal policy
   d. foreign income
   e. the foreign exchange rate

6. Which of the following shifts the aggregate demand curve leftward?
   a. a decrease in government expenditure on goods and services
   b. an increase in the price level
   c. a tax cut
   d. an increase in foreign income
   e. a decrease in the price level

7. When investment increases, the ____ in aggregate demand is ____ the change in investment.
   a. increase; greater than
   b. increase; smaller than
   c. increase; the same as
   d. decrease; the same as
   e. decrease; greater than

Complete the graph

■ **FIGURE 13.5**

Price level (GDP price index, 2005 = 100)

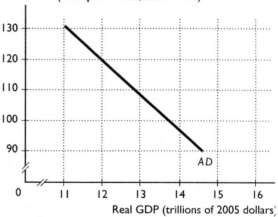

1. Figure 13.5 shows an aggregate demand curve.
   a. Suppose that government expenditure on goods and services increase. In Figure 13.5, illustrate the effect of this fiscal policy.
   b. Suppose the Federal Reserve decreases the quantity of money. In Figure 13.5, illustrate the effect of this monetary policy.

Short answer and numeric questions

1. Why does an increase in the price level decrease the quantity of real GDP demanded?
2. Expected future profit increases. Explain the effect on aggregate demand.
3. The government increases its taxes. What is the effect on aggregate demand?
4. What is the aggregate demand multiplier?

Additional Exercises (also in MyEconLab Test A)

1. Explain the effect on Japan's aggregate demand of each of the following events, one at a time.
   a. The price level in Japan rises.
   b. The Asian economies experience very strong growth.
   c. Japan adopts an expansionary fiscal policy and cuts taxes.
2. Explain the effect on China's aggregate demand of each of the following events, one at a time.
   a. The United States goes into recession.
   b. Japanese and European firms establish new plants in China.
   c. The Chinese yuan strengthens against the U.S. dollar.

CHECKPOINT 13.3

■ **Explain how trends and fluctuations in aggregate demand and aggregate supply bring economic growth, inflation, and the business cycle.**

Quick Review

- *Recessionary gap* A gap that exists when potential GDP exceeds real GDP. To restore full employment, the money wage rate falls and aggregate supply increases.
- *Inflationary gap* A gap that exists when real GDP exceeds potential GDP. To restore full employment, the money wage rate rises and aggregate supply decreases.

Additional Practice Problem 13.3

1. The table has the U.K. aggregate demand and aggregate supply schedules.

Price level (GDP price index)	Real GDP demanded	Real GDP supplied
		(billions of 2005 pounds)
90	800	650
100	775	700
110	750	750
120	725	800
130	700	850

   a. Plot the aggregate demand curve and the aggregate supply curve in the figure.

   Price level (GDP price index)

   130
   120
   110
   100
   90

   0   650 700 750 800 850
   Real GDP
   (billions of 2005 pounds)

   b. What is the macroeconomic equilibrium?
   c. If U.K. potential GDP is £800 billion, what is the type of macroeconomic equilibrium?
   d. If the government increases its expenditure on goods and services, what is the effect on the British economy?

Solution to Additional Practice Problems 13.3

1a. The aggregate demand curve is in the figure. It has a negative slope, so as the price level falls, the quantity of real GDP demanded increases. The aggregate supply curve also is plotted in the figure. It has a positive slope, so as the price level rises, the quantity of real GDP supplied increases.

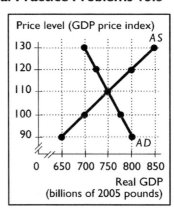

Price level (GDP price index)

130
120
110
100
90

0   650 700 750 800 850
Real GDP
(billions of 2005 pounds)

1b. The macroeconomic equilibrium is at a price level of 110 and real GDP of £750 billion. The macroeconomic equilibrium is at the intersection of the aggregate supply curve and the aggregate demand curve.

1c. Potential GDP is £800 billion and the macroeconomic equilibrium real GDP is £750 billion, so as the figure shows, the economy is in a below full-employment equilibrium. Real GDP is less than potential GDP.

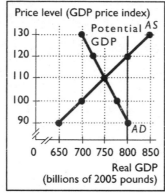

1d. If the government increases its expenditure on goods and services, aggregate demand increases and the aggregate demand curve shifts rightward. The price level rises and real GDP increases, moving the nation closer to a full-employment equilibrium.

■ Self Test 13.3

Fill in the blanks

Macroeconomic equilibrium occurs where the AD curve intersects _____ (the AS curve; potential GDP line). When real GDP exceeds potential GDP, _____ (an inflationary; a recessionary) gap exists. When potential GDP exceeds real GDP, _____ (an inflationary; a recessionary) gap exists. If aggregate demand grows more rapidly than potential GDP, the result is _____. An increase in government expenditure on goods and services might start a _____ (demand-pull; cost-push) inflation. An increase in the money price of oil might start a _____ (demand-pull; cost-push) inflation. Stagflation is a combination of _____ (expansion; recession) and a _____ (falling; rising) price level. During the _____ (Great Depression; financial crisis of 2008) the Fed took no action.

True or false

1. A recessionary gap has a shortage of labor.

2. In the AS-AD model, economic growth is demonstrated by persisting rightward movements of the AD curve.

3. Aggregate demand fluctuations are the main source of the business cycle.

4. Demand-pull inflation starts with an increase in aggregate demand that leads to an inflationary gap.

5. To persist, cost-push inflation does not need persisting increases in aggregate demand.

6. In the financial crisis of 2008, the Fed took action to bail out financial institutions and doubled the monetary base.

Multiple choice

1. If the quantity of real GDP supplied equals the quantity of real GDP demanded, then
   a. nominal GDP must equal real GDP.
   b. real GDP must equal potential GDP.
   c. real GDP must be greater than potential GDP.
   d. real GDP might be greater than, equal to, or less than potential GDP.
   e. real GDP must be less than potential GDP.

2. An inflationary gap is created when
   a. real GDP is greater than potential GDP.
   b. real GDP equal to potential GDP.
   c. the inflation rate is less than potential inflation.
   d. the price level exceeds the equilibrium price level.
   e. potential GDP is greater than real GDP.

3. The economy is at full employment. Aggregate demand increases, so _____ is created and the adjustment to full employment occurs because _____.
   a. an inflationary gap; the AS curve shifts leftward as the money wage rate rises
   b. an inflationary gap; the AD curve shifts leftward
   c. an inflationary gap; potential GDP increases to close the gap
   d. a recessionary gap; the AS curve shifts leftward as the money wage rate falls
   e. a recessionary gap; the AS curve shifts leftward as the money wage rate rises

■ **FIGURE 13.6**

Price level (GDP price index, 2005 = 100)

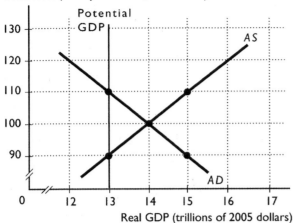

4. In Figure 13.6, the equilibrium price level is ____ and the equilibrium real GDP is ____ trillion.
   a. 110; $13
   b. 110; $15
   c. 100; $14
   d. 90; $13
   e. 90; $15

5. Figure 13.6 shows
   a. a full-employment equilibrium.
   b. an above full-employment equilibrium with an inflationary gap.
   c. an above full-employment equilibrium with a recessionary gap.
   d. a below full-employment equilibrium with an inflationary gap.
   e. a below full-employment equilibrium with a recessionary gap.

6. The adjustment from a recessionary gap to full employment requires the money wage rate to ____, which then ____.
   a. rise; decreases aggregate supply
   b. rise; increases aggregate demand
   c. fall; decreases aggregate demand
   d. fall; increases potential GDP
   e. fall; increases aggregate supply

7. The main source of business cycle fluctuations is
   a. fluctuations in aggregate demand.
   b. persisting growth in aggregate demand.
   c. persisting growth in potential GDP
   d. fluctuations in aggregate supply.
   e. persisting growth in aggregate supply.

8. A cost-push inflation can be started by ____.
   a. an increase in the quantity of money
   b. a fall in the money price of oil
   c. an increase in potential GDP
   d. a rise in the money price of oil
   e. an increase in U.S. exports

9. Stagflation is a combination of ____ real GDP and a ____ price level.
   a. increasing; rising
   b. increasing; falling
   c. decreasing; rising
   d. decreasing; falling
   e. no change in; rising

Complete the graph

■ **FIGURE 13.7**

Price level (GDP price index, 2005 = 100)

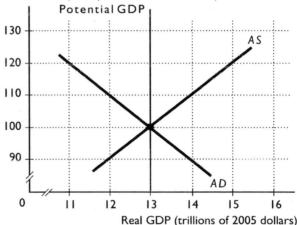

1. Use Figure 13.7 to show the effect of an increase in expected future profit on the price level and real GDP. Does this change create an inflationary gap or a recessionary gap? In the figure, show how the economy returns to potential GDP.

© 2013 Pearson Education, Inc. Publishing as Addison Wesley

■ **FIGURE 13.8**

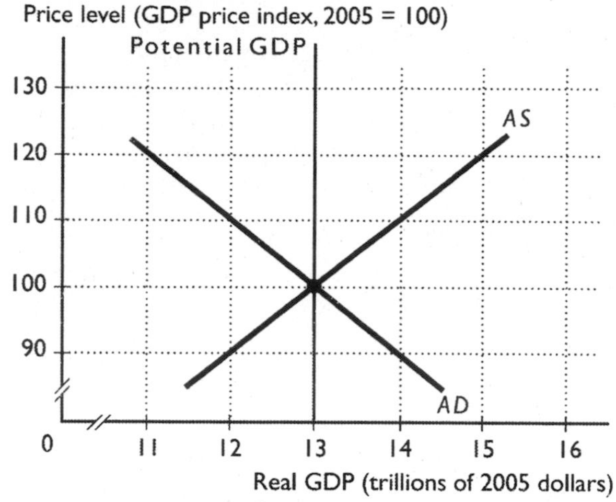

Price level (GDP price index, 2005 = 100)

2. Use Figure 13.8 to show the effect a rise in the price of oil has on the price level and real GDP. Does this change create an inflationary gap or a recessionary gap?

Short answer and numeric questions

1. What is an inflationary gap and how is it eliminated?

2. Why is growth in the quantity of money necessary to sustain a demand-pull inflation?

3. What is the difference between a demand-pull inflation and a cost-push inflation? How are they similar?

4. What is stagflation? What can create stagflation?

5. What was the difference in the Fed's behavior during the Great Depression contrasted to the Fed's behavior during the 2008 financial crisis?

6. The Eye on Your Life on discussed some of the uses you can make of the AS-AD model. Another use lies in the political arena. For instance, if a politician is running a campaign in which he or she suggests raising taxes, using the AS-AD model, what do you expect will happen to real GDP if this campaign promise is carried out?

Additional Exercises (also in MyEconLab Test A)

The Canadian economy is at full employment when the following events occur:

  a. The world economy goes into a strong expansion.

  b. Canadian businesses expect future profits to rise.

1. Explain the effect of each event separately on real GDP, the price level, and unemployment in Canada in the short run.

2. If the events occur separately, explain the adjustment that occurs in each case in the long run.

3. Explain the combined effect of these events on Canadian real GDP and price level.

SELF TEST ANSWERS

■ CHECKPOINT 13.1

Fill in the blanks

Moving along the aggregate supply curve, as the price level rises, the quantity of real GDP supplied <u>increases</u> because the real wage rate <u>falls</u>. Moving along the potential GDP line, the money wage rate <u>does not change</u> when the price level changes. When potential GDP increases, a <u>shift of</u> the *AS* curve occurs. When the money wage rate changes, a <u>shift of</u> the *AS* curve occurs.

True or false

1. False; pages 322-323
2. False; pages 322-323
3. True; page 325
4. True; page 325

Multiple choice

1. c; pages 322-323
2. a; page 323
3. d; pages 322-323
4. a; page 324
5. e; page 326
6. a; page 325
7. c; page 326

Complete the graph

■ FIGURE 13.9

Price level (GDP price index, 2005 = 100)

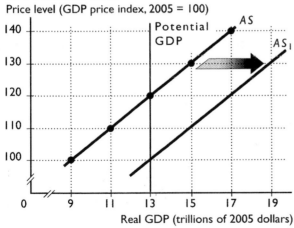

1. a. Figure 13.9 labels the axes. The aggregate

supply curve is labeled *AS*; page 323.

b. The fall in the money wage rate has no effect on potential GDP, so the potential GDP line does not change. Aggregate supply, however, increases so the *AS* curve shifts rightward, to an *AS* curve such as *AS*₁; page 326.

■ FIGURE 13.10

Price level (GDP price index, 2005 = 100)

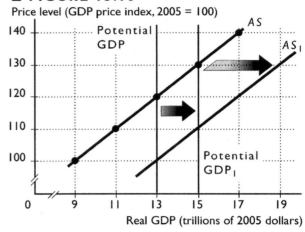

Real GDP (trillions of 2005 dollars)

c. Figure 13.10 labels the axes. The aggregate supply curve is labeled *AS*; page 323.

d. The potential GDP line shifts rightward by $2 trillion, as indicated by the shift to Potential GDP₁. The aggregate supply curve also shifts rightward by $2 trillion, as shown by the shift to *AS*₁; page 325.

Short answer and numeric questions

1. A movement along the *AS* curve brings a change in the real wage rate (and changes in the real cost of other resources whose money prices are fixed).

   If the price level rises and the money wage rate does not change, an extra hour of labor that was previously unprofitable becomes profitable. So, the quantity of labor demanded increases and production increases.

   In addition, if the price level rises and the money wage rate does not change, the real wage rate falls. A fall in the real wage rate boosts firms' profits. With the increase in profit, the number of firms in business increases. Finally fewer firms will shut down and more firms will open. All these changes increase the quantity of real GDP supplied. So as the price level rises, the quantity of real GDP supplied increases; pages 322-324.

2. An increase in the money wage rate increases firms' costs. The higher are firms' costs, the smaller is the quantity that firms are willing to supply at each price level. Aggregate supply decreases and the *AS* curve shifts leftward. A change in the money wage rate does not change potential GDP. Potential GDP depends only on the economy's real ability to produce and on the full-employment quantity of labor, which occurs at the equilibrium real wage rate. The equilibrium real wage rate can occur at any money wage rate; pages 325-326.

3. If the money price of oil rises, firm's costs increase. The higher firms' costs, the smaller the quantity of goods and services that firms will supply at each price level. Aggregate supply decreases and the aggregate supply curve shifts leftward; page 326.

Additional Exercises (also in MyEconLab Test A)

1. a. Establishing more branches of businesses within South Africa increases the number of business and increases aggregate supply; page 324.
   b. In the short run, the increase in the price level increases the aggregate quantity supplied; page 325.
   c. As unemployment decreases and employment increases, production increases and aggregate supply increases; page 322.
   d. An increase in money wage rates decreases aggregate supply; pages 325-326 .
   e. As tourism increases and new hotels are built, the quantity capital increases so that potential GDP increases and thereby aggregate supply increases; pages 322, 325.
   f. The spread of AIDS decreases the quantity of labor. As a result, potential GDP decreases so that aggregate supply decreases; page 322.

■ CHECKPOINT 13.2

Fill in the blanks

An increase in the price level <u>decreases</u> the quantity of real GDP demanded and a <u>movement along</u> the aggregate demand curve occurs. An increase in expected future income shifts the *AD* curve <u>rightward</u>. A tax cut shifts the *AD* curve <u>rightward</u>. A decrease in foreign income shifts the *AD* curve <u>leftward</u>.

True or false

1. True; page 328
2. False; page 330
3. False; page 331
4. False; page 332

Multiple choice

1. d; page 328
2. c; pages 328-329
3. b; pages 329-330
4. a; page 331
5. b; pages 330-331
6. a; pages 330-331
7. a; page 332

Complete the graph

■ **FIGURE 13.11**

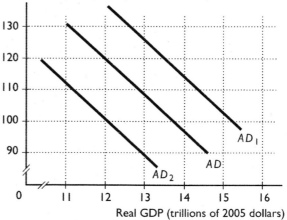

1. a. An increase in government expenditure on goods and services increases aggregate demand and shifts the *AD* curve rightward, in Figure 13.11 from *AD* to *AD₁*; page 331.

b. A decrease in the quantity of money decreases aggregate demand and shifts the AD curve leftward, in Figure 13.11 from AD to AD2; page 331.

Short answer and numeric questions

1. An increase in the price level decreases the quantity of real GDP demanded because an increase in the price level lowers the buying power of money, raises the real interest rate, raises the real prices of exports, and lowers the real price of imports; pages 328-330.

2. An increase in expected future profit increases the firms' investment and thereby increases aggregate demand; page 330.

3. The government can influence aggregate demand by changing taxes. When the government increases taxes, aggregate demand decreases; page 331.

4. The aggregate demand multiplier is an effect that magnifies changes in expenditure and increases fluctuations in aggregate demand. For example, an increase in investment increases aggregate demand and increases income. The increase in income induces an increase in consumption expenditure so aggregate demand increases by more than the initial increase in investment; page 332.

Additional Exercises (also in MyEconLab Test A)

1. a. The increase in the Japanese price level makes Japanese-made goods more expensive. Japan's exports decrease and Japan's imports increase, and there is a movement up along Japan's AD curve; page 330.

   b. As the rest of Asia experiences strong economic growth, the demand for Japanese exports increases. Japan's aggregate demand increases and the AD curve shifts rightward; page 332.

   c. An expansionary fiscal policy and tax cuts increase aggregate demand and the AD curve shifts rightward; page 331.

2. a. As the United States goes into recession, the demand for Chinese exports decreases. China's aggregate demand decreases and the AD curve shifts leftward; page 332.

   b. The new plants will have the first order effect of increasing China's potential GDP and its aggregate supply.

   c. A stronger yuan makes China's exports more expensive and imports from the United States cheaper to residents of China. Chinese exports decrease and imports increase, which decreases China's aggregate demand and shifts the AD curve leftward; page 331.

■ CHECKPOINT 13.3

Fill in the blanks

Macroeconomic equilibrium occurs where the AD curve intersects the AS curve. When real GDP exceeds potential GDP, an inflationary gap exists. When potential GDP exceeds real GDP, a recessionary gap exists. If aggregate demand grows more rapidly than potential GDP, the result is inflation. An increase in government expenditure on goods and services might start a demand-pull inflation. An increase in the money price of oil might start a cost-push inflation. Stagflation is a combination of recession and a rising price level. During the Great Depression the Fed took no action.

True or false

1. False; page 335
2. False; page 336
3. True; page 337
4. True; page 338
5. False; page 339
6. True; page 340

Multiple choice

1. d; page 335
2. a; page 335
3. a; page 335
4. c; page 335
5. b; page 335
6. e; page 335
7. a; page 337
8. d; page 339
9. c; page 339

© 2013 Pearson Education, Inc. Publishing as Addison Wesley

Complete the graph

■ FIGURE 13.12

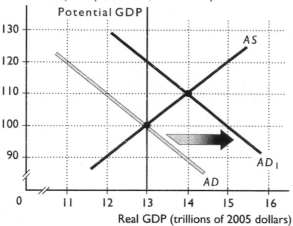

■ FIGURE 13.13

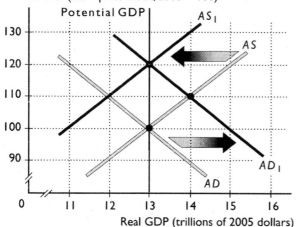

1. An increase in expected profit increases firms' investment. Investment is part of aggregate demand, so the increase in investment increases aggregate demand. The aggregate demand curve shifts rightward, from *AD* to *AD₁* in Figure 13.12. Aggregate supply does not change, so in the figure the equilibrium price level rises to 110 and equilibrium real GDP increases to $14 trillion. An inflationary gap now exists because there is an above-full employment equilibrium. The money wage rate rises and aggregate supply decreases. This change is illustrated

in Figure 13.13, in which the *AS* curve shifts leftward. Eventually the *AS* curve shifts to *AS₁*. Real GDP returns to potential GDP, $13 trillion, and the price level rises to 120; pages 330, 335.

■ FIGURE 13.14

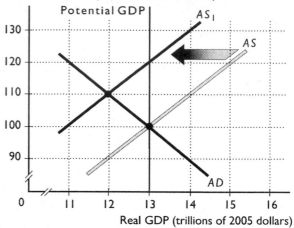

2. Figure 13.14 shows the effect of a rise in the price of oil. Aggregate supply decreases and the *AS* curve shifts leftward from *AS* to *AS₁*. Real GDP decreases to $12 trillion and the price level rises to 110. A recessionary gap is created because real GDP is less than potential GDP; pages 326, 335.

Short answer and numeric questions

1. An inflationary gap exists when real GDP exceeds potential GDP. Employment in the labor market exceeds full employment, so the money wage rate starts to rise. As the money wage rate rises, aggregate supply decreases and the aggregate supply curve shifts leftward. Eventually, real GDP returns to potential GDP and the inflationary gap is eliminated; page 335.

2. Demand-pull inflation starts with an increase in aggregate demand which raises the price level. In order for an inflation to occur, the price level must persistently continue to rise. The only factor that can create an on-going increase in the price level is (persisting) increases in the quantity of money because

they create (persisting) increases in aggregate demand and thereby (persisting) increases in the price level; page 338

3. The difference between demand-pull and cost-push inflation can be traced to what starts the inflationary process. In a demand-pull inflation, the inflation starts with an event that increases aggregate demand. In a cost-push inflation, the inflation starts with an event that decreases aggregate supply. A demand-pull inflation and cost-push inflation are similar because both need constant increases in the quantity of money to create a persisting inflation; pages 338-339.

4. Stagflation is a combination of recession (falling real GDP) and inflation (rising price level). Stagflation can be created by a decrease in aggregate supply, that is, a leftward shift of the aggregate supply curve; page 339.

5. During the Great Depression, the Fed did little or nothing. The quantity of money contracted by a huge amount and aggregate demand collapsed. The result was that real GDP plummeted. During the financial crisis of 2008, the Fed actively bailed out financial institutions and doubled the monetary base so that the quantity of money continued to grow. Aggregate demand decreased but did not collapse; page 340.

6. If the politician is elected and, as a result, taxes are raised, then aggregate demand decreases and the *AD* curve shifts leftward. As a result, real GDP decreases.

Additional Exercises (also in MyEconLab Test A)

1. a. A strong expansion in the world economy increases Canada's aggregate demand because it increases Canadian exports. The price level and real GDP both increase. In the short run, unemployment decreases; pages 331-332, 335.

b. A rise in expected future profits increases Canada's aggregate demand. The price level and real GDP both increase. In the short run, unemployment decreases; pages 330-331, 335.

2. a. A strong expansion in the world economy increases Canada's aggregate demand and, in the short run, tightens the labor market so there is a shortage of labor. As time passes, the money wage rate rises, raising the real wage rate and decreasing aggregate supply. In the long run the money wage rate has risen enough to decrease aggregate supply and shift the *AS* curve enough so that real GDP returns to potential GDP. The price level rises so that in the long run it is higher than what it was both initially and in the short run; page 335.

b. A rise in expected future profits increases Canada's aggregate demand and, in the short run, tightens the labor market so there is a shortage of labor. The shortage of labor puts upward pressure on the money wage rate, so the money wage rate rises. As the money wage rate rises, aggregate supply decreases and the *AS* curve shifts leftward. In the long run, real GDP returns to potential GDP. The price level, however, rises so that in the long run it is higher than what it was both initially and in the short run; page 335.

3. In the short run, both events increase Canada's real GDP and the price level, so Canada's real GDP and the price level rise. In the long run, for both events Canada's real GDP returns to potential GDP and the price level rises, so in the long run there is no change in Canada's real GDP but the price level rises; pages 330-332, 335.

Aggregate Expenditure Multiplier

Chapter 14

1 Explain how real GDP influences expenditure plans.

Aggregate planned expenditure is planned consumption expenditure plus planned investment plus planned government expenditures plus planned net exports. The consumption function is the relationship between consumption expenditure and disposable income; when disposable income increases, consumption expenditure increases. The marginal propensity to consume, *MPC*, is the fraction of a change in disposable income that is spent on consumption. The slope of the consumption function equals the *MPC*. When real GDP increases, imports increase. The marginal propensity to import is the fraction of an increase in real GDP spent on imports.

2 Explain how real GDP adjusts to achieve equilibrium expenditure.

Autonomous expenditure are the components of aggregate planned expenditure that do not change when real GDP changes; induced expenditure are the components of aggregate planned expenditure that change when real GDP changes. Equilibrium expenditure occurs when aggregate *planned* expenditure equals real GDP which is at the point where the *AE* curve intersects the 45° line. If aggregate planned expenditure exceeds real GDP, an unplanned decrease in inventories occurs. Firms increase production and real GDP increases until equilibrium expenditure is reached. If aggregate planned expenditure is less than real GDP, an unplanned increase in inventories occurs. Firms decrease production and real GDP decreases until equilibrium expenditure is reached.

3 Explain the expenditure multiplier.

The expenditure multiplier is the amount by which a change in any component of autonomous expenditure is multiplied to determine the change that it generates in equilibrium expenditure and real GDP. The multiplier is greater than 1 because an increase in autonomous expenditure induces further changes in aggregate expenditure. Ignoring income taxes and imports, the multiplier equals $1/(1 - MPC)$. The multiplier is larger if the *MPC* is larger. Imports and income taxes reduce the size of the multiplier. In general, the multiplier equals 1/(1 − slope of *AE* curve). A business cycle expansion is triggered by an increase in autonomous expenditure that increases aggregate planned expenditure and real GDP; a business cycle recession is triggered by a decrease in autonomous expenditure.

4 Derive the *AD* curve from equilibrium expenditure.

The *AE* curve is the relationship between aggregate planned expenditure and real GDP. The *AD* curve is the relationship between the quantity of real GDP demanded and the price level. When the price level rises, aggregate planned expenditure decreases, the *AE* curve shifts downward, and equilibrium expenditure decreases. When the price level rises, aggregate planned expenditure increases, the *AE* curve shifts upward, and equilibrium expenditure increases. Each point of equilibrium expenditure corresponds to a point on the *AD* curve.

CHECKPOINT 14.1

■ Explain how real GDP influences expenditure plans.

Quick Review

- *Autonomous expenditure* The components of aggregate expenditure that do not change when real GDP changes.
- *Induced expenditure* The components of aggregate expenditure that change when real GDP changes
- *Consumption function* The relationship between consumption expenditure and disposable income, other things remaining the same.
- *Marginal propensity to consume, MPC* The fraction of a change in disposable income that is spent on consumption, which equals the change in consumption expenditure divided by the change in disposable income that brought it about.

Additional Practice Problems 14.1

1. Suppose disposable income increases by $1.5 trillion.
   a. If the marginal propensity to consume (*MPC*) is 0.8, what is the change in consumption expenditure?
   b. If the *MPC* equals 0.6, what is the change in consumption expenditure?
   c. What is the relationship between the *MPC* and the change in consumption expenditure for a given change in disposable income?

2. The figure shows the consumption function for a small nation. Use the figure to calculate the marginal propensity to consume and autonomous consumption in the nation.

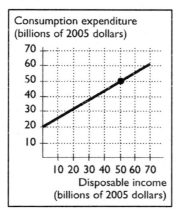

Consumption expenditure (billions of 2005 dollars)

Disposable income (billions of 2005 dollars)

Solutions to Additional Practice Problems 14.1

1a. The change in consumption expenditure equals the *MPC* multiplied by the change in disposable income. When the *MPC* is 0.8, the change in consumption expenditure equals ($1.5 trillion) × (0.8), which is $1.2 trillion.

1b. When the *MPC* is 0.6, the change in consumption expenditure is ($1.5 trillion) × (0.6), which is $0.9 trillion.

1c. The larger the *MPC*, the greater the change in consumption expenditure for a given change in disposable income.

2. The *MPC* is the slope of the consumption function and equals the change in consumption expenditure divided by the change in disposable income that brought it about. The figure shows that when disposable income increases from $0 to $50 billion, consumption expenditure increases from $20 billion to $50 billion. The *MPC* equals ($30 billion) ÷ ($50 billion), which is 0.60. Autonomous consumption is the amount of consumption when income equals zero and equals the *y*-axis intercept, $20 billion.

■ Self Test 14.1

Fill in the blanks

The components of aggregate expenditure that change when real GDP changes are ____ (induced; autonomous) expenditure. The components of aggregate expenditure that do not change when real GDP changes are ____ (induced; autonomous) expenditure. The ____ is the relationship between consumption expenditure and disposable income. The marginal propensity to consume equals the change in consumption expenditure ____ (plus; multiplied by; divided by) the change in disposable income that brought it about. The slope of the consumption function equals the ____. A change in disposable income is shown by a ____ (shift in; movement along) the consumption function, and a change in expected future income is shown by a ____ (shift in; movement along) the consumption function. Imports ____ (are; are not) part of induced expenditure.

True or false

1. Induced expenditure increases as real GDP increases.
2. The slope of the consumption function line is less than the slope of the 45° line.
3. The marginal propensity to consume equals total consumption expenditure divided by total disposable income.
4. The consumption function shifts when wealth changes.

Multiple choice

1. The components of aggregate expenditure are consumption expenditure,
   a. interest, gross spending, and net spending.
   b. investment, government expenditure on goods and services, and net income.
   c. interest, government expenditure on goods and services, and net exports.
   d. investment, government expenditure on goods and services, and net exports.
   e. investment, government expenditure on goods and services, and net taxes.

2. Autonomous expenditure is the component of
   a. aggregate expenditure that changes when real GDP changes.
   b. induced expenditure that changes when real GDP changes.
   c. aggregate planned expenditure that changes only when government expenditure on goods and services change.
   d. aggregate expenditure that does not change when real GDP changes.
   e. aggregate expenditure that does not change when the interest rate changes.

3. The components of aggregate expenditure that change when real GDP changes are
   a. unplanned expenditure.
   b. induced expenditure.
   c. planned expenditure.
   d. autonomous expenditure.
   e. changeable expenditure.

4. The consumption function is the relationship between ____, other things remaining the same.
   a. consumption expenditure and saving
   b. consumption expenditure and the price level
   c. consumption expenditure and disposable income
   d. net taxes and disposable income
   e. consumption expenditure and net taxes

5. When disposable income increases from $9 trillion to $10 trillion, consumption expenditure increases from $6 trillion to $6.8 trillion. The *MPC* is
   a. 1.00.
   b. 0.80.
   c. 0.60.
   d. 0.68.
   e. $6.8 trillion.

■ **FIGURE 14.1**

Consumption expenditure (billions of 2005 dollars)

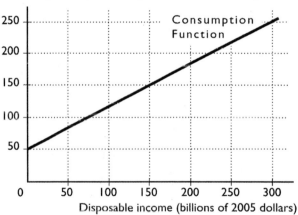

6. Figure 14.1 shows a consumption function. What is the amount of autonomous consumption?
   a. $0
   b. $50 billion
   c. $100 billion
   d. $150 billion
   e. $200 billion

7. Figure 14.1 shows a consumption function. What is the amount of induced consumption when disposable income equals $150 billion?
   a. $0
   b. $50 billion
   c. $100 billion
   d. $150 billion
   e. $200 billion

8. Figure 14.1 shows a consumption function. What does the *MPC* equal?
   a. 1.00
   b. 0.80
   c. 0.67
   d. 0.60
   e. 0.50

9. Consumption expenditure _____ and the consumption function shifts _____ when wealth _____.
   a. increases; upward; increases
   b. increases; upward; decreases
   c. decreases; downward; increases
   d. decreases; upward; decreases
   e. increases; downward; increases

Complete the graph

Disposable income (trillions of 2005 dollars)	Consumption expenditure, (trillions of 2005 dollars)
0.0	0.4
1.0	1.2
2.0	2.0
3.0	2.8
4.0	3.6
5.0	4.4

1. The table above has data on consumption expenditure and disposable income.
   a. Using the data, label the axes and plot the consumption function in Figure 14.2.
   b. Indicate the amount of autonomous consumption expenditure in Figure 14.2.
   c. What is the amount of saving if disposable income equals $1.0 trillion? $4.0 trillion?
   d. Calculate the marginal propensity to consume.
   e. Suppose the real interest rate falls and consumers increase their consumption by

■ **FIGURE 14.2**

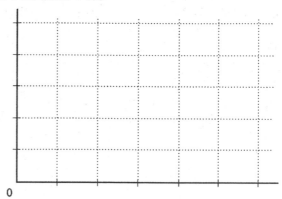

0

$0.6 trillion at every level of disposable income. Draw the new consumption function in Figure 14.2. What is the amount of autonomous consumption now?

Short answer and numeric questions

1. What does aggregate planned expenditure equal?
2. What is the difference between autonomous expenditure and induced expenditure?
3. In a graph with a consumption function, what does the *MPC* equal? What does autonomous consumption equal?

Change in disposable income (trillions of 2005 dollars)	Change in consumption expenditure (trillions of 2005 dollars)	Marginal propensity to consume, *MPC*
2	1.8	_____
1	0.9	_____
4	3.0	_____

4. The table above shows the change in consumption expenditure when a change in disposable income occurs. Complete the table by calculating the marginal propensities to consume.

Additional Exercises (also in MyEconLab Test A)

1. The marginal propensity to consume in Japan is less than that in the United States, and for any amount of real GDP, Americans spend more on consumption than do the Japanese. Compare the consumption functions in Japan and the United States.

2. As China becomes richer, the marginal propensity to consume in China will decrease. Explain how the consumption function in China will change.

3. Autonomous consumption in the United Kingdom was £150 billion and the marginal propensity to consume was 0.9. Plot the U.K. consumption function and explain how a rise in the real interest rate will influence it.

4. The marginal propensity to import is higher in Singapore than it is in the United States. The growth rate of real GDP in Singapore exceeds that in the United States. Which country's imports grow more quickly and why?

CHECKPOINT 14.2

■ **Explain how real GDP adjusts to achieve equilibrium expenditure.**

Quick Review

- *Equilibrium expenditure* The level of aggregate expenditure that occurs when aggregate planned expenditure equals real GDP.

Additional Practice Problem 14.2

GDP	C	I	G	X	M
50	50	20	25	25	10
100	85	20	25	25	15
150	120	20	25	25	20
200	155	20	25	25	25
250	190	20	25	25	30
300	225	20	25	25	35

1. The table gives the components of real GDP in billions of dollars.
   a. Draw the aggregate expenditure curve.
   b. What is equilibrium expenditure?
   c. At what levels of GDP does aggregate planned expenditure exceed real GDP? At what levels does real GDP exceed aggregate planned expenditure?
   d. At what levels of GDP is unplanned inventory change negative? At what levels is unplanned inventory change positive?

e. What is the relationship between your answers to parts (c) and (d)?
f. By what process is the equilibrium expenditure reached?

Solution to Additional Practice Problem 14.2

1a. Aggregate planned expenditure is equal to C + I + G + X − M. To construct the AE curve, use the formula for each level of real GDP. The AE curve is illustrated in the figure along with a 45° line.

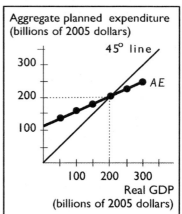

1b. Equilibrium expenditure occurs at the level of real GDP where the AE curve intersects the 45° line. The equilibrium expenditure is $200 billion.

1c. For all GDP less than $200 billion, aggregate planned expenditure exceeds real GDP. For all GDP greater than $200 billion, aggregate planned expenditure exceeds real GDP.

1d. For all GDP less than $200 billion, unplanned inventory change is negative. For all GDP greater than $200 billion, unplanned inventory change is positive.

1e. For all levels of GDP for which aggregate planned expenditure exceeds real GDP, unplanned inventory change is negative. And for all levels of GDP for which real GDP exceeds aggregate planned expenditure, unplanned inventory change is positive.

1f. If aggregate planned expenditure exceeds real GDP, unplanned inventory change is negative so firms increase production and real GDP increases. Eventually real GDP increases enough so that it equals aggregate planned expenditure and equilibrium is reached. If aggregate planned expenditure is less than real GDP, unplanned inventory change is positive and so firms decrease production and real GDP decreases. Eventually real GDP decreases by enough so that it equals aggregate planned expenditure and equilibrium is reached. When real GDP reaches $200 billion, aggregate planned expenditure equals real GDP. The economy is at equilibrium expenditure. The unplanned inventory change is zero and firms have no reason to change production.

■ Self Test 14.2

Fill in the blanks

Aggregate planned expenditure equals _____ plus _____ plus _____ plus _____ minus _____. As real GDP increases, aggregate planned expenditure _____ (increases; does not change; decreases). Equilibrium expenditure occurs when aggregate planned expenditure is the level of aggregate expenditure that equals _____. When aggregate planned expenditure exceeds real GDP, an unplanned _____ (increase; decrease) in inventories occurs and firms _____ (increase; decrease) production.

True or false

1. Equilibrium expenditure occurs at the intersection of the aggregate expenditure curve and the 45° line.

2. If aggregate planned expenditure is less than real GDP, unplanned inventories increase.

3. If aggregate planned expenditure exceeds real GDP, inventories decrease and firms decrease production.

4. If unplanned investment occurs, then the aggregate expenditure is not at its equilibrium level.

Multiple choice

1. When aggregate planned expenditure exceeds real GDP, there is
   a. a planned decrease in inventories.
   b. a planned increase in inventories.
   c. an unplanned decrease in inventories.
   d. an unplanned increase in inventory.
   e. an unplanned decrease in the price level.

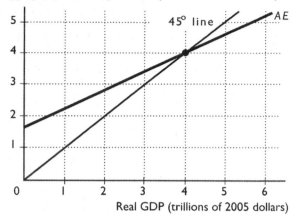

■ **FIGURE 14.3**
Aggregate planned expenditure (trillions of 2005 dollars)

2. In Figure 14.3, equilibrium expenditure equals _____ trillion.
   a. $1
   b. $2
   c. $3
   d. $4
   e. $5

3. In Figure 14.3, if real GDP is $5 trillion, then
   a. the economy is at its equilibrium.
   b. inventories are above their target.
   c. inventories are below their target
   d. the price level will rise to restore equilibrium.
   e. the price level will fall to restore equilibrium.

4. If aggregate planned expenditure is greater than real GDP,
   a. an unplanned decrease in inventories leads to an increase in production.
   b. an unplanned increase in inventories leads to a decrease in production.
   c. a planned decrease in inventories leads to an decrease in production.
   d. a planned increase in inventories leads to an increase in production.
   e. an unplanned decrease in inventories leads to an increase in the price level.

5. If real GDP equals aggregate planned expenditure, then inventories are
   a. above their target levels.
   b. below their target levels.
   c. equal their target levels.
   d. are either above or below their target levels but more information is needed to determine which.
   e. None of the above answers is necessarily correct because there is no relationship between inventories and aggregate planned expenditure.

6. Equilibrium expenditure is the level of expenditure at which
   a. firms' inventories are zero.
   b. firms' inventories are at the desired level.
   c. firms produce more output than they sell.
   d. aggregate planned expenditure minus planned changes in inventories equals real GDP.
   e. aggregate planned expenditure plus planned changes in inventories equals real GDP.

Complete the graph

GDP	C	I	G	X	M	AE
0.0	0.6	0.4	0.2	0.2	0.2	___
1.0	1.2	0.4	0.2	0.2	0.4	___
2.0	1.8	0.4	0.2	0.2	0.6	___
3.0	2.4	0.4	0.2	0.2	0.8	___
4.0	3.0	0.4	0.2	0.2	1.0	___
5.0	3.6	0.4	0.2	0.2	1.2	___

1. The table above gives the components of aggregate planned expenditure in trillions of 2005 dollars.
   a. Complete the table.
   b. Label the axes in Figure 14.4 (at the top of the next column) and plot the AE curve.
   c. In Figure 14.4, show the equilibrium expenditure.
   d. Over what range of GDP is there an unplanned increase in inventories? Over what range of GDP is there an unplanned decrease in inventories?
   e. What is the amount of planned and actual investment when GDP equals $3.0 trillion?

■ **FIGURE 14.4**

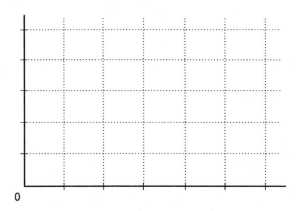

Short answer and numeric questions

1. What is the relationship between aggregate planned expenditure and real GDP? Explain the relationship.

2. In a diagram with an *AE* curve, what does the 45° line represent? Why is equilibrium expenditure determined by the intersection of the aggregate expenditure curve and the 45° line?

3. If aggregate planned expenditure is less than real GDP, what forces drive the economy to equilibrium expenditure?

Additional Exercises (also in MyEconLab Test A)

■ **FIGURE 14.5**

Aggregate planned expenditure (trillions of 2005 dollars)

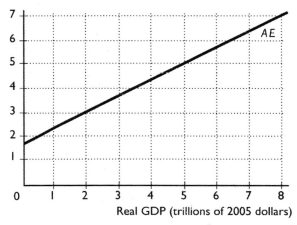

Real GDP (trillions of 2005 dollars)

Figure 14.5 shows aggregate planned expenditure.
1. What is aggregate planned expenditure

when real GDP is $8 billion and when real GDP is $2 billion?

2. Calculate equilibrium expenditure.

3. If real GDP is $8 billion, explain the process that moves the economy toward equilibrium expenditure.

4. If real GDP is $2 billion, explain the process that moves the economy toward equilibrium expenditure.

CHECKPOINT 14.3

■ **Explain the expenditure multiplier.**

Quick Review

- *Multiplier* The expenditure multiplier is the amount by which a change in any component of autonomous expenditure is magnified or multiplied to determine the change that it generates in equilibrium expenditure and real GDP.

- *Basic multiplier formula* The defining multiplier formula is:

$$\text{Multiplier} = \frac{\text{Change in equilibrium expenditure}}{\text{Change in autonomous expenditure}}.$$

- *Multiplier and the MPC* With no imports or income taxes, the multiplier is:

$$\text{Multiplier} = \frac{1}{(1 - MPC)}.$$

- *Multiplier, imports and income taxes* With imports and income taxes, the multiplier is:

$$\text{Multiplier} = \frac{1}{(1 - \text{slope of the } AE \text{ curve})}.$$

Additional Practice Problems 14.3

1. An economy has no imports or taxes, the *MPC* is 0.90, and real GDP is $12 trillion. If businesses increase investment by $0.1 trillion:
   a. Calculate the multiplier.
   b. Calculate the change in real GDP.
   c. Calculate the new level of real GDP.

2. An increase in autonomous expenditure of $2 trillion increases equilibrium expenditure by $4 trillion:

   a. Calculate the multiplier.
   b. Calculate the slope of the *AE* curve.

3. Suppose there are no income taxes or imports. How would the following events affect equilibrium expenditure and real GDP?
   a. Investment increases by $40 billion and the *MPC* equals 0.6.
   b. The president and Congress agree to increase military spending by $100 billion and the *MPC* is 0.8.

Solutions to Additional Practice Problems 14.3

1a. With no taxes or imports, the multiplier equals $1/(1 - MPC)$. The *MPC* is 0.9, so the multiplier equals $1/(1 - 0.9)$, which equals 10.0.

1b. The change in real GDP is equal to the multiplier times the change in investment, which is $10 \times \$0.1$ trillion = $1 trillion.

1c. Real GDP increases by $1 trillion from $12 trillion to $13 trillion.

2a. The multiplier equals the change in equilibrium expenditure divided by the change in autonomous expenditure. The multiplier equals $4 trillion ÷ $2 trillion, which is 2.

2b. The expenditure multiplier equals $1/(1 - \text{slope}$ of the *AE* curve). The multiplier is 2, so $2 = 1/(1 - \text{slope of the } AE \text{ curve})$. Multiply both sides by $(1 - \text{slope of the } AE \text{ curve})$ to get $2 \times (1 - \text{slope of the } AE \text{ curve}) = 1$. Solve for the slope of the *AE* curve, which is that the slope of the *AE* curve is 0.50.

3a. The increase in investment is an increase in autonomous expenditure. The change in equilibrium expenditure and real GDP equals the multiplier times the change in autonomous expenditure. The multiplier equals $1/(1 - MPC) = 1/(1 - 0.6) = 2.5$. The change in equilibrium expenditure and real GDP equals $(2.5 \times \$40$ billion), which is $100 billion. Equilibrium expenditure and real GDP increase by $100 billion.

3b. The increase in military spending is an increase in government purchases and is an increase in autonomous expenditure. The change in equilibrium expenditure and real

GDP equals the multiplier times the change in autonomous expenditure. The multiplier equals 1/(1 − MPC). Because the MPC equals 0.8, the multiplier is 5.0. The change in equilibrium expenditure and real GDP equals (5.0 × $100 billion), which is $500 billion.

■ Self Test 14.3

Fill in the blanks

The multiplier equals the change in equilibrium expenditure ____ (minus; divided by; multiplied by) the change in autonomous expenditure. The multiplier is ____ (less than; greater than) 1. If there are no taxes or imports, the multiplier equals 1 divided by 1 minus the ____. Imports and income taxes make the multiplier ____ (larger; smaller). A recession is started by ____ (an increase; a decrease) in autonomous expenditure.

True or false

1. The multiplier is greater than 1.

2. If the multiplier equals 4, then a $0.25 trillion increase in investment increases real GDP by $1.0 trillion.

3. The smaller the marginal propensity to consume, the larger is the multiplier.

4. A country that has a high marginal tax rate has a larger multiplier than a country with a low marginal tax rate, other things being the same.

Multiple choice

1. The multiplier is equal to the change in ____ divided by the change in ____.
   a. autonomous expenditure; equilibrium expenditure
   b. dependent expenditure; autonomous expenditure
   c. real GDP; equilibrium expenditure
   d. equilibrium expenditure; autonomous expenditure
   e. the price level; real GDP

2. The multiplier is larger than one because
   a. an increase in autonomous expenditure induces further increases in aggregate expenditure.
   b. additional expenditure induces lower incomes.
   c. an increase in autonomous expenditure brings about a reduction in the real interest rate.
   d. an increase in autonomous expenditure induces further decreases in aggregate expenditure.
   e. the price level rises, thereby reinforcing the initial effect.

3. The multiplier equals 5 and there is a $3 million increase in investment. Equilibrium expenditure
   a. decreases by $15 million.
   b. increases by $3 million.
   c. increases by $5 million.
   d. increases by $15 million.
   e. increases by $0.60 million.

4. In an economy with no income taxes or imports, the marginal propensity to consume is 0.80. The multiplier is
   a. 0.20.
   b. 0.80.
   c. 1.25.
   d. 5.00.
   e. 10.00.

5. An increase in the marginal tax rate
   a. increases the multiplier.
   b. decreases the multiplier but cannot make it negative.
   c. has no effect on the multiplier.
   d. can either increase or decrease the multiplier.
   e. decreases the multiplier and can make it negative.

6. Which of the following increases the size of the multiplier?
   a. a decrease in the marginal propensity to consume
   b. an increase in autonomous spending
   c. an increase in the marginal income tax rate
   d. a decrease in the marginal propensity to import
   e. an increase in investment

7. If the slope of the *AE* curve is 0.5, then the expenditure multiplier equals
   a. 5.
   b. 4.
   c. 3.
   d. 2.
   e. 0.5.

8. At the beginning of a recession, the multiplier
   a. offsets the initial cut in autonomous expenditure and slows the recession.
   b. reinforces the initial cut in autonomous expenditure and adds force to the recession.
   c. offsets the initial cut in autonomous expenditure and reverses the recession.
   d. reinforces the initial cut in autonomous expenditure and reverses the recession.
   e. has no effect on the recession.

Complete the graph

■ **FIGURE 14.6**
Aggregate planned expenditure (trillions of 2005 dollars)

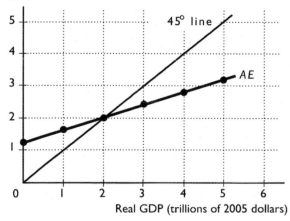

1. Figure 14.6 has the aggregate planned ex-

penditure curve for a nation. (This curve is the same curve you plotted in the "Complete the Graph" problem in Checkpoint 14.2.) Suppose that government expenditure on goods and services increases by $1.2 trillion.
   a. In Figure 14.6 plot the new aggregate expenditure curve.
   b. What is the new equilibrium expenditure? By how much did equilibrium expenditure change?
   c. What is the slope of the *AE* curve?
   d. What is the multiplier? Use the multiplier to find the change in equilibrium expenditure.

Short answer and numeric questions

Marginal propensity to consume, MPC	Multiplier
0.9	——
0.8	——
0.7	——
0.6	——
0.5	——
0.4	——

1. The table gives various values for the marginal propensity to consume. Suppose there are no income taxes or imports. Complete the table by calculating the values of the multiplier. What is the relationship between the *MPC* and the multiplier?

2. Why is the multiplier greater than 1?

3. How does the multiplier affect business cycle turning points?

Additional Exercises (also in MyEconLab Test A)
An economy has no imports and no income taxes. The marginal propensity to consume is 0.60, and real GDP is $100 billion. Businesses decrease investment by $10 billion. Use this information to answer Exercises 1 and 2.
1. Calculate the multiplier and the change in real GDP.
2. Calculate the new level of real GDP and explain why real GDP decreases by more than $10 billion.

An economy has no imports and no income taxes. Autonomous expenditure increases by $2 trillion and the multiplier is 1.25. Use this information to answer Exercises 3 and 4.

3. Calculate the change in real GDP and the marginal propensity to consume.

4. If the government opens the country to international trade, explain how international trade influences the multiplier.

CHECKPOINT 14.4

■ **Derive the AD curve from equilibrium expenditure.**

Quick Review

- *Equilibrium expenditure* The level of aggregate expenditure that occurs when aggregate planned expenditure equals real GDP.

- *Aggregate demand* The aggregate demand schedule is real GDP at equilibrium expenditure and the associated price level.

Additional Practice Problem 14.4

■ **FIGURE 14.7**
Aggregate planned expenditure (trillions of 2005 dollars)

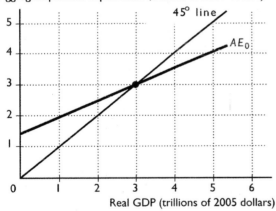

1. Figure 14.7 shows the *AE* curve, *AE*₀, when the price level is 100.

    a. In the figure, show what occurs when the price level rises to 110 and aggregate planned expenditure decreases by $1 trillion at every level of real GDP. What is the new equilibrium expenditure?

b. In the figure, show what occurs when the price level falls to 90 and aggregate planned expenditure increases by $1 trillion at every level of real GDP. What is the new equilibrium expenditure?

c. Use the results from parts (a) and (b) to draw an aggregate demand curve in Figure 14.8.

■ **FIGURE 14.8**
Price level (GDP price index, 2005 = 100)

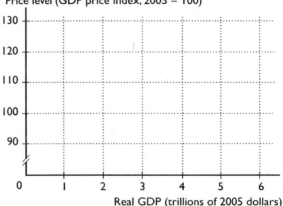

Solution to Additional Practice Problem 14.4

■ **FIGURE 14.9**
Aggregate planned expenditure (trillions of 2005 dollars)

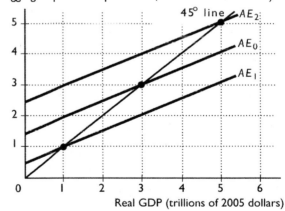

1a. Figure 14.9 shows the new aggregate expenditure curve, labeled *AE*₁. The new equilibrium expenditure is $1 trillion, where the *AE*₁ curve intersects the 45° line.

1b. Figure 14.9 shows the new aggregate expenditure curve, labeled AE_2. The new equilibrium expenditure is $5 trillion.

■ **FIGURE 14.10**

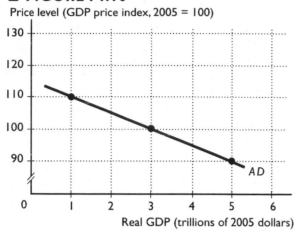

Price level (GDP price index, 2005 = 100)

Real GDP (trillions of 2005 dollars)

1c. Points on the aggregate demand schedule are the points of equilibrium expenditure. So each point of equilibrium expenditure corresponds to a point on the *AD* curve. When the price level is 110, real GDP is $1 trillion. When the price level is 100, real GDP is $3 trillion. And when the price level is 90, real GDP is $5 trillion. These points and the aggregate demand curve are shown Figure 14.10. The aggregate demand curve has been derived from the equilibrium expenditure model.

■ **Self Test 14.4**

Fill in the blanks

The _____ (*AE; AD*) curve is derived from the _____ (*AE; AD*) curve. The _____ (*AE; AD*) curve is the relationship between aggregate planned expenditure and real GDP. The _____ (*AE; AD*) curve is the relationship between the quantity of real GDP demanded and the price level. The _____ (*AE; AD*) curve is upward sloping and the _____ (*AE; AD*) curve is downward sloping. The _____ (*AE; AD*) curve shifts when the price level changes. There is a movement along the _____ (*AE; AD*) curve when the price level changes.

True or false

1. There is no relationship between equilibrium expenditure and the *AD* curve.

2. A change in the price level results in a movement along the *AD* curve.

3. A change in the price level results in a movement along the *AE* curve.

4. Each point of equilibrium expenditure on the *AE* curve corresponds to a point on the *AD* curve.

Multiple choice

1. A movement along the *AE* curve arises from a change in ____ and a movement along the *AD* curve arises from a change in ____.
   a. real GDP; the price level
   b. real GDP; investment
   c. the price level; the price level
   d. the price level; investment
   e. investment; the price level

2. A change in the price level
   a. shifts the *AE* curve and creates a movement along the *AD* curve.
   b. creates a movement along the *AE* curve and shifts the *AD* curve.
   c. shifts the *AE* curve and the *AD* curve in the same direction.
   d. shifts the *AE* curve and the *AD* curve in opposite directions.
   e. creates a movement along both the *AE* curve and the *AD* curve.

3. The *AD* curve is the relationship between
   a. aggregate planned expenditure and the price level.
   b. aggregate planned expenditure and the quantity of real GDP demanded.
   c. the quantity of real GDP demanded and the quantity of real GDP supplied.
   d. the quantity of real GDP demanded and the unemployment rate.
   e. aggregate planned expenditure and real GDP when the price level is fixed.

Complete the graph

■ **FIGURE 14.11**

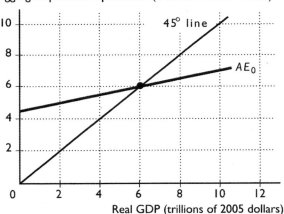

1. Figure 14.11 has the aggregate planned expenditure curve for a nation when the price level is 100. Autonomous expenditure equals $4.25 trillion.

   a. Suppose the price level rises to 120 and aggregate planned expenditure decreases by $0.75 trillion at every level of real GDP. In the figure, show the new aggregate expenditure line. What does equilibrium expenditure now equal?

   b. Suppose that the price level falls to 100 and, compared to the situation when the price level equaled 110, aggregate planned expenditure increases by $0.75 trillion at every level of real GDP. In the figure, show the new aggregate expenditure line. What does equilibrium expenditure now equal?

   c. Use the results from parts (a) and (b) to draw an aggregate demand curve in Figure 14.12.

■ **FIGURE 14.12**

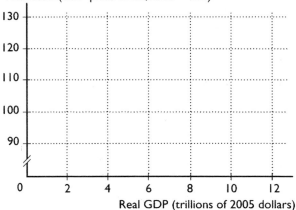

Short answer and numeric questions

1. What is the relationship between the AE curve and the AD curve?

2. What is the effect on the AE curve when the price level rises? What is the effect on the AD curve when the price level rises?

Additional Exercises (also in MyEconLab Test A)

Real GDP (trillions of 2005 dollars)	Aggregate planned expenditure when the price level is (trillions of 2005 dollars)		
	110	100	90
0	1.0	1.5	2.0
1	1.5	2.0	2.5
2	2.0	2.5	3.0
3	2.5	3.0	3.5
4	3.0	3.5	4.0
5	3.5	4.0	4.5
6	4.0	4.5	5.0

In the economy described in the table above, autonomous expenditure increases by $0.5 trillion.

1. Make a graph to show three new AE curves. On the graph, mark equilibrium expenditure at each price level.

2. Construct the aggregate demand schedule and plot the AD curve.

3. Calculate the magnitude of the multiplier.

■ CHECKPOINT 14.1

Fill in the blanks

The components of aggregate expenditure that change when real GDP changes are induced expenditure. The components of aggregate expenditure that do not change when real GDP changes are autonomous expenditure. The consumption function is the relationship between consumption expenditure and disposable income. The marginal propensity to consume equals the change in consumption expenditure divided by the change in disposable income that brought it about. The slope of the consumption function equals the marginal propensity to consume. A change in disposable income is shown by a movement along the consumption function, a change in expected future income is shown by a shift in the consumption function. Imports are a part of induced expenditure.

True or false

1. True; page 348
2. True; page 349
3. False; page 350
4. True; page 351

Multiple choice

1. d; page 348
2. d; page 348
3. b; page 348
4. c; page 348
5. b; page 350
6. b; pages 348-349
7. c; pages 348-349
8. c; page 350
9. a; page 351

Complete the graph

1. a. Figure 14.13 plots the consumption function, labeled CF_0; page 349.
   b. Autonomous consumption is $0.4 trillion, the y-intercept of curve CF_0 in Figure 14.13; pages 348-349.

■ **FIGURE 14.13**

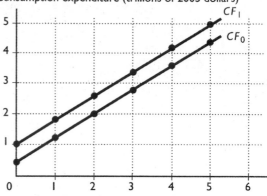

Consumption expenditure (trillions of 2005 dollars)

Disposable income (trillions of 2005 dollars)

c. If disposable income is $1.0 trillion, consumption expenditure is $1.2 trillion, so saving is –$0.2 trillion. If disposable income is $4.0 trillion consumption expenditure is $3.6 trillion, so saving is $0.4 trillion; page 349.
d. The marginal propensity to consume is 0.80; page 350.
e. The new consumption function is labeled CF_1 in Figure 14.13. Autonomous consumption is $1 trillion; pages 348, 351.

Short answer and numeric questions

1. Aggregate planned expenditure equals planned consumption expenditure plus planned investment plus planned government expenditures plus planned exports minus planned imports; page 348.
2. Autonomous expenditures are the components of aggregate expenditure that do not change when real GDP changes. Induced expenditures are the components of aggregate expenditure that change when real GDP changes; page 348.
3. The MPC equals the slope of the consumption function. Autonomous consumption equals the y-axis intercept; pages 348, 350.

Change in disposable income (trillions of 2005 dollars)	Change in consumption expenditure (trillions of 2005 dollars)	Marginal propensity to consume, MPC
2	1.8	0.90
1	0.9	0.90
4	3.0	0.75

4. The completed table is above. The marginal propensity to consume is equal to the change in consumption expenditure divided by the change in disposable income that brought it about; page 350.

Additional Exercises (also in MyEconLab Test A)

1. The U.S. consumption function and the Japanese consumption function differ in two aspects. First, because the marginal propensity to consume is less in Japan, the U.S. consumption function is steeper than the Japanese consumption function. Second, because for any level of real GDP, Americans spend more on consumption than do the Japanese, U.S. autonomous consumption exceeds Japanese autonomous consumption. So, the U.S. consumption function lies above the Japanese consumption function; page 350.

2. The decrease in the Chinese marginal propensity to consume makes the Chinese consumption function become less steep; page 350.

■ FIGURE 14.14

Consumption expenditure (billions of 2005 pounds)

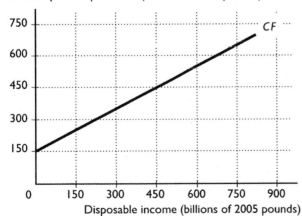

3. The U.K. consumption function is in Figure

14.14. The intercept on the *y*-axis is £150 billion, which is the amount of autonomous consumption expenditure. The slope is 0.90, which is the U.K. marginal propensity to consume. If the real interest rate rises, the consumption function shifts downward; pages 348-350.

4. Imports are related to a nation's real GDP via the marginal propensity to import. The higher the marginal propensity to import, the greater the amount of imports from any given real GDP. The growth rate of real GDP in Singapore exceeds that in the United States, so the growth of imports in Singapore will exceed the growth of imports in the United States; page 352.

■ CHECKPOINT 14.2

Fill in the blanks

Aggregate planned expenditure equals con-sumption expenditure plus investment plus government purchases of goods and services plus exports minus imports. As real GDP increases, aggregate planned expenditure in-creases. Equilibrium expenditure is the level of aggregate expenditure that occurs when aggregate planned expenditure equals real GDP. When aggregate planned expenditure exceeds real GDP, an unplanned decrease in inventories occurs and firms increase production.

True or false

1. True; page 356
2. True; page 357
3. False; page 357
4. True; page 357

Multiple choice

1. c; page 357
2. d; page 356
3. b; page 357
4. a; page 357
5. c; page 357
6. b; page 357

Complete the graph

GDP	C	I	G	X	M	AE
0.0	0.6	0.4	0.2	0.2	0.2	1.2
1.0	1.2	0.4	0.2	0.2	0.4	1.6
2.0	1.8	0.4	0.2	0.2	0.6	2.0
3.0	2.4	0.4	0.2	0.2	0.8	2.4
4.0	3.0	0.4	0.2	0.2	1.0	2.8
5.0	3.6	0.4	0.2	0.2	1.2	3.2

1. a. Aggregate planned expenditure equals $C + I + G + X - M$. The completed table is above; pages 354-355.

■ FIGURE 14.15
Aggregate planned expenditure (trillions of 2005 dollars)

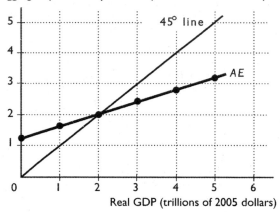

b. Figure 14.15 shows the aggregate expenditure curve; page 355.

c. A 45° line has been added to Figure 14.15. Equilibrium expenditure is where the 45° line intersects the aggregate expenditure curve, so equilibrium expenditure is $2 trillion; page 356.

d. An unplanned increase in inventories occurs when real GDP exceeds aggregate planned expenditure. In Figure 14.15, real GDP exceeds planned expenditure when real GDP is greater than $2 trillion; page 356.

An unplanned decrease in inventories occurs when real GDP is less than aggregate planned expenditure. In Figure 14.15, real GDP is less than planned expenditure when real GDP is less than $2 trillion; page 356.

e. When GDP is $3 trillion, planned invest-

ment is $0.4 trillion. When GDP is $3 trillion, aggregate planned expenditure is $2.4 trillion, so there is an unplanned increase in inventories of $0.6 trillion. The actual investment is $1 trillion, the sum of planned investment plus the unplanned change in inventories; page 357.

Short answer and numeric questions

1. As real GDP increases, aggregate planned expenditure increases, so there is a positive relationship between real GDP and aggregate planned expenditure. Aggregate planned expenditure increases when real GDP increases because, as real GDP increases, induced expenditure increases; pages 354-355.

2. Along the 45° line real GDP equals aggregate planned expenditure. Equilibrium expenditure occurs when aggregate planned expenditure equals real GDP, which is the point where the AE curve intersects the 45° line; page 356.

3. If aggregate planned expenditure is less than real GDP, total expenditure is less than what firms are producing. There is an unplanned increase in inventories. Firms decrease production, and real GDP decreases. Firms continue to decrease production until the unplanned inventory change is zero. When this occurs, real GDP and aggregate expenditure are in equilibrium; page 357.

Additional Exercises (also in MyEconLab Test A)

1. Aggregate planned expenditure when real GDP is $8 billion is $7 billion. Aggregate planned expenditure when real GDP is $2 billion is $3 billion; page 356.

2. Equilibrium expenditure occurs where aggregate planned expenditure equals real GDP. (Equivalently, equilibrium expenditure occurs where the AE curve intersects the 45° line.) Aggregate planned expenditure equals real GDP at $5 billion, so $5 billion is equilibrium expenditure; page 356.

3. If real GDP equals $8 billion, real GDP exceeds aggregate planned expenditure. Firms find that they are not selling all that they

produce and inventories are climbing above their target levels. The unplanned inventory accumulation leads firms to decrease their production, so that real GDP decreases and the economy converges toward its equilibrium of $5 billion; page 357.

4. If real GDP equals $2 billion, aggregate planned expenditure exceeds real GDP. Firms find their inventories falling below the target levels. In response, firms increase production to restore their inventories to their target levels. Real GDP increases and the economy moves toward its equilibrium expenditure of $5 billion; page 357.

■ CHECKPOINT 14.3

Fill in the blanks

The multiplier equals the change in equilibrium expenditure <u>divided by</u> the change in autonomous expenditure. The multiplier is <u>greater than 1</u>. If there are no taxes or imports, the multiplier equals 1 divided by 1 minus the <u>marginal propensity to consume</u>. Imports and income taxes make the multiplier <u>smaller</u>. A recession is started by <u>a decrease</u> in autonomous expenditure.

True or false

1. True; pages 360-361
2. True; page 361
3. False; pages 361-362
4. False; page 362

Multiple choice

1. d; page 361
2. a; page 361
3. d; page 361
4. d; page 362
5. b; page 362
6. d; page 362
7. d; page 362
8. b; page 365

Complete the graph

■ FIGURE 14.16

Aggregate planned expenditure (trillions of 2005 dollars)

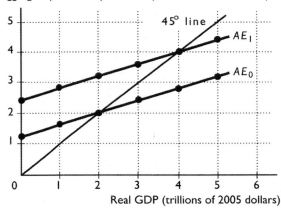

1. a. Figure 14.16 has the new AE curve, labeled AE₁ and the initial curve labeled AE₀; page 361.

 b. Equilibrium expenditure increases by $2 trillion to $4 trillion; page 361.

 c. The slope of the AE curve equals ($0.4 trillion) ÷ ($1.0 trillion), which is 0.40; page 361.

 d. The formula for the multiplier is given by $\frac{1}{(1-\text{slope of the }AE\text{ curve})}$. Thus the multiplier is $\frac{1}{(1-0.4)}$ = 1.67. The change is equal to the multiplier multiplied by the change in autonomous expenditure, which is (1.67) × ($1.2 trillion). The change in equilibrium expenditure is $2.0 trillion; pages 360, 362.

Short answer and numeric questions

Marginal propensity to consume, MPC	Multiplier
0.9	10.0
0.8	5.0
0.7	3.3
0.6	2.5
0.5	2.0
0.4	1.7

1. The multiplier equals 1 ÷ (1 − MPC). The

completed table is above. As the *MPC* increases in size, the multiplier increases in size; pages 361-362.

2. The multiplier exceeds 1 because an initial change in autonomous expenditure leads to changes in induced expenditure. As a result, the change in aggregate expenditure exceeds the initial change in autonomous expenditure; page 361.

3. The forces that bring business-cycle turning points are the swings in autonomous expenditure such as investment and exports. The multiplier gives momentum to the economy's new direction; page 364.

Additional Exercises (also in MyEconLab Test A)

1. Because the economy has no imports or taxes, the multiplier equals $\frac{1}{(1-MPC)}$, which is

$\frac{1}{(1-0.6)} = \frac{1}{0.4} = 2.5$. The change in real GDP =

change in investment × multiplier = −$10 billion × 2.5 = −$25 billion. Real GDP decreases by $25 billion; pages 361-362.

2. The new level of real GDP is $100 billion −$25 billion, which is $75 billion. Real GDP decreases by more than the $10 billion because the initial decrease in investment decreases real GDP. And the decrease in real GDP decreases induced expenditure, which decreases real GDP even more; page 361.

3. The change in real GDP equals the multiplier × the change in autonomous expenditure. Therefore the change in real GDP= 1.25 × $2 trillion = $2.5 trillion.

Because there are no taxes or imports, the multiplier = $\frac{1}{(1-MPC)}$. We know that the multiplier equals 1.25, so 1.25 = $\frac{1}{(1-MPC)}$.

Solve this formula for the *MPC*. Multiplying both sides by (1 − *MPC*) gives 1.25 × (1 − *MPC*) = 1. Multiplying both sides of the equation by 1.25 gives 1.25 − 1.25 × *MPC* = 1.

Subtracting 1.25 from both sides gives −1.25 × *MPC* = −.25. Dividing both sides by −1.25 gives *MPC* = 0.2; pages 361-362.

4. Opening the economy to trade decreases the magnitude of the multiplier; page 362.

■ CHECKPOINT 14.4

Fill in the blanks

The *AD* curve is derived from the *AE* curve. The *AE* curve is the relationship between aggregate planned expenditure and real GDP. The *AD* curve is the relationship between the quantity of real GDP demanded and the price level. The *AE* curve is upward sloping and the *AD* curve is downward sloping. The *AE* curve shifts when the price level changes. There is a movement along the *AD* curve when the price level changes.

True or false

1. False; pages 366-367.
2. True; pages 366-367.
3. False; pages 366-367.
4. True; pages 366-367.

Multiple choice

1. a; page 366
2. a; pages 366-367
3. c; page 366

Complete the graph

1. a. Figure 14.17 (on the next page) has the new *AE* curve, labeled *AE1* and the initial curve labeled *AE0* Equilibrium expenditure decreases by $2 trillion to $4 trillion; pages 366-367.

   b. Figure 14.17 has the new *AE* curve, labeled *AE2* Equilibrium expenditure increases by $2 trillion to $8 trillion; pages 366-367.

   c. Figure 14.18 (on the next page) shows the aggregate demand curve. The three points identified have been derived from Figure 14.17 and equilibrium expenditure. When the price level is 120, equilibrium expenditure and real GDP is $4 trillion. When the

■ **FIGURE 14.17**
Aggregate planned expenditure (trillions of 2005 dollars)

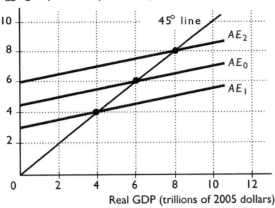

■ **FIGURE 14.18**
Price level (GDP price index, 2005 = 100)

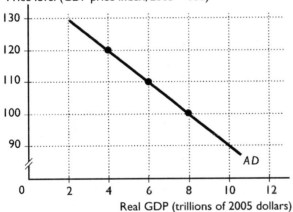

price level is 110, equilibrium expenditure and real GDP is $6 trillion. And when the price level is 100, equilibrium expenditure and real GDP is $8 trillion; page 367

Short answer and numeric questions

1. The *AE* curve is used to derive the *AD* curve. Each point of equilibrium expenditure on the *AE* curve corresponds to a point on the *AD* curve; page 366.

2. When the price level rises, the *AE* curve shifts downward and there is a movement up along the *AD* curve. When the price level falls, the *AE* curve shifts upward and there is a movement down along the *AD* curve; pages 366-367.

Additional Exercises (also in MyEconLab Test A)

■ **FIGURE 14.19**
Aggregate planned expenditure (trillions of 2005 dollars)

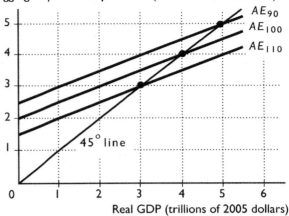

■ **FIGURE 14.20**
Price level (GDP price index, 2005 = 100)

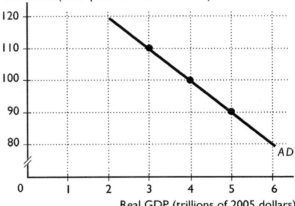

1. Figure 14.19 illustrates the three new *AE* curves. Figure 14.19 also shows the equilibrium expenditures. The equilibrium expenditure when the price level is 90 is $5 trillion. The equilibrium expenditure when the price level is 100 is $4 trillion. The equilibrium expenditure when the price level is 110 is $3 trillion; pages 366-367.

Price level	Quantity of real GDP demanded (trillions of 2005 dollars)
90	5
100	4
110	3

2. A table with the aggregate demand schedule

is above. It shows the aggregate quantity demanded, which equals aggregate expenditure, at each price level. Figure 14.20 (on the previous page) plots the aggregate demand curve; pages 366-367.

3. Each $0.5 trillion increase in autonomous expenditure increased equilibrium GDP by $1 trillion. So, for each AE curve, the multiplier is 2.0; pages 366-367.

The Short-Run Policy Tradeoff

Chapter 15

1 Describe the short-run tradeoff between inflation and unemployment.

The short-run Phillips curve shows the relationship between the inflation rate and the unemployment rate when the natural unemployment rate and the expected inflation rate remain constant. The downward-sloping short-run Phillips curve indicates a tradeoff between inflation and unemployment: lower unemployment can be attained, but at the cost of higher inflation. The short-run Phillips curve is another way of looking at the upward-sloping aggregate supply curve, because a change in aggregate demand, which leads to a movement along the aggregate supply curve, changes real GDP so that the unemployment rate changes and changes the price level so that the inflation rate changes. For instance, moving up the aggregate supply curve, larger real GDP corresponds to lower unemployment and the higher price level corresponds to higher inflation. The relationship between output and unemployment is called Okun's Law. Okun's Law states that for each percentage point that the unemployment rate is above the natural unemployment rate, real GDP is two percentage points below potential GDP.

2 Distinguish between the short-run and the long-run Phillips curves and describe the shifting tradeoff between inflation and unemployment.

The long-run Phillips curve is a vertical line that shows the relationship between inflation and unemployment when the economy is at full employment. At full employment, the unemployment rate is the natural unemployment rate, but the inflation rate can take on any value. Along the long-run Phillips curve, there is no long-run tradeoff between inflation and unemployment. The short-run Phillips curve intersects the long-run Phillips at the expected inflation rate. If the expected inflation rate changes, the short-run Phillips curve shifts upward or downward to intersect the long-run Phillips curve at the new expected inflation rate. The natural rate hypothesis is the proposition that when the inflation rate changes, the unemployment rate changes temporarily and eventually returns to the natural unemployment rate. If the natural unemployment rate increases, both the long-run Phillips curve and the short-run Phillips curve shift rightward; if it decreases, both curves shift leftward.

3 Explain how the Fed can influence the inflation rate and the unemployment rate.

The expected inflation rate helps set the money wage rate and other money prices. To forecast inflation, people use data about past inflation and other relevant variables, as well as economic science. If the Fed tries to lower unemployment to less than the natural rate, the expected inflation rate rises. Eventually the unemployment rate will return to the natural unemployment rate but the inflation rate is permanently higher. If the Fed then lowers the inflation rate, unemployment temporarily rises above the natural rate as the economy moves into a recession. Ultimately the unemployment rate will return to the natural unemployment rate and the inflation rate will be lower.

CHECKPOINT 15.1

■ **Describe the short-run tradeoff between inflation and unemployment.**

Quick Review

- *Short-run Phillips curve* A curve that shows the relationship between the inflation rate and the unemployment rate when the natural unemployment rate and the expected inflation rate remain constant.
- *Okun's Law* For each percentage point that the unemployment rate is above (below) the natural unemployment rate, real GDP is two percentage points below (above) potential GDP.

Additional Practice Problems 15.1

1. For a nation, the table describes five possible situations that might arise in 2013, depending on the level of aggregate demand in that year. In this nation potential GDP is $7 trillion, and the natural unemployment rate is 5 percent.

	Price level (2010 = 100)	Unemployment rate (percentage)
A	101.5	9
B	104.0	6
C	105.0	5
D	106.5	4
E	109.0	3

   a. Calculate the inflation rate for each possible outcome.
   b. Use Okun's Law to find the real GDP associated with each unemployment rate in the table.
   c. Plot the short-run Phillips curve for 2013.
   d. Plot the aggregate supply curve for 2013.
   e. Mark the points *A, B, C, D,* and *E* on each curve that correspond to the data provided in the table and the data that you have calculated.

2. In the Practice Problem, what is the role played the aggregate demand curve? In the figure you have drawn with the aggregate supply curve, show an aggregate demand curve that would create an inflation rate of 5 percent. To what point on the Phillips curve does this aggregate demand/aggregate supply equilibrium correspond?

Solutions to Additional Practice Problems 15.1

1a. The inflation rate equals the change in the price level divided by the initial price level, all multiplied by 100. So, for row *A*, the inflation rate equals $\frac{101.5 - 100.0}{100.0} \times 100$, or 1.5

	Inflation rate (percent per year)
A	1.5
B	4.0
C	5.0
D	6.5
E	9.0

percent. The rest of the inflation rates are calculated similarly.

1b. Okun's Law states that for each percentage point the unemployment rate is above the natural unemployment rate, there is a 2 percent gap between real GDP and potential GDP. In row *A* of the table, the unemployment rate is 9 percent. The natural unemployment rate is 5 percent, so the unemployment rate is 4 percentage points above the natural unemployment rate. Based on Okun's law, real GDP is (2) × (4 percent) = 8 percent below potential GDP. Potential GDP is $7 trillion, so real GDP is (8 percent) × ($7 trillion) = $0.56 trillion dollars below potential GDP. In this case, real GDP equals $7 trillion minus $0.56 trillion, $6.44 trillion, as in the table to the right. The rest of the calculations of real GDP are similar.

	Real GDP (trillions of 2010 dollars)
A	6.44
B	6.86
C	7.00
D	7.14
E	7.28

1c. The figure plots the Phillips curve. The short-run Phillips curve shows the relationship between the inflation rate and the unemployment rate.

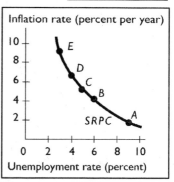

The unemployment rates are given in the table in the problem and the associated inflation rates are given in the answer to part (a).

© 2013 Pearson Education, Inc. Publishing as Addison Wesley

1d. The aggregate supply curve for 2013 is plotted in the figure. The price levels are given in the problem and the corresponding real GDPs are calculated from Okun's Law in part (b).

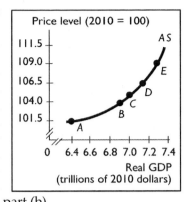

1e. The figures in part (e) and part (f) have the points labeled.

2. When aggregate demand increases, everything else remaining the same, there is a movement up along the aggregate supply curve. Real GDP increases and the price level rises. At the same time, the unemployment rate decreases and the inflation rate rises. There is a movement up along the short-run Phillips curve.

When aggregate demand decreases, everything else remaining the same, there is a movement down along the aggregate supply curve. Real GDP decreases and the price level falls. At the same time, the unemployment rate increases and the inflation rate falls. There is a movement down along the short-run Phillips curve.

Because the current price level is 100, to create an inflation rate of 5 percent, the aggregate demand curve must intersect the aggregate supply at a price level of 105. The figure shows this aggregate demand curve. This price level corresponds to point C, so this aggregate demand/aggregate supply equilibrium corresponds to point C on the short-run Phillips curve

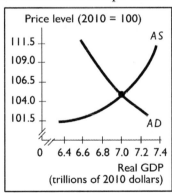

■ Self Test 15.1

Fill in the blanks

The short-run Phillips curve is the curve that shows the relationship between the ____ (price level; inflation rate; nominal interest rate) and the ____ (quantity of real GDP supplied; unemployment rate; real interest rate) when the natural unemployment rate and expected inflation rate remain constant. The short-run Phillips curve is ____ (downward; upward) sloping. Okun's Law states that for each percentage point that the unemployment rate is above the natural unemployment rate, there is a ____ (2; 6) percent gap between real GDP and potential GDP. A change in aggregate demand that leads to a movement along the aggregate supply curve also leads to a ____ (shift in; movement along) the short-run Phillips curve.

True or false

1. The short-run Phillips curve shows the tradeoff between the natural unemployment rate and the expected inflation rate.

2. Moving along a short-run Phillips curve, the cost of a lower unemployment rate is a higher inflation rate.

3. Okun's Law states that for each percentage point that real GDP is less than potential GDP, the unemployment rate is 2 percentage points above the natural unemployment rate.

4. Points on the short-run Phillips curve correspond to points on the aggregate supply curve.

5. Aggregate demand fluctuations bring movements along the aggregate supply curve and along the short-run Phillips curve.

Multiple choice

1. The short-run Phillips curve shows the relationship between the
   a. inflation rate and the interest rate.
   b. inflation rate and real GDP.
   c. unemployment rate and the interest rate.
   d. inflation rate and the unemployment rate.
   e. price level and real GDP.

2. The short-run Phillips curve is
   a. vertical at the natural unemployment rate.
   b. upward sloping.
   c. downward sloping.
   d. horizontal at the expected inflation rate.
   e. U-shaped.

3. Moving along the short-run Phillips curve, as the unemployment rate increases the inflation rate
   a. decreases.
   b. increases.
   c. remains unchanged.
   d. initially decreases and then increases.
   e. initially increases and then decreases.

4. If real GDP exceeds potential GDP, then employment is ____ full employment and the unemployment rate is ____ the natural unemployment rate.
   a. below; above
   b. equal to; below
   c. above; below
   d. above; above
   e. equal to; equal to

5. According to Okun's Law, if the natural unemployment rate is 5 percent, the actual unemployment rate is 4 percent, and potential GDP is $15 trillion, then actual real GDP is
   a. $12.0 trillion.
   b. $15.0 trillion.
   c. $14.7 trillion.
   d. $15.4 trillion.
   e. $15.3 trillion.

6. When a movement up along the aggregate supply curve occurs, there is also
   a. a movement down along the short-run Phillips curve.
   b. a movement up along the short-run Phillips curve.
   c. a rightward shift of the short-run Phillips curve.
   d. a leftward shift of the short-run Phillips curve.
   e. neither a movement along nor a shift in the short-run Phillips curve.

7. When aggregate demand increases, there is a movement ____ along the AS curve and ____.
   a. up; a movement up along the short-run Phillips curve
   b. up; a movement down along the short-run Phillips curve
   c. up; an upward shift of the short-run Phillips curve
   d. down; a downward shift of the short-run Phillips curve
   e. down; a movement down along the short-run Phillips curve

Complete the graph

Inflation rate (percent per year)	Unemployment rate (percentage)
2	12
3	8
4	5
5	3
6	2

■ **FIGURE 15.1**

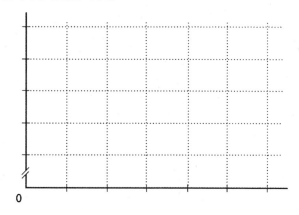

1. The table above has data on the inflation rate and the unemployment rate.
   a. Using the data, label the axes and plot the short-run Phillips curve in Figure 15.1. Label the curve SRPC.
   b. What is the effect of a decrease in the unemployment rate from 8 percent to 5 percent? Show the effect in Figure 15.1.
   c. How does your answer to question (b) indicate the presence of a tradeoff?

Short answer and numeric questions

1. What does the slope of the short-run Phillips curve indicate about the tradeoff between inflation and unemployment?

Unemployment rate (percentage)	Real GDP (trillions of 2005 dollars)
4	___
5	___
6	___
7	___

2. The table above gives data for an economy. Suppose that for this economy the natural unemployment rate is 5 percent and potential GDP is $8 trillion.

   a. What is Okun's Law?

   b. Using Okun's Law, complete the table by calculating real GDP for each unemployment rate.

3. What is the effect on the aggregate supply curve and on the short-run Phillips curve of an increase in aggregate demand?

Additional Exercises (also in MyEconLab Test A)

	Price level (2005 = 100)	Unemployment rate (percentage)
A	108	9
B	113	6
C	115	5
D	118	4
E	123	3

The table shows five possible outcomes for 2011 depending on the level of aggregate demand in that year. Potential GDP in 2011 is $11.0 trillion and the natural unemployment rate is 6 percent. The price level in 2010 was 105.

1. Calculate the inflation rate for each possible outcome.

2. Use Okun's Law to find the real GDP at each unemployment rate in the table.

3. What are the expected inflation rate and the expected price level in 2011?

4. Plot the short-run Phillips curve for 2011. Mark the points A, B, C, D, and E that corre-

spond to the data in the table and that you have calculated.

5. Plot the aggregate supply curve for 2011. Mark the points A, B, C, D, and E that correspond to the data in the table.

CHECKPOINT 15.2

■ **Distinguish between the short-run and the long-run Phillips curves and describe the shifting tradeoff between inflation and unemployment.**

Quick Review

- *Long-run Phillips curve* The vertical line that shows the relationship between inflation and unemployment when the economy is at full employment.
- *Factor that shifts the long-run Phillips curve* An increase (decrease) in the natural unemployment rate shifts the long-run (and short-run) Phillips curve rightward (leftward).
- *Natural rate hypothesis* When the inflation rate changes, the unemployment rate changes temporarily and eventually returns to the natural unemployment rate.

Additional Practice Problems 15.2

1. The figure shows a short-run Phillips curve and a long-run Phillips curve.

   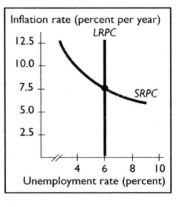

   a. What is the expected inflation rate?

   b. What is the natural unemployment rate?

   c. If the expected inflation rate falls to 2.5 percent a year, show the new short-run and long-run Phillips curves.

   d. If the natural unemployment rate decreases to 4 percent but the expected inflation rate does not change from what it is in the figure above, show the new short-run and long-run Phillips curves.

2. Explain how the inflation rate and unemployment rate might simultaneously increase.

Solutions to Additional Practice Problems 15.2

1a. The expected inflation rate is the inflation rate where the short-run Phillips curve and the long-run Phillips curve intersect. The expected inflation rate is 7.5 percent a year.

1b. The long-run Phillips curve is vertical at the natural unemployment rate. The natural unemployment rate is 6 percent.

1c. When the expected inflation rate decreases to 2.5 percent a year, the short-run Phillips curve shifts downward but the long-run Phillips curve does not shift. The figure 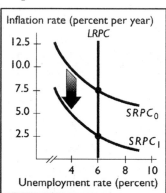 shows that the short-run Phillips curve shifts downward from $SRPC_0$ to $SRPC_1$. The new short-run Phillips curve intersects the long-run Phillips curve at the new expected inflation rate, 2.5 percent.

1d. A decrease in the natural unemployment rate shifts *both* the short-run Phillips curve and the long-run Phillips curve leftward. In the figure the long-run Phillips curve 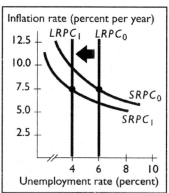 shifts leftward from $LRPC_0$ to $LRPC_1$ and the short-run Phillips curve shifts leftward from $SRPC_0$ to $SRPC_1$. The new short-run Phillips

curve intersects the new long-run Phillips curve at the expected inflation rate.

2. If the natural unemployment rate increases, the short-run Phillips curves shifts rightward. If simultaneously the inflation rate rises, it is possible to move from a point on its old short-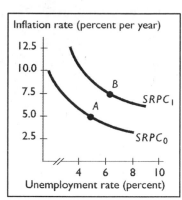run Phillips curve to a point on the new short-run Phillips curve such that both the inflation rate and the unemployment rate increase. For instance, in the figure the short-run Phillips curve shifts and the inflation rate rises from 5.0 percent to 7.5 percent. The movement from point *A* on the initial short-run Phillips curve $SRPC_0$ to point *B* on the new short-run Phillips curve $SRPC_1$ shows how both the unemployment rate and inflation rate can simultaneously increase.

■ Self Test 15.2

Fill in the blanks

The long-run Phillips curve is a ____ (vertical; horizontal) line that shows the relationship between inflation and unemployment when the economy is at full employment. The long-run Phillips curve tells us that ____ (any; only one) inflation rate is possible at the natural unemployment rate. A change in the expected inflation rate ____ (shifts; does not shift) the long-run Phillips curve and ____ (shifts; does not shift) the short-run Phillips curve. The ____ (natural rate hypothesis; constant natural unemployment rate theory) is the proposition that when the inflation rate changes, the unemployment rate ____ (permanently; temporarily) changes. A change in the natural unemployment rate ____ (shifts; does not shift) the long-run Phillips curve and also ____ (shifts; does not shift) the short-run Phillips curve.

True or false

1. The long-run Phillips curve is horizontal because it shows that at the expected inflation rate, any unemployment rate might occur.

2. An increase in the expected inflation rate shifts the long-run Phillips curve.

3. An increase in the expected inflation rate shifts the short-run Phillips curve.

4. The natural rate hypothesis states that an increase in the inflation rate temporarily decreases the unemployment rate but does not permanently change the unemployment rate.

5. A change in the natural unemployment rate shifts both the short-run and long-run Phillips curves.

Multiple choice

1. The long-run Phillips curve is the relationship between
   a. unemployment and the price level at full employment.
   b. unemployment and the inflation rate at the expected price level.
   c. inflation and real GDP at full employment.
   d. inflation and unemployment when the economy is at full employment.
   e. inflation and the expected inflation rate.

2. The long-run Phillips curve is
   a. upward sloping.
   b. downward sloping.
   c. horizontal.
   d. vertical.
   e. upside-down U-shaped.

3. The inflation rate that is used to set the money wage rate and other money prices is the
   a. natural inflation rate.
   b. actual inflation rate.
   c. expected inflation rate.
   d. cost of living inflation rate.
   e. wage inflation rate.

4. When the expected inflation rate ____, the short-run Phillips curve ____.
   a. falls; shifts upward
   b. rises; shifts upward
   c. rises; shifts downward
   d. falls; does not shift
   e. rises; might shift upward or downward depending on how the long-run Phillips curve shifts

■ **FIGURE 15.2**

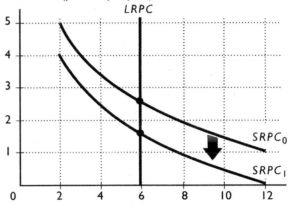

5. The shift in Figure 15.2 is the result of
   a. an increase in the expected inflation rate.
   b. a decrease in the expected inflation rate.
   c. an increase in the natural unemployment rate.
   d. a decrease in the natural unemployment rate.
   e. an increase in the inflation rate.

6. The natural rate hypothesis states that
   a. only natural economic policies can bring a permanent reduction in the unemployment rate.
   b. changes in the inflation rate temporarily change the unemployment rate.
   c. it is natural for the unemployment rate to exceed the inflation rate.
   d. it is natural for the unemployment rate to be less than the natural unemployment rate.
   e. changes in the inflation rate temporarily change the natural unemployment rate.

7. If the natural unemployment rate decreases, then the short-run Phillips curve ____ and the long-run Phillips curve ____.
   a. does not shift; shifts leftward
   b. shifts leftward; shifts leftward
   c. shifts rightward; shifts leftward
   d. shifts rightward; shifts rightward
   e. shifts leftward; does not shift

8. The natural unemployment rate
   a. increases when job search increases.
   b. never changes.
   c. always increases.
   d. decreases when the inflation rate rises.
   e. increases when the expected inflation rate rises.

Complete the graph

Inflation rate (percent per year)	Unemployment rate (percentage)
2	12
3	8
4	5
5	3
6	2

■ **FIGURE 15.3**

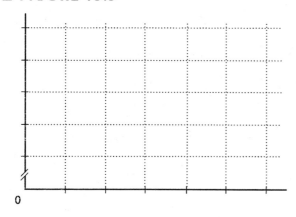

1. The table above has data on a nation's short-run Phillips curve. In this nation, the natural unemployment rate equals 5 percent.
   a. Label the axes and then draw both the short-run Phillips curve and long-run Phillips curve in Figure 15.3.
   b. What is the expected inflation rate?
   c. Suppose the expected inflation rate falls

by 1 percentage point. Show the effect of this change on the short-run Phillips curve and long-run Phillips curve in Figure 15.3.

2. In Figure 15.4, redraw your initial short-run and long-run Phillips curves from Figure 15.3. Suppose that the natural unemployment rate falls to 3 percent and the expected inflation rate does not change. In Figure 15.4, show the effect of this change.

■ **FIGURE 15.4**

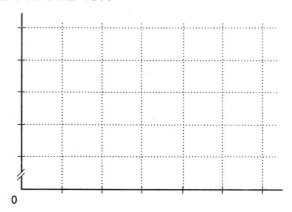

Short answer and numeric questions

1. In the *AS-AD* model, does the aggregate demand curve, the aggregate supply curve, or the potential GDP line best correspond to the long-run Phillips curve?

2. What are the key points about the long-run Phillips curve and the relationship between the long-run Phillips curve and the short-run Phillips curve?

3. How does an increase in the expected inflation rate change the short-run and long-run Phillips curves?

4. What is the natural rate hypothesis?

5. How does an increase in the natural unemployment rate change the short-run and long-run Phillips curves?

Additional Exercises (also in MyEconLab Test A)
In an economy, the natural unemployment rate is 7 percent and the expected inflation rate is 4 percent a year.
1. Draw a graph of the short-run Phillips curve and long-run Phillips curve.

2. If the expected inflation rate changes to 3 percent a year, show the new short-run and long-run Phillips curves.

3. If the natural unemployment rate becomes 6 percent, show the new short-run and long-run Phillips curves.

4. Aggregate demand growth slows and eventually the inflation rate falls to 2 percent a year. Explain how unemployment and inflation change.

CHECKPOINT 15.3

■ **Explain how the Fed can influence the inflation rate and the unemployment rate.**

Quick Review

- *Expected inflation rate* The inflation rate people forecast and use to set the money wage rate and other money prices.

Additional Practice Problem 15.3

1. The figure shows the short-run and long-run Phillips curves. The current inflation rate is 7.5 percent a year and the current unemployment rate is the natural unemployment rate, 5 percent. Suppose that the Fed believes that this inflation is too high and wants to lower it to 5 percent.

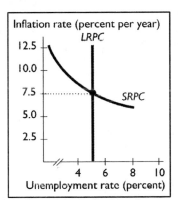

a. What policy will the Fed undertake to lower the inflation rate?

b. What will be the effect of the Fed's policy in the short run?

c. What will be the effect of the Fed's policy in the long run?

Solutions to Additional Practice Problem 15.3

1a. To lower the inflation rate, the Fed must slow the growth of aggregate demand by slowing the money growth rate and raising the interest rate.

1b. In the short run, the Fed's action does not change the expected inflation rate, so the short-run Phillips curve does not shift. The economy moves along its short-run Phillips curve from point A to point B. The inflation rate falls to 5 percent and, as the economy moves into a recession, the unemployment rate rises to 8 percent.

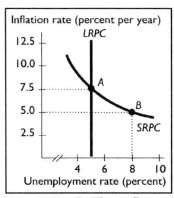

1c. In the long run, the expected inflation rate falls. The short-run Phillips curve shifts downward as illustrated in the figure. The economy moves to point C. The inflation rate falls to 5 percent a year and the unemployment rate returns to the natural unemployment rate of 5 percent. The reduction in the inflation rate had no lasting effect on the unemployment rate but there was a temporary recession with an increase in unemployment.

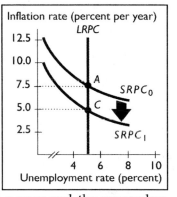

■ **Self Test 15.3**

Fill in the blanks

When all the relevant data and economic science are used to forecast inflation, the forecast is called _____ (an accurate prediction; a rational expectation; an accurate expectation). An increase in the inflation rate ____ (raises; lowers) the unemployment rate. The effect on the unemployment rate from a higher inflation rate is ____ (permanent; temporary).

True or false

1. The expected inflation rate never changes.

2. One factor that can be used to predict inflation is the Fed's monetary policy.

3. To lower the unemployment rate in the short run, the Fed will speed up the growth rate of money.

4. If the Fed tries to lower the unemployment rate to be less than the natural rate, increasing deflation can result.

5. When the Fed slowed inflation in 1981, the consequence was recession.

Multiple choice

1. A rational expectation of the inflation rate is
   a. a forecast based on the forecasted actions of the Fed and other relevant determinant factors.
   b. an expected inflation rate between 1 percent and 5 percent.
   c. a forecast based only on the historical evolution of inflation over the last 100 years.
   d. an expected inflation rate between 5 percent and 10 percent.
   e. always correct.

2. Because money growth is a major component determining the inflation rate, in order to forecast inflation we should forecast actions by the
   a. Office of the Treasury.
   b. president.
   c. Congress.
   d. Fed.
   e. U.S. Mint.

3. If the Fed tries to lower the unemployment rate so it is lower than the natural unemployment rate, before the expected inflation rate changes, the inflation rate ____ and the unemployment rate ____.
   a. does not change; falls
   b. falls; falls
   c. rises; falls
   d. rises; does not change
   e. falls; rises

4. If the Fed tries to lower the unemployment rate so it is less than the natural unemployment rate, in the short run before the expected inflation rate changes, the SRPC ____ and the LRPC ____.
   a. does not change; does not change
   b. shifts downward; shifts leftward
   c. shifts upward; does not change
   d. shifts downward; does not change
   e. does not change; shifts rightward

5. If the Fed tries to lower the unemployment rate so it is less than the natural unemployment rate, in the long run the SRPC ____ and the LRPC ____.
   a. does not change; does not change
   b. shifts downward; shifts leftward
   c. shifts upward; does not change
   d. shifts downward; does not change
   e. does not change; shifts rightward

6. In 1981, the Fed
   a. created an expected inflation reduction policy and created an expansion.
   b. created an unexpected inflation reduction policy and created a recession.
   c. publicly announced an inflation reduction policy and created a recession.
   d. publicly announced an inflation reduction policy and created an expansion.
   e. took no action so that the inflation rate skyrocketed.

Complete the graph

■ **FIGURE 15.5**

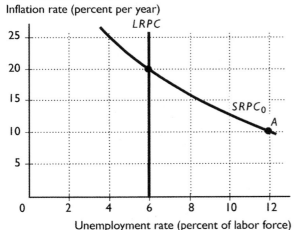

1. Figure 15.5 shows a nation's short-run and long-run Phillips curves. In this nation, the natural unemployment rate equals 6 percent and the actual and expected inflation rate is 20 percent. The nation's government decides to take actions to lower the inflation rate to 10 percent.

   a. In the figure, show what happens in the short run when the expected inflation rate does not change from 20 percent. Indicate the combination of the inflation rate and unemployment rate by labeling it point A.

   b. In the figure, show what happens in the short run when the expected inflation rate falls to 10 percent. Draw any new Phillips curve you need and indicate the new inflation rate and unemployment rate combination by labeling it B.

Short answer and numeric questions

1. Suppose the Fed tries to lower the unemployment rate to be less than the natural rate. What are short-run effects of this policy on the short-run and long-run Phillips curve if there is no change in the expected inflation rate? What are the short-run effects on the inflation rate and the unemployment rate? What long-run effects does the policy have?

2. Why can the short-run effects of an increase in the inflation rate be different from the long-run effects?

3. The Eye on Your Life discusses how the short-run tradeoff between inflation and unemployment can affect your life. Another impact it can have might be more immediate. Would you rather look for a job when the Fed had just slowed the inflation rate? Based on your answer, what sort of policy would you prefer the Fed follow: One in which it keeps the inflation rate low and this fact is widely known or one in which the Fed occasionally slows the inflation rate when the slowing is unexpected by the public?

Additional Exercises (also in MyEconLab Test A)

■ **FIGURE 15.6**

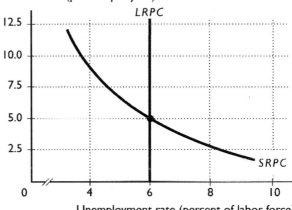

In Figure 15.6, the current and expected inflation rate is 5 percent a year. The Fed decides it wants to lower the unemployment rate to 4 percent.

1. What are the short-run effects of the Fed's policy on inflation and unemployment?

2. What are the long-run effects of the Fed's policy on inflation and unemployment?

3. Comment on the temporary versus permanent nature of the changes in unemployment and inflation.

SELF TEST ANSWERS

■ CHECKPOINT 15.1

Fill in the blanks

The short-run Phillips curve is the curve that shows the relationship between the <u>inflation rate</u> and the <u>unemployment rate</u> when the natural unemployment rate and expected inflation rate remain constant. The short-run Phillips curve is <u>downward</u> sloping. Okun's Law states that for each percentage point that the unemployment rate is above the natural unemployment rate, there is a <u>2</u> percent gap between real GDP and potential GDP. A change in aggregate demand that leads to a movement along the aggregate supply curve also leads to a <u>movement along</u> the short-run Phillips curve.

True or false

1. False; page 374
2. True; page 374
3. False; page 375
4. True; pages 375-376
5. True; page 375

Multiple choice

1. d; page 374
2. c; page 374
3. a; page 374
4. c; page 375
5. e; page 375
6. b; pages 375-376
7. a; page 377

Complete the graph

1. a. Figure 15.7 plots the short-run Phillips curve, labeled *SRPC*; page 374.

   b. The decrease in the unemployment rate brings a rise in the inflation rate. There is a movement along the short-run Phillips curve, as indicated by the movement from point *A* to point *B*; page 374.

   c. The movement indicates a tradeoff because a decrease in the unemployment rate has a rise in the inflation rate as the price; page 374.

■ FIGURE 15.7

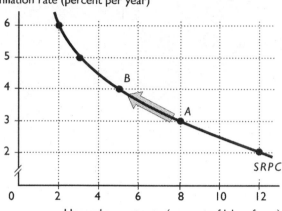

Short answer and numeric questions

1. The slope of the short-run Phillips curve is negative, which indicates that as the unemployment rate decreases, the inflation rate increases. So the cost of a lower unemployment rate is a higher inflation rate; page 374.

2. a. Okun's Law states that for each percentage point that the unemployment rate is above the natural unemployment rate, there is a 2 percent gap between real GDP and potential GDP; page 375.

Unemployment rate (percentage)	Real GDP (trillions of 2005 dollars)
4	8.16
5	8.00
6	7.84
7	7.68

   b. The completed table is above. When the unemployment rate is 7 percent, it is 2 percentage points above the natural unemployment rate. According to Okun's Law, real GDP is (2) × (2 percent) or 4 percent below potential GDP. So real GDP is (4 percent) × ($8 trillion) or $0.32 trillion below potential GDP. Real GDP is $8 trillion minus $0.32 trillion, which is $7.68 trillion; page 375.

3. When aggregate demand increases, the aggregate demand curve shifts rightward and there is a movement up along the aggregate supply curve. The price level rises and real GDP increases. As the price level rises the inflation rate rises and as real GDP increases the unemployment rate decreases. There is a movement up along the short-run Phillips curve; page 377.

Additional Exercises (also in MyEconLab Test A)

	Inflation rate (percent per year)	Unemployment rate (percentage)	Price level	Real GDP (trillions of 2005 dollars)
A	2.9	9	108	10.34
B	7.6	6	113	11.00
C	9.5	5	115	11.22
D	12.4	4	118	11.44
E	17.1	3	123	11.66

1. The table gives the inflation rates for the different possible price levels. The inflation rates have been calculated starting with an initial price level of 105, which was the price level in 2010. So the inflation rate for possibility A is [(108 − 105) ÷ 105] × 100, which is 2.9 percent; page 375.

2. The real GDP associated with each unemployment rate is in the above table. Okun's Law states that for each percentage point that the unemployment rate is above the natural unemployment rate, real GDP is 2 percentage points below potential GDP. In row A of the table, when the unemployment rate is 9 percent, the unemployment rate is 3 percent above the natural unemployment rate. So real GDP is (2 × 3 percent) = 6 percent below potential GDP. As a result, real GDP is (6 percent × $11 trillion) = $0.66 trillion below potential GDP, so that real GDP = ($11 trillion − $0.66 trillion) = $10.34 trillion. The rest of the answers are calculated similarly; page 375.

3. The expected inflation rate is 7.6 percent a year because that is the inflation rate that corresponds with the price level at potential GDP, which is full employment and the nat-

■ FIGURE 15.8

Inflation rate (percent per year)

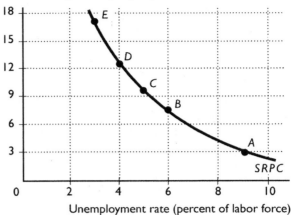

Unemployment rate (percent of labor force)

■ FIGURE 15.9

Price level (GDP price index, 2005 = 100)

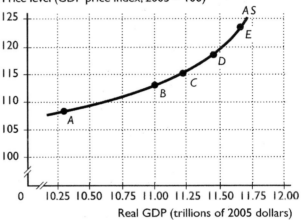

Real GDP (trillions of 2005 dollars)

ural unemployment rate. The corresponding price level is 113; page 376.

4. The Phillips curve in Figure 15.8 plots these inflation rates and unemployment rates; pages 375-376.

5. To plot the aggregate supply curve, real GDP is needed. These data are in the table above. The aggregate supply curve is then plotted in Figure 15.9 using the data from the table; pages 375-376.

■ CHECKPOINT 15.2

Fill in the blanks

The long-run Phillips curve is a <u>vertical</u> line that shows the relationship between inflation and unemployment when the economy is at full employment. The long-run Phillips curve tells us that <u>any</u> inflation rate is possible at the natural unemployment rate. A change in the expected inflation rate <u>does not shift</u> the long-run Phillips curve and <u>shifts</u> the short-run Phillips curve. The <u>natural rate hypothesis</u> is the proposition that when the inflation rate changes, the unemployment rate <u>temporarily</u> changes. A change in the natural unemployment rate <u>shifts</u> the long-run Phillips curve and also <u>shifts</u> the short-run Phillips curve.

True or false

1. False; page 380
2. False; pages 381-382
3. True; pages 381-382
4. True; page 382
5. True; pages 383-384

Multiple choice

1. d; page 380
2. d; page 380
3. c; page 381
4. b; pages 381-382
5. b; pages 381-382
6. b; page 382
7. b; pages 383-384
8. a; page 384

Complete the graph

1. a. Figure 15.10 plots the short-run Phillips curve, labeled *SRPC*0 and the long-run Phillips curve, labeled *LRPC*; page 381.

   b. The expected inflation rate is 4 percent a year because that is the inflation rate at which the short-run Phillips curve intersects the long-run Phillips curve; page 381.

   c. The new short-run Phillips curve is illustrated as *SRPC*1; pages 381-382.

2. The initial short-run Phillips curve is labeled

■ FIGURE 15.10

Inflation rate (percent per year)

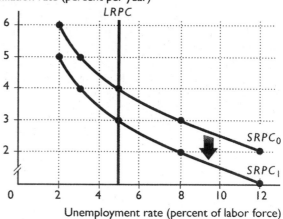

Unemployment rate (percent of labor force)

■ FIGURE 15.11

Inflation rate (percent per year)

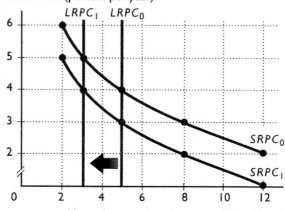

Unemployment rate (percent of labor force)

*SRPC*0 and the initial long-run Phillips curve is labeled *LRPC*0 in Figure 15.11. The decrease in the natural unemployment rate by 2 percentage points shifts both the long-run Phillips curve leftward from *LRPC*0 to *LRPC*1 and the short-run Phillips curve leftward from *SRPC*0 to *SRPC*1. The new short-run Phillips curve and the new long-run Phillips curve intersect at the expected inflation rate; pages 383-384.

Short answer and numeric questions

1. The potential GDP line best corresponds to the long-run Phillips curve. The potential GDP line shows that a change in the price

level does not change potential GDP and has no effect on the natural unemployment rate. The long-run Phillips curve shows that a change in the inflation rate does not change the natural unemployment rate; page 380.

2. There are several key points: First, the long-run Phillips curve is vertical at the natural unemployment rate. Next, the short-run Phillips curve intersects the long-run Phillips curve at the expected inflation rate. Finally, changes in the expected inflation rate shift only the short-run Phillips curve, while changes in the natural unemployment rate shift both the short-run and long-run Phillips curves; pages 380-383.

3. An increase in the expected inflation rate shifts the short-run Phillips curve upward but does not change the long-run Phillips curve; pages 381-382.

4. The natural rate hypothesis is the proposition that when the inflation rate changes, the unemployment rate changes temporarily and eventually returns to the natural unemployment rate. An increase in the inflation rate temporarily lowers the unemployment rate but eventually the unemployment rate returns to the natural unemployment rate. The fall in the unemployment rate was only temporary. Similarly, a decrease in the inflation rate temporarily raises the unemployment rate but eventually the unemployment rate returns to the natural unemployment rate. The rise in the unemployment rate was only temporary; page 382.

5. An increase in the natural unemployment rate shifts *both* the long-run and short-run Phillips curves rightward; pages 383-384.

Additional Exercises (also in MyEconLab Test A)

1. Figure 15.12 shows the short-run and long-run Phillips curves. The long-run Phillips curve, *LRPC*, is vertical at the natural unemployment rate, 7 percent. The short-run Phillips curve, *SRPC*, intersects the long-run Phillips curve at the expected inflation rate, 4 percent a year; page 381.

2. When the expected inflation rate falls, the

■ **FIGURE 15.12**

Inflation rate (percent per year)

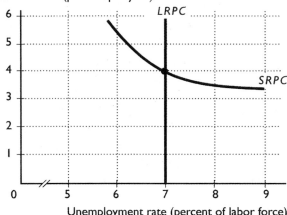

■ **FIGURE 15.13**

Inflation rate (percent per year)

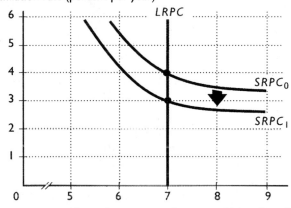

short-run Phillips curve shifts downward, as shown in Figure 15.13. In Figure 15.13, the new short-run Phillips curve, $SRPC_1$, intersects the long-run Phillips curve at the new expected inflation rate, 3 percent a year; page 381.

3. When the natural unemployment rate changes, both the long-run and the short-run Phillips curves shift. In Figure 15.14 (on the next page) the decrease in the natural unemployment rate to 6 percent shifts the long-run and short-run Phillips curves leftward by an equal amount. The new short-run Phillips curve, $SRPC_1$, intersects the new long-run Phillips curve, $LRPC_1$, where the inflation rate equals 4 percent a year because the ex-

■ **FIGURE 15.14**

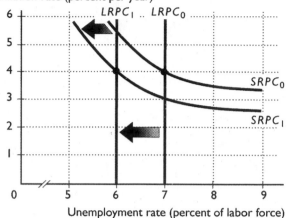

Inflation rate (percent per year)

pected inflation rate has not changed; pages 383-384.

4. When aggregate demand begins to grow more slowly, the inflation rate starts to drop. However, people will not immediately change their expected inflation rate so unemployment rises. Eventually, as the inflation rate reaches and then remains at 2 percent, the expected inflation rate is revised downward and the short-run Phillips curve (gradually) shifts downward. In the long run, the inflation rate falls to 2 percent and the unemployment rate returns to the natural unemployment rate; pages 382-383.

■ CHECKPOINT 15.3

Fill in the blanks

When all the relevant data and economic science are used to forecast inflation, the forecast is called a rational expectation. An increase in the inflation rate lowers the unemployment rate. The effect on the unemployment rate from a higher inflation rate is temporary.

True or false
1. False; page 387
2. True; page 387
3. True; page 388
4. False; page 388
5. True; page 389

Multiple choice
1. a; page 387
2. d; page 387
3. c; page 388
4. a; page 388
5. c; page 388
6. b; page 389

Complete the graph

■ **FIGURE 15.15**

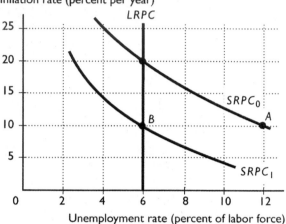

Inflation rate (percent per year)

1. a. In the short run, because the expected inflation rate does not change, the short-run Phillips curve does not change. The economy moves along its short-run Phillips curve $SRPC_0$ to point A in Figure 15.15. The inflation rate is 10 percent and the unemployment rate is 12 percent; page 388.

   b. In the long run, the expected rate falls to 10 percent. With the fall in the expected inflation rate, the short-run Phillips curve shifts downward, in the figure to $SRPC_1$. It intersects the long-run Phillips curve at the new expected inflation rate. The economy moves to point B. The inflation rate is 10 percent and the unemployment rate is the natural rate of 6 percent; page 388.

Short answer and numeric questions
1. In the short run, the Fed's policy increases the inflation rate and does not change the short-run or long-run Phillips curve. The economy moves up along the short-run Phil-

lips curve. The inflation rate rises and the unemployment rate falls. In the long run, the increase in the inflation rate is matched by an increase in the expected inflation rate. The short-run Phillips curve shifts upward. The long-run Phillips curve does not change. The inflation rate permanently rises and the unemployment rate returns to the natural unemployment rate; page 388

2. In the short run, the expected inflation rate might well not change. With people expected lower inflation than is actually the case, the money wage will not rise as much. Workers' real wage rates will fall and, in response, firms will boost employment so the unemployment rate falls to be less than the natural rate. But in the long run the expected inflation rate rises to equal the actual inflation rate. Once this occurs, the rise in the money wage matches the inflation rate. The real wage rate is no longer lower, so firms slash employment and the unemployment rate rises back to equal the natural rate; page 388.

3. If the Fed slows the inflation rate and the expected inflation rate does not change, then, the economy moves along its short-run Phillips curve and the unemployment rate rises. Looking for a job when the unemployment is

high is not a pleasant experience! Based on this consideration, you might prefer that the Fed concentrate on keeping the inflation rate low so that the Fed does not need to unexpectedly lower the inflation rate when the Fed fears that inflation is getting out of hand.

Additional Exercises (also in MyEconLab Test A)

1. If the expected inflation rate does not change, then the short-run Phillips curve does not shift and the economy moves upward along *SRPC* to a lower unemployment rate, 4 percent, and a higher inflation rate, 9 percent. The Fed has successfully lowered the unemployment rate. However, the inflation rate has risen; page 388.

2. In the long run, the expected inflation rate rises to match the actual inflation rate. When this occurs, the short-run Phillips curve shifts upward. In the long run, the unemployment rate returns to its natural rate, 6 percent, but the inflation rate remains permanently higher, 9 percent; page 388.

3. The result in problem 2 demonstrates that the Fed's lowering of the unemployment rate is only temporary but the increase in the inflation rate is permanent; page 388.

Chapter

Fiscal Policy

16

1 **Describe the federal budget process and the recent history of tax revenues, outlays, deficits, and debts.**

If tax revenues exceed outlays, the government has a budget surplus and if outlays exceed tax revenues, the government has a budget deficit. A budget deficit adds to the national debt, which is the total amount of government debt outstanding from past budget deficits. The government's Social Security and Medicare obligations are estimated at $80 trillion, much more than the national debt of $12.1 trillion.

2 **Explain how fiscal stimulus is used to fight a recession.**

The Keynesian view is that fiscal stimulus (an increase in government outlays or a decrease in tax revenues) has a multiplier effect and boosts real GDP and employment. The mainstream view is that the multiplier from fiscal stimulus is lower than Keynesians believe and that the long-run effects from a fiscal stimulus are lower potential GDP and a slower real GDP growth rate. Fiscal policy can be discretionary, policy initiated by an act of Congress, or automatic, policy that is triggered by the state of the economy. Automatic stabilizers are features of fiscal policy, such as induced taxes and needs-tested spending, that stabilize real GDP without explicit action. Discretionary policy can be changes in government outlays or tax revenues. The government expenditure multiplier, tax multiplier, and transfer payments multiplier conclude that aggregate demand changes by more than an initiating change in government expenditures, taxes, or transfer payments. The balanced budget multiplier shows that an increase in government expenditure balanced by an equal sized increase in taxes still increases aggregate demand. If real GDP is less than potential GDP, fiscal stimulus can move the economy to potential GDP. The use of discretionary fiscal policy is hampered by law-making time lags, by the shrinking area of law-maker discretion, by difficulties in estimating potential GDP, and by economic forecasting.

3 **Explain the supply-side effects of fiscal policy on employment, potential GDP, and the economic growth rate.**

The effects of fiscal policy on potential GDP and the real GDP growth rate are the supply-side effects. A tax cut or an increase in government expenditure on productive services have supply-side effects that increase potential GDP and aggregate supply. An increase in the income tax on labor income increases the tax wedge between the before-tax and the after-tax wage rate and decreases the supply of labor, thereby decreasing employment and potential GDP. An increase in the income tax on interest income increases the interest rate tax wedge. The real-after tax real interest rate falls, thereby decreasing the quantity of saving and investment and slowing the growth rate of real GDP. The combined demand-side and supply-side effects of fiscal policy show that both the aggregate demand and aggregate supply curves shift in response to fiscal policy. Fiscal stimulus has large long-run negative effects if investment is crowded out by budget deficits.

CHECKPOINT 16.1

■ **Describe the federal budget process and the recent history of tax revenues, outlays, deficits, and debts.**

Quick Review

- *Budget surplus* When tax revenues exceed outlays.
- *Budget deficit* When outlays exceed tax revenues.
- *National debt* The amount of government debt outstanding that has arisen from past budget deficits.

Additional Practice Problems 16.1

1. What is the relationship between the budget deficit or surplus and the national debt?
2. Can the national debt rise when the government is running a budget surplus?

Solutions to Additional Practice Problems 16.1

1. The budget deficit or surplus shows the government's budget situation for that year. The national debt is the total accumulated amount of debt the government owes from all past budget deficits. If the government has a budget deficit, so that its expenditures exceed its tax revenues, then the national debt rises. If it has a budget surplus, so that tax revenues exceed expenditures, then the national debt decreases.
2. The national debt cannot rise when the government has a budget surplus. The national debt increases when the government has a budget deficit and decreases when the government has a budget surplus.

■ Self Test 16.1

Fill in the blanks

The ____ (President; Congress) proposes the budget each February. The government has a budget ____ (surplus; deficit) when tax revenues are less than outlays. The national debt is ____ (tax revenues minus outlays; the amount of debt outstanding that arises from past budget deficits). In recent years, the government has had a budget ____ (surplus; deficit).

True or false

1. The national debt and budget deficit are different names for the same thing.
2. If government outlays and taxes revenues increase by the same amount, the government's budget balance does not change.
3. Social Security and Medicare obligations are less than U.S. GDP.
4. For the past decade, the U.S. federal government has had a budget deficit.

Multiple choice

1. The annual statement of the outlays, tax revenues, and surplus or deficit of the government of the United States is the federal
   a. surplus record.
   b. deficit record.
   c. budget.
   d. spending.
   e. debt to the public.

2. When government outlays are less than tax revenues, the government has
   a. a budget with a positive balance.
   b. a budget deficit.
   c. a budget surplus.
   d. a budget with a negative debt.
   e. an illegal budget because outlays must exceed tax revenues.

3. National debt decreases in a given year when a country has
   a. a budget deficit.
   b. a balanced budget.
   c. a budget supplement.
   d. a budget surplus.
   e. no government budget.

Short answer and numeric questions

1. What happens to the national debt if the government has a $1,400 billion budget deficit?
2. As a percent of GDP, how does the U.S. budget deficit compare to the budget deficits of other nations?
3. What is the amount of the U.S. Social Security and Medicare obligations? What actions might the government take to pay this debt?

Additional Exercises (also in MyEconLab Test A)

1. What is fiscal policy? What roles do the President and Congress play in making it? What is the time line for U.S. fiscal policy and is the federal budget in deficit or surplus?

CHECKPOINT 16.2

■ **Explain how fiscal stimulus is used to fight a recession.**

Quick Review

- *Fiscal stimulus* An increase in government outlays or a decrease in tax revenue designed to boost real GDP.

- *Automatic fiscal policy* Fiscal policy that is triggered by the state of the economy.

- *Discretionary fiscal policy* Fiscal policy initiated by an act of Congress.

- *Government expenditure multiplier* The magnification effect of a change in government expenditure on aggregate demand.

- *Tax multiplier* The magnification effect of a change in taxes on aggregate demand.

Additional Practice Problems 16.2

1. The figure shows the U.S. economy in 2016.

   a. What is the equilibrium price level and real GDP?

   b. What sorts of fiscal policies might be used to move the economy to potential GDP?

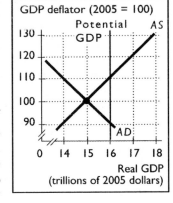

   c. In the figure, show the effect of these policies after real GDP equals potential GDP. What is the new equilibrium price level and real GDP?

2. What is the balanced budget multiplier and why is it greater than zero?

Solutions to Additional Practice Problems 16.2

1a. The equilibrium price level and real GDP are determined by the intersection of the aggregate demand, *AD*, curve and the aggregate supply, *AS*, curve. The figure shows that the equilibrium price is 100 and the equilibrium quantity of real GDP is $15 trillion.

1b. To move the economy to potential GDP, the government can use fiscal stimulus. Potential policy includes a decrease in taxes and/or an increase in government expenditures.

1c. The figure shows the effect of the fiscal stimulus. A decrease in taxes and an increase in government expenditure both increase aggregate demand. The aggregate demand curve shifts rightward,

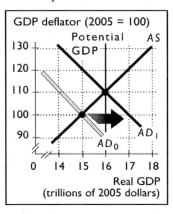

from AD_0 to AD_1 in the figure. As a result, the price level rises from 100 to 110 and real GDP increases from $15 trillion back to potential GDP of $16 trillion.

2. The balanced budget multiplier is the magnification effect on aggregate demand of *simultaneous* changes in government expenditures and taxes that leave the budget balance unchanged. The balanced budget multiplier is not zero—it is positive—because the size of the government expenditure multiplier is larger than the size of the tax multiplier. That is, a $1 increase in government expenditures increases aggregate demand by more than a $1 increase in taxes decreases aggregate demand. So when both government expenditures and taxes increase by $1, aggregate demand still increases.

■ **Self Test 16.2**

Fill in the blanks

(Automatic; Discretionary) ____ fiscal policy is a fiscal policy action that is initiated by an act of

Congress; ____ (automatic; discretionary) fiscal policy is a fiscal policy action triggered by the state of the economy. The government expenditures multiplier is the magnification of a change in government expenditures on aggregate ____ (demand; supply). A tax cut ____ (increases; decreases) aggregate demand and shifts the *AD* curve ____ (rightward; leftward). One limitation of discretionary fiscal policy is the ____ (needs-tested lag; law-making time lag).

True or false

1. Automatic stabilizers are features of fiscal policy that work to stabilize real GDP without explicit action by the government.

2. The cyclical deficit is larger when the economy is in a recession.

3. The government expenditure multiplier is the magnification effect that a change in aggregate demand has on government expenditures on goods and services.

4. A tax cut is a possible fiscal stimulus designed to increase GDP.

5. Estimating potential GDP is a limitation of automatic fiscal policy.

Multiple choice

1. The ____ view says that fiscal stimulus has a multiplier effect that makes it a ____ tool to fight a deep recession.
   a. mainstream; powerful
   b. "free lunch"; powerful
   c. Keynesian; powerful
   d. Keynesian; weak
   e. None of the above answers is correct.

2. An example of automatic fiscal policy is
   a. an interest rate cut, initiated by an act of Congress.
   b. an increase in the quantity of money.
   c. a tax cut, initiated by an act of Congress.
   d. a decrease in tax revenues, triggered by the state of the economy.
   e. any change tax revenues, regardless of the cause.

3. If the structural deficit is $800 billion and the cyclical deficit is $600 billion, the actual budget deficit is ____.
   a. $200 billion
   b. $600 billion
   c. $800 billion
   d. $1,400 billion
   e. None of the above answers are correct.

4. The government expenditure multiplier reflects the magnification effect on ____ from a change in government expenditure on goods and services.
   a. aggregate demand
   b. the budget deficit
   c. tax revenues
   d. aggregate supply
   e. potential GDP

5. The magnitude of the tax multiplier is ____ the magnitude of the government expenditure multiplier.
   a. equal to
   b. greater than
   c. smaller than
   d. the inverse of
   e. exactly one half

6. An example of a discretionary fiscal stimulus policy is
   a. the automatic increase in needs-tested spending in a recession.
   b. induced taxes.
   c. decreasing government expenditure.
   d. decreasing needs-tested spending.
   e. cutting taxes.

7. A fiscal stimulus works to close a recessionary gap by shifting the
   a. *AD* curve leftward.
   b. *AS* curve leftward.
   c. *AD* curve leftward and the *AS* curve leftward.
   d. *AD* curve rightward.
   e. potential GDP line leftward.

■ **FIGURE 16.1**

Price level (GDP price index, 2005 = 100)

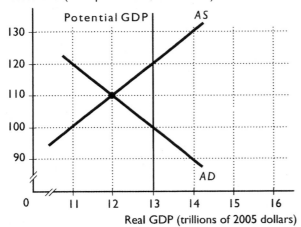

■ **FIGURE 16.2**

Price level (GDP price index, 2005 = 100)

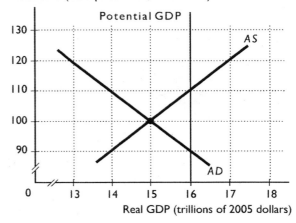

8. In Figure 16.1, a fiscal stimulus designed to restore GDP to potential GDP could be ____, which shifts the ____ curve ____.
   a. an increase in government expenditure; *AS*; leftward
   b. a tax hike; *AD*; leftward
   c. an increase in government expenditure; *AS*; rightward
   d. a tax hike; *AS*; rightward
   e. an increase in government expenditure; *AD*; rightward

9. Discretionary fiscal policy is handicapped by
   a. induced taxes and automatic stabilizers.
   b. law-making time lags, estimation of potential GDP, and economic forecasting.
   c. economic forecasting, law-making time lags, and induced taxes.
   d. automatic stabilizers, law-making time lags, and potential GDP estimation.
   e. automatic stabilizers and induced taxes.

Complete the graph

1. Figure 16.2 (at the top of the next column) illustrates the situation in the United States in 2016. What type of fiscal stimulus might be used to restore this economy to full employment? In Figure 16.2, illustrate the effect of the policy you suggested.

Short answer and numeric questions

1. What are automatic stabilizers? Can they eliminate a recession?

2. What is the relationship between the actual budget deficit, structural deficit, and cyclical deficit?

3. Why does government expenditure have a multiplier effect?

4. What are the demand-side effects of a tax cut?

5. How can the government use fiscal stimulus to eliminate a recessionary gap?

6. It is not easy to determine potential GDP. Why does this fact hamper the use of discretionary fiscal policy?

Additional Exercises (also in MyEconLab Test A)

1. Classify each of the following items as discretionary fiscal policy or automatic fiscal policy or neither.
   a. The imposition of huge fines on tobacco companies
   b. A cut in the gas tax
   c. A cut in cross-border (custom) taxes
   d. An increase in payments to unemployed people

2. Explain the effects of a $100 billion decrease in government expenditure on aggregate demand.

3. Use an *AS-AD* graph to show the effects of a $100 billion decrease in taxes.

4. Use an *AS-AD* graph to show the effects of a simultaneous decrease in government expenditure and taxes of $100 billion.

CHECKPOINT 16.3

■ **Explain the supply-side effects of fiscal policy on employment and potential GDP.**

Quick Review

- *Supply-side effects* The effects of fiscal policy on potential GDP.
- *Tax wedge* The gap created by taxes between what a buyer pays and a seller receives.

Additional Practice Problem 16.3

1. The figure shows the U.S. labor market when there is no income tax.

   a. What is the equilibrium real wage rate and amount of employment?

   b. Suppose the government imposes an income tax rate on labor income of $2 per hour. Show the effect in the figure.

   c. With the income tax, what is the before-tax real wage rate and what is the after-tax real wage rate? What is the amount of the tax wedge?

   d. With the income tax, what is equilibrium employment? How does the income tax affect potential GDP?

Solutions to Additional Practice Problem 16.3

1a. The equilibrium real wage rate is $22 an hour and the equilibrium level of employment is 200 billion hours.

1b. The figure shows the effect of the tax. The supply of labor decreases and the labor supply curve shifts to *LS*tax. The new labor supply curve lies above the initial labor supply curve by the amount of the tax, in this case, by $2.

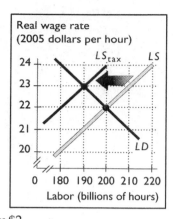

1c. The before-tax real wage rate is $23 per hour, determined by the intersection of the labor supply curve with the tax, *LS*tax, and the labor demand curve, *LD*. From this wage rate $2 must be sent to the government as the tax, so the after-tax real wage rate is $21 per hour. The tax wedge equals the difference in the wage rates, which is $2.

1d. Equilibrium employment is 190 billion hours. Because the equilibrium employment decreases with the tax, potential GDP also decreases.

■ Self Test 16.3

Fill in the blanks

If the income tax rate is 20 percent and the tax rate on consumption expenditure is 15 percent, the tax wedge is ____ (35; 5) percent. An income tax cut ____ (increases; decreases) employment, ____ (increases; decreases) aggregate supply and shifts the *AS* curve ____ (rightward; leftward). Taxes on interest income ____ (increase; decrease) the growth rate of potential GDP. A tax cut ____ (increases; decreases; does not change aggregate demand and ____ (increases; decreases, does not change) aggregate supply.

True or false

1. Income taxes create a wedge between the wage rate paid by firms and the wage rate workers take home.

2. An income tax hike decreases the supply of labor but has no effect on employment or potential GDP.

3. An income tax cut increases potential GDP by shifting the nation's production function upward.

4. Taxes on interest income can drive a wedge between the interest rate borrowers pay and the interest rate lenders receive.

5. An increase in the budget deficit can raise the real interest rate and crowd out private investment.

6. A tax cut increases aggregate demand and decreases aggregate supply.

Multiple choice

1. The quantity of employment is determined in the ____ and that quantity, along with the ____, determines potential GDP.
   a. loanable funds market; production function
   b. goods and services market; labor market
   c. labor market; tax rate
   d. labor market; production function
   e. labor market; tax wedge

2. If the income tax rate is 20 percent and the tax rate on consumption expenditure is 15 percent, then the tax wedge is
   a. 2 percent.
   b. 5 percent.
   c. 35 percent.
   d. 300 percent.
   e. None of the above answers is correct.

3. Increasing the income tax rate ____ the ____.
   a. decreases; demand for labor
   b. increases; supply of labor
   c. decreases; supply of labor
   d. does not change; supply of labor
   e. increases; demand for labor

4. Increasing the income tax rate ____ the before-tax real wage rate and ____ the after-tax real wage rate.
   a. raises; raises
   b. does not change; raises
   c. lowers; lowers
   d. lowers; raises
   e. raises; lowers

5. The supply-side effects of an income tax cut ____ potential GDP and ____ aggregate supply.
   a. increase; increase
   b. increase; decrease
   c. decrease; increase
   d. decrease; decrease
   e. increases; do not change

6. An income tax on labor income decreases the ____ of potential GDP and a tax on interest income decreases the ____ of potential GDP.
   a. level; growth rate
   b. growth rate; level
   c. level; level
   d. growth rate; growth rate
   e. None of the above answers is correct.

7. If the nominal interest rate is 10 percent, the inflation rate is 6 percent, and the tax rate on interest income is 25 percent, what is the after-tax real interest rate?
   a. 4.0 percent
   b. 6.0 percent
   c. 3.0 percent
   d. 1.5 percent
   e. 3.5 percent

8. An income tax cut ____ aggregate demand and ____ aggregate supply.
   a. increases; increases
   b. increases; decreases
   c. decreases; increases
   d. decreases; decreases
   e. does not change; increases

9. If fiscal stimulus creates a large budget ____, then in the long run economic growth ____.
   a. surplus; increases
   b. surplus; decreases
   c. deficit; increases
   d. deficit; decreases
   e. None of the above answers is correct

Complete the graph

■ FIGURE 16.3

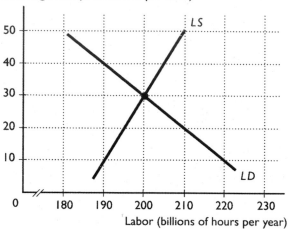

1. Figure 16.3 illustrates the labor market. Suppose that the government cuts taxes so that the supply of labor changes by 15 billion hours at each wage rate. Show the effects from the tax cut in the figure.

■ FIGURE 16.4

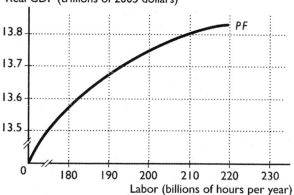

2. Figure 16.4 shows the nation's production function. Employment is initially 200 billion hours. If employment increases by 10 billion hours, show the effect on potential GDP.

3. Based on the previous two questions, how will a tax cut affect the aggregate supply curve?

■ FIGURE 16.5

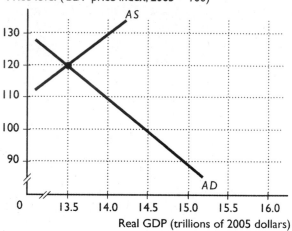

4. Figure 16.5 illustrates the economy. Potential GDP is $15 trillion. Suppose that the government cuts its taxes and that the supply-side effects are larger than the demand-side effects. If the economy moves back to potential GDP, in Figure 16.5, illustrate the effect of this government policy.

Short answer and numeric questions

1. What are the supply-side effects of a tax cut? Why does a tax cut have supply-side effects?

2. What is the tax wedge on labor income? How does the tax wedge affect potential GDP? Why does the tax wedge affect potential GDP?

3. Suppose the tax rate on interest income is 25 percent.
   a. If the real interest rate is 4 percent and the inflation rate is zero percent, what is the nominal interest rate and the after-tax real interest rate? What is the true tax rate on interest income?
   b. If the real interest rate is 4 percent and the inflation rate is 4 percent, what is the nominal interest rate and the after-tax real

interest rate? What is the true tax rate on interest income?

c. How has higher inflation affected the true tax rate on interest income?

4. What is the effect on aggregate demand and aggregate supply of a tax cut? What is the effect on real GDP and the price level of a tax cut?

5. What can be the long-run adverse effects from a fiscal stimulus that increases the budget deficit?

6. The Eye on Your Life discusses how you can think about how fiscal policy relates to your values and opinions. You can also use this thought to make predictions about the future. For instance, if you think the election of a Presidential candidate who supports tax hikes for the rich is likely, how do you think that would affect the cruise industry? High-end clothing retailers? Expensive jewelers?

Additional Exercises (also in MyEconLab Test A)

1. The government raises the income tax rate. Explain the effects of this action on the supply of labor, the demand for labor, the equilibrium level of employment, the real wage rate, and potential GDP.

2. The government raises the income tax rate. Explain the effects of this action on saving, investment, the real interest rate, and the growth rate of real GDP.

3. Explain why inflation increases the true tax rate on interest income. What is the true income tax rate on interest income if the real interest rate is 3 percent, the inflation rate is 2 percent, and the tax rate on nominal interest is 25 percent?

4. The government increases its outlays but keeps tax revenue unchanged. Explain the effects of this action on saving, investment, the real interest rate, and the growth rate of real GDP.

SELF TEST ANSWERS

■ CHECKPOINT 16.1

Fill in the blanks

The <u>President</u> proposes the budget each February. The government has a budget <u>deficit</u> when tax revenues are less than outlays. The national debt is <u>the amount of debt outstanding that arises from past budget deficits</u>. In recent years, the government has had a budget <u>deficit</u>.

True or false

1. False; pages 396-397
2. True; page 396
3. False; page 398
4. True; page 399

Multiple choice

1. c; page 396
2. c; page 396
3. d; page 397

Short answer and numeric questions

1. If the government has a $1,400 billion budget deficit, the national debt increases by $1,400 billion; page 397.
2. The United States has a government deficit that, as percent of GDP, is large compared to other countries. The U.S. budget deficit is 6 percent of GDP. Only Japan has a larger deficit (8 percent) while the U.K. deficit is about equal to that of the United States. But the budget deficits of New Zealand, the Euro area, and Canada are much less than that in the United States; page 400.
3. Social Security and Medicare obligations are huge: $80 trillion. To pay the debt, the government must either raise income taxes, raise Social Security taxes, cut Social Security spending, and/or cut other federal government spending; page 398.

Additional Exercises (also in MyEconLab Test A)

1. Fiscal policy is using the federal budget, expenditures and taxes, to achieve sustained economic growth and full employment. The President proposes a budget to Congress each February. The Congress then passes budget acts in September. The President then either signs or vetoes the acts. The President's role is to propose potential fiscal policy while the Congress then enacts legislation that incorporates fiscal policy. The President can approve or disapprove of Congress's actions. The federal budget today is in deficit; pages 396-397.

■ CHECKPOINT 16.2

Fill in the blanks

<u>Discretionary</u> fiscal policy is a fiscal policy action that is initiated by an act of Congress; <u>automatic</u> fiscal policy is a fiscal policy action triggered by the state of the economy. The government expenditure multiplier is the magnification of a change in government expenditures on aggregate <u>demand</u>. A tax cut <u>increases</u> aggregate demand and shifts the *AD* curve <u>rightward</u>. One limitation of discretionary fiscal policy is the <u>law-making time lag</u>.

True or false

1. True; page 402
2. True; page 403
3. False; page 404
4. True; page 405
5. False; page 406

Multiple choice

1. c; page 401
2. d; page 402
3. d; page 403
4. a; page 404
5. c; page 404
6. e; page 404
7. d; page 405
8. e; page 405
9. b; page 406

Complete the graph

1. There is a recessionary gap because real GDP is less than potential GDP. An expansionary fiscal stimulus, such as increasing govern-

■ **FIGURE 16.6**

Price level (GDP price index, 2005 = 100)

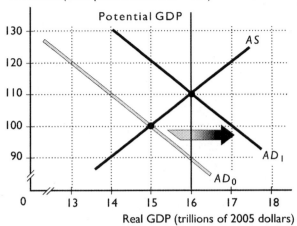

Real GDP (trillions of 2005 dollars)

ment expenditure on goods and services, increasing transfer payments, and/or cutting taxes, could be applied to return the economy to potential GDP. Aggregate demand increases and, as Figure 16.6 shows, the AD curve shifts rightward from AD_0 to AD_1. Real GDP increases from $15 trillion to $16 trillion and the price level rises from 100 to 110; page 405.

Short answer and numeric questions

1. Automatic stabilizers are features of fiscal policy that stabilize real GDP without explicit action by the government. Automatic stabilizers include induced taxes and needs-tested spending. Induced taxes and needs-tested spending decrease the multiplier effect of a change in autonomous expenditure. Because they decrease the multiplier, they moderate both expansions and recessions and make real GDP more stable but they cannot eliminate a recession; page 402.

2. The actual budget deficit is equal to the sum of the structural deficit (the budget deficit that would occur if the economy was at full employment) plus the cyclical deficit (the budget deficit that arises because revenues and outlays are not at their full-employment levels); page 403.

3. Government expenditure has a multiplier effect because it induces further changes in consumption expenditure. For instance, an increase in government expenditure increases people's disposable income, which then increases their consumption expenditure; page 404.

4. A tax cut increases disposable income, which increases consumption expenditure and aggregate demand; page 405.

5. A recessionary gap exists when real GDP is less than potential GDP. The government can eliminate the recessionary gap by using a fiscal stimulus to increase aggregate demand. The government can increase aggregate demand by increasing its expenditures on goods and services and/or by cutting taxes; page 405.

6. Because it is not easy to tell whether real GDP is below, above, or at potential GDP a discretionary fiscal action might move real GDP *away* from potential GDP instead of toward it; page 406.

Additional Exercises (also in MyEconLab Test A)

1. a. Huge fines on tobacco companies are not a fiscal policy because they are the judgment of a court; page 402.

   b. A cut in the gas tax is a discretionary fiscal policy because the cut requires an act of Congress; page 404.

   c. A cut in the cross-border (custom) taxes would be classified as a discretionary fiscal policy because the tax cut requires an act of Congress; page 404.

   d. An increase in payments to unemployed people is an automatic fiscal policy; page 403.

2. Figure 16.7 (on the next page) illustrates the effect of a $100 billion decrease in government expenditure. The decrease in government expenditure decreases aggregate demand and shifts the AD curve leftward from AD_0 to AD_1. The magnitude of the shift of the AD curve, $300 billion, exceeds the initial $100 billion decrease in government expenditure because of the multiplier effect; pages 404-405.

■ **FIGURE 16.7**

Price level (GDP price index, 2005 = 100)

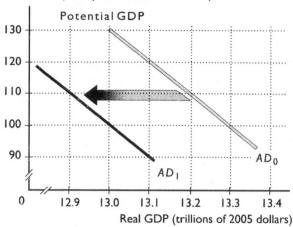

■ **FIGURE 16.8**

Price level (GDP price index, 2005 = 100)

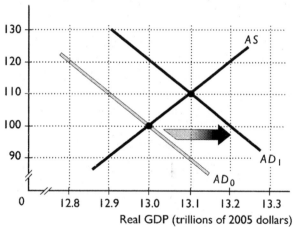

3. Figure 16.8 illustrates the effect of a $100 billion decrease in taxes. The decrease in taxes increases aggregate demand and shifts the AD curve rightward from AD_0 to AD_1. The magnitude of the shift in the AD curve, $200 billion, exceeds $100 billion because of the multiplier effect. The AS curve might also shift rightward as a result of the lower taxes, but once again because the conventional view is that the shift is small, the AS curve is not changed in Figure 16.8. The tax cut increases real GDP and raises the price level; page 405.

■ **FIGURE 16.9**

Price level (GDP price index, 2005 = 100)

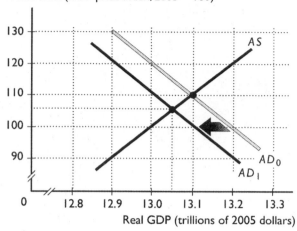

4. When the government decreases its expenditure *and* cuts its taxes by $100 billion, the effect on aggregate demand from the decrease in government expenditure exceeds the effect from the cut in taxes. Therefore, as shown in Figure 16.9, in accord with the balanced budget multiplier aggregate demand decreases and the aggregate demand curve shifts leftward, though the shift is not as large as in Exercise 2. The AS curve might shift in this case, but the direction of the shift is likely to be small and also is ambiguous. So once again the AS curve in Figure 16.9 is not changed. As the figure illustrates, the aggregate demand curve shifts leftward so the price level falls and real GDP decreases; pages 404–405.

■ **CHECKPOINT 16.3**

Fill in the blanks

If the income tax rate is 20 percent and the tax rate on consumption expenditure is 15 percent, the tax wedge is <u>35</u> percent. An income tax cut <u>increases</u> employment, <u>increases</u> aggregate supply and shifts the AS curve <u>rightward</u>. Taxes on interest income <u>decrease</u> the growth rate of potential GDP. A tax cut <u>increases</u> aggregate demand and <u>increases</u> aggregate supply.

True or false

1. True; page 410
2. False; pages 410-411
3. False; pages 410-411
4. True; page 412
5. True; page 412
6. False; page 414

Multiple choice

1. d; page 408
2. c; page 409
3. c; pages 410-411
4. e; page 410
5. a; page 411
6. a; pages 411-412
7. d; page 412
8. a; page 414
9. d; page 415

Complete the graph

■ **FIGURE 16.10**

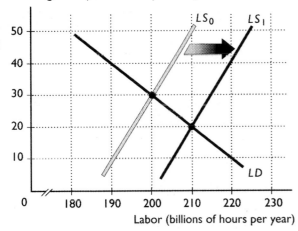

Real wage rate (2005 dollars per hour)

1. The cut in taxes increase the supply of labor so, as Figure 16.10 shows, the supply of labor curve shifts rightward by 15 billion hours of labor from LS_0 to LS_1. Equilibrium employment increases from 200 billion hours of labor to 210 billion hours and the real wage rate falls from $30 per hour to $20 per hour; pages 410-411.

■ **FIGURE 16.11**

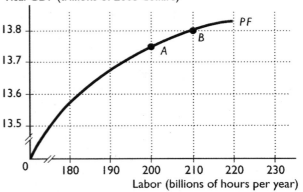

Real GDP (trillions of 2005 dollars)

2. Figure 16.11 shows the results of the increase in employment. Potential GDP increases from $13.75 trillion at point A on the production function to $13.8 trillion at point B on the production function; page 411.

3. The tax cut increases potential GDP so the tax cut also increases aggregate supply. The aggregate supply curve shifts rightward; page 411.

■ **FIGURE 16.12**

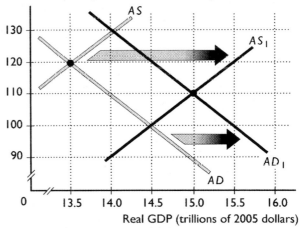

Price level (GDP price index, 2005 = 100)

4. The tax cut increases both aggregate demand and aggregate supply, so in Figure 16.12, the aggregate demand curve shifts rightward from AD to AD_1 and the aggregate supply curve shifts rightward from AS to AS_1. Because the effect on aggregate supply exceeds the effect on aggregate demand, the shift of

the AS curve is larger than the shift of the AD curve. Real GDP increases and the price level falls. The exact fall of the price level depends on the precise sizes of the shifts but in the figure it falls to 100; page 414.

Short answer and numeric questions

1. A tax cut increases the incentive to work and save by decreasing the tax wedges. A tax cut increases the supply of labor and the supply of saving. An increase in the supply of labor increases equilibrium employment, which increases potential GDP. An increase in the supply of saving increases the equilibrium quantity of investment and capital. With larger quantities of labor and capital, potential GDP grows more rapidly; pages 409-412.

2. The tax wedge on labor income is the difference in the real wage rate paid by employers and the real wage rate received by employees. It equals the sum of the income tax rate on labor income plus the tax rate on consumption expenditure.

   The tax wedge decreases potential GDP because it decreases the supply of labor, which decreases equilibrium employment; pages 409-410.

3. a. The nominal interest rate is 4 percent (since the inflation rate is 0 percent) and the after-tax real interest rate is 3 percent. The true tax rate on interest income is 25 percent; page 412.

   b. The nominal interest rate is 10 percent (it equals the sum of the inflation rate plus the real interest rate). The after-tax real interest rate is 1.5 percent because the tax (which equals the 25 percent tax rate multiplied by the 10 percent nominal interest rate, or 2.5 percent) must be subtracted from the real interest rate. The tax has lowered the real interest rate by 1.5 percent (from 4 percent to 2.5 percent) so the true tax rate is (1.5 percent ÷ 4 percent) × 100, which is 37.5 percent; page 412.

   c. The increase in the inflation rate raised the true tax rate paid on interest income; page 412.

4. A tax cut increases both aggregate demand and aggregate supply. As a result, real GDP unambiguously increases but the effect on the price level is uncertain. If the increase in aggregate demand exceeds the increase in aggregate supply, the price level rate rises; if the increase in aggregate demand equals the increase in aggregate supply, the price level does not change; and, if the increase in aggregate demand is less than the increase in aggregate supply, the price level falls; pages 414-415.

5. If the budget deficit crowds out investment, the long-run negative consequences from the fiscal stimulus can be severe. With less investment, the economy will have less capital and so its economic growth rate slows. If the large budget deficit persists, the government might be tempted to instruct the central bank to make open market purchases of the debt, in which case inflation could soar; page 415.

6. The cruise industry, high-end clothing retailers, and expensive jewelry stores would all be harmed by taxes being increased on the rich. If you were thinking of making an investment in any of these endeavors—or other similar areas—you might well want to delay until you have more information about the extent of the tax increases. On the other hand, investment in a "dollar store" sort of opportunity ought not to be affected by the proposed taxes on the rich.

Additional Exercises (also in MyEconLab Test A)

1. The higher income tax rate decreases the supply of labor. The demand for labor does not change. As a result, the equilibrium level of employment falls so that potential GDP decreases. The before-tax real wage rate rises but the after-tax real wage rate falls; pages 410-411.

2. The higher income tax rate decreases the quantity of saving and investment. The after-tax real interest rate, which is the interest rate that is relevant to saving and investment, falls. Because there is less investment, the growth rate of real GDP decreases; page 412.

3. The tax on interest income is applied to the nominal interest rate. So the after-tax real interest rate equals the nominal interest rate minus the inflation rate (which equals the before-tax real interest rate) minus the tax paid on the interest income. When the inflation rate rises, the nominal interest rate rises. The higher nominal interest rate increases the tax paid on the interest rate, which decreases the after-tax real interest rate and thereby increases the true tax rate on interest income.

If the real interest rate is 3 percent and the inflation rate is 2 percent, then the nominal interest rate is 5 percent. If the tax rate on nominal interest income is 25 percent, then of the 5 percent nominal interest rate, 1.25 percent is paid as taxes. The after-tax real interest rate equals the real interest rate minus the amount paid as taxes, which is 3 percent − 1.25 percent, or 1.75 percent. The tax lowers the real interest rate from 3 percentage points to 1.75 percentage points, which is a fall of 1.25 percentage points for a true tax rate on interest income of 42 percent; page 412.

4. By increasing its outlays and keeping its tax revenue unchanged, the government budget deficit rises. This action decreases the supply of loanable funds to firms, which raises the real interest rate. The quantity of saving increases but the quantity of investment decreases—crowded out by the higher budget deficit. With less investment, the growth rate of real GDP slows; page 412.

Chapter

Monetary Policy

17

1 Describe the objectives of U.S. monetary policy, the framework for achieving those objectives, and the Fed's monetary policy actions.

The goals of monetary policy are "maximum employment, stable prices, and moderate long-term interest rates." Financial stability is a necessary prerequisite for obtaining the Fed's goals which is why the Fed pursued that goal intensively in Fall 2008. The Fed uses the output gap, which is the percentage deviation of real GDP from potential GDP, as its "maximum employment" goal. It uses the core inflation rate, which is the annual inflation rate calculated using the PCE deflator *excluding* the prices of food and fuel, as its "stable prices" goal. The Fed's monetary policy instrument is the federal funds rate. The Fed uses a targeting strategy in which it sets the federal funds rate at a level that makes the Fed's forecast of its ultimate policy goals, the core inflation rate and the GDP gap, equal to their targeted goals. The Fed changes the federal funds rate using open market operations to change banks' reserves. During the global financial crisis the demand for reserves skyrocketed so to keep the federal funds rate from rising, the Fed responded with quantitative easing, a massive increase in reserves.

2 Explain the transmission channels through which the Fed influences real GDP and the inflation rate.

The transmission channel tells how monetary policy affects real GDP and the inflation rate. For instance, when the Fed lowers the federal funds rate, other short term interest rates fall and the exchange rate also falls. The quantity of money and the supply of loanable funds increase. The increase in the supply of loanable funds lowers the long-term real interest rate, which boosts consumption expenditure and investment. The lower exchange rate increases net exports. The increases in these three components of aggregate expenditure increase aggregate demand so that real GDP growth and the inflation rate rise. The effect of an increase in the federal funds rate is the opposite of what was just outlined. When the Fed fights a recession, it lowers the federal funds rate in order to boost aggregate demand and raise real GDP; when the Fed fights inflation, it raises the federal funds rate in order to decrease aggregate demand and lower the inflation rate. The links along the transmission channel can take a lengthy and variable time until they affect real GDP and the inflation rate.

3 Explain and compare alternative monetary policy strategies.

Using rules rather than discretion enable the Fed to keep inflation expectations anchored close to the inflation rate target. The Fed could have chosen to use an inflation targeting rule, which is similar to the Fed's current procedure but requires the Fed to make public its inflation target. Or the Fed could opt for a monetary targeting rule such as the *k*-percent rule, but if the demand for money is unstable money targeting is unreliable. The Fed could also use a nominal GDP targeting rule, under which the Fed would attempt to hit a target for nominal GDP growth (which is a variety of inflation targeting).

CHECKPOINT 17.1

■ **Describe the objectives of U.S. monetary policy, the framework for achieving those objectives, and the Fed's monetary policy actions.**

Quick Review

- *Core inflation rate* The annual inflation rate calculated using the PCE deflator excluding the prices of food and fuel.
- *Monetary policy instrument* A variable that the Fed can directly control or closely target and that influences the economy in desirable ways.
- *Federal funds rate* The interest rate at which banks can borrow and lend reserves in the federal funds market.

Additional Practice Problems 17.1

1. Why does the Fed focus on the core inflation rate rather than the overall inflation rate?
2. What is the role of the President and the Congress in making monetary policy decisions?

Solutions to Additional Practice Problems 17.1

1 The Fed focuses on the core inflation rate because the Fed believes that this inflation rate is a better indicator of whether price stability is being achieved. The price of fuel is heavily influenced by oil prices and the price of food is heavily influenced by harvest conditions. Both of these events are outside of the economy's control, so the Fed uses the core inflation rate to better measure the stability of the prices that it can influence.

2. Neither the President nor the Congress has a direct role in making monetary policy decisions. These decisions are left to the Federal Reserve. But some U.S. Presidents have tried to influence the Fed and the Fed is required to report twice a year to Congress.

■ **Self Test 17.1**

Fill in the blanks

The Fed's goals are ____ employment, ____ prices, and ____ long-term interest rates. The key to achieving them is ____ (maximum employment; stable prices). Financial stability ____ (is; is not) necessary for the Fed to meet its employment and price level goals. To meet its price level goal, the Fed uses the ____ (CPI inflation rate; core inflation rate). The President of the United States ____ (has; does not have) direct control over the Fed's monetary policy. The Fed has selected the ____ (federal funds rate; monetary base) as its monetary policy instrument. To lower the federal funds rate, the Fed will ____ (increase; decrease) banks' reserves using ____.

True or false

1. By law, the Fed is required to keep inflation equal to or less than 2 percent per year.
2. The core inflation rate excludes the cost of housing and medical care.
3. The Fed's monetary policy instrument is the federal funds rate.
4. The Fed uses a targeting rule in which it sets the federal funds at the level that makes the forecasts of its policy goals equal to their targets.
5. To change the federal funds rate, the Fed uses open market operations.

Multiple choice

1. Maximum employment and moderate long-term interest rates are best achieved with
   a. high and stable inflation rates.
   b. high and variable inflation rates.
   c. high real interest rates.
   d. high short-term interest rates.
   e. price stability.

2. The operational goals the Fed uses for its monetary policy objectives are the
   a. federal funds rate and the supply of reserves.
   b. the demand for reserves and the supply of reserves.
   c. supply of reserves and the output gap.
   d. core inflation rate and the output gap.
   e. federal funds rate and the core inflation rate.

3. Which of the following is the Fed's monetary policy instrument?
   a. the output gap
   b. the core inflation rate
   c. the federal funds rate
   d. the supply of reserves
   e. the demand for reserves

4. To lower the federal funds rate, the Fed conducts an open market _____ of securities which _____.
   a. sale; increases the demand for reserves
   b. sale; increases the supply of reserves
   c. purchase; increases the demand for reserves
   d. purchase; decreases the demand for reserves
   e. None of the above answers are correct

Complete the graph

■ **FIGURE 17.1**

Federal funds rate (percent per year)

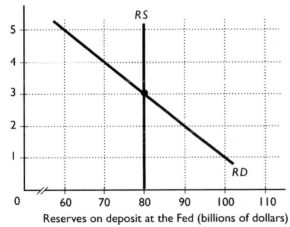

1. Figure 17.1 shows the market for reserves.
   a. What is the equilibrium federal funds rate?
   b. If the Fed wants to change the federal funds rate to 2 percent, what can the Fed do?
   c. Through what method will the Fed change the federal funds rate to 2 percent?

Short answer and numeric questions

1. Why do stable prices help the Fed meet its goals for employment and long-term interest rates?

2. What are the Fed's objectives for employment and the price level? What does it use as operational goals for these targets?

3. What does the Fed use as its monetary policy instrument? How was this instrument used during the financial crisis of 2008?

4. What is the difference between an instrument rule and a target rule? Which rule does the Fed use?

5. How does the Fed change the supply of reserves? What happened in the market for reserves during the financial crisis of 2008?

Additional Exercises (also in MyEconLab Test A)

1. What does the Federal Reserve Act say that the Fed must try to achieve and the means that it must use?

2. If the price of housing was rising much faster than other prices, would the core inflation measure exclude housing costs?

3. Consider two situations, A and B: In A, the output gap is positive (an inflationary gap) and the core inflation rate is 3 percent a year; and in B, the output gap is negative (a recessionary gap) and the core inflation rate is 1 percent a year. In which situation is the Fed likely to have the higher federal funds rate target and why?

■ **FIGURE 17.2**

Federal funds rate (percent per year)

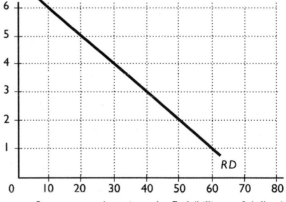

4. If in Figure 17.2 the quantity of reserves supplied is $40 billion and the Fed wants to set the federal funds rate at 5 percent a year,

does it buy or sell securities in the open market? By how much must it change banks' reserves?

CHECKPOINT 17.2

■ **Explain the transmission channels through which the Fed influences real GDP and the inflation rate.**

Quick Review

- *Monetary policy transmission* When the Fed raises the federal funds rate, other short-term interest rates and the exchange rate rise. The quantity of money and supply of loanable funds decrease so that the long-term real interest rate rises. Consumption expenditure, investment, and net exports decrease so aggregate demand decreases. The real GDP growth rate and the inflation rate decrease.

Additional Practice Problems 17.2

1. The figure shows the market for reserves. Suppose the Fed becomes concerned that the inflation rate is too high and wants to change the quantity of reserves by $20 billion.

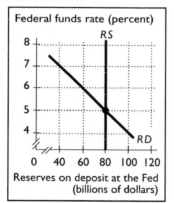

   a. Will the Fed want to raise or lower the federal funds rate? How will the Fed make this change? In the figure, show how the Fed's policy will the change the market for reserves.

   b. What will be the effect of the policy on the quantity of money, the supply of loanable funds and the real interest rate?

   c. What will be the effect of the policy on aggregate demand and on the growth rate real GDP and the inflation rate?

2. In reality, can monetary policy offset fluctuations in aggregate demand so that neither the price level nor real GDP changes? Explain your answer.

Solutions to Additional Practice Problems 17.2

1a. Because the Fed is concerned with inflation, the Fed will raise the federal funds rate. To do so, the Fed will use open market purchases of securities. The figure shows that the Fed will decrease the quantity of reserves.

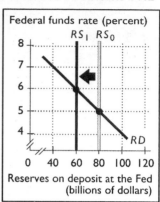

The federal funds rate will rise from 5 percent to 6 percent.

1b. The quantity of money decreases as does the supply of loanable funds. The decrease in the supply of loanable funds raises the real long-term interest rate.

1c. The rise in the long-term real interest rate decreases consumption expenditure and investment. Net exports also decreases, so for these three reasons aggregate demand decreases. The growth rate of real GDP slows and the inflation rate falls.

2. It is not possible for monetary policy to offset fluctuations in aggregate demand so that neither the price level nor real GDP changes. Because monetary policy must work through many linkages before it affects the economy, there are long and variable lags between the Fed's policy action and its impact on the economy. As a consequence, policy that eliminates all changes in the price level and real GDP is impossible.

■ Self Test 17.2

Fill in the blanks

When the Fed lowers the federal funds rate, other short-term interest rates _____ (fall; rise) and the exchange rate _____ (falls; rises). When the Fed lowers the federal funds rate, the quantity of money _____ (increases; decreases) and the supply of loanable funds _____ (increases; decreases). When the Fed lowers the federal funds rate, the long-term real interest rate _____ (falls; rises) so that consumption expenditure and investment _____ (increase; decrease). When the Fed lowers the federal funds rate, it aims to _____ (increase; decrease) aggregate _____ (demand; supply). To fight a recession, the Fed will _____ (raise; lower) the federal funds rate and to fight inflation the Fed will _____ (raise; lower) the federal funds rate. The linkage between changes in the federal funds rate and changes in real GDP and inflation is _____ (short and tight; long and variable).

True or false

1. When the Fed lowers the federal funds rate, other short-term interest rates quickly fall.

2. If the Fed raises the federal funds rate, the quantity of money and the supply of loanable funds both decrease

3. The Fed has immediate and direct control over the long-term real interest rate.

4. When the Fed lowers the federal funds rate, its policy affects real GDP and the price level by changing aggregate supply.

5. If the Fed raises the federal funds rate, it is aiming to decrease aggregate demand and thereby decrease the inflation rate.

6. On average, the Fed's actions take about 3 to 4 months before they have an impact on the inflation rate.

Multiple choice

1. When the Fed lowers the federal funds rate, which of the following economic variables responds most rapidly?
   a. consumption expenditure
   b. the supply of loanable funds
   c. the long-term real interest rate
   d. other short-term interest rates
   e. the inflation rate

2. When the Fed lowers the federal funds rate, which of the following economic variables responds most slowly?
   a. consumption expenditure
   b. the supply of loanable funds
   c. the long-term real interest rate
   d. other short-term interest rates
   e. the inflation rate

3. When the Fed lowers the federal funds rate, in the short run the quantity of money _____ and the supply of loanable funds _____.
   a. increases; increases
   b. increases; decreases
   c. decreases; decreases
   d. decreases; increases
   e. increases; does not change

4. When the Fed raises the federal funds rate, consumption expenditure _____ and investment _____.
   a. does not change; does not change
   b. does not change; decreases
   c. increases; decreases
   d. increases; increases
   e. decreases; decreases

5. When the Fed raises the federal funds rate, the exchange rate _____ and net exports _____.
   a. does not change; does not change
   b. does not change; decreases
   c. increases; decreases
   d. increases; increases
   e. decreases; decreases

6. A change in the federal funds rate _____ the supply of loanable funds, _____ the long-term real interest rate, and _____ investment.
   a. affects; affects; affects
   b. affects; affects; does not affect
   c. does not affect; affect; does not affect
   d. affects; does not affect; affects
   e. does not affect; does not affect; does not affect

7. If the Fed wants to fight a recession, it will ____ the federal funds rate in order to ____.
   a. raise; increase aggregate demand
   b. raise; decrease aggregate supply
   c. raise; increase aggregate supply
   d. lower; increase aggregate supply
   e. lower; increase aggregate demand

8. If the Fed wants to fight inflation, it will ____ the federal funds rate in order to ____.
   a. raise; decrease aggregate demand
   b. raise; decrease aggregate supply
   c. raise; increase aggregate supply
   d. lower; increase aggregate supply
   e. lower; decrease aggregate demand

Complete the graph

■ **FIGURE 17.3**

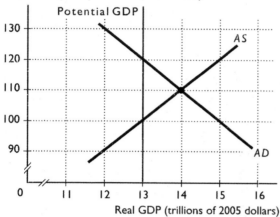

1. Figure 17.3 shows the economy in its initial equilibrium.
   a. What is the equilibrium real GDP and price level? To move the economy back to potential GDP, should the Fed raise or lower the federal funds rate? Why?
   b. Supposing that the Fed undertakes the correct policy to restore real GDP to potential GDP. In Figure 17.2 show the effect of that policy.

2. Use Figures 17.4 through 17.7 to show the effect of the Fed conducting an open market purchase that increases the supply of reserves by $1 billion.

■ **FIGURE 17.4**

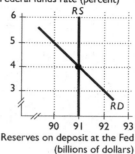

■ **FIGURE 17.5**

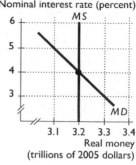

■ **FIGURE 17.6**

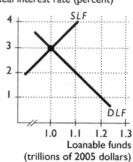

■ **FIGURE 17.7**

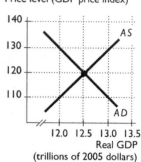

Short answer and numeric questions

1. Does the Fed's monetary policy aim to change aggregate demand or aggregate supply? Why?

2. How does monetary policy affect the exchange rate? In your answer, explain the case in which the Fed raises the interest rate and assume that the Fed's monetary policy is the only factor that changes.

3. Suppose the Fed is concerned that the economy is entering a recession. What policy can the Fed pursue and what is the effect of the policy on real GDP and the price level?

4. Suppose it takes two years for monetary policy to have an effect and recessions last for only one year. What implication does this have for monetary policy?

Additional Exercises (also in MyEconLab Test A)

1. List the sequence of events in the transmission from a fall in the federal funds rate to a change in the inflation rate.

For the next two exercises, suppose the Fed thinks that an inflationary gap is emerging and takes actions to avoid its consequences.

2. What action does the Fed take? Illustrate the effects of the Fed's actions in the money market and the loanable funds market.

3. Explain how the Fed's actions change aggregate demand and real GDP.

CHECKPOINT 17.3

■ **Explain and compare alternative monetary policy strategies.**

Quick Review

- *Discretionary monetary policy* A monetary policy that is based on the expert assessment of the current economic situation.

- *k-percent rule* A monetary policy that makes the quantity of money grow at k percent per year, where k is the growth rate of potential GDP.

- *Inflation targeting* A monetary policy framework that combines an announced target range for the inflation rate with the publication of the central bank's economic forecasts and analysis.

Additional Practice Problems 17.3

1. What is the major drawback of discretionary monetary policy?

2. If a central bank is using a k-percent rule, how does it respond to a recession?

Solutions to Additional Practice Problems 17.3

1. People must make long-term plans for the future. Firms and workers must determine wages while savers and borrowers must determine interest rates. These plans are best made when inflation is correctly anticipated. Discretionary monetary policy makes it difficult to correctly anticipate inflation, so this type of policy can lead to poor economic outcomes.

2. A k-percent rule calls for the central bank to ignore recessions and keep the quantity of money growing at k percent. So the central bank would not respond to a recession; the growth rate of the quantity of money would stay at k percent.

■ Self Test 17.3

Fill in the blanks

Monetary policy that assesses the current situation and then bases the policy on that assessment is _____ (a k-percent rule; discretionary monetary policy). If a central bank uses an inflation targeting rule, the central bank _____ (must; must not) make its inflation rate target public. A strength of inflation targeting is that it _____ (helps people ignore inflation; helps manage people's inflation expectations; easily can be used to fight recessions).

True or false

1. Discretionary policy must be implemented using an inflation targeting rule.

2. Inflation targeting aims to keep the inflation rate within an announced target range.

3. The k-percent rule says that the growth rate of the quantity of money must equal the inflation rate minus k percent.

4. The United States is currently targeting nominal GDP.

Multiple choice

1. Discretionary monetary policy has the drawback that it
   a. must lead to very high inflation.
   b. is currently illegal in the United States.
   c. makes inflation expectations harder to manage.
   d. cannot be implemented using changes in the federal funds rate.
   e. None of the above answers are correct.

2. To work well, which monetary policy rule needs the demand for money to be stable?
   a. discretionary monetary policy
   b. nominal GDP targeting
   c. k-percent rule
   d. inflation targeting rule
   e. No monetary policy rule requires the demand for money to be stable.

3. Under a nominal GDP targeting rule, the Federal Reserve
   a. cannot use the federal funds rate to conduct monetary policy.
   b. lowers its interest rate when nominal GDP falls below the target.
   c. changes the interest rate only when real GDP, and hence nominal GDP, is off target.
   d. loses its ability to influence the inflation rate.
   e. must publish its expected inflation rate.

4. Inflation targeting requires the central bank to
   a. use a short-term interest rate as its policy instrument.
   b. adopt a *k*-percent rule for the inflation rate.
   c. avoid changing the amount of the monetary base.
   d. publicize its targeted inflation rate.
   e. set a fixed target for nominal GDP.

Short answer and numeric questions

1. What is inflation targeting? Why does the central bank announce its inflation rate targets?
2. What are the drawbacks of the *k*-percent rule for monetary policy?

Additional Exercises (also in MyEconLab Test A)

1. Why do monetary policy rules beat discretionary monetary policy?
2. What are the main differences between the way the Fed and the Bank of England conduct monetary policy?

SELF TEST ANSWERS

■ CHECKPOINT 17.1

Fill in the blanks

The Fed's goals are <u>maximum</u> employment, <u>stable</u> prices, and <u>moderate</u> long-term interest rates. The key to achieving them is <u>stable prices</u>. Financial stability <u>is</u> necessary for the Fed to meet its employment and price level goals. To meet its price level goal, the Fed uses the <u>core inflation rate</u>. The President of the United States <u>does not have</u> direct control over the Fed's monetary policy. The Fed has selected the <u>federal funds rate</u> as its monetary policy instrument. To lower the federal funds rate, the Fed will <u>increase</u> banks' reserves using <u>open market operations</u>.

True or false

1. False; page 422
2. False; page 423
3. True; page 424
4. True; page 426
5. True; page 427

Multiple choice

1. e; page 422
2. d; page 423
3. c; page 424
4. e; page 428

Complete the graph

1. a. The equilibrium federal funds rate is 3 percent; page 427.
   b. As Figure 17.8 (at the top of the next column) shows, for the Fed lower the federal funds rate to 2 percent, the Fed must increase the quantity of reserves to by $10 billion to $90 billion; pages 427-428.
   c. The Fed will increase the quantity of reserves by using an open market purchase of securities; page 428.

Short answer and numeric questions

1. The Fed seeks "maximum employment" and "moderate long-term interest rates." If the Fed can achieve stable prices, then the inflation rate will be low. A low inflation rate helps people makes the best decisions about

■ FIGURE 17.8

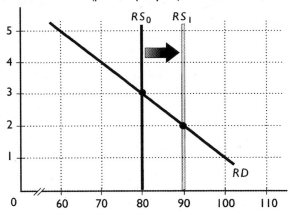

Federal funds rate (percent per year)

Reserves on deposit at the Fed (billions of dollars)

savings and investment and so helps promote economic growth and maximum employment. Because the long-term interest rate equals the real interest rate plus the inflation rate, low inflation also makes the long-term interest lower than otherwise; page 422.

2. The Fed seeks "maximum employment, stable prices ...". For use as an operational "maximum employment" goal, the Fed uses percentage output gap. For use as an operational "stable prices" goal, the Fed uses the core inflation rate; page 423.

3. The Fed uses the federal funds rate—the interest rate at which banks can borrow and lend reserves—as its policy instrument. The federal funds rate has fluctuated since 1990. Since 2009 the Fed has set the federal funds at an unprecedentedly low level of near 0 percent; pages 424-425.

4. An instrument rule sets the policy instrument according to a formula. For instance, the Taylor rule sets the federal funds rate according to the inflation rate and the output gap. A targeting rule sets the policy instrument at the level that makes the forecasts of the ultimate policy goals equal to their targets. A targeting rule need not be a specific quantitative rule. The Fed currently uses a targeting rule; page 426.

5. The Fed changes the supply of reserves by using open market operations, its purchases or sales of securities. In the financial crisis of 2008, increased risk vastly raised banks' demand for reserves. To keep the interest rate low, the Fed responded with a huge increase in the quantity of reserves; pages 427-428.

Additional Exercises (also in MyEconLab Test A)

1. The Federal Reserve Act says that "The Board of Governors of the Federal Reserve System and the Federal Open Market Committee shall maintain long-run growth of the monetary and credit aggregates commensurate with the economy's long-run potential to increase production, so as to promote effectively the goals of maximum employment, stable prices, and moderate long-term interest rates." In this statement, the Fed's goals are specified as "maximum employment, stable prices, and moderate long-term interest rates." In order to reach these goals, the act specifies that the Fed should focus upon the "long-run growth of the monetary and credit aggregates"; page 422.

2. The core inflation is defined as excluding the effects from changes in the prices of food and fuel. So the core inflation rate does not exclude the effect of higher housing costs; page 423.

3. The Fed will have a higher federal funds rate target in situation *A*. A higher federal funds rate target aims to reduce aggregate demand and thereby lower the price level and inflation. In situation *A* the inflation rate is higher than in situation *B*, so the Fed efforts to lower the inflation rate will be more strenuous in situation *A*; page 426.

4. If the Fed wants the federal funds rate to equal its target of 5 percent a year, banks must posses $20 billion of reserves. Because banks presently have $40 billion of reserves, the Fed must decrease banks' reserves by $20 billion. In order to decrease reserves, the Fed sells securities in the open market. So to decrease reserves by $20 billion, the Fed must sell $20 billion of securities; page 427.

■ CHECKPOINT 17.2

Fill in the blanks

When the Fed lowers the federal funds rate, other short-term interest rates <u>fall</u> and the exchange rate <u>falls</u>. When the Fed lowers the federal funds rate, the quantity of money <u>increases</u> and the supply of loanable funds <u>increases</u>. When the Fed lowers the federal funds rate, the long-term real interest rate <u>falls</u> so that consumption expenditure and investment <u>increase</u>. When the Fed lowers the federal funds rate, it aims to <u>increase</u> aggregate <u>demand</u>. To fight a recession, the Fed will <u>lower</u> the federal funds rate and to fight inflation the Fed will <u>raise</u> the federal funds rate. The linkage between changes in the federal funds rate and changes in real GDP and inflation is <u>long and variable</u>.

True or false
1. True; page 430
2. True; pages 430-431
3. False; page 432
4. False; page 431
5. True; pages 436-437
6. False; page 438

Multiple choice
1. d; page 431
2. e; page 431
3. a; pages 432-433
4. e; pages 432-433
5. d; page 432
6. a; pages 432-433
7. e; pages 434-435
8. a; pages 436-437

Complete the graph
1. a. The equilibrium real GDP is $14 trillion and the equilibrium price level is 110. To move the economy back to potential GDP, $13 trillion, the Fed should raise the federal fund rate. By raising the federal funds rate, the Fed decreases aggregate demand, which decreases real GDP (and lowers the inflation rate); pages 436-437.

■ **FIGURE 17.9**

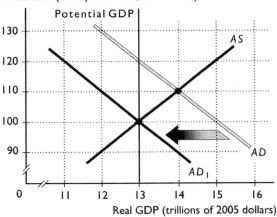

Price level (GDP price index, 2005 = 100)

■ **FIGURE 17.10**

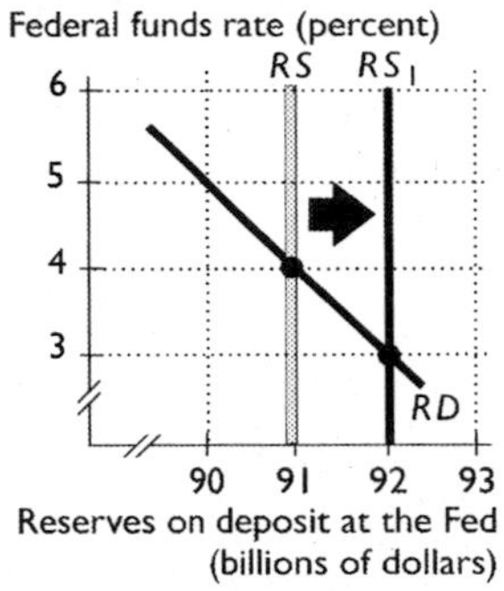

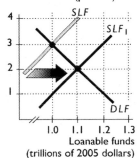

Federal funds rate (percent)

Reserves on deposit at the Fed
(billions of dollars)

■ **FIGURE 17.11**

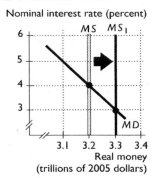

Nominal interest rate (percent)

Real money
(trillions of 2005 dollars)

b. Figure 17.9 shows the effect of the Fed's policy. The increase in the federal funds rate and the multiplier effect shift the *AD* leftward to *AD*1 and real GDP falls back to potential GDP, $13 trillion; pages 436-437.

2. Figures 17.10 through 17.13 show the effects from the Fed's open market operation that increases the supply of reserves by $1 billion. In Figure 17.10 this policy shifts the supply of reserves curve rightward and the federal funds rate falls from 4 percent to 3 percent. This policy also increases the supply of money, so in Figure 17.11, the quantity of money increases and the interest rate falls. The policy increases the supply of loanable funds. Figure 17.12 shows that the supply of loanable funds curve shifts rightward to *SLF*1 so that the real interest rate falls to 2 percent. Finally, the fall in the real interest rate increases consumption expenditure and investment, so these increases, combined with the multiplier effect, increases aggregate demand. In Figure 17.13 the aggregate demand curve shifts rightward to *AD*1. Real GDP increases and the price level rises; pages 434-435.

Short answer and numeric questions

1. The Fed's monetary policy affects aggregate demand. The Fed controls the federal funds rate. Through this control the Fed can influence the exchange rate and the long-term real

■ **FIGURE 17.12**

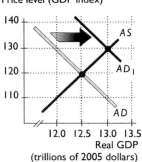

Real interest rate (percent)

Loanable funds
(trillions of 2005 dollars)

■ **FIGURE 17.13**

Price level (GDP index)

Real GDP
(trillions of 2005 dollars)

interest rate, which in turn affect net exports, consumption expenditure, and investment. Changes in all three of these variables change aggregate demand, so the Fed's policy allows it to influence aggregate demand. The Fed has no such influence over aggregate supply; page 430.

2. If the U.S. interest rate rises relative to the interest rate in other countries, some people will want to move funds into the United States from other countries to take advantage of the higher interest rate they can now earn on U.S. bank deposits and bonds. To move money into the United States, people must buy dollars and sell other currencies. With more dollars demanded, the U.S. exchange rate rises; page 432.

3. When the Fed is concerned that the economy is entering a recession, it makes an open market purchase of government securities in order to lower the federal funds rate and increases reserves. The quantity of money and

the supply of loanable funds increase. The long-term real interest rate falls so that consumption expenditure and investment increase. The exchange rate falls so that net exports also increases. With the increase in consumption expenditure, investment, and net exports, the multiplier effect increases aggregate demand by even more. The increase in aggregate demand raises the growth rate of real GDP and also raises the inflation rate; pages 434-435.

4. If it takes two years for monetary policy to have an effect and recessions last for only one year, for the Fed to help offset a recession, the Fed must be able to predict recessions a year in advance. If it cannot, then the long and variable lags make it possible for monetary policy to boost inflation rather than fight recession; page 438.

Additional Exercises (also in MyEconLab Test A)

1. When the Fed lowers the federal funds rate, the Fed increases banks' reserves. Other short-term interest rates fall and the exchange rate falls. Because the Fed increases banks' reserves, the quantity of money and supply of loanable funds increase so that the long-term real interest rate falls. Consumption expenditure and investment increase because of the lower real interest rate. The U.S. exchange rate falls so that net exports increase. With the increase in consumption expenditure, investment, and net exports, aggregate demand increases, and eventually the real GDP growth rate and the inflation rate increase; page 433.

2. Because the Fed is worried about an inflationary gap, the Fed will raise the federal funds rate and decrease banks' reserves. Decreasing banks' reserves decreases the quantity of money so, as illustrated in Figure 17.14, the supply of money decreases, in the figure from $3.1 trillion to $2.9 trillion, and the interest rate rises, in the figure from 3 percent to 4 percent.

In the market for loanable funds, the higher federal funds rate and lower quantity of re-

■ **FIGURE 17.14**

Federal funds rate (percent per year)

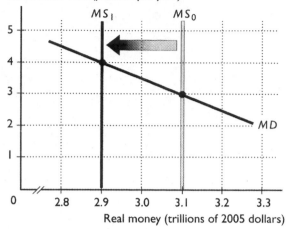

■ **FIGURE 17.15**

Real interest rate (percent per year)

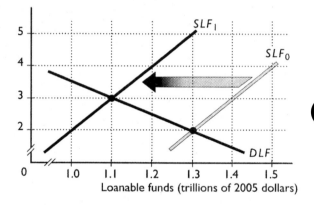

serves decrease the supply of banks' loans, which decreases the supply of loanable funds. As Figure 17.15 then shows, the supply of loanable funds curve shifts leftward. The real interest rate rises, from 2 percent to 3 percent in the figure, and the quantity of loanable funds decreases, from $1.3 trillion to $1.1 trillion in the figure; page 436.

3. The higher real interest rate decreases consumption expenditure and investment. It also leads to a higher U.S. exchange rate, which decreases net exports. On all counts, aggregate demand decreases. The multiplier effect decreases aggregate demand by more so

■ **FIGURE 17.16**

Price level (GDP price index, 2005 = 100)

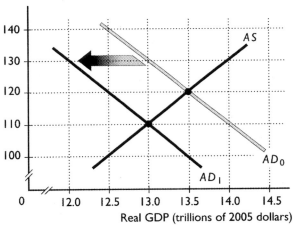

Real GDP (trillions of 2005 dollars)

that the *AD* curve shifts leftward, as illustrated in Figure 17.16. In the short run, aggregate supply does not change. Real GDP decreases, in the figure from $13.5 trillion to $13.0 trillion, and the price level falls, in the figure from 120 to 110. In addition to the fall in the price level, the inflation rate also falls; pages 436-437.

■ **CHECKPOINT 17.3**

Fill in the blanks

Monetary policy that assesses the current situation and then bases the policy on that assessment is <u>discretionary monetary policy</u>. If a central bank uses an inflation targeting rule, the central bank <u>must</u> make its inflation rate target public. A strength of inflation targeting is that it <u>helps manage people's inflation expectations</u>.

True or false

  1. False; page 440
  2. True; page 440
  3. False; page 441
  4. False; page 443

Multiple choice

  1. c; page 440
  2. d; pages 440-441
  3. c; page 443
  4. b; page 443

Short answer and numeric questions

  1. Inflation targeting is a monetary policy framework in which the central bank announces a target range for the inflation rate and publicizes its economic forecasts and analysis. The central bank commits to keeping the inflation rate within its target zone. The target is announced because the announcement gives the people and businesses an anchor for their inflation expectations and thereby helps the central bank manage these expectations; pages 440-441.

  2. For a *k*-percent rule to work well, the demand for money needs to be stable and predictable. If the demand for money is not stable, then the interest rate will fluctuate whenever the demand changes. In turn, the changes in the interest rate would lead to fluctuations in aggregate demand. The Fed believes that the demand for money is not stable. As a result, the Fed does not use this policy strategy because the Fed believes this policy would introduce undesirable fluctuations in the interest rate. And, ultimately, the policy would result in unnecessary fluctuations in real GDP growth and the inflation rate; page 443.

Additional Exercises (also in MyEconLab Test A)

  1. Rules are superior to discretion because people make long-term plans. These plans, such as employment contracts and long-term loans depend on people's view of inflation. Rules help make future inflation more predictable, and so enable people to make better plans for the future. When people's expectations are more accurate, the economic outcomes are more desirable; page 440.

  2. The Bank of England targets inflation, so it makes its inflation target public, commits to hitting the target, and explains how its policy actions will allow it to met its target. The Federal Reserve, however, does not make public its inflation target, does not commit to meeting its target, and does not explain how its actions will enable it to hit its (unannounced) target; pages 440-441.

Chapter

International Trade Policy

18

CHAPTER CHECKLIST

Chapter 18 shows that all countries can benefit from free trade but countries nevertheless restrict trade.

1 Explain how markets work with international trade and identify the gains from international trade and its winners and losers.

Imports are the goods and services that firms in one country buy from households and firms in other countries; exports are the goods and services that firms in one country sell to households and firms in other countries. In 2009 total U.S. exports were $1.5 trillion, about 11 percent of the value of U.S. production, and total U.S. imports were $1.9 trillion, about 13 percent of the value of total expenditure in the United States. Comparative advantage enables countries to gain from trade. A nation has a comparative advantage in producing a good if it can produce that good at a lower opportunity cost than any other country. In this case the domestic no-trade price is lower than the world price. The United States imports goods and services for which the U.S. no-trade price is higher than the world price. U.S. consumers gain from U.S. imports while U.S. producers lose. The United States exports goods and services for which the U.S. no-trade price is lower than the world price. U.S. producers gain from U.S. exports while U.S. consumers lose. For both imports and exports, the gains to the gainers exceed the losses to the losers, so international trade provides a net gain for the United States.

2 Explain the effects of international trade barriers.

A tariff is a tax that is imposed on a good when it is imported. A tariff reduces imports, decreases domestic consumption of the good, increases domestic production of the good, yields revenue for the government, and reduces the society's gain from international trade. An import quota is a quantitative restriction on the import of a good that limits the maximum quantity of a good that may be imported in a given period. An import quota reduces imports, decreases domestic consumption of the good, increases domestic production of the good, and reduces the society's gain from international trade. Health, safety, and regulation barriers and voluntary export restraints are two other barriers to trade.

3 Explain and evaluate arguments used to justify restricting international trade.

Three traditional arguments for protection and restriction of international trade are the: national security argument; the infant-industry argument (the claim that it is necessary to protect a new industry to enable it to grow into a mature industry that can compete in world markets); and the dumping argument (when a foreign firm sells its exports at a lower price than its cost of production). Each of these arguments is flawed. Other new arguments for protection are that protection: saves jobs; allows us to compete with cheap foreign labor (but high-wage U.S. workers effectively compete in industries in which they are more productive than foreigners); brings diversity and stability; and, penalizes lax environmental standards. These arguments also are flawed. However international trade is restricted because of rent seeking—lobbying and other political activity that aims to capture the gains from trade.

CHECKPOINT 18.1

■ **Explain how markets work with international trade and identify the gains from international trade and its winners and losers.**

Quick Review

- *Imports* The goods and services that firms in one country buy from people and firms in other countries.
- *Exports* The goods and services that people and firms in one country sell to firms in other countries.
- *Comparative advantage* A nation has a comparative advantage in a good when its opportunity cost of producing the good is lower than any other nation's opportunity cost of producing the good.

Additional Practice Problem 18.1

1. The figure shows the market for CPU chips in the United States with no international trade. The world price for a CPU chip is $150.

    Price (dollars per CPU chip)

    200 ···········S
    150 ············
    100 ············
    50 ·············
                       D
      5 10 15 20 25
    Quantity (millions per year)

    a. Does the United States have a comparative advantage in producing CPU chips? How can you tell?
    b. If international trade is allowed, will the United States import or export CPU chips?
    c. Will the quantity of CPU chips produced in the United States increase or decrease? By how much?
    d. Will the quantity of CPU chips consumed in the United States increase or decrease? By how much?
    e. How many CPU chips will the United States import or export?

Solution to Additional Practice Problem 18.1

1a. Because the price of a CPU chip in the United States is lower than the world price, the

United States has a comparative advantage in producing CPU chips.

1b. Because the United States has a comparative advantage in producing CPU chips, the United States will export CPU chips.

1c. With international trade, the price of a CPU chip in the United States will be $150. At this price, the supply curve shows that the quantity of chips produced will equal 20 million per year. With no international trade, the equilibrium quantity of CPU chips produced is 15 million, so international trade leads to 5 million more chips being produced.

1d. With international trade, the price of a CPU chip in the United States will be $150. At this price, the demand curve shows that the quantity of chips demanded will equal 10 million per year. With no international trade, the equilibrium quantity of CPU chips consumed is 15 million, so international trade leads to 5 million fewer chips being consumed.

1e. The quantity of CPU chips exported equals the difference between the quantity of CPU chips produced, 20 million per year, and the quantity consumed, 10 million per year. So the United States will export 20 million CPU chips − 10 million CPU chips, which is 10 million CPU chips.

■ **Self Test 18.1**

Fill in the blanks

Global international trade accounts for about ____ (27; 52; 67) percent of global production. If a country can produce a good at a lower opportunity cost than any other country, the country has ____ (an export advantage; a comparative advantage) in the production of that good. The United States will export a good if its price in the United States with no international trade is ____ (lower; higher) than its world price. If the United States imports a good, then U.S. production of the good ____ (increases; decreases) and U.S. consumption of the good ____ (increases; decreases). Producers ____ (gain; lose) from imports and consumers (gain; lose) ____ from imports. On net, society ____ (gains; loses) from international trade.

True or false

1. The United States is the world's largest international trader.

2. If a nation can produce a service at lower opportunity cost than any other nation, the nation has a national comparative advantage in producing that service.

3. If the price of a good in the United States with no international trade is higher than the world price, then with international trade the United States will export that good.

4. U.S. production of goods exported from the United States increases and the U.S. production of goods imported into the United States decreases.

5. Everyone in a nation gains from exports.

Multiple choice

1. Goods and services that we buy from firms in other countries are called our
   a. imports.
   b. exports.
   c. inputs.
   d. raw materials.
   e. obligations.

2. If the United States exports planes to Brazil and imports ethanol from Brazil, the price received by U.S. producers of planes ____ and the price received by Brazilian producers of ethanol ____.
   a. does not change; does not change
   b. rises; rises
   c. rises; falls
   d. falls; rises
   e. falls; falls

3. When Italy buys Boeing jets, the price Italy pays is ____ if it produced their own jets and the price Boeing receives is ____ than it could receive from an additional U.S. buyer.
   a. lower than; lower
   b. higher than; higher
   c. lower than; higher
   d. higher than; lower
   e. the same as; higher

4. A nation will import a good if its no-trade, domestic
   a. price is equal to the world price.
   b. price is less than the world price.
   c. price is greater than the world price.
   d. quantity is less than the world quantity.
   e. quantity is greater than the world quantity.

5. When a good is imported, the domestic production of it ____ and the domestic consumption of it ____.
   a. increases; increases
   b. increases; decreases
   c. decreases; increases
   d. decreases; decreases
   e. increases; does not change

6. The United States exports a good if its no-trade U.S. price is ____ its world price. With international trade, U.S. production of the good ____ compared to the level of no-trade production.
   a. higher than; does not change
   b. higher than; increases
   c. lower than; increases
   d. the same as; increases
   e. the same as; does not change

7. When a country imports a good, the ____ to consumers is ____ the ____ to producers.
   a. loss; larger than; gain
   b. loss; smaller than; gain
   c. gain; smaller than; loss
   d. gain; equal to; loss
   e. gain; larger than; loss

Complete the graph

■ **FIGURE 18.1**

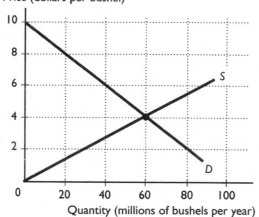

1. Figure 18.1 shows the U.S. demand and supply curves for wheat.
   a. In the absence of international trade, what is the price of a bushel of wheat in the United States?
   b. If the world price of a bushel of wheat is $6 a bushel, will the United States import or export wheat? Above what world price for wheat will the United States export wheat? Below what world price for wheat will the United States import wheat?

Short answer and numeric questions

1. French cheese is sold in the United States. Classify this transaction from the vantage point of the United States and from the vantage point of France.

Price (dollars per ton)	Quantity supplied (tons per year)	Quantity demanded (tons per year)
400	38	58
500	42	52
600	46	46
700	50	40
800	54	34
900	58	28

2. The table above has the U.S. demand and supply schedules for potatoes.
   a. If there is no international trade, what is the equilibrium price and quantity of potatoes?
   b. If the world price of potatoes is $800 a ton,

what is the quantity supplied and the quantity demanded in the United States? Does the United States import or export potatoes? What quantity?
   c. If the world price of potatoes rises to $900 a ton, what is the U.S. quantity supplied and the U.S. quantity demanded? Does the United States import or export potatoes? What quantity?
   d. Would the United States ever import potatoes?

3. How does international trade affect the domestic production and domestic consumption of goods imported into the country?
4. Why do consumers gain from imports?
5. Why doesn't everyone in a nation gain from exporting a good?

Additional Exercises (also in MyEconLab Test A)

1. Suppose that the world price of bananas is 18 U.S. cents a pound and that when Australia does not trade bananas internationally, their equilibrium price in Australia is 12 U.S. cents a pound. If Australia opens up to international trade, does it export or import bananas? Explain how the price of bananas in Australia changes. How does the quantity of bananas consumed in Australia change? How does the quantity of bananas grown in Australia change?

2. Both the United States and Canada produce lumber and wine. Canada exports lumber and imports wine. The United States imports lumber and exports wine. If the United States and Canada did not trade internationally, compare the equilibrium prices of lumber and wine in the two countries with the world prices of lumber and wine. Compare the quantities of lumber that Americans buy with and without international trade, and compare the quantities of wine that Canadians buy with and without international trade. Also compare the quantities of lumber that Americans produce with and without international trade, and compare the quantities of wine that Canadians produce with and without international trade.

CHECKPOINT 18.2

■ Explain the effects of international trade barriers.

Quick Review

- *Tariff* A tariff is a tax imposed on a good when it is imported.
- *Import Quota* An import quota is a quantitative restriction on the import of a good that limits the maximum quantity of a good that may be imported in a given period.

Additional Practice Problems 18.2

Price (dollars per ton of plywood)	U.S. quantity supplied (tons per month)	U.S. quantity demanded (tons per month)
1,000	600	1,400
750	500	1,600
500	300	1,800
250	100	2,000

1. The table above shows the U.S. supply and demand schedules for plywood. The United States also can buy plywood from Canada at the world price of $500 per ton.

   a. If there are no tariffs or nontariff barriers, what is the price of a ton of plywood in the United States? How much plywood is produced in the United States and how much is consumed? How much plywood is imported from Canada?

   b. Suppose that the United States imposes a $250 per ton tariff on all plywood imported into the country. What now is the price of a ton of plywood in the United States? How much plywood is produced in the United States and how much is consumed? How much plywood is imported from Canada?

   c. Who has gained from the tariff and who has lost?

2. For many years Japan conducted extremely slow, detailed, and costly safety inspections of *all* U.S. cars imported into Japan. In terms of trade, what was the effect of this inspection? How did the inspection affect the price and quantity of cars in Japan?

Solutions to Additional Practice Problems 18.2

1a. With no tariffs or nontariff barriers, the price of a ton of plywood is equal to the world price, $500 per ton. At this price, 300 tons per month are produced in the United States and 1,800 tons per month are consumed. The difference between the quantity consumed and the quantity produced, which is 1,500 tons per month, is imported from Canada.

1b. If a $250 per ton tariff is imposed, the price in the United States rises to $750 per ton. At this price, 500 tons per month are produced in the United States and 1,600 tons per month are consumed. The difference between the quantity consumed and the quantity produced, which is 1,100 tons per month, is imported from Canada.

1c. Gainers from the tariff are U.S. producers of plywood, who have a higher price for plywood and therefore increase their production, and the U.S. government, which gains tariff revenue. Losers are U.S. consumers, who consume less plywood with the tariff, and Canadian producers of plywood, who wind up exporting less plywood to the United States.

2. Japan's safety inspection (which has since been eliminated) was an example of a nontariff barrier to trade. It served a role similar to tariffs and import quotas. The safety inspection added to the cost of selling cars in Japan. It raised the price of U.S. produced cars in Japan and decreased the quantity of U.S. cars sold.

■ Self Test 18.2

Fill in the blanks

A tax on a good that is imposed when the good is imported is ____ (an import quota; a tariff) and a specified maximum amount of a good that may be imported in a given period of time is ____ (an import quota; a tariff). A tariff ____ (raises; lowers) the price paid by domestic consumers and ____ (increases; decreases) the quantity produced by domestic producers. An import quota ____ (raises; lowers) the price paid by domestic consumers and ____ (increases; decreases) the quantity produced by domestic producers.

True or false

1. If the United States imposes a tariff, the price paid by U.S. consumers does not change.

2. If a country imposes a tariff on rice imports, domestic production of rice will increase and domestic consumption of rice will decrease.

3. A tariff increases the gains from trade for the exporting country.

4. An import quota specifies the minimum quantity of the good that can be imported in a given period.

Multiple choice

1. A tax on a good that is imposed when it is imported is called
   a. an import tax quota.
   b. a nontariff barrier.
   c. a tariff.
   d. a sanction.
   e. a border tax.

2. The average U.S. tariff was highest in the
   a. 1930s.
   b. 1940s.
   c. 1970s.
   d. 1980s.
   e. 1990s.

3. Suppose the world price of a shirt is $10. If the United States imposes a tariff of $5 a shirt, then the price of a shirt in the
   a. United States falls to $5.
   b. United States rises to $15.
   c. world falls to $5.
   d. world rises to $5.
   e. world rises to $15.

4. When a tariff is imposed on a good, the _____ increases.
   a. domestic quantity purchased
   b. domestic quantity produced
   c. quantity imported
   d. quantity exported
   e. world price

5. When a tariff is imposed on a good, domestic consumers of the good _____ and domestic producers of the good _____.
   a. win; lose
   b. lose; win
   c. win; win
   d. lose; lose
   e. lose; neither win nor lose

6. When an import quota is imposed on a good, domestic consumers of the good _____ and domestic producers of the good _____.
   a. win; lose
   b. lose; win
   c. win; win
   d. lose; lose
   e. lose; neither win nor lose

Complete the graph

■ **FIGURE 18.2**

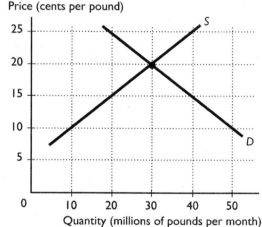

1. Figure 18.2 shows the supply of and demand for sugar in the United States.

   a. If the world price of sugar is 10¢ a pound, draw the world price line in the figure. What is the quantity consumed in the United States, the quantity produced in the United States, and the quantity imported?

   b. Suppose the government imposes a 5¢ a pound tariff on sugar. Show the effect of the tariff in Figure 18.2. After the tariff, what is the quantity consumed in the

United States, the quantity produced in the United States, and the quantity imported?

Short answer and numeric questions

Price (dollars per ton of steel)	U.S. quantity supplied (tons per month)	U.S. quantity demanded (tons per month)
1,000	20,000	20,000
750	17,000	22,000
500	14,000	24,000
250	11,000	26,000

1. The table above gives the U.S. supply and the U.S. demand schedules for steel. Suppose the world price of steel is $500 per ton.

   a. If there are no tariffs or nontariff barriers, what is the price of steel in the United States, the quantity of steel consumed in the United States, the quantity produced in the United States, and the quantity imported into the United States?

   b. If the U.S. government imposes a tariff of $250 per ton of steel, what is the price of steel in the United States, the quantity of steel consumed in the United States, the quantity produced in the United States, and the quantity imported into the United States?

   c. Instead of a tariff, if the U.S. government imposes an import quota of 5,000 tons of steel per month, what is the price of steel in the United States, the quantity of steel consumed in the United States, the quantity produced in the United States, and the quantity imported into the United States?

   d. Comparing your answers to parts (b) and (c), are U.S. consumers better off with the tariff or the import quota? Are U.S. producers better off with the tariff or the import quota? Is the U.S. government better off with the tariff or the import quota?

2. Suppose the U.S. government imposes a tariff on sugar. How does the tariff affect the price of sugar? How does it affect U.S. sugar consumers? U.S. sugar producers?

3. Suppose the U.S. government imposes an import quota on sugar. How does the import quota affect the price of sugar? How does it

affect U.S. sugar consumers? U.S. sugar producers?

4. Why do consumers lose from a tariff?

Additional Exercises (also in MyEconLab Test A)

Suppose that in response to huge job losses in the U.S. textile industry, Congress imposes a 100 percent tariff on imports of textiles from China. Use this formation to answer exercises 1 and 2.

1. Explain how the tariff on textiles will change the price of textiles, the quantity of textiles imported, and the quantity of textiles produced in the United States.

2. Explain how the U.S. and Chinese gains from trade will change. Who in the United States will lose and who will gain?

3. With free international trade between Australia and the United States, Australia would export beef to the United States. But the United States imposes an import quota on Australia beef. Explain how this import quota influences the price that U.S. consumers pay for beef, the quantity of beef produced in the United States, and the U.S. and Australian gains from trade. Who in the United States gains from the import quota on beef imports and who loses?

CHECKPOINT 18.3

■ **Explain and evaluate arguments used to justify restricting international trade.**

Quick Review

- *Rent seeking* Lobbying and other political activity that seeks to capture the gains from trade.

Additional Practice Problems 18.3

1. Pork is a popular food in China. China has occasionally limited U.S. exports of pork to China, most recently when swine flu was in the news. What argument might China make to limit imports of pork? Who in China would lose from this restriction of trade? Who would gain?

2. The United States has, from time to time, limited imports of lumber from Canada. What is the argument that the United States has used to justify this import quota? Who wins from this restriction? Who loses?

3. In each of the first two Practice Problems, identify who is rent seeking.

Solutions to Additional Practice Problems 18.3

1. The primary argument China has made involves the health of Chinese consumers. In particular, China argues that it must prohibit pork imports from the United States because Chinese consumers might catch swine flu from it. This argument is scientifically flawed because swine flu is not transmitted through pork products. The losers from the Chinese limitations are Chinese consumers who must pay a higher price for the pork they buy. The gainers are the Chinese pork farmers and processors who enjoy a higher price for pork.

2. In past decades, the United States asserted that the lumber industry was needed because it played a major role in national defense. With the use of more exotic materials in defense armaments, the national defense argument has passed into history. More recently, the United States has set import quotas and tariffs allegedly for environmental reasons and allegedly because the Canadian government was subsidizing the production of lumber. Both of these arguments are likely not the true reason for the quotas. The import quotas and limitations are the result of political lobbying by lumber producers and lumber workers. The winners from the import quotas and tariffs are the lumber producers and lumber workers. The losers are all U.S. lumber consumers.

3. Rent seeking is lobbying and other political activity that seeks to capture the gains from trade. In Practice Problem 1, the Chinese producers of pork are rent seeking. In Practice Problem 2, the U.S. lumber producers and U.S. lumber workers are rent seeking. It is important to keep in mind that free trade promotes prosperity for all countries. Protection reduces the potential gains from trade

■ Self Test 18.3

Fill in the blanks

The assertion that it is necessary to protect a new industry to enable it to grow into a mature industry that can compete in world markets is the ____ (infant-industry; maturing-industry) argument. Dumping occurs when ____ (U.S. jobs are lost to cheap foreign labor; a foreign firm sells its exports at a lower price than its cost of production). Protection ____ (is; is not) necessary to bring diversity and stability to our economy. Protection ____ (is; is not) necessary to penalize countries with lax environmental standards. The major reason why international trade is restricted is because ____ (foreign countries protect their industries; of rent seeking).

True or false

1. The national security argument is the only valid argument for protection.

2. Dumping by a foreign producer is easy to detect.

3. Protection saves U.S. jobs at no cost.

Multiple choice

1. The national security argument is used by those who assert they want to
   a. increase imports as a way of strengthening their country.
   b. increase exports as a way of earning money to strengthen their country.
   c. limit imports that compete with domestic producers important for national defense.
   d. limit exports to control the flow of technology to third world nations.
   e. limit all imports.

2. The argument that it is necessary to protect a new industry to enable it to grow into a mature industry that can compete in world markets is the
   a. national security argument.
   b. diversity argument.
   c. infant-industry argument.
   d. environmental protection argument.
   e. national youth protection argument.

3. ____ occurs when a foreign firm sells its exports at a lower price than its cost of production.
   a. Dumping
   b. The trickle-down effect
   c. Rent seeking
   d. Tariff avoidance
   e. Nontariff barrier protection

4. The United States
   a. needs tariffs to allow us to compete with cheap foreign labor.
   b. does not need tariffs to allow us to compete with cheap foreign labor.
   c. should not trade with countries that have cheap labor.
   d. will not benefit from trade with countries that have cheap labor.
   e. avoids trading with countries that have cheap labor.

5. What is a major reason international trade is restricted?
   a. rent seeking
   b. to allow competition with cheap foreign labor
   c. to save jobs
   d. to prevent dumping
   e. for national security

Short answer and numeric questions

1. What is the dumping argument for protection? What is its flaw?

2. How do you respond to a speaker who says that we need to limit auto imports from Japan in order to save U.S. jobs?

3. Why is it incorrect to assert that trade with countries that have lax environmental standards needs to be restricted?

4. The Eye on Your Life discusses the role international trade plays in your life. Suppose you get a job working for Frito Lay, the maker of corn chips (and other snacks). Frito Lay is a big user of corn. Corn can also be used to produce ethanol and increasingly more ethanol is being used as a replacement (or additive) fuel for gasoline. Currently the U.S. government places a hefty tariff on ethanol imported from Brazil. As a representative of Frito Lay, would you be in favor of this tariff? Explain your answer.

Additional Exercises (also in MyEconLab Test A)

1. Venezuelan president Hugo Chavez opposes the creation of a Free Trade Area of the Americas (FTAA). Why? Who does he think will gain and lose? Do you think he is correct?

2. At the Summit of the Americas in November 2005, President George W. Bush made no progress in his bid to create the FTAA. What are the main obstacles to establishing the FTAA?

3. Hong Kong has never restricted trade. What gains has Hong Kong reaped by unilaterally adopting free trade with all nations? Is there any argument for restricted trade that might have benefited Hong Kong?

SELF TEST ANSWERS

■ CHECKPOINT 18.1

Fill in the blanks

Global international trade accounts for about <u>27</u> percent of global production. If a country can produce a good at a lower opportunity cost than any other country, the country has <u>a comparative advantage</u> in the production of that good. The United States will export a good if its price in the United States with no international trade is <u>lower</u> than its world price. If the United States imports a good, then U.S. production of the good <u>decreases</u> and U.S. consumption of the good <u>increases</u>. Producers <u>lose</u> from imports and consumers <u>gain</u> from imports. On net, society <u>gains</u> from international trade.

True or false

1. True; page 450
2. True; page 450
3. False; pages 452-453
4. True; pages 452-453
5. False; pages 454-455

Multiple choice

1. a; page 450
2. b; pages 452-453
3. c; page 453
4. c; page 452
5. c; page 452
6. c; page 453
7. e; pages 454-455

Complete the graph

1. a. In the absence of international trade, the equilibrium price of a bushel of wheat in the United States is $4; pages 451-453.
   b. If the world price of a bushel of wheat is $6 a bushel, the United States will export wheat because the world price exceeds the no-trade price. If the price of wheat exceeds $4 a bushel, the United States will export wheat. If the price of wheat is less than $4 a bushel, the United States will import wheat; pages 451-453.

Short answer and numeric questions

1. From the U.S. vantage, the cheese is an imported good. From the French vantage, the cheese is an exported good; page 450.
2. a. In the absence of international trade, the equilibrium price is $600 a ton and the equilibrium quantity is 46 tons; page 453.
   b. In the United States, the quantity supplied is 54 tons and the quantity demanded is 34 tons. The United States exports 20 tons of potatoes; page 453.
   c. In the United States, the quantity supplied is 58 tons and the quantity demanded is 28 tons. The United States exports 30 tons of potatoes; page 453.
   d. The United States would import potatoes if the world price is less than $600 a ton; page 452.
3. International trade lowers the domestic price of imported goods. The lower price increases the quantity domestic demanders consume and decreases the quantity domestic suppliers produce; page 452.
4. Consumers gain from imports because international trade lowers the prices of imported goods and services. Consumers gain because the price is lower and because the lower price leads consumers to buy more of the good or service; page 454.
5. When a good is exported, its domestic price rises. Producers gain from the higher price but consumers lose. (The gain to the producers, however, is larger than the loss to consumers.) So not everyone gains when a good is exported because consumers of that good lose; pages 454-455.

Additional Exercises (also in MyEconLab Test A)

1. With no international trade, the price in Australia is less than that in the world, so Australia has a comparative advantage in producing bananas. As a result, if Australia opens up to international trade, it will export bananas. With international trade, the price of bananas in Australia rises. The higher

price leads to a decrease in the quantity of bananas consumed in Australia. The higher price also leads to an increase in the quantity of bananas grown in Australia; page 453.

2. Canada exports wood, so Canada has a comparative advantage in producing wood. If Canada did not trade internationally, the price of wood in Canada would be less than the world price. Canada imports wine, so Canada does *not* have a comparative advantage in producing wine. If Canada did not trade internationally, the price of wine in Canada would be higher than the world price. The United States exports wine, so the United States has a comparative advantage in producing wine. If the United States did not trade internationally, the price of wine in the United States would be less than the world price. The United States imports wood, so the United States does *not* have a comparative advantage in producing wood. If the United States did not trade internationally, the price of wood in the United States would be higher than the world price.

With international trade, Americans buy more wood because the price of wood is lower in the United States with international trade than it would be without international trade. With international trade, Canadians buy more wine because the price of wine is lower in Canada with international trade than it would be without international trade.

With international trade, the quantity of wood produced in the United States is less than it would be without international trade because international trade lowers the price of wood in the United States. With international trade, the quantity of wine produced in Canada is less than it would be without international trade because international trade lowers the price of wine in Canada; pages 452-453.

■ CHECKPOINT 18.2

Fill in the blanks

A tax on a good that is imposed when the good is imported is <u>a tariff</u> and a specified maximum amount of a good that may be imported in a given time period is <u>an import quota</u>. A tariff <u>raises</u> the price paid by domestic consumers and <u>increases</u> the quantity produced by domestic producers. An import quota <u>raises</u> the price paid by domestic consumers and <u>increases</u> the quantity produced by domestic producers.

True or false

1. False; pages 458-459
2. True; pages 458-459
3. False; page 459
4. False; page 460

Multiple choice

1. c; page 457
2. a; page 457
3. b; page 458
4. b; pages 458-459
5. b; page 459
6. b; page 461

Complete the graph

■ **FIGURE 18.3**

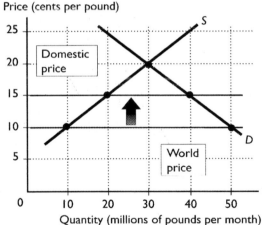

1. a. The world price line is shown in Figure 18.3. 50 million pounds of sugar are consumed in the United States, 10 million pounds are produced in the United States, and 40 million pounds are imported into the United States; page 458.

   b. The tariff increases the domestic price, as shown in the figure. The quantity consumed in the United States decreases to 40 million pounds, the quantity produced in the United States increases to 20 million pounds, and the amount imported decreases to 20 million pounds; page 458.

Short answer and numeric questions

1. a. The price is the world price, $500 per ton. At this price, the quantity consumed in the United States is 24,000 tons per month, the quantity produced in the United States is 14,000 tons per month, and the quantity imported is the difference, 10,000 tons per month; page 458.

   b. With a $250 per ton tariff, the price is $750 per ton. At this price, the quantity consumed in the United States is 22,000 tons per month, the quantity produced in the United States is 17,000 tons per month, and the quantity imported is the difference, 5,000 tons per month; page 458.

   c. With an import quota of 5,000 tons per month, the total supply schedule equals the U.S. supply schedule plus 5,000 tons per month. The price of steel is $750 per ton because this is the price that sets the U.S. quantity demanded (22,000 tons) equal to the U.S. quantity supplied (17,000 tons) plus the quantity that can be imported (5,000 tons). At this price, the quantity consumed in the United States is 22,000 tons per month and the quantity produced in the United States is 17,000 tons per month; page 460.

   d. U.S. consumers are no better off or worse off with the tariff or the import quota because both raise the price to $750 per ton and decrease the quantity consumed to 22,000 tons. Similarly U.S. producers are no better off or worse off because both raise the price to $750 per ton and increase the quantity produced to 17,000 tons. The U.S. government is better off with the tariff because it receives revenue with the tariff; pages 459, 461.

2. The tariff raises the price of sugar. U.S. sugar consumers decrease the quantity they purchase and U.S. sugar producers increase the quantity they produce; pages 458-459.

3. The import quota has the same effects as the tariff in the previous question. The import quota raises the price of sugar. U.S. sugar consumers decrease the quantity purchased and U.S. sugar producers increase the quantity produced; pages 460-461.

4. Consumers lose from a tariff because the tariff raises the price they pay and the quantity bought decreases. The tariff makes people pay more than the opportunity cost of the good; page 459.

Additional Exercises (also in MyEconLab Test A)

1. Higher tariffs increase the price U.S. consumers pay for textiles imported from China. Because the price of Chinese imported textiles rises, the quantity imported decreases. The quantity of textiles produced in the United States increases; pages 458-459.

2. This trade restriction means that the U.S. and Chinese gains from trade definitely decrease. Textile workers and owners of textile firms will gain from the higher price. Textile consumers will lose from the higher price; page 459.

3. By restricting the amount of beef imported into the United States, the import quota raises the price of beef to U.S. consumers. The quantity of beef produced in the United States increases. The U.S. and Australian gains from trade are reduced by the U.S. import quota. U.S. beef producers and their workers gain from the import quota on beef. In addition, the importers who have the right to import beef gain. U.S. consumers lose from the higher price of beef; pages 460-461.

■ CHECKPOINT 18.3

Fill in the blanks

The assertion that it is necessary to protect a new industry to enable it to grow into a mature industry that can compete in world markets is the <u>infant-industry</u> argument. Dumping occurs when <u>a foreign firm sells its exports at a lower price than its cost of production</u>. Protection <u>is</u>

<u>not</u> necessary to bring diversity and stability to our economy. Protection <u>is not</u> necessary to penalize countries with lax environmental standards. The major reason why international trade is restricted is because <u>of rent seeking</u>.

True or false
1. False; page 463
2. False; page 464
3. False; page 466

Multiple choice
1. c; page 463
2. c; page 463
3. a; page 464
4. b; pages 465-466
5. a; pages 466-465

Short answer and numeric questions
1. Dumping occurs when a foreign firm sells its exports at a lower price than its cost of production. The dumping argument is flawed for the following reasons. First, it is virtually impossible to detect dumping because it is hard to determine a firm's costs and the fair market price. Second, it is hard to think of a good that is produced by a global monopoly. Third, if a firm truly was a global monopoly, the best way to deal with it would be by regulation; page 464.

2. Saving jobs is one of the oldest arguments in favor of protection. It is also incorrect. Protecting a particular industry will likely save jobs in that industry but will cost many other jobs in other industries. The cost to consumers of saving a job is many times the wage rate of the job saved; page 465.

3. The assertion that trade with developing countries that have lax environmental standards should be restricted to "punish" the nation for its lower standards is weak. Everyone wants a clean environment, but not every country can afford to devote resources toward this goal. The rich nations can afford this expenditure of resources, but for many poor nations protecting the environment takes second place to more pressing prob-

lems such as feeding their people. These nations must develop and grow economically in order to be able to afford to protect their environment. One important way to help these nations grow is by trading with them. Through trade these nations' incomes will increase and with this increase will also increase their ability and willingness to protect the environment; page 466.

4. The tariff on ethanol imported from Brazil severely limits the quantity of ethanol that can be imported and, by so doing, keeps the price of ethanol high in the United States. The high price for ethanol increases the demand for U.S. corn to be processed into ethanol. The higher demand for corn means that the tariff on ethanol keeps the price of corn in the United States higher than it would be in the absence of the tariff. As a representative of Frito Lay, your interest lies in lowering the price of corn. So you would be in favor of lowering or eliminating entirely this tariff.

Additional Exercises (also in MyEconLab Test A)
1. Mr. Chavez argues against the Free Trade Area of the Americas because he thinks that poor workers in nations such as Venezuela and other countries will be harmed by the trade. He also worries that U.S. firms will come to dominate markets in other countries. He is likely incorrect on both counts. First, poor workers in Venezuela will benefit from increased trade with the United States because the trade will increase the demand for their labor and thereby lead to higher wage rates. Second, it is unlikely U.S. firms will be able to dominate markets in other countries because to do so U.S. firms would need some sort of cost advantage over their foreign rivals, which is unlikely; pages 464-466.

2. Former-president Bush faced opposition from opponents who believe they will be harmed by a Free Trade Area of the Americas (FTAA). The losers under such an arrangement would be the inefficient industries (and, in the short term, the workers

within these industries) in each member country, that is those industries without a comparative advantage. These potential losers lobby and protest intensively in opposition to the FTAA. In addition, there is political opposition from leaders such as Hugo Chavez who worry that U.S. businesses would dominate markets in many of the countries and that this domination would increase U.S. influence; pages 466-467.

3. Hong Kong has one of the most successful economies in the world as a result of adopting unilateral free trade. Both its exports and imports increased a result. There really isn't any argument for restricted free trade that might have benefited Hong Kong; page 467.

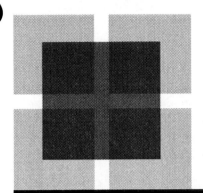

Chapter

International Finance

19

Chapter 19 studies how nations keep their international accounts, what determines the balance of payments, and how the value of the dollar is determined in the foreign exchange market.

1 **Describe a country's balance of payments accounts and explain what determines the amount of international borrowing and lending.**

There are three balance of payments accounts: the current account, the capital account, and the official settlements account. The current account balance equals exports minus imports, plus net interest and transfers received from abroad. The capital account is a record of foreign investment in the United States minus U.S. investment abroad. The official settlements account is a record of the change in U.S. official reserves. The sum of the balances on the three accounts always equals zero. We pay for imports that exceed the value of our exports by borrowing from the rest of the world. A net borrower is a country that is borrowing more from the rest of the world than it is lending to the rest of the world and a net lender is a country that is lending more to the rest of the world than it is borrowing from the rest of the world. A debtor nation is a country that during its entire history has borrowed more from the rest of the world than it has lent to it and a creditor nation is a country that during its entire history has invested more in the rest of the world than other countries have invested in it. Net exports, $X - M$, equals the sum of the private sector balance, $S - I$, and the government sector balance, $NT - G$.

2 **Explain how the exchange rate is determined and why it fluctuates.**

Foreign currency is needed to buy goods or invest in another country. The foreign exchange rate is the price at which one currency exchanges for another. It is determined by demand and supply in the foreign exchange market. The quantity of dollars demanded increases when the exchange rate falls. The demand for dollars changes and the demand curve for dollars shifts if the U.S. interest rate differential or the expected future exchange rate changes. A rise in either increases the demand for dollars. The quantity of dollars supplied increases when the exchange rate rises. The supply of dollars changes and the supply curve of dollars shifts if the U.S. interest rate differential or the expected future exchange rate changes. A rise in either decreases the supply of dollars. At the equilibrium exchange rate, the quantity of dollars demanded equals the quantity of dollars supplied. The exchange rate is volatile because factors that change the demand also change the supply. Exchange rate expectations are influenced by purchasing power parity, a situation in which money buys the same amount of goods and services in different currencies, and interest rate parity, a situation in which the interest rate in one currency equals the interest rate in another currency once exchange rate changes are taken into account. The Fed and other central banks can intervene directly in the foreign exchange market by pegging the exchange rate. If the peg overvalues the exchange rate, the central bank runs out of foreign reserves; if the peg undervalues the exchange rate, the central bank accumulates foreign reserves.

CHECKPOINT 19.1

■ **Describe a country's balance of payments accounts and explain what determines the amount of international borrowing and lending.**

Quick Review

- *Current account balance* The current account balance equals net exports plus net interest plus net transfers received from abroad.
- *Capital account balance* The capital account balance equals foreign investment in the United States minus U.S. investment abroad.

Additional Practice Problems 19.1

In 2006 the U.S. economy recorded the following transactions:

Imports of goods and services, $2,203 billion; net interest, $36 billion; net transfers –$90 billion; decrease in U.S. official reserves, –$2 billion; exports of goods and services, $1,446 billion; statistical discrepancy –$18 billion; foreign investment in the United States, $1,882 billion; and, U.S. investment abroad, $1,055 billion.

   a. Calculate the current account balance.
   b. Calculate the capital account balance.
   c. Calculate the official settlements account balance.
   d. To what do these balances sum?
   e. Was the United States a debtor or a creditor nation in 2006?

2. Suppose the official settlements account equals zero. In this case, what is the relationship between the current account and the capital account? Why does this relationship exist?

Solutions to Additional Practice Problems 19.1

1a. The current account balance equals exports plus net interest plus net transfers minus imports. So the current account balance equals $1,446 billion + $36 billion + (–$90 billion) – $2,203 billion = –$811 billion.

1b. The capital account balance equals foreign investment in the United States minus U.S. investment abroad plus any statistical discrepancy. So the capital account balance equals $1,882 billion – $1,055 billion + (–$18 billion) = $809 billion.

1c. The official settlements account balance is the negative of the change in U.S. official reserves. When reserves decrease by $2 billion, the official settlements account balance is $2 billion.

1d. Keep in mind that the sum of the current account, capital account, and official settlements account is zero. So, if the previous answers are correct, they will sum to zero. Fortunately, they do: –$811 billion + $809 billion + $2 billion = $0.

1e. Interest payments reflect the value of outstanding debts. The United States is a debtor nation because the value of interest payments received from the rest of the world is less than the value of interest payments made to the rest of the world.

2. If the official settlements account equals zero, then the deficit in the current account equals the surplus in the capital account. Or, if the official settlements account equals zero, then the surplus in the current account equals the deficit in the capital account. This relationship exists because the sum of the current account, capital account, and the official settlements account equals zero. If the official settlements account equals zero, the current account balance must equal the negative of the capital account balance.

■ Self Test 19.1

Fill in the blanks

The _____ (current; capital; official settlements) account records payments for the imports of goods and services. The _____ (current; capital; official settlements) account records foreign investment in the United States minus U.S. investment abroad. The sum of the balances on current account, capital account, and the official settlements account always equals _____ (zero;

100 percent). The United States is a ____ (debtor; creditor) nation. The United States is borrowing for ____ (consumption; investment).

True or false

1. If foreign investment in the United States increases, and U.S. investment in the rest of the world decreases, the current account shows an increase in exports and a decrease in imports.

2. The official settlements account balance is negative if U.S. official reserves increase.

3. If the United States has a surplus in its capital account and a deficit in its current account, the balance in its official settlements account is zero.

4. At the present time, the United States has a current account deficit.

5. The United States is a net lender and a debtor nation.

6. If the United States started to run a current account surplus that continued indefinitely, it would immediately become a net lender and would eventually become a creditor nation.

7. Net exports equals the private sector balance minus the government sector balance.

8. In 2010, U.S. borrowing from abroad financed investment.

Multiple choice

1. A country's balance of payments accounts records its
   a. tax receipts and expenditures.
   b. tariffs and nontariff revenue and government purchases.
   c. international trading, borrowing, and lending.
   d. its tariff receipts and what it pays in tariffs to other nations.
   e. international exports and imports and nothing else.

2. Which of the following are balance of payments accounts?
   i. capital account
   ii. tariff account
   iii. current account
   a. i only.
   b. ii only.
   c. iii only.
   d. i and iii.
   e. ii and iii.

3. Which balance of payments account records payments for imports and receipts from exports?
   a. current account
   b. capital account
   c. official settlements account
   d. reserves account
   e. trade account

4. The current account balance is equal to
   a. imports − exports + net interest + net transfers.
   b. imports − exports + net interest − net transfers.
   c. exports − imports − net interest + net transfers.
   d. exports − imports + net interest + net transfers.
   e. exports − imports − net interest − net transfers.

5. If an investment of $100 million from the United Kingdom is made in the United States, in the U.S balance of payments accounts the $100 million is listed as a ____ entry in the ____ account.
   a. positive; current
   b. negative; capital
   c. positive; capital
   d. negative; current
   e. positive; official settlements

6. If the United States receives $200 billion of foreign investment and at the same time invests a total of $160 billion abroad, then the U.S.
   a. capital account balance increases by $40 billion.
   b. current account must be in surplus.
   c. balance of payments must be negative.
   d. capital account balance decreases by $40 billion.
   e. official settlements account balance increases by $40 billion.

7. In the balance of payments accounts, changes in U.S. official reserves are recorded in the
   a. current account.
   b. capital account.
   c. official settlements account.
   d. international currency account.
   e. international reserves account.

8. If a country has a current account balance of $100 billion and the official settlements account balance is zero, then the country's capital account balance must be
   a. equal to $100 billion.
   b. positive but not necessarily equal to $100 billion.
   c. equal to –$100 billion.
   d. negative but not necessarily equal to –$100 billion.
   e. zero.

9. A country that is borrowing more from the rest of the world than it is lending is called a
   a. net lender.
   b. net borrower.
   c. net debtor.
   d. net creditor.
   e. net loaner country.

10. A debtor nation is a country that
    a. borrows more from the rest of the world than it lends to it.
    b. lends more to the rest of the world than it borrows from it.
    c. during its entire history has invested more in the rest of the world than other countries have invested in it.
    d. during its entire history has borrowed more from the rest of the world than it has lent to it.
    e. during its entire history has consistently run a capital account deficit.

11. Comparing the U.S. balance of payments in 2010 to the rest of the world, we see that the
    a. United States has the largest current account surplus.
    b. U.S. current account is similar in size to most developed nations.
    c. United States has the largest capital account deficit.
    d. United States has the largest current account deficit.
    e. U.S. current account is similar in size to most developed nations and has a deficit.

12. According to the U.S. balance of payments accounts in 2010, U.S. international borrowing is used for
    a. private and public investment.
    b. private consumption.
    c. government expenditure.
    d. private and public saving.
    e. private saving and public consumption.

Short answer and numeric questions

1. What is recorded in the U.S. current account? In its capital account? In its official settlements account?

2. If its official settlements account equals zero, what will a country's capital account equal if it has a $350 billion current account deficit?

Item	(billions of dollars)
U.S. investment abroad	400
Exports of goods and services	1,000
Net transfers	0
Change in official reserves	10
Net interest	0
Foreign investment in the United States	800

3. The table above has balance of payment data for the United States.

   a. What is the capital account balance?

   b. What is the official settlements balance?

   c. What is the current account balance?

   d. What is the value of imports of goods and services?

4. What is a net borrower? A debtor nation? Is it possible for a nation to be net borrower and yet not be a debtor nation?

Item	(billions of dollars)
Saving	1,600
Investment	1,900
Government expenditures	1,300
Net taxes	1,400

5. The table above has data for the United States.

   a. What is the private sector balance?

   b. What is the government sector balance?

   c. What is net exports?

Additional Exercises (also in MyEconLab Test A)

It is 2016, and the U.S. economy records the following transactions: Exports of goods and services, $1,800 billion; interest payments to the rest of the world, $550 billion; interest received from the rest of the world, $350 billion; decrease in U.S. official reserves, $10 billion; government sector balance, $200 billion; saving, $1,800 billion; investment, $2,000 billion; net transfers are zero.

1. Calculate the current account balance, the capital account balance, the official settlements account balance, and imports of goods and services.

2. Is the United States a debtor or creditor nation in 2016?

3. If net taxes increase by $100 billion, what happens to the capital account balance?

CHECKPOINT 19.2

■ **Explain how the exchange rate is determined and why it fluctuates.**

Quick Review

- *U.S. interest rate differential* In the foreign exchange market, an increase in the U.S. interest rate differential increases the demand for dollars and decreases the supply of dollars.

- *Expected future exchange rate* In the foreign exchange market, a rise in the expected future exchange rate increases the demand for dollars and decreases the supply of dollars.

Additional Practice Problems 19.2

1. The figure shows the supply and demand curves for dollars in the foreign exchange market.

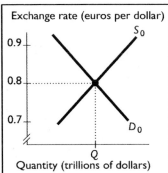

   a. What is the equilibrium exchange rate?

   b. Suppose the U.S. interest rate rises so that the U.S. interest rate differential increases. Assume that the effect on the supply is the same as the effect on the demand. In the figure, show the effect of this change. Does the equilibrium exchange rate rise or fall? Does the equilibrium quantity of dollars exchanged increase or decrease?

2. How and why does an increase in the expected future exchange rate change the *current* demand for U.S. dollars and the demand curve for dollars? How and why does an increase in the expected future exchange rate change the supply of U.S. dollars and the supply curve of dollars? What is the effect on the equilibrium exchange rate?

Solutions to Additional Practice Problems 19.2

1a. The figure shows that the initial equilibrium exchange rate is 0.8 euros per dollar.

1b. The increase in the U.S. interest rate differential increases the demand for U.S. dollars and simultaneously decreases the supply of U.S. dollars. As a result the de-

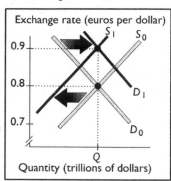

mand curve for dollars shifts rightward, from D_0 to D_1 and the supply curve of dollars shifts leftward, from S_0 to S_1. The exchange rate rises. In the figure the exchange rate rises to 0.9 euros per dollar. Because the effect on the demand is the same as the effect on the supply, the curves shift by the same amount, so the equilibrium quantity of dollars exchanged does not change.

2. An increase in the expected future exchange rate increases the demand for U.S. dollars and shifts the demand curve rightward. The demand for U.S. dollars increases because at the current exchange rate people want to buy U.S. dollars now and sell them in the future at the higher expected exchange rate. An increase in the expected future exchange rate decreases the supply of U.S. dollars and shifts the supply curve leftward. The supply of U.S. dollars decreases because people would rather keep the dollars until they can sell them in the future at the higher expected exchange rate. Because the demand for dollars increases and the supply of dollars decreases, the current equilibrium exchange rate rises.

■ Self Test 19.2

Fill in the blanks

The price at which one currency exchanges for another is called a foreign _____ (exchange rate;

interest rate). If the dollar falls in value against the Mexican peso, the dollar has _____ (appreciated; depreciated). A rise in exchange rate _____ (decreases; increases) the quantity of U.S. dollars demanded. An increase in the demand for dollars shifts the demand curve for dollars _____ (leftward; rightward) and an increase in the supply of dollars shifts the supply curve of dollars _____ (leftward; rightward). The exchange rate is volatile because an influence that changes the demand for dollars often _____ (changes; does not change) the supply of dollars. An increase in the expected future exchange rate _____ (raises; lowers) the equilibrium exchange rate. Purchasing power parity is equal value of _____ (interest rates; money). If the Fed buys dollars on the foreign exchange market, the exchange rate _____ (rises; falls).

True or false

1. The U.S. foreign exchange rate changes infrequently.

2. If the exchange rate increases from 0.9 euros per dollar to 1.1 euros per dollar, the dollar has appreciated.

3. The larger the value of U.S. exports, the larger is the quantity of U.S. dollars demanded.

4. An increase in the U.S. exchange rate from 1.10 euros per dollar to 1.20 euros per dollar increases the supply of U.S. dollars and shifts the supply curve of dollars rightward.

5. A rise in the expected future exchange rate increases the demand for dollars and also the supply of dollars and might raise or lower the exchange rate.

6. The equilibrium U.S. exchange rate is the exchange rate that sets the quantity of dollars demanded equal to the quantity of dollars supplied.

7. An increase in the U.S. interest rate differential raises the U.S. exchange rate.

8. To prevent the price of the euro from falling, the European Central Bank might sell euros on the foreign exchange market.

Multiple choice

1. The foreign exchange market is the market in which
    a. all international transactions occur.
    b. currencies are exchanged solely by governments.
    c. goods and services are exchanged between governments.
    d. the currency of one country is exchanged for the currency of another.
    e. the world's governments collect their tariff revenue.

2. When Del Monte, an American company, purchases Mexican tomatoes, Del Monte pays for the tomatoes with
    a. Canadian dollars.
    b. Mexican pesos.
    c. gold.
    d. Mexican goods and services.
    e. euros.

3. If today the exchange rate is 1.00 euro per dollar and tomorrow the exchange rate is 0.98 euros per dollar, then the dollar ____ and the euro____.
    a. appreciated; appreciated
    b. appreciated; depreciated
    c. depreciated; appreciated
    d. depreciated; depreciated
    e. depreciated; did not change

4. In the foreign exchange market, as the U.S. exchange rate rises from 0.95 euros per dollar to 1.05 euros per dollar, other things remaining the same, the
    a. quantity of dollars demanded increases.
    b. demand curve for dollars shifts rightward.
    c. demand curve for dollars shifts leftward.
    d. quantity of dollars demanded decreases.
    e. supply curve of dollars shifts rightward.

5. In the foreign exchange market, the demand for dollars increases and the demand curve for dollars shifts rightward if the
    a. U.S. interest rate differential increases.
    b. expected future exchange rate falls.
    c. foreign interest rate rises.
    d. U.S. interest rate falls.
    e. exchange rate falls.

6. As the exchange rate ____, the quantity of U.S. dollars supplied ____.
    a. rises; increases
    b. falls; increases
    c. falls; remains the same
    d. rises; decreases
    e. rises; remains the same

7. In the foreign exchange market, the supply curve of dollars is
    a. upward sloping.
    b. downward sloping.
    c. vertical.
    d. horizontal.
    e. identical to the demand curve for dollars.

8. Everything else remaining the same, in the foreign exchange market which of the following increases the supply of U.S. dollars?
    a. The European interest rate rises.
    b. The expected future exchange rate rises.
    c. The U.S. interest rate rises.
    d. The U.S. interest rate differential increases.
    e. The exchange rate falls.

9. When there is a shortage of dollars in the foreign exchange market, the
    a. demand curve for dollars shifts leftward to restore the equilibrium.
    b. U.S. exchange rate will appreciate.
    c. U.S. exchange rate will depreciate.
    d. supply curve of dollars shifts leftward to restore the equilibrium.
    e. supply curve of dollars shifts rightward to restore the equilibrium.

10. In the foreign exchange market, when the U.S. interest rate rises, the supply of dollars ____ and the foreign exchange rate ____.
    a. increases; rises
    b. increases; falls
    c. decreases; rises
    d. decreases; falls
    e. increases; does not change

11. A situation in which money buys the same amount of goods and services in different currencies is called
    a. exchange rate equilibrium.
    b. purchasing power parity.
    c. exchange rate surplus.
    d. exchange rate balance.
    e. a fixed exchange rate.

12. Interest rate parity occurs when
    a. the interest rate in one currency equals the interest rate in another currency when exchange rate changes are taken into account.
    b. interest rate differentials are always maintained across nations.
    c. interest rates are equal across nations.
    d. prices are equal across nations when exchange rates are taken into account.
    e. the interest rate in one country changes in tandem with the interest rate in the other country.

Complete the graph

1. Figure 19.1 shows the foreign exchange market for U.S. dollars.
    a. What is the equilibrium exchange rate?
    b. The U.S. interest rate differential rises. In Figure 19.1, illustrate the effect of this change. What happens to the exchange rate?

2. Figure 19.2 shows the foreign exchange market for U.S. dollars. Suppose people expect that the future exchange rate will be lower. In Figure 19.2, illustrate the effect of this change. What happens to the exchange rate? Has the exchange rate appreciated or depreciated?

■ FIGURE 19.1

Exchange rate (euros per dollar)

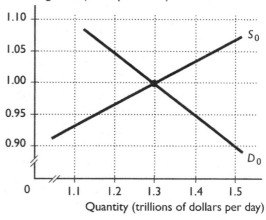

Quantity (trillions of dollars per day)

■ FIGURE 19.2

Exchange rate (euros per dollar)

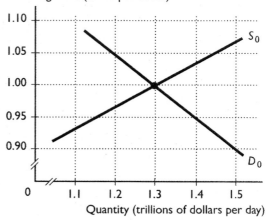

Quantity (trillions of dollars per day)

Short answer and numeric questions

1. If the exchange rate rises from 0.90 euros per dollar to 1.00 euros per dollar, has the dollar appreciated or depreciated? Has the euro appreciated or depreciated?

2. What is the relationship between the value of U.S. exports and the quantity of U.S. dollars demanded? Why does this relationship exist?

3. What is the relationship between the value of U.S. imports and the quantity of U.S. dollars supplied? Why does this relationship exist?

4. Everything else remaining the same, how will a rise in the European interest rate affect the demand for dollars, the supply of dollars, and the U.S. exchange rate?

5. If the Fed believes the exchange rate is too low and wants to raise it, what action does the Fed undertake in the foreign exchange market? What limits the extent to which the Fed can undertake this action?

Additional Exercises (also in MyEconLab Test A)

Use the following for the next 3 exercises. Suppose that yesterday, the Canadian dollar ($C) was trading on the foreign exchange market at $0.85 U.S. per $C. Today, the Canadian dollar is trading at $0.80 U.S. per $C.

1. Which of the two currencies (the Canadian dollar or the U.S. dollar) has appreciated and which has depreciated today?

2. List the events that could have caused today's change in the value of the Canadian dollar on the foreign exchange market. Did the events on you list increase or decrease the demand for Canadian dollars, the supply of Canadian dollars, or both the demand for and supply of Canadian dollars?

3. If the Bank of Canada had tried to stabilize the value of the Canadian dollar at $0.85 U.S., what action would it have taken? What effect would the Bank of Canada's actions have had on Canadian official reserves?

■ SELF TEST ANSWERS

■ CHECKPOINT 19.1

Fill in the blanks

The <u>current</u> account records payments for the imports of goods and services. The <u>capital</u> account records foreign investment in the United States minus U.S. investment abroad. The sum of the balances on current account, capital account, and the official settlements account always equals <u>zero</u>. The United States is a <u>debtor</u> nation. The United States is borrowing for <u>investment</u>.

True or false

1. False; page 474
2. True; page 474
3. False; page 474
4. True; page 475
5. False; page 476
6. True; page 477
7. False; pages 478-479
8. True; page 479

Multiple choice

1. c; page 474
2. d; page 474
3. a; page 474
4. d; page 474
5. c; page 474
6. a; page 474
7. c; page 474
8. c; page 474
9. b; page 476
10. d; page 476
11. d; page 479
12. a; page 479

Short answer and numeric questions

1. The current account records payments for imports, receipts from exports, net interest and net transfers received from abroad. The capital account records foreign investment in the United States minus U.S. investments abroad. The official settlements account records changes in U.S. official reserves, the government's holding of foreign currency; page 474.

2. The current account balance plus the capital account balance plus official settlements account balance sums to zero. So if the official settlements account equals zero, a $350 billion current account deficit means there is a $350 billion capital account surplus; page 474.

3. a. The capital account balance equals foreign investment in the United States minus U.S. investment abroad, which is $400 billion; pages 474-475.

   b. The official settlements balance is the negative of the change in official reserves, or −$10 billion; pages 474-475.

   c. The sum of the current account balance, the capital account balance, and the official settlements account balance is zero. The capital account balance is $400 billion and the official settlements account balance is −$10 billion, so the current account balance is −$390 billion; pages 474-475.

   d. The current account balance equals exports minus imports plus net interest plus net transfers received from abroad. Net interest and net transfers are given as zero. The current account balance is −$390 billion and exports are $1,000 billion, so imports equal $1,390 billion; pages 474-475.

4. A net borrower is a country that is borrowing more from the rest of the world than it is lending to the rest of the world. A debtor nation is a country that during its entire history has borrowed more from the rest of the world than it has lent to it. It is possible for a nation to be a net borrower but not be a debtor nation. A country can be a creditor nation and a net borrower. This situation occurs if a creditor nation is, during a particular year, borrowing more from the rest of the world than it is lending to the rest of the world; page 476.

5. a. The private sector balance equals saving minus investment, so the private sector balance is –$300 billion; page 479.

   b. The government sector balance equals net taxes minus government expenditures on goods and services, so the government sector balance is $100 billion; page 479.

   c. The sum of the private sector balance plus the government sector balance equals net exports, so net exports equals –$200 billion; page 479.

Additional Exercises (also in MyEconLab Test A)

1. The current account balance equals net exports plus net interest (which is –$200 billion) plus net transfers (which is zero). Net exports equals the government sector balance ($200 billion) plus the private sector balance. The private sector balance equals saving ($1,800 billion) minus investment ($2,000 billion), which is –$200 billion. So net exports equals ($200 billion) + (–$200 billion) = $0. So the current account balance equals –$200 billion.

   The capital account equals –(current account balance + official settlements account balance). The official settlements account equals $10 billion because official U.S. reserves decreased by $10 billion. So the capital account balance equals –(–$200 billion + $10 billion) = –(–$190 billion) = $190 billion.

   The official settlements account balance is $10 billion.

   Net exports equal exports minus imports. Exports are $1,800 billion and net exports are –$200 billion, so imports = $2,000 billion; pages 474-475.

2. The United States is a debtor nation because interest payments to the rest of the world exceed interest payments to the United States; pages 476-477 .

3. If net taxes increase by $100 billion, the government surplus increases by $100 billion and so the current account deficit shrinks. With no change in the official settlements account balance, the capital account surplus decreases; pages 478-479.

■ CHECKPOINT 19.2

Fill in the blanks

The price at which one currency exchanges for another is called a foreign exchange rate. If the dollar falls in value against the Mexican peso, the dollar has depreciated. A rise in the exchange rate decreases the quantity of U.S. dollars demanded. An increase in the demand for dollars shifts the demand curve for dollars rightward and an increase in the supply of dollars shifts the supply curve of dollars rightward. The exchange rate is volatile because an influence that changes the demand for dollars often changes the supply of dollars. An increase in the expected future exchange rate raises the equilibrium exchange rate. Purchasing power parity is equal value of money. If the Fed buys dollars on the foreign exchange market, the exchange rate rises.

True or false

1. False; page 481
2. True; page 481
3. True; page 482
4. False; page 486
5. False; pages 484, 487, 489
6. True; page 488
7. True; page 489
8. False; page 492

Multiple choice

1. d; page 481
2. b; page 481
3. c; pages 481-482
4. d; page 482
5. a; page 484
6. a; page 485
7. a; page 486
8. a; page 487
9. b; page 488
10. c; pages 487, 489
11. b; page 490
12. a; page 492

Complete the graph

■ FIGURE 19.3

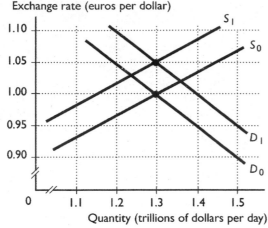

1. a. The equilibrium exchange rate is 1.00 euro per dollar; page 488.
   b. The increase in the U.S. interest rate differential increases the demand for dollars and shifts the demand curve from D_0 to D_1 in Figure 19.3. The increase in the U.S. interest rate differential also decreases the supply of dollars and shifts the supply curve from S_0 to S_1. The exchange rate rises. In the figure, the exchange rate rises to 1.05 euros per dollar; pages 484, 487, 489.

■ FIGURE 19.4

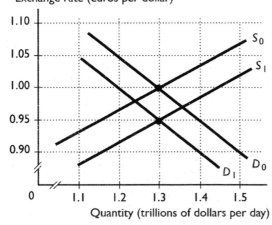

2. The fall in the expected future exchange rate decreases the demand for dollars and in-

creases the supply of dollars. The demand curve shifts leftward from D_0 to D_1 and the supply curve shifts rightward from S_0 to S_1. The exchange falls from 1.00 euro per dollar to 0.95 euros per dollar in Figure 19.4. The exchange rate depreciates; pages 484, 487, 489.

Short answer and numeric questions

1. When the exchange rate rises from 0.90 euros per dollar to 1.00 euro per dollar, the dollar appreciates because the dollar buys more euros. The euro depreciates because it now takes 1 euro to buy a dollar instead of 0.9 euros to buy a dollar; pages 481-482.

2. The larger the value of U.S. exports, the larger is the quantity of U.S. dollars demanded. This relationship exists because U.S. firms want to be paid for their goods and services in dollars; page 482.

3. The larger the value of U.S. imports, the larger the quantity of U.S. dollars supplied. This relationship exists because U.S. consumers must pay for their imports in foreign currency. To obtain foreign currency, U.S. consumers supply dollars; page 485.

4. An increase in the European interest rate decreases the U.S. interest rate differential. The smaller the U.S. interest rate differential, the smaller is the demand for U.S. assets and the smaller the demand for dollars. And the smaller the U.S. interest rate differential, the greater is the demand for foreign assets and the greater is the supply of dollars. So when the European interest rate rises, the demand for dollars decreases, the supply of dollars increases, and the equilibrium exchange rate falls; pages 484, 487, 489.

5. If the Fed wants to raise the exchange rate, it will buy dollars. The Fed would have to sell U.S. official reserves to buy dollars. The Fed is limited by its quantity of official reserves. If the Fed persisted in this action, eventually it would run out of reserves and would be forced to stop buying dollars; page 492.

Additional Exercises (also in MyEconLab Test A)

1. Yesterday a Canadian dollar purchased 85 U.S. cents; today a Canadian dollar buys only 80 U.S. cents. The Canadian dollar buys fewer U.S. cents and so the Canadian dollar has depreciated. The U.S. dollar has appreciated; pages 481-482.

2. The main events that might have caused the appreciation of the U.S. dollar and the depreciation of the Canadian dollar are an increase in the U.S. interest rate, a decrease in the Canadian interest rate, or concern that the Canadian dollar will depreciate (the U.S. dollar will appreciate) even more in the future.

   The foreign exchange market is unlike other markets because the factors that affect the supply also affect the demand. So the factors listed in part (b) all affected both the demand for Canadian dollars as well as the supply of Canadian dollars. All the factors listed decreased the demand for Canadian dollars and increased the supply; pages 483-485, 486-487.

3. To stabilize the value of the Canadian dollar at 85 U.S. cents, the Bank of Canada would have needed to decrease the supply of Canadian dollars. The Bank of Canada would have needed to buy Canadian dollars.

   When the Bank of Canada buys Canadian dollars, it decreases Canadian official reserves; pages 492-493.